2007

Bed & Breakfast Stops in Britain

With supplements for Non-Smokers, Disabled & Special Diets

For Contents see pages 2-3

Index of towns/ counties see page 347-350

Contents

ENGLAND

Contents

SCOTLAND

WALES

Special Welcome Supplements

ISBN 1 85055 390 4
978-1-85055-390-8

Typeset by FHG Guides Ltd, Paisley.
Printed and bound in Malaysia by Imago

Distribution. Book Trade: ORCA Book Services, Stanley House,
3 Fleets Lane, Poole, Dorset BH15 3AJ
(Tel: 01202 665432; Fax: 01202 666219)
e-mail: mail@orcabookservices.co.uk
Published by FHG Guides Ltd., Abbey Mill Business Centre,
Seedhill, Paisley PA1 ITJ (Tel: 0141-887 0428 Fax: 0141-889 7204).
e-mail: admin@fhguides.co.uk

Bed & Breakfast Stops
is published by FHG Guides Ltd,
part of Kuperard Group.

Cover design: FHG Guides
Cover pictures courtesy of: Arches Guesthouse, Whitby
Caebetran Farm, Brecon
Bolden's Wood, Ashford
Acton Scott Farm, Church Stretton
Yorkshire Bridge Inn, Bamford

Foreword

This new and colourful edition of Bed & Breakfast stops contains a large selection of accommodation offering town and country hospitality for the holiday or business traveller. The entries give a clear description of the properties and of the facilities offered – bedrooms, bathrooms etc – and at least an indication of price. We hope that all of our advertisers provide friendly service – we ask them to vouch for this when we confirm their entry – and if they have official approval or other grading from the Tourism Authority or the AA we would certainly make this clear in the entry.

Our supplements will direct you quickly to accommodation for non-smokers, the disabled or those requiring special diets, and to add to your holiday enjoyment we have arranged with the proprietors and managers of a range of holiday attractions to offer our readers FREE or REDUCED RATE entry during 2007. We hope that you find this useful.

Anne Cuthbertson, **Editor**

Canal at Newbury, Berkshire. Picture courtesy of Berkshire Tourism

Ratings & Awards

For the first time ever the AA, VisitBritain, VisitScotland, and the Wales Tourist Board will use a single method of assessing and rating serviced accommodation. Irrespective of which organisation inspects an establishment the rating awarded will be the same, using a common set of standards, giving a clear guide of what to expect. The RAC is no longer operating an Hotel inspection and accreditation business.

Accommodation Standards: Star Grading Scheme

Using a scale of 1-5 stars the objective quality ratings give a clear indication of accommodation standard, cleanliness, ambience, hospitality, service and food, This shows the full range of standards suitable for every budget and preference, and allows visitors to distinguish between the quality of accommodation and facilities on offer in different establishments. All types of board and self-catering accommodation are covered, including hotels, B&Bs, holiday parks, campus accommodation, hostels, caravans and camping, and boats.

The more stars, the higher level of quality

★★★★★
exceptional quality, with a degree of luxury

★★★★
excellent standard throughout

★★★
very good level of quality and comfort

★★
good quality, well presented and well run

★
acceptable quality; simple, practical, no frills

VisitBritain and the regional tourist boards, **enjoyEngland.com, VisitScotland** and **VisitWales,** and **the AA** have full details of the grading system on their websites

enjoy**England**.com

visit**Wales**.com

National Accessible Scheme

If you have particular mobility, visual or hearing needs, look out for the National Accessible Scheme. You can be confident of finding accommodation or attractions that meet your needs by looking for the following symbols.

Typically suitable for a person with sufficient mobility to climb a flight of steps but would benefit from fixtures and fittings to aid balance

Typically suitable for a person with restricted walking ability and for those that may need to use a wheelchair some of the time and can negotiate a maximum of three steps

Typically suitable for a person who depends on the use of a wheelchair and transfers unaided to and from the wheelchair in a seated position. This person may be an independent traveller

Typically suitable for a person who depends on the use of a wheelchair in a seated position. This person also requires personal or mechanical assistance (eg carer, hoist).

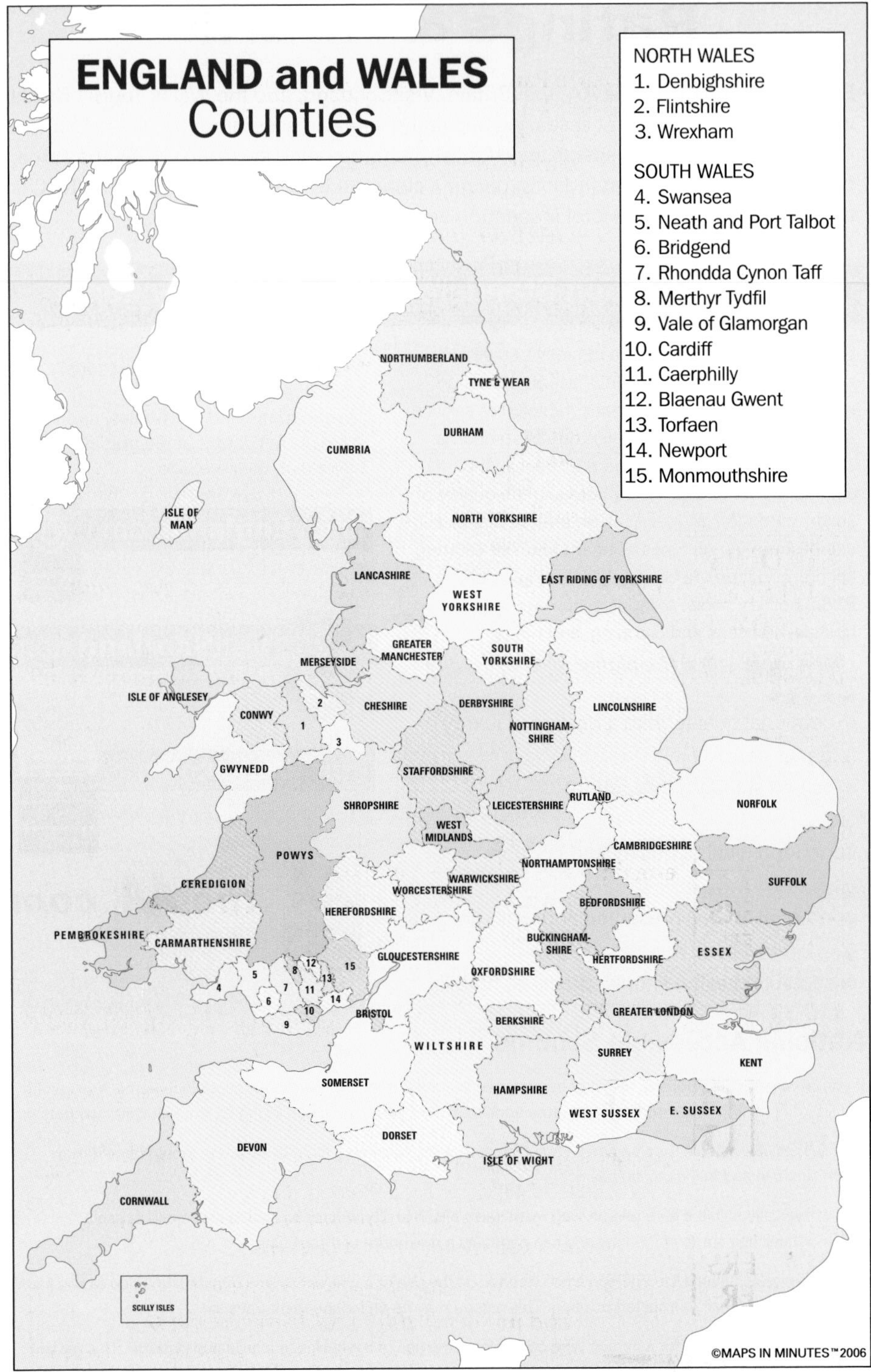

ENGLAND and WALES
Counties
NORTH WALES
1. Denbighshire
2. Flintshire
3. Wrexham
SOUTH WALES
4. Swansea
5. Neath and Port Talbot
6. Bridgend
7. Rhondda Cynon Taff
8. Merthyr Tydfil
9. Vale of Glamorgan
10. Cardiff
11. Caerphilly
12. Blaenau Gwent
13. Torfaen
14. Newport
15. Monmouthshire
NORTHUMBERLAND
TYNE & WEAR
DURHAM
CUMBRIA
ISLE OF MAN
NORTH YORKSHIRE
LANCASHIRE
WEST YORKSHIRE
EAST RIDING OF YORKSHIRE
GREATER MANCHESTER
SOUTH YORKSHIRE
MERSEYSIDE
ISLE OF ANGLESEY
CONWY
CHESHIRE
DERBYSHIRE
LINCOLNSHIRE
NOTTINGHAMSHIRE
GWYNEDD
STAFFORDSHIRE
SHROPSHIRE
LEICESTERSHIRE
RUTLAND
NORFOLK
WEST MIDLANDS
POWYS
CAMBRIDGESHIRE
NORTHAMPTONSHIRE
WARWICKSHIRE
CEREDIGION
WORCESTERSHIRE
SUFFOLK
BEDFORDSHIRE
HEREFORDSHIRE
PEMBROKESHIRE
CARMARTHENSHIRE
BUCKINGHAMSHIRE
HERTFORDSHIRE
ESSEX
GLOUCESTERSHIRE
OXFORDSHIRE
BRISTOL
GREATER LONDON
BERKSHIRE
WILTSHIRE
SURREY
KENT
SOMERSET
HAMPSHIRE
WEST SUSSEX
E. SUSSEX
DORSET
DEVON
ISLE OF WIGHT
CORNWALL
SCILLY ISLES
©MAPS IN MINUTES™2006

FHG

K·U·P·E·R·A·R·D

READERS' OFFER 2007

LEIGHTON BUZZARD RAILWAY

Page's Park Station, Billington Road,
Leighton Buzzard, Bedfordshire LU7 4TN
Tel: 01525 373888
e-mail: info@buzzrail.co.uk
www.buzzrail.co.uk

One FREE adult/child with full-fare adult ticket
Valid 11/3/2007 - 28/10/2007

NOT TO BE USED IN CONJUNCTION WITH ANY OTHER OFFER

FHG

K·U·P·E·R·A·R·D

READERS' OFFER 2007

BEKONSCOT MODEL VILLAGE & RAILWAY

Warwick Road, Beaconsfield,
Buckinghamshire HP9 2PL
Tel: 01494 672919
e-mail: info@bekonscot.co.uk
www.bekonscot.com

Bekonscot
Model Village
& Railway

One child FREE when accompanied by full-paying adult
Valid February to October 2007

NOT TO BE USED IN CONJUNCTION WITH ANY OTHER OFFER

READERS' OFFER 2007

BUCKINGHAMSHIRE RAILWAY CENTRE

Quainton Road Station, Quainton,
Aylesbury HP22 4BY
Tel & Fax: 01296 655720
e-mail: bucksrailcentre@btopenworld.com
www.bucksrailcentre.org

BUCKINGHAMSHIRE RAILWAY CENTRE

One child FREE with each full-paying adult
Not valid for Special Events

NOT TO BE USED IN CONJUNCTION WITH ANY OTHER OFFER

FHG

K·U·P·E·R·A·R·D

READERS' OFFER 2007

THE RAPTOR FOUNDATION

The Heath, St Ives Road,
Woodhurst, Huntingdon, Cambs PE28 3BT
Tel: 01487 741140 • Fax: 01487 841140
e-mail: heleowl@aol.com
www.raptorfoundation.org.uk

The Raptor Foundation

TWO for the price of ONE
Valid until end 2007 (not Bank Holidays)

NOT TO BE USED IN CONJUNCTION WITH ANY OTHER OFFER

A 70-minute journey into the lost world of the English narrow gauge light railway. Features historic steam locomotives from many countries.

PETS MUST BE KEPT UNDER CONTROL AND NOT ALLOWED ON TRACKS

Open: Sundays and Bank Holiday weekends 11 March to 28 October. Additional days in summer.

Directions: on A4146 towards Hemel Hempstead, close to roundabout junction with A505.

FHG GUIDES, ABBEY MILL BUSINESS CENTRE, PAISLEY PA1 1TJ • www.holidayguides.com

Be a giant in a magical miniature world of make-believe depicting rural England in the 1930s. "A little piece of history that is forever England."

Open: 10am-5pm daily mid February to end October.

Directions: Junction 16 M25, Junction 2 M40.

FHG GUIDES, ABBEY MILL BUSINESS CENTRE, PAISLEY PA1 1TJ • www.holidayguides.com

A working steam railway centre. Steam train rides, miniature railway rides, large collection of historic preserved steam locomotives, carriages and wagons.

Open: Sundays and Bank Holidays April to October, plus Wednesdays in school holidays 10.30am to 5.30pm.

Directions: off A41 Aylesbury to Bicester Road, 6 miles north west of Aylesbury.

FHG GUIDES, ABBEY MILL BUSINESS CENTRE, PAISLEY PA1 1TJ • www.holidayguides.com

Birds of Prey Centre offering audience participation in flying displays which are held 3 times daily. Tours, picnic area, gift shop, tearoom, craft shop.

Open: 10am-5pm all year except Christmas and New Year.

Directions: follow brown tourist signs from B1040.

FHG GUIDES, ABBEY MILL BUSINESS CENTRE, PAISLEY PA1 1TJ • www.holidayguides.com

FHG

·K·U·P·E·R·A·R·D·

READERS' OFFER 2007

SACREWELL FARM & COUNTRY CENTRE

Sacrewell, Thornhaugh,
Peterborough PE8 6HJ
Tel: 01780 782254
e-mail: info@sacrewell.fsnet.co.uk
www.sacrewell.org.uk

One child FREE with one full paying adult
Valid from March 1st to October 1st 2007

NOT TO BE USED IN CONJUNCTION WITH ANY OTHER OFFER

READERS' OFFER 2007

GEEVOR TIN MINE

Pendeen, Penzance,
Cornwall TR19 7EW
Tel: 01736 788662 • Fax: 01736 786059
e-mail: bookings@geevor.com
www.geevor.com

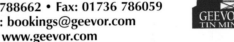

TWO for the price of ONE or £3.75 off a family ticket
Valid 02/01/2007 to 20/12/2007

NOT TO BE USED IN CONJUNCTION WITH ANY OTHER OFFER

READERS' OFFER 2007

TAMAR VALLEY DONKEY PARK

St Ann's Chapel, Gunnislake,
Cornwall PL18 9HW
Tel: 01822 834072
e-mail: info@donkeypark.com
www.donkeypark.com

50p OFF per person, up to 6 persons
Valid from Easter until end October 2007

NOT TO BE USED IN CONJUNCTION WITH ANY OTHER OFFER

READERS' OFFER 2007

NATIONAL SEAL SANCTUARY

NATIONAL SEAL SANCTUARY

Gweek, Helston,
Cornwall TR12 6UG
Tel: 01326 221361
e-mail: seals@sealsanctuary.co.uk
www.sealsanctuary.co.uk

TWO for ONE - on purchase of another ticket of equal or greater value. Valid until December 2007.

NOT TO BE USED IN CONJUNCTION WITH ANY OTHER OFFER

Farm animals, 18th century watermill and farmhouse, farm artifacts, caravan and camping, children's play areas. Restaurant and gift shop.	**Open:** all year. 9.30am to 5pm 1st March -30th Sept 10am-4pm 1st Oct to 28th Feb **Directions:** signposted off both A47 and A1.

FHG GUIDES, ABBEY MILL BUSINESS CENTRE, PAISLEY PA1 1TJ • www.holidayguides.com

Geevor is the largest mining history site in the UK in a spectacular setting on Cornwall's Atlantic coast. Guided underground tour, many surface buildings, museum, cafe, gift shop. Free parking.	**Open:** daily except Saturdays 10am to 4pm **Directions:** 7 miles from Penzance beside the B3306 Land's End to St Ives coast road

FHG GUIDES, ABBEY MILL BUSINESS CENTRE, PAISLEY PA1 1TJ • www.holidayguides.com

Cornwall's only Donkey Sanctuary set in 14 acres overlooking the beautiful Tamar Valley. Donkey rides, rabbit warren, goat hill, children's playgrounds, cafe and picnic area. New all-weather play barn.	**Open:** Easter to end Oct: daily 10am to 5.30pm. Nov to March: weekends and all school holidays 10.30am to 4.30pm **Directions:** just off A390 between Callington and Gunnislake at St Ann's Chapel.

FHG GUIDES, ABBEY MILL BUSINESS CENTRE, PAISLEY PA1 1TJ • www.holidayguides.com

Britain's leading grey seal rescue centre	**Open:** daily (except Christmas Day) from 10am **Directions:** from A30 follow signs to Helston, then brown tourist signs to Seal Sanctuary.

FHG GUIDES, ABBEY MILL BUSINESS CENTRE, PAISLEY PA1 1TJ • www.holidayguides.com

FHG

KUPERARD

READERS' OFFER 2007

CARS OF THE STARS MOTOR MUSEUM

Standish Street, Keswick,
Cumbria CA12 5HH
Tel: 017687 73757
e-mail: cotsmm@aol.com
www.carsofthestars.com

One child free with two paying adults
Valid during 2007

NOT TO BE USED IN CONJUNCTION WITH ANY OTHER OFFER

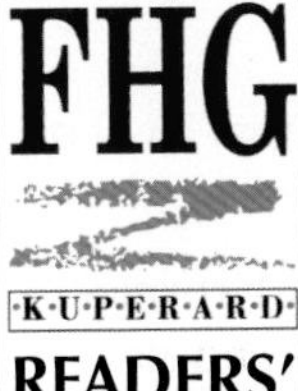

KUPERARD

READERS' OFFER 2007

ESKDALE HISTORIC WATER MILL

Mill Cottage, Boot, Eskdale,
Cumbria CA19 1TG
Tel: 019467 23335
e-mail: david.king403@tesco.net
www.eskdale.info

Eskdale Historic Water Mill

Two children FREE with two adults
Valid during 2007

NOT TO BE USED IN CONJUNCTION WITH ANY OTHER OFFER

KUPERARD

READERS' OFFER 2007

CRICH TRAMWAY VILLAGE

Crich, Matlock
Derbyshire DE4 5DP
Tel: 01773 854321 • Fax: 01773 854320
e-mail: enquiry@tramway.co.uk
www.tramway.co.uk

One child FREE with every full-paying adult
Valid during 2007

NOT TO BE USED IN CONJUNCTION WITH ANY OTHER OFFER

KUPERARD

READERS' OFFER 2007

THE BIG SHEEP

Abbotsham, Bideford,
Devon EX39 5AP
Tel: 01237 472366
e-mail: info@thebigsheep.co.uk
www.thebigsheep.co.uk

Admit one child FREE with each paying adult
Valid during 2007

NOT TO BE USED IN CONJUNCTION WITH ANY OTHER OFFER

A collection of cars from film and TV, including Chitty Chitty Bang Bang, James Bond's Aston Martin, Del Boy's van, Fab1 and many more.

PETS MUST BE KEPT ON LEAD

Open: daily 10am-5pm. Open February half term, Ist April to end November, also weekends in December.

Directions: in centre of Keswick close to car park.

FHG GUIDES, ABBEY MILL BUSINESS CENTRE, PAISLEY PA1 1TJ • www.holidayguides.com

The oldest working mill in England with 18th century oatmeal machinery running daily.

DOGS ON LEADS

Open: 11am to 5pm April to Sept. (may be closed Saturdays).

Directions: near inland terminus of Ravenglass & Eskdale Railway or over Hardknott Pass.

FHG GUIDES, ABBEY MILL BUSINESS CENTRE, PAISLEY PA1 1TJ • www.holidayguides.com

A superb family day out in the atmosphere of a bygone era. Explore the recreated period street and fascinating exhibitions. Unlimited tram rides are free with entry. Play areas, woodland walk and sculpture trail, shops, tea rooms, pub, restaurant and lots more.

Open: daily April to October 10 am to 5.30pm, weekends in winter.

Directions: eight miles from M1 Junction 28, follow brown and white signs for "Tramway Museum".

FHG GUIDES, ABBEY MILL BUSINESS CENTRE, PAISLEY PA1 1TJ • www.holidayguides.com

"England for Excellence" award-winning family entertainment park. Highlights: hilarious shows including the famous sheep-racing and the duck trials; the awesome Ewetopia indoor adventure playground for adults and children; brewery; mountain boarding; great local food.

Open: daily, 10am to 6pm April - Oct Phone for Winter opening times and details.

Directions: on A39 North Devon link road, two miles west of Bideford Bridge.

FHG GUIDES, ABBEY MILL BUSINESS CENTRE, PAISLEY PA1 1TJ • www.holidayguides.com

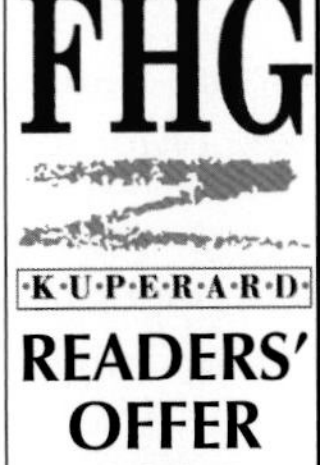

READERS' OFFER 2007

DEVONSHIRE COLLECTION OF PERIOD COSTUME

Totnes Costume Museum,
Bogan House, 43 High Street,
Totnes,
Devon TQ9 5NP

FREE child with a paying adult with voucher
Valid from Spring Bank Holiday to end of Sept 2007

NOT TO BE USED IN CONJUNCTION WITH ANY OTHER OFFER

READERS' OFFER 2007

CREALY ADVENTURE PARK

Sidmouth Road, Clyst St Mary, Exeter,
Devon EX5 1DR
Tel: 0870 116 3333• Fax: 01395 233211
e-mail: fun@crealy.co.uk
www.crealy.co.uk

FREE superkart race or panning for gold.
Height restrictions apply. Valid until 31/10/07.
Photocopies not accepted. One voucher per person.

NOT TO BE USED IN CONJUNCTION WITH ANY OTHER OFFER

READERS' OFFER 2007

KILLHOPE LEAD MINING MUSEUM

Cowshill, Upper Weardale,
Co. Durham DL13 1AR
Tel: 01388 537505
e-mail: killhope@durham.gov.uk
www.durham.gov.uk/killhope

One child FREE with full-paying adult
Valid April to October 2007 (not Park Level Mine)

NOT TO BE USED IN CONJUNCTION WITH ANY OTHER OFFER

READERS' OFFER 2007

AVON VALLEY RAILWAY

Bitton Station, Bath Road, Bitton,
Bristol BS30 6HD
Tel: 0117 932 5538
e-mail: info@avonvalleyrailway.org
www.avonvalleyrailway.org

One FREE child with every fare-paying adult
Valid May - Oct 2007 (not 'Day Out with Thomas' events)

NOT TO BE USED IN CONJUNCTION WITH ANY OTHER OFFER

Themed exhibition, changed annually, based in a Tudor house. Collection contains items of dress for women, men and children from 17th century to 1980s, from high fashion to everyday wear.

Open: Open from Spring Bank Holiday to end September. 11am to 5pm Tuesday to Friday.

Directions: centre of town, opposite Market Square. Mini bus up High Street stops outside.

FHG GUIDES, ABBEY MILL BUSINESS CENTRE, PAISLEY PA1 1TJ • www.holidayguides.com

Maximum fun, magic and adventure. An unforgettable family experience, with Tidal Wave log flume, rollercoaster, Queen Bess pirate ship, techno race karts, bumper boats, Vicorian carousel, animal handling, and huge indoor and outdoor play areas. The South-West's favourite family attraction!

Open: Summer: daily 10am to 5pm
High season: daily 10am to 7pm
Winter (Nov-March): Wed-Sun 10am -5pm

Directions: minutes from M5 J30 on the A3052 Sidmouth road, near Exeter

FHG GUIDES, ABBEY MILL BUSINESS CENTRE, PAISLEY PA1 1TJ • www.holidayguides.com

Voted 'Most Family-Friendly Museum 2004' and 'Most Welcome Experience 2005', Killhope is Britain's best preserved lead mining site, with lots to see and do. Underground Experience is something not to be missed.

Open: April 1st to October 31st 10.30am to 5pm daily.

Directions: alongside A689, midway between Stanhope and Alston in the heart of the North Pennines.

FHG GUIDES, ABBEY MILL BUSINESS CENTRE, PAISLEY PA1 1TJ • www.holidayguides.com

The Avon Valley Railway offers a whole new experience for some, and a nostalgic memory for others.

PETS MUST BE KEPT ON LEADS AND OFF TRAIN SEATS

Open: Steam trains operate every Sunday, Easter to October, plus Bank Holidays and Christmas.

Directions: on the A431 midway between Bristol and Bath at Bitton.

FHG GUIDES, ABBEY MILL BUSINESS CENTRE, PAISLEY PA1 1TJ • www.holidayguides.com

FHG

·K·U·P·E·R·A·R·D·

READERS' OFFER 2007

NOAH'S ARK ZOO FARM

Failand Road, Wraxall,
Bristol BS48 1PG
Tel: 01275 852606 • Fax: 01275 857080
e-mail: info@noahsarkzoofarm.co.uk
www.noahsarkzoofarm.co.uk

One FREE child for each group of 4 or more persons
Valid until October 2007 (closed in winter)

NOT TO BE USED IN CONJUNCTION WITH ANY OTHER OFFER

READERS' OFFER 2007

CIDER MUSEUM & KING OFFA DISTILLERY

21 Ryelands Street,
Hereford HR4 0LW
Tel: 01432 354207 • Fax: 01432 371641
e-mail: enquiries@cidermuseum.co.uk
www.cidermuseum.co.uk

50p reduction on entry fee
Valid during 2007

NOT TO BE USED IN CONJUNCTION WITH ANY OTHER OFFER

READERS' OFFER 2007

MUSEUM OF KENT LIFE

MUSEUM OF KENT LIFE

Lock Lane, Sandling, Maidstone,
Kent ME14 3AU
Tel: 01622 763936 • Fax: 01622 662024
e-mail: enquiries@museum-kentlife.co.uk
www.museum-kentlife.co.uk

Two tickets for the price of one (cheapest ticket FREE)
Valid from March to November 2007

NOT TO BE USED IN CONJUNCTION WITH ANY OTHER OFFER

READERS' OFFER 2007

QUEX MUSEUM, HOUSE & GARDENS

Quex Park,
Birchington
Kent CT7 0BH

Tel: 01843 842168 • Fax: 01843 846661
e-mail: pcmuseum@btconnect.com

One adult FREE with each full-paying adult on presentation of voucher. Valid until 31 December 2007

NOT TO BE USED IN CONJUNCTION WITH ANY OTHER OFFER

Fantastic 'hands-on' adventure zoo farm for all ages and all weathers. 80 different species from chicks and lambs to camels and rhinos. New indoor and outdoor mazes (longest in world and educational). Family-friendly cafe and shop.

Open: from February half-term to end October 10.30am to 5pm Mon to Sat. Check open days on website

Directions: on B3128 between Bristol and Clevedon or Exit 19/20 M5

FHG GUIDES, ABBEY MILL BUSINESS CENTRE, PAISLEY PA1 1TJ • www.holidayguides.com

Discover the fascinating history of cider making. There is a programme of temporary exhibitions and events plus free samples of Hereford cider brandy.

Open: April to Oct 10am to 5pm ; Nov to March 11am to 3pm. Closed Sun and Mon excluding Bank Holiday weekends.

Directions: situated west of Hereford off the A438 Hereford to Brecon road.

FHG GUIDES, ABBEY MILL BUSINESS CENTRE, PAISLEY PA1 1TJ • www.holidayguides.com

Kent's award-winning open air museum is home to a collection of historic buildings which house interactive exhibitions on life over the last 150 years.

Open: seven days a week from February to start November, 10am to 5pm.

Directions: Junction 6 off M20, follow signs to Aylesford.

FHG GUIDES, ABBEY MILL BUSINESS CENTRE, PAISLEY PA1 1TJ • www.holidayguides.com

World-ranking Museum incorporating Kent's finest Regency house. Gardens with peacocks, woodland walk, walled garden, maze and fountains. Children's activities and full events programme. Tearoom and gift shop. Full events programme.

Open: mid-March-Nov: Sun-Thurs 11am-5pm (House opens 2pm). Winter: Sundays 1-3.30pm (Museum and Gardens only).

Directions: A2 to Margate, on entering Birchington turn right at church into Park Lane; Powell-Cotton Museum signposted.

FHG GUIDES, ABBEY MILL BUSINESS CENTRE, PAISLEY PA1 1TJ • www.holidayguides.com

FHG

·K·U·P·E·R·A·R·D·

READERS' OFFER 2007

DOCKER PARK FARM

Arkholme, Carnforth,
Lancashire LA6 1AR
Tel & Fax: 015242 21331
e-mail: info@dockerparkfarm.co.uk
www.dockerparkfarm.co.uk

One FREE child per one paying adult (one voucher per child)
Valid from January to December 2007

NOT TO BE USED IN CONJUNCTION WITH ANY OTHER OFFER

READERS' OFFER 2007

NATIONAL FISHING HERITAGE CENTRE

Alexandra Dock, Grimsby
N.E. Lincs DN31 1UZ
Tel: 01472 323345 • Fax: 01472 323555
nfhc@nelincs.gov.uk
www.nelincs.gov.uk

One child FREE with every paying adult.
Valid until August 2007 (not Bank Holidays)

NOT TO BE USED IN CONJUNCTION WITH ANY OTHER OFFER

SKEGNESS NATURELAND SEAL SANCTUARY

North Parade, Skegness,
Lincolnshire PE25 1DB
Tel: 01754 764345
e-mail: natureland@fsbdial.co.uk
www.skegnessnatureland.co.uk

Natureland Seal Sanctuary

Free entry for one child when accompanied by full-paying adult. Valid during 2007.

NOT TO BE USED IN CONJUNCTION WITH ANY OTHER OFFER

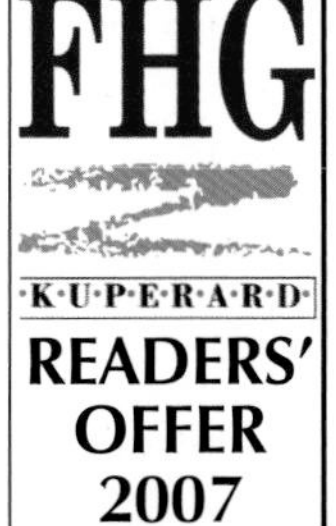

DINOSAUR ADVENTURE PARK

Weston Park, Lenwade, Norwich,
Norfolk NR9 5JW
Tel: 01603 876310 • Fax: 01603 876315
e-mail: info@dinosaurpark.co.uk
www.dinosaurpark.co.uk

Dinosaur Adventure Park

50p off standard admission prices for up to six people
Valid until end of October 2007

NOT TO BE USED IN CONJUNCTION WITH ANY OTHER OFFER

We are a working farm, with lots of animals to see and touch. Enjoy a walk round the Nature Trail or refreshments in the tearoom. Lots of activities during school holidays.	**Open:** Summer: daily 10.30am- 5pm. Winter: weekends only 10.30am-4pm. **Directions:** Junction 35 off M6, take B6254 towards Kirkby Lonsdale, then follow the brown signs.

FHG GUIDES, ABBEY MILL BUSINESS CENTRE, PAISLEY PA1 1TJ • www.holidayguides.com

Sign on as a crew member for an incredible journey of discovery that will take you to the edge of disaster and the extremes of the elements to witness at first hand the depths of human endurance. Plot your course, take the wheel in the Skipper's Wheelhouse, study maps and charts, try the radio, send a Morse Code message - and lots more.	**Open:** Apr-Oct: Mon-Fri 10am to 5pm, Sat-Sun 10.30am-5.30pm. Please phone for winter opening hours. **Directions:** A180 Corporation Road towards Sainsbury's.

FHG GUIDES, ABBEY MILL BUSINESS CENTRE, PAISLEY PA1 1TJ • www.holidayguides.com

Well known for rescuing and rehabilitating orphaned and injured seal pups found washed ashore on Lincolnshire beaches. Also: penguins, aquarium, pets' corner, reptiles, Floral Palace (tropical birds and butterflies etc).	**Open:** daily from 10am. Closed Christmas/Boxing/New Year's Days. **Directions:** at the north end of Skegness seafront.

FHG GUIDES, ABBEY MILL BUSINESS CENTRE, PAISLEY PA1 1TJ • www.holidayguides.com

It's time you came-n-saurus for a monster day out of discovery, adventure and fun. Enjoy the adventure play areas, dinosaur trail, secret animal garden and lots more.	**Open:** Please call for specific opening times or see our website. **Directions:** 9 miles from Norwich, follow the brown signs to Weston Park from the A47 or A1067

FHG GUIDES, ABBEY MILL BUSINESS CENTRE, PAISLEY PA1 1TJ • www.holidayguides.com

READERS' OFFER 2007

THE COLLECTORS WORLD OF ERIC ST JOHN-FOTI

Hermitage Hall, Downham Market,
Norfolk PE38 0AU
Tel: 01366 383185 • Fax: 01366 386519
www.collectors-world.org

50p off adult admission - 25p off child admission
Valid during 2007

NOT TO BE USED IN CONJUNCTION WITH ANY OTHER OFFER

READERS' OFFER 2007

THE TALES OF ROBIN HOOD

30 - 38 Maid Marian Way,
Nottingham NG1 6GF
Tel: 0115 9483284 • Fax: 0115 9501536
e-mail: robinhoodcentre@mail.com
www.robinhood.uk.com

One FREE child with full paying adult per voucher
Valid from January to December 2007

NOT TO BE USED IN CONJUNCTION WITH ANY OTHER OFFER

READERS' OFFER 2007

NEWARK AIR MUSEUM

The Airfield, Winthorpe, Newark,
Nottinghamshire NG24 2NY
Tel: 01636 707170
e-mail: newarkair@onetel.com
www.newarkairmuseum.co.uk

Party rate discount for every voucher (50p per person off normal admission). Valid during 2007.

NOT TO BE USED IN CONJUNCTION WITH ANY OTHER OFFER

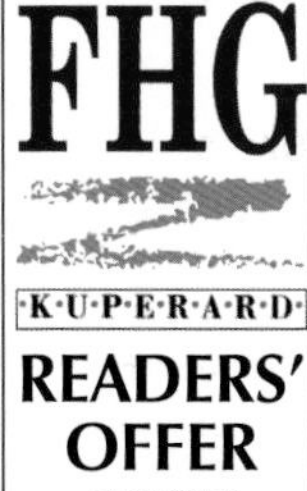

READERS' OFFER 2007

DIDCOT RAILWAY CENTRE

Didcot,
Oxfordshire OX11 7NJ
Tel: 01235 817200 • Fax: 01235 510621
e-mail: didrlyc@globalnet.co.uk
www.didcotrailwaycentre.org.uk

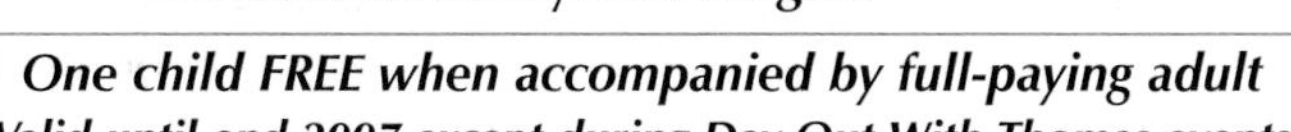
One child FREE when accompanied by full-paying adult
Valid until end 2007 except during Day Out With Thomas events

NOT TO BE USED IN CONJUNCTION WITH ANY OTHER OFFER

The collections of local eccentric Eric St John-Foti (Mr Norfolk Punch himself!) on view and the Magical Dickens Experience. Two amazing attractions for the price of one. Somewhere totally different, unique and interesting.

Open: 11am to 5pm (last entry 4pm) Open all year.

Directions: one mile from town centre on the A1122 Downham/ Wisbech Road.

FHG GUIDES, ABBEY MILL BUSINESS CENTRE, PAISLEY PA1 1TJ • www.holidayguides.com

Travel back in time with Robin Hood and his merry men on an adventure-packed theme tour, exploring the intriguing and mysterious story of their legendary tales of Medieval England. Enjoy film shows, live performances, adventure rides and even try archery! Are you brave enough to join Robin on his quest for good against evil?

Open: 10am-5.30pm, last admission 4.30pm.

Directions: follow the brown and white tourist information signs whilst heading towards the city centre.

FHG GUIDES, ABBEY MILL BUSINESS CENTRE, PAISLEY PA1 1TJ • www.holidayguides.com

A collection of 70 aircraft and cockpit sections from across the history of aviation. Extensive aero engine and artefact displays.

Open: daily from 10am (closed Christmas period and New Year's Day).

Directions: follow brown and white signs from A1, A46, A17 and A1133.

FHG GUIDES, ABBEY MILL BUSINESS CENTRE, PAISLEY PA1 1TJ • www.holidayguides.com

See the steam trains from the golden age of the Great Western Railway. Steam locomotives in the original engine shed, a reconstructed country branch line, and a re-creation of Brunel's original broad gauge railway. On Steam Days there are rides in the 1930s carriages.

Open: Sat/Sun all year; daily 23 June to 2 Sept + school holidays. 10am-5pm weekends and Steam Days, 10am-4pm other days and in winter.

Directions: at Didcot Parkway rail station; on A4130, signposted from M4 (Junction 13) and A34

FHG GUIDES, ABBEY MILL BUSINESS CENTRE, PAISLEY PA1 1TJ • www.holidayguides.com

FHG
·K·U·P·E·R·A·R·D·
READERS' OFFER 2007

THE HELICOPTER MUSEUM

The Heliport, Locking Moor Road,
Weston-Super-Mare BS24 8PP
Tel: 01934 635227• Fax: 01934 645230
e-mail: office@helimuseum.fsnet.co.uk
www.helicoptermuseum.co.uk

One child FREE with two full-paying adults
Valid from April to October 2007

NOT TO BE USED IN CONJUNCTION WITH ANY OTHER OFFER

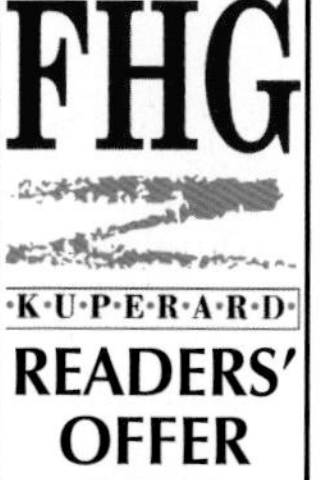

READERS' OFFER 2007

EXMOOR FALCONRY & ANIMAL FARM

Allerford, Near Porlock, Minehead,
Somerset TA24 8HJ
Tel: 01643 862816
e-mail: exmoor.falcon@virgin.net
www.exmoorfalconry.co.uk

Exmoor Falconry

10% off entry to Falconry Centre
Valid during 2007

NOT TO BE USED IN CONJUNCTION WITH ANY OTHER OFFER

READERS' OFFER 2007

TROPIQUARIA

Washford Cross, Watchet
Somerset TA23 0QB
Tel: 01984 640688 • Fax: 01984 641105
e-mail: info@tropiquaria.co.uk
www.tropiquaria.co.uk

TROPIQUARIA Animals & Adventure!

One FREE child per full paying adult
(one child per voucher). Valid during 2007

NOT TO BE USED IN CONJUNCTION WITH ANY OTHER OFFER

FHG
·K·U·P·E·R·A·R·D·
READERS' OFFER 2007

FLEET AIR ARM MUSEUM

RNAS Yeovilton, Ilchester,
Somerset BA22 8HT
Tel: 01935 840565
e-mail: enquiries@fleetairarm.com
www.fleetairarm.com

Fleet Air Arm Museum

One child FREE with full paying adult
Valid during 2007 except Bank Holidays

NOT TO BE USED IN CONJUNCTION WITH ANY OTHER OFFER

The world's largest helicopter collection - over 70 exhibits, includes two royal helicopters, Russian Gunship and Vietnam veterans plus many award-winning exhibits. Cafe, shop. Flights.

PETS MUST BE KEPT UNDER CONTROL

Open: Wednesday to Sunday 10am to 5.30pm. Daily during school Easter and Summer holidays and Bank Holiday Mondays. November to March: 10am to 4.30pm

Directions: Junction 21 off M5 then follow the propellor signs.

FHG GUIDES, ABBEY MILL BUSINESS CENTRE, PAISLEY PA1 1TJ • www.holidayguides.com

Falconry centre with animals - flying displays, animal handling, feeding and bottle feeding - in 15th century NT farmyard setting on Exmoor. Also falconry and outdoor activities, hawk walks and riding.

Open: 10.30am to 5pm daily

Directions: A39 west of Minehead, turn right at Allerford, half a mile along lane on left.

FHG GUIDES, ABBEY MILL BUSINESS CENTRE, PAISLEY PA1 1TJ • www.holidayguides.com

Animal and adventure park where you can hold snakes and tarantulas in the Tropical Hall. Visit the Aquarium, Puppet Theatre and Radio Museum.
Play on our two full-size pirate ships and indoor playcastle.

Open: daily Easter-Sept 10am-6pm.
Sept - end Oct: 11am-5pm;
Nov - Easter: weekends and school holidays.

Directions: on A39 between Williton and Minehead. Look for tall pirate ship masts. Buses: 14, 28, 38.

FHG GUIDES, ABBEY MILL BUSINESS CENTRE, PAISLEY PA1 1TJ • www.holidayguides.com

Europe's largest naval aviation collection with over 40 aircraft on display , including Concorde 002 and Ark Royal Aircraft Carrier Experience. Situated on an operational naval air station.

Open: open daily April to October 10am-5.30pm; November to March 10am-4.30pm (closed Mon and Tues).

Directions: just off A303/A37 on B3151 at Ilchester. Yeovil rail station 10 miles.

FHG GUIDES, ABBEY MILL BUSINESS CENTRE, PAISLEY PA1 1TJ • www.holidayguides.com

Stay and play all day at Somerset's top all-weather family day out. Cuddle pets and baby animals, mega playbarn with 3 levels of fun and exciting giant slides! Acres of friendly animals to meet and feed, farm walks, massive play park with trampolines, free train rides and lots, lots more! See website for event days.	**Open:** 10am-5.30pm daily all year except 24-26 December. **Directions:** from M5 J22 head for Berrow/Brean; follow Animal Farm signs.

FHG GUIDES, ABBEY MILL BUSINESS CENTRE, PAISLEY PA1 1TJ • www.holidayguides.com

Discover 'Planet Earth' for an unforgettable experience. A unique Museum of Life, Dinosaur Safari, beautiful Water Gardens with fish and wildfowl, plant houses, themed gardens, Heritage Trail, miniature railway. Playzone includes crazy golf and adventure play areas. Garden Centre and Terrace Cafe.	**Open:** open daily, except Christmas Day and Boxing Day. **Directions:** signposted off A26 and A259.

FHG GUIDES, ABBEY MILL BUSINESS CENTRE, PAISLEY PA1 1TJ • www.holidayguides.com

The past is brought to life at one of the South East's best loved family attractions. 100,000+ nostalgic artefacts, set in a charming 15th century house and country garden. New attractions and tearooms.	**Open:** 9.30am to 6pm (last admission 4.45pm, one hour earlier in winter). Closing times may vary – phone or check website. **Directions:** just off A21 in Battle High Street opposite the Abbey.

FHG GUIDES, ABBEY MILL BUSINESS CENTRE, PAISLEY PA1 1TJ • www.holidayguides.com

18-hole American Adventure Golf set in ⅓ acre landscaped surroundings. Played on different levels including water features.	**Open:** April until end October 10am until dusk. **Directions:** on the seafront ¼ mile east of Eastbourne Pier.

FHG GUIDES, ABBEY MILL BUSINESS CENTRE, PAISLEY PA1 1TJ • www.holidayguides.com

FHG
·K·U·P·E·R·A·R·D·
READERS' OFFER 2007

WILDERNESS WOOD

Hadlow Down, Near Uckfield, East Sussex TN22 4HJ
Tel: 01825 830509• Fax: 01825 830977
e-mail: enquiries@wildernesswood.co.uk
www.wildernesswood.co.uk

one FREE admission with a full-paying adult
Valid during 2007 (not for Special Events)

NOT TO BE USED IN CONJUNCTION WITH ANY OTHER OFFER

FHG
·K·U·P·E·R·A·R·D·
READERS' OFFER 2007

WASHINGTON WETLAND CENTRE

Washington Wetland Centre

Pattinson, Washington, Tyne & Wear NE38 8LE
Tel: 0191 416 5454
e-mail: info.washington@wwt.org.uk
www.wwt.org.uk

One FREE admission with full-paying adult
Valid from 1st Jan to 30th Sept 2007

NOT TO BE USED IN CONJUNCTION WITH ANY OTHER OFFER

READERS' OFFER 2007

HATTON COUNTRY WORLD FARM VILLAGE

Dark Lane, Hatton, Near Warwick, Warwickshire CV35 8XA
Tel: 01926 843411

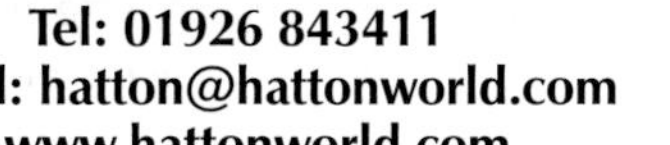

e-mail: hatton@hattonworld.com
www.hattonworld.com

Admit one child FREE with one full-paying adult day ticket.
Admission into Shopping Village free. Valid during 2007

NOT TO BE USED IN CONJUNCTION WITH ANY OTHER OFFER

FHG
·K·U·P·E·R·A·R·D·
READERS' OFFER 2007

STRATFORD BUTTERFLY FARM

Swan's Nest Lane, Stratford-upon-Avon Warwickshire CV37 7LS
Tel: 01789 299288 • Fax: 01789 415878
e-mail: sales@butterflyfarm.co.uk
www.butterflyfarm.co.uk

Admit TWO for the price of ONE
Valid until 31/12/2007

NOT TO BE USED IN CONJUNCTION WITH ANY OTHER OFFER

Wilderness Wood is a unique family-run working woodland in the Sussex High Weald. Explore trails and footpaths, enjoy local cakes and ices, try the adventure playground. Many special events and activities. Parties catered for.

Open: daily 10am to 5.30pm or dusk if earlier.

Directions: on the south side of the A272 in the village of Hadlow Down. Signposted with a brown tourist sign.

FHG GUIDES, ABBEY MILL BUSINESS CENTRE, PAISLEY PA1 1TJ • www.holidayguides.com

Conservation site with 100 acres of stunning wetland and woodland, home to rare wildlife. Waterside cafe, play area, gift shop.

Open: every day except Christmas Day

Directions: signposted from A19, A195, A1231 and A182.

FHG GUIDES, ABBEY MILL BUSINESS CENTRE, PAISLEY PA1 1TJ • www.holidayguides.com

Two attractions side-by-side. Hatton Farm Village has fun for the whole family, with animals, demonstrations and adventure play. Hatton Shopping Village has 25 craft and gift shops, an antiques centre, a factory-style store, and two restaurants. Free parking.

Open: daily 10am to 5pm. Open until 4pm Christmas Eve; 11am-4pm 27 Dec-1st Jan incl; closed Christmas Day & Boxing Day.

Directions: 5 minutes from M40 (J15), A46 towards Coventry, then just off A4177 (follow brown tourist signs).

FHG GUIDES, ABBEY MILL BUSINESS CENTRE, PAISLEY PA1 1TJ • www.holidayguides.com

Wander through a tropical rainforest with a myriad of multicoloured butterflies, sunbirds and koi carp. See fascinating animals in Insect City and view deadly spiders in perfect safety in Arachnoland.

Open: daily except Christmas Day.
10am-6pm summer,
10am-dusk winter.

Directions: on south bank of River Avon opposite Royal Shakespeare Theatre. Easily accessible from town centre, 5 minutes' walk.

FHG GUIDES, ABBEY MILL BUSINESS CENTRE, PAISLEY PA1 1TJ • www.holidayguides.com

READERS' OFFER 2007

AVONCROFT MUSEUM

AVONCROFT MUSEUM OF HISTORIC BUILDINGS

Stoke Heath,
Bromsgrove,
Worcestershire B60 4JR
Tel: 01527 831363 • Fax: 01527 876934
www.avoncroft.org.uk

One FREE child with one full-paying adult
Valid from March to November 2007

NOT TO BE USED IN CONJUNCTION WITH ANY OTHER OFFER

READERS' OFFER 2007

YORKSHIRE DALES FALCONRY & WILDLIFE CONSERVATION CENTRE

YORKSHIRE DALES FALCONRY & WILDLIFE CONSERVATION CENTRE

Crow's Nest, Giggleswick, Near Settle LA2 8AS
Tel: 01729 822832• Fax: 01729 825160
e-mail: info@falconryandwildlife.com
www.falconryandwildlife.com

One child FREE with two full-paying adults
Valid until end 2007

NOT TO BE USED IN CONJUNCTION WITH ANY OTHER OFFER

READERS' OFFER 2007

WORLD OF JAMES HERRIOT

HERRIOT

23 Kirkgate, Thirsk,
North Yorkshire YO7 1PL
Tel: 01845 524234
Fax: 01845 525333
www.worldofjamesherriot.org

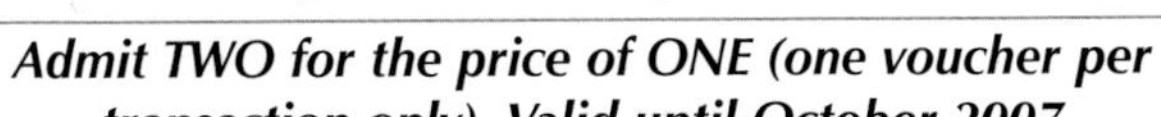
Admit TWO for the price of ONE (one voucher per transaction only). Valid until October 2007

NOT TO BE USED IN CONJUNCTION WITH ANY OTHER OFFER

READERS' OFFER 2007

EMBSAY & BOLTON ABBEY STEAM RAILWAY

EMBSAY & BOLTON ABBEY STEAM RAILWAY

Bolton Abbey Station, Skipton,
North Yorkshire BD23 6AF
Tel: 01756 710614
e-mail: embsay.steam@btinternet.com
www.embsayboltonabbeyrailway.org.uk

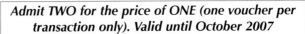

One adult travels FREE when accompanied by a full fare paying adult (does not include Special Event days). Valid during 2007.

NOT TO BE USED IN CONJUNCTION WITH ANY OTHER OFFER

A fascinating world of historic buildings covering 7 centuries, rescued and rebuilt on an open-air site in the heart of the Worcestershire countryside.

PETS ON LEADS ONLY

Open: July and August all week. March to November varying times, please telephone for details.

Directions: A38 south of Bromsgrove, near Junction 1 of M42, Junction 5 of M5.

FHG GUIDES, ABBEY MILL BUSINESS CENTRE, PAISLEY PA1 1TJ • www.holidayguides.com

All types of birds of prey exhibited here, from owls and kestrels to eagles and vultures. Special flying displays 12 noon, 1.30pm and 3pm. Bird handling courses arranged for either half or full days.

GUIDE DOGS ONLY

Open: 10am to 4.30pm summer 10am to 4pm winter

Directions: on main A65 trunk road outside Settle. Follow brown direction signs.

FHG GUIDES, ABBEY MILL BUSINESS CENTRE, PAISLEY PA1 1TJ • www.holidayguides.com

Visit James Herriot's original house recreated as it was in the 1940s. Television sets used in the series 'All Creatures Great and Small'. There is a children's interactive gallery with life-size model farm animals and three rooms dedicated to the history of veterinary medicine.

Open: daily. Easter-Oct 10am-5pm; Nov-Easter 11am to 4pm

Directions: follow signs off A1 or A19 to Thirsk, then A168, off Thirsk market place

FHG GUIDES, ABBEY MILL BUSINESS CENTRE, PAISLEY PA1 1TJ • www.holidayguides.com

Steam trains operate over a 4½ mile line from Bolton Abbey Station to Embsay Station. Many family events including Thomas the Tank Engine take place during major Bank Holidays.

Open: steam trains run every Sunday throughout the year and up to 7 days a week in summer. 10.30am to 4.30pm

Directions: Embsay Station signposted from the A59 Skipton by-pass; Bolton Abbey Station signposted from the A59 at Bolton Abbey.

FHG GUIDES, ABBEY MILL BUSINESS CENTRE, PAISLEY PA1 1TJ • www.holidayguides.com

READERS' OFFER 2007

MUSEUM OF RAIL TRAVEL

Ingrow Railway Centre, Near Keighley,
West Yorkshire BD22 8NJ
Tel: 01535 680425
e-mail: admin@vintagecarriagestrust.org
www.vintagecarriagestrust.org • www.museumofrailtravel.co.uk

"ONE for ONE" free admission
Valid during 2007 except during special events (ring to check)

NOT TO BE USED IN CONJUNCTION WITH ANY OTHER OFFER

READERS' OFFER 2007

THE COLOUR MUSEUM

Colour Museum

Perkin House, PO Box 244, Providence Street,
Bradford BD1 2PW
Tel: 01274 390955 • Fax: 01274 392888
e-mail: museum@sdc.org.uk
www.colour-experience.org

TWO for ONE
Valid during 2007

NOT TO BE USED IN CONJUNCTION WITH ANY OTHER OFFER

READERS' OFFER 2007

THACKRAY MUSEUM

THACKRAY museum

Beckett Street, Leeds LS9 7LN
Tel: 0113 244 4343
Fax: 0113 247 0219
e-mail: info@thackraymuseum.org
www.thackraymuseum.org

TWO for ONE on the purchase of a full adult ticket
Valid until July 2007 excluding Bank Holidays

NOT TO BE USED IN CONJUNCTION WITH ANY OTHER OFFER

READERS' OFFER 2007

EUREKA! THE MUSEUM FOR CHILDREN

Discovery Road, Halifax,
West Yorkshire HX1 2NE
Tel: 01422 330069
e-mail: info@eureka.org.uk
www.eureka.org

243 - £6.50 ticket
244 - £1.95 ticket

One child FREE with one adult paying full price.
Valid Saturdays and Sundays only during 2007

NOT TO BE USED IN CONJUNCTION WITH ANY OTHER OFFER

A fascinating display of railway carriages and a wide range of railway items telling the story of rail travel over the years.

ALL PETS MUST BE KEPT ON LEADS

Open: daily 11am to 4.30pm

Directions: approximately one mile from Keighley on A629 Halifax road. Follow brown tourist signs

FHG GUIDES, ABBEY MILL BUSINESS CENTRE, PAISLEY PA1 1TJ • www.holidayguides.com

The Colour Museum is unique. Dedicated to the history, development and technology of colour, it is the ONLY museum of its kind in Europe. A truly colourful experience for both kids and adults, it's fun, it's informative and it's well worth a visit.

Open: Tuesday to Saturday 10am to 4pm (last admission 3.30pm).

Directions: just off Westgate on B6144 from the city centre to Haworth.

FHG GUIDES, ABBEY MILL BUSINESS CENTRE, PAISLEY PA1 1TJ • www.holidayguides.com

The Thackray Museum has been England's Visitor Attraction of the Year and is a fantastic day out, transporting you into a living experience of health and medicine, past, present and future. Experience life as a character in the Victorian Slums of 1840, where you will be flabbergasted at the incredible lotions and potions once offered as cures, then see how this has evolved into modern medicine. Then step inside the human body in the interactive Life Zone!

Open: daily 10am till 5pm, closed 24th-26th + 31st Dec and 1st Jan.

Directions: from M621 follow signs for York (A64), then follow brown tourist signs. From the north, take A58 towards city, then follow brown tourist signs.

FHG GUIDES, ABBEY MILL BUSINESS CENTRE, PAISLEY PA1 1TJ • www.holidayguides.com

The UK's first and foremost museum for children under 11, where hundreds of interactive exhibits let them make fascinating discoveries about themselves and the world around them.

Open: daily 10am to 5pm (closed 24-26 December)

Directions: next to Halifax railway station, five minutes from J24 M62

FHG GUIDES, ABBEY MILL BUSINESS CENTRE, PAISLEY PA1 1TJ • www.holidayguides.com

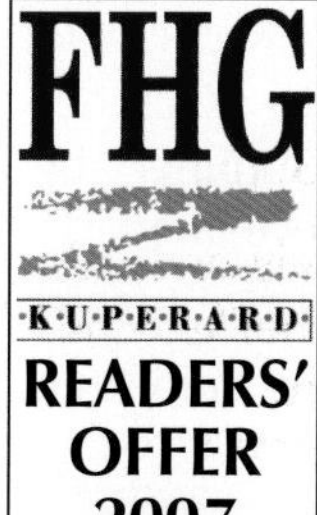

THE GRASSIC GIBBON CENTRE

Arbuthnott, Laurencekirk,
Aberdeenshire AB30 1PB
Tel: 01561 361668
e-mail: lgginfo@grassicgibbon.com
www.grassicgibbon.com

The Grassic Gibbon Centre

TWO for the price of ONE entry to exhibition (based on full adult rate only). Valid during 2007 (not groups)

NOT TO BE USED IN CONJUNCTION WITH ANY OTHER OFFER

STORYBOOK GLEN

Maryculter,
Aberdeen
Aberdeenshire AB12 5FT
Tel: 01224 732941

www.storybookglenaberdeen.co.uk

10% discount on all admissions
Valid until end 2007

NOT TO BE USED IN CONJUNCTION WITH ANY OTHER OFFER

OBAN RARE BREEDS FARM PARK

Glencruitten, Oban,
Argyll PA34 4QB
Tel: 01631 770608
e-mail: info@obanrarebreeds.com
www.obanrarebreeds.com

Oban Rare Breeds Farm Park

20% DISCOUNT on all admissions
Valid during 2007

NOT TO BE USED IN CONJUNCTION WITH ANY OTHER OFFER

INVERARAY JAIL

Church Square, Inveraray,
Argyll PA32 8TX
Tel: 01499 302381 • Fax: 01499 302195
e-mail: info@inverarayjail.co.uk
www.inverarayjail.co.uk

One child FREE with one full-paying adult
Valid until end 2007

NOT TO BE USED IN CONJUNCTION WITH ANY OTHER OFFER

Visitor Centre dedicated to the much-loved Scottish writer Lewis Grassic Gibbon. Exhibition, cafe, gift shop. Outdoor children's play area. Disabled access throughout.	**Open:** daily April to October 10am to 4.30pm. Groups by appointment including evenings. **Directions:** on the B967, accessible and signposted from both A90 and A92.

FHG GUIDES, ABBEY MILL BUSINESS CENTRE, PAISLEY PA1 1TJ • www.holidayguides.com

28-acre theme park with over 100 nursery rhyme characters, set in beautifully landscaped gardens. Shop and restaurant on site.	**Open:** 1st March to 31st October: daily 10am to 6pm; 1st Nov to end Feb: Sat/Sun only 11am to 4pm **Directions:** 6 miles west of Aberdeen off B9077

FHG GUIDES, ABBEY MILL BUSINESS CENTRE, PAISLEY PA1 1TJ • www.holidayguides.com

Rare breeds of farm animals, pets' corner, conservation groups, tea room, woodland walk in beautiful location	**Open:** 10am to 6pm mid-March to end October **Directions:** two-and-a-half miles from Oban along Glencruitten road

FHG GUIDES, ABBEY MILL BUSINESS CENTRE, PAISLEY PA1 1TJ • www.holidayguides.com

19th century prison with fully restored 1820 courtroom and two prisons. Guides in uniform as warders, prisoners and matron. Remember your camera!	**Open:** April to October 9.30am-6pm (last admission 5pm); November to March 10am-5pm (last admission 4pm) **Directions:** A83 to Campbeltown

FHG GUIDES, ABBEY MILL BUSINESS CENTRE, PAISLEY PA1 1TJ • www.holidayguides.com

FHG

·K·U·P·E·R·A·R·D·

READERS' OFFER 2007

SCOTTISH MARITIME MUSEUM

Harbourside, Irvine,
Ayrshire KA12 8QE
Tel: 01294 278283
Fax: 01294 313211
www.scottishmaritimemuseum.org

Scottish Maritime Museum

TWO for the price of ONE
Valid from April to October 2007

NOT TO BE USED IN CONJUNCTION WITH ANY OTHER OFFER

JEDFOREST DEER & FARM PARK

Mervinslaw Estate, Camptown, Jedburgh,
Borders TD8 6PL
Tel: 01835 840364
e-mail: mervinslaw@ecosse.net
www.aboutscotland.com/jedforest

Jedforest Deer and Farm Park JEDBURGH

One FREE child with two full-paying adults
Valid May/June and Sept/Oct 2007

NOT TO BE USED IN CONJUNCTION WITH ANY OTHER OFFER

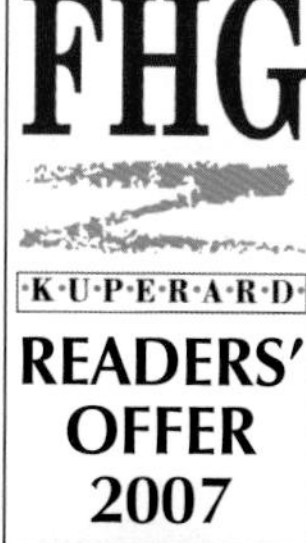

SCOTTISH SEABIRD CENTRE

The Harbour, North Berwick,
East Lothian EH39 4SS
Tel: 01620 890202 • Fax: 01620 890222
e-mail: info@seabird.org
www.seabird.org

Scottish Seabird Centre

20% OFF any admission
Valid until 1st October 2007

NOT TO BE USED IN CONJUNCTION WITH ANY OTHER OFFER

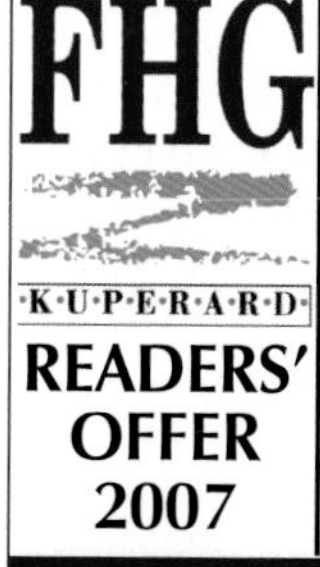

THE SCOTTISH MINING MUSEUM

Lady Victoria Colliery, Newtongrange,
Midlothian EH22 4QN
Tel: 0131-663 7519 • Fax: 0131-654 0952
visitorservices@scottishminingmuseum.com
www.scottishminingmuseum.com

Scottish Mining Museum

One child FREE with full-paying adult
Valid January to December 2007

NOT TO BE USED IN CONJUNCTION WITH ANY OTHER OFFER

Scotland's seafaring heritage is among the world's richest and you can relive the heyday of Scottish shipping at the Maritime Museum.

Open: 1st April to 31st October - 10am-5pm

Directions: situated on Irvine harbourside and only a 10 minute walk from Irvine train station.

FHG GUIDES, ABBEY MILL BUSINESS CENTRE, PAISLEY PA1 1TJ • www.holidayguides.com

Working farm with visitor centre showing rare breeds, deer herds, ranger-led activities, and walks. Birds of prey displays and tuition. Corporate activities. Shop and cafe.

Open: daily Easter to August 10am to 5.30pm; Sept/Oct 11am to 4.30pm.

Directions: 5 miles south of Jedburgh on A68.

FHG GUIDES, ABBEY MILL BUSINESS CENTRE, PAISLEY PA1 1TJ • www.holidayguides.com

Get close to Nature with a visit to this award-winning Centre. With panoramic views across islands and sandy beaches, the area is a haven for wildlife. Live cameras zoom in close to see wildlife including gannets, puffins and seals. Wildlife boat safaris, new Environmental Zone and Flyway.

Open: daily from 10am

Directions: from A1 take road for North Berwick; near the harbour; Centre signposted.

FHG GUIDES, ABBEY MILL BUSINESS CENTRE, PAISLEY PA1 1TJ • www.holidayguides.com

visitscotland 5-Star Attraction with two floors of interactive exhibitions, a 'Magic Helmet' tour of the pithead, re-created coal road and coal face, and new Big Stuff tour. Largest working winding engine in Britain.

Open: daily. Summer: 10am to 5pm (last tour 3.30pm). Winter: 10am to 4pm (last tour 2.30pm)

Directions: 5 minutes from Sherrifhall Roundabout on Edinburgh City Bypass on A7 south

FHG GUIDES, ABBEY MILL BUSINESS CENTRE, PAISLEY PA1 1TJ • www.holidayguides.com

FHG

·K·U·P·E·R·A·R·D·

READERS' OFFER 2007

BO'NESS & KINNEIL RAILWAY

Bo'ness Station, Union Street,
Bo'ness, West Lothian EH51 9AQ
Tel: 01506 822298
e-mail: enquiries.railway@srps.org.uk
www.srps.org.uk

FREE child train fare with one paying adult/concession. Valid 31st March-31st Oct 2007. Not Thomas events or Santa Steam trains

NOT TO BE USED IN CONJUNCTION WITH ANY OTHER OFFER

READERS' OFFER 2007

MYRETON MOTOR MUSEUM

MYRETON
MOTOR
MUSEUM

Aberlady,
East Lothian
EH32 0PZ
Tel: 01875 870288

One child FREE with each paying adult
Valid during 2007

NOT TO BE USED IN CONJUNCTION WITH ANY OTHER OFFER

READERS' OFFER 2007

GLASGOW SCIENCE CENTRE

50 Pacific Quay
Glasgow
G51 1EA
Tel: 0871 540 1000
www.glasgowsciencecentre.org

£1 off entry to Science Mall or IMAX Cinema (not valid for feature-length films; not with group tickets). Valid until 30/5/2007

NOT TO BE USED IN CONJUNCTION WITH ANY OTHER OFFER

READERS' OFFER 2007

SPEYSIDE HEATHER GARDEN & VISITOR CENTRE

Speyside
HEATHER
GARDEN

Speyside Heather Centre, Dulnain Bridge,
Inverness-shire PH26 3PA
Tel: 01479 851359 • Fax: 01479 851396
e-mail: enquiries@heathercentre.com
www.heathercentre.com

FREE entry to 'Heather Story' exhibition
Valid during 2007

NOT TO BE USED IN CONJUNCTION WITH ANY OTHER OFFER

Steam and heritage diesel passenger trains from Bo'ness to Birkhill for guided tours of Birkhill fireclay mines. Explore the history of Scotland's railways in the Scottish Railway Exhibition. Coffee shop and souvenir shop.

Open: weekends April to October, daily July and August.

Directions: in the town of Bo'ness. Leave M9 at Junction 3 or 5, then follow brown tourist signs.

FHG GUIDES, ABBEY MILL BUSINESS CENTRE, PAISLEY PA1 1TJ • www.holidayguides.com

On show is a large collection, from 1899, of cars, bicycles, motor cycles and commercials. There is also a large collection of period advertising, posters and enamel signs.

Open: March-November - open daily 11am to 4pm. December-February - weekends 11am to 3pm or by special appointment.

Directions: off A198 near Aberlady. Two miles from A1.

FHG GUIDES, ABBEY MILL BUSINESS CENTRE, PAISLEY PA1 1TJ • www.holidayguides.com

Hundreds of interactive exhibits, live science shows and Scotland's only IMAX cinema - a great day out whatever the weather!

Open: 10am-6pm 7 days until 28/10/06.
From 29/10/06 to 30/3/2007 open 10am-6pm Tues-Sun.

Directions: J24 M8, J21 M77.
Nearest Underground: Cessnock.
Train - Exhibition Centre.

FHG GUIDES, ABBEY MILL BUSINESS CENTRE, PAISLEY PA1 1TJ • www.holidayguides.com

Award-winning attraction with unique 'Heather Story' exhibition, gallery, giftshop, large garden centre selling 300 different heathers, antique shop, children's play area and famous Clootie Dumpling restaurant.

Open: all year except Christmas Day.

Directions: just off A95 between Aviemore and Grantown-on-Spey.

FHG GUIDES, ABBEY MILL BUSINESS CENTRE, PAISLEY PA1 1TJ • www.holidayguides.com

FHG

K·U·P·E·R·A·R·D

READERS' OFFER 2007

NEW LANARK WORLD HERITAGE SITE

New Lanark Mills, Lanark,
Lanarkshire ML11 9DB
Tel: 01555 661345• Fax: 01555 665738
e-mail: visit@newlanark.org
www.newlanark.org

NEW LANARK

One FREE child with one full price adult
Valid until 31st October 2007

NOT TO BE USED IN CONJUNCTION WITH ANY OTHER OFFER

READERS' OFFER 2007

LLANBERIS LAKE RAILWAY

Gilfach Ddu, Llanberis,
Gwynedd LL55 4TY
Tel: 01286 870549
e-mail: info@lake-railway.co.uk
www.lake-railway.co.uk

One pet travels FREE with each full fare paying adult
Valid Easter to October 2007

NOT TO BE USED IN CONJUNCTION WITH ANY OTHER OFFER

PILI PALAS - BUTTERFLY PALACE & NATURE WORLD

Menai Bridge
Isle of Anglesey LL59 5RP
Tel: 01248 712474
e-mail: info@pilipalas.co.uk
www.pilipalas.co.uk

One child FREE with two adults paying full entry price
Valid March to October 2007

NOT TO BE USED IN CONJUNCTION WITH ANY OTHER OFFER

READERS' OFFER 2007

FELINWYNT RAINFOREST CENTRE

Felinwynt, Cardigan,
Ceredigion SA43 1RT
Tel: 01239 810882/810250
e-mail: dandjdevereux@btinternet.com
www.butterflycentre.co.uk

TWO for the price of ONE (one voucher per party only)
Valid until end October 2007

NOT TO BE USED IN CONJUNCTION WITH ANY OTHER OFFER

A beautifully restored cotton mill village close to the Falls of Clyde. Explore the fascinating history of the village, try the 'Millennium Experience', a magical ride which takes you back in time to discover what life used to be like.

Open: 11am-5pm daily. June-August 10.30am-5pm daily. Closed Christmas Day and New Year's Day.

Directions: 25 miles from Glasgow and 35 miles from Edinburgh; well signposted on all major routes.

FHG GUIDES, ABBEY MILL BUSINESS CENTRE, PAISLEY PA1 1TJ • www.holidayguides.com

A 60-minute ride along the shores of beautiful Padarn Lake behind a quaint historic steam engine. Magnificent views of the mountains from lakeside picnic spots.

DOGS MUST BE KEPT ON LEAD AT ALL TIMES ON TRAIN

Open: most days Easter to October. Free timetable leaflet on request.

Directions: just off A4086 Caernarfon to Capel Curig road at Llanberis; follow 'Country Park' signs.

FHG GUIDES, ABBEY MILL BUSINESS CENTRE, PAISLEY PA1 1TJ • www.holidayguides.com

Visit Wales' top Butterfly House, with Bird House, Snake House, Ant Avenue, Tropical Hide, shop, cafe, adventure playground, indoor play area, picnic area, nature trail etc.

Open: March to end Oct: 10am - 5.30pm daily; Nov/Dec 11am-3pm

Directions: follow brown and white signs when crossing to Anglesey; one-and-a- half miles from Bridge

FHG GUIDES, ABBEY MILL BUSINESS CENTRE, PAISLEY PA1 1TJ • www.holidayguides.com

Mini-rainforest full of tropical plants and exotic butterflies. Personal attention of the owner, Mr John Devereux. Gift shop, cafe, video room, exhibition. Suitable for disabled visitors. WTB Quality Assured Visitor Attraction.

PETS NOT ALLOWED IN TROPICAL HOUSE ONLY

Open: daily Easter to end October 10.30am to 5pm

Directions: West Wales, 7 miles north of Cardigan off Aberystwyth road. Follow brown tourist signs on A487.

FHG GUIDES, ABBEY MILL BUSINESS CENTRE, PAISLEY PA1 1TJ • www.holidayguides.com

FHG

·K·U·P·E·R·A·R·D·

READERS' OFFER 2007

NATIONAL CYCLE COLLECTION

Automobile Palace, Temple Street,
Llandrindod Wells, Powys LD1 5DL
Tel: 01597 825531
e-mail: cycle.museum@powys.org.uk
www.cyclemuseum.org.uk

TWO for the price of ONE
Valid during 2007 except Special Event days

NOT TO BE USED IN CONJUNCTION WITH ANY OTHER OFFER

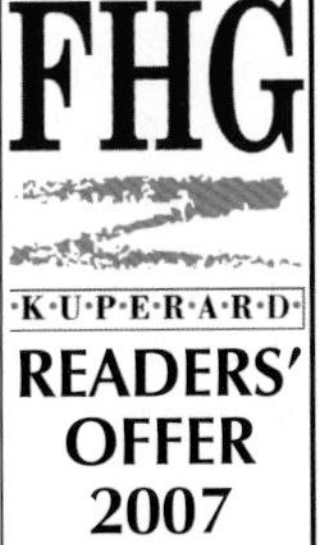

READERS' OFFER 2007

RHONDDA HERITAGE PARK

Lewis Merthyr Colliery, Coed Cae Road,
Trehafod, Near Pontypridd CF37 7NP
Tel: 01443 682036
e-mail: info@rhonddaheritagepark.com
www.rhonddaheritagepark.com

Two adults or children for the price of one when accompanied by a full paying adult. Valid until end 2007 for full tours only. Not valid on special event days/themed tours.

NOT TO BE USED IN CONJUNCTION WITH ANY OTHER OFFER

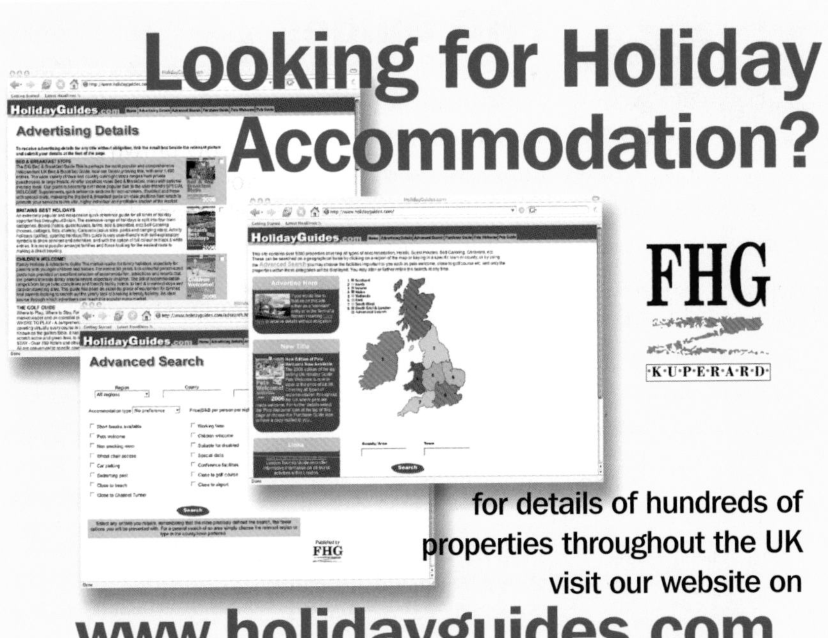

Looking for Holiday Accommodation?
HolidayGuides.com
Advertising Details
Advanced Search
FHG
·K·U·P·E·R·A·R·D·
for details of hundreds of properties throughout the UK visit our website on
www.holidayguides.com

Journey through the lanes of cycle history and see bicycles from Boneshakers and Penny Farthings up to modern Raleigh cycles. Over 250 machines on display

PETS MUST BE KEPT ON LEADS

Open: 1st March to 1st November daily 10am onwards.

Directions: brown signs to car park. Town centre attraction.

FHG GUIDES, ABBEY MILL BUSINESS CENTRE, PAISLEY PA1 1TJ • www.holidayguides.com

Make a pit stop whatever the weather! Join an ex-miner on a tour of discovery, ride the cage to pit bottom and take a thrilling ride back to the surface. Multi-media presentations, period village street, children's adventure play area, restaurant and gift shop. Disabled access with assistance.

Open: Open daily 10am to 6pm (last tour 4pm). Closed Mondays Oct - Easter, also Dec 25th to 2nd Jan incl.

Directions: Exit Junction 32 M4, signposted from A470 Pontypridd. Trehafod is located between Pontypridd and Porth.

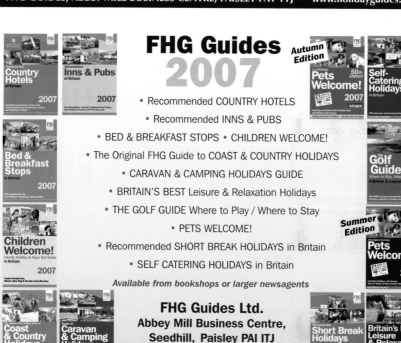

FHG GUIDES, ABBEY MILL BUSINESS CENTRE, PAISLEY PA1 1TJ • www.holidayguides.com

London

(Central & Greater)

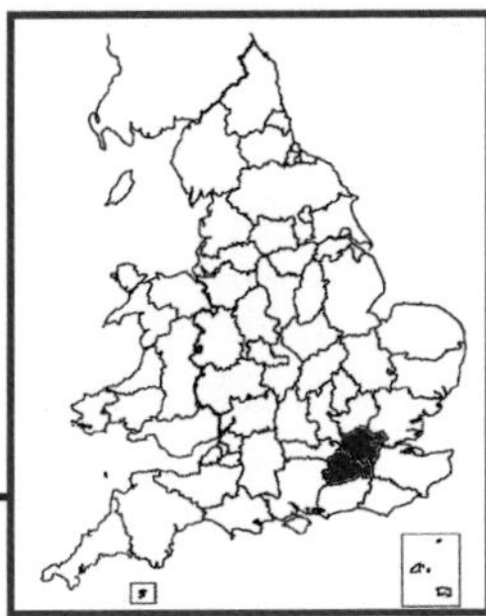

CENTRAL LONDON. Manor Court Hotel, 7 Clanricarde Gardens, London W2 4JJ (020 7792 3361 or 020 7727 5407; Fax: 020 7229 2875).
Situated off the Bayswater Road, opposite Kensington Palace. Family-run B&B Hotel within walking distance of Hyde Park and Kensington Gardens. Very near to Notting Hill underground. All rooms have colour TV and telephone. We accept Visa, Mastercard, Diners Club and American Express Cards.
Rates: terms from £25 to £40 single, £40 to £50 double, £55 to £65 triple and £75 for a quad room.
• Open all year.
ETC ◆
e-mail: enquiries@manorcourthotel.com

Comfortable well furnished rooms in small private home, full central heating. Two double and one single rooms, all non-smoking. Extra single beds for double rooms available.

8 bus routes; one minute for Trafalgar Square, Westminster, St Paul's. Piccadilly Line underground few minutes' walk. Direct Piccadilly and Heathrow. 1½ miles King's Cross, Euston and St Pancras Main Line Stations. 4½ miles Piccadilly, 3 miles London Zoo and Hampstead Heath. 2 minutes A1. King's Cross for Gatwick. Central for all tourist attractions. Full English Breakfast.

Terms: £24.00 per person per night. Children over 10 years. Minimum stay two nights. SAE, please.

Mrs B. Merchant,
562 Caledonian Road,
Holloway, London N7 9SD
Tel: 020 7607 0930

WHITE LODGE HOTEL

White Lodge Hotel is situated in a pleasant North London suburb, with easy access via tube and bus to all parts of London. Alexandra Palace is the closest landmark and buses pass the front door. Prices are kept as low as possible for people on low budget holidays, whilst maintaining a high standard of service and cleanliness. Many guests return year after year which is a good recommendation. Six single, ten double bedrooms, four family bedrooms (eight rooms en suite), all with washbasins; three showers, six toilets; sittingroom; diningroom

Cot, high chair, babysitting and reduced rates for children.
No pets, please.
Open all year for Bed and Breakfast from £32 single, £42 double.

White Lodge Hotel, No. 1 Church Lane, Hornsey, London N8 7BU
e-mail: info@whitelodgehornsey.co.uk • www.whitelodgehornsey.co.uk
Tel: 020 8348 9765 / 4259 • Fax: 020 8340 7851

• • • some fun days out in LONDON

BA London Eye • 0870 990 8883 • www.londoneye.com
Thames Barrier Park • 020 7511 4111 • www.thamesbarrierpark.org.uk
Tate Modern • 020 7887 8888 • www.tate.org.uk/modern
The London Dungeon • 020 7403 7221 • www.thedungeons.com

Bedfordshire

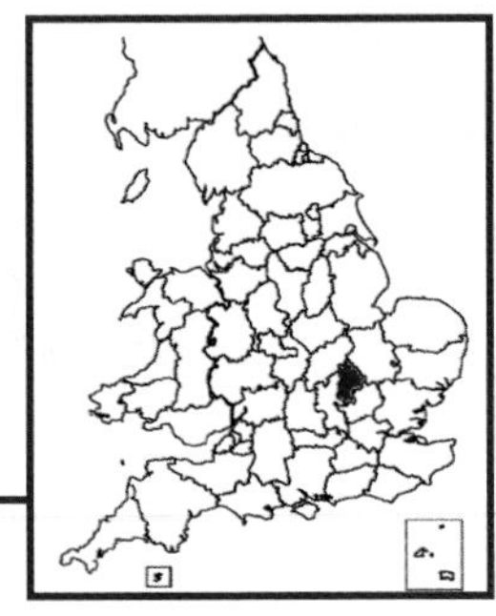

Bedfordshire - 'go wild' and come face to face with some of the world's rarest and most endangered species at Woburn Safari Park and Whipsnade Wild Animal Park. There are fun farms to visit with favourites such as rabbits, pigs and lambs, or head to Bedford Butterfly Park, where amid tropical foliage you are surrounded by colourful, free-flying butterflies.

Bedfordshire offers a unique tapestry of green, pleasant countryside, rich in wildlife, with gentle rolling chalk hills, open commons, ancient woodlands, prosperous agricultural land and peaceful canals. A criss cross of paths including long distance walks exist alongside many shorter routes suitable for families with young children, and wheelchair users.

The county is noted for its peaceful waterways and picturesque villages of thatch and half-timbered houses. Antique lovers will love to browse in the quaint shops of Georgian Ampthill and Woburn where you can also visit the magnificent Abbey. Follow the WW11 'Airfield Trail' around the north of the county, once alive with the Big Band sound of Glenn Miller (who was stationed here during the war). For a real 'vintage' experience, visit the Shuttleworth Collection where aircraft are kept in full flying order and can often be seen 'looping the loop' in the skies above Old Warden.

Bedford

THE KNIFE & CLEAVER

Deep in the heart of rural Bedfordshire, this friendly country inn offers a warm welcome to locals and visitors alike, and proves equally popular with both. One of the main reasons for its enviable reputation is the quite exceptional Victorian-style conservatory restaurant, where the finest of fresh ingredients are prepared with care and imagination by first-class chefs and where the accompanying wine list has been selected with quality and value as the highest priorities. Nine well-appointed en suite bedrooms, all with power shower, satellite television and a full range of amenities, provide comfortable accommodation for those wishing to explore this lovely area.

The Grove, Houghton Conquest, Bedford, Bedfordshire MK45 3LA • Tel: 01234 740387
Fax: 01234 740900 • e-mail: info@knifeandcleaver.com • www.knifeandcleaver.com

Please mention **FHG Guides** when making enquiries about accommodation featured in these pages

Wicks B&B

Bed and Breakfast accommodation situated just 10 minutes from Luton Airport, just off the M1 Junction 10 and close to the A505. Near town centre and railway stations (Town Centre and Parkway); 25 minutes' train journey to Central London. Large bungalow with double rooms; tea/coffee making equipment and colour TV. Overnight parking available. Close to local pubs, restaurants and shops. Children welcome.
A warm welcome awaits.

Mr and Mrs Wicks, 19 Wigmore Lane, Stopsley, Luton LU2 8AA • Tel: 01582 423419
e-mail: wicks-bandb@hotmail.co.uk

GUESTACCOM "GOOD ROOM" AWARD.
BEST ETC B&B REGIONAL WINNER FOR EASTERN COUNTIES.
Gold

Tranquil welcoming atmosphere on attractive arable farm. Set well back off A1 giving quiet, peaceful seclusion yet within easy reach of the RSPB, the Shuttleworth Collection, the Greensand Ridge Walk, Grafham Water and Woburn Abbey. Cambridge 22 miles, London 50 miles.

All rooms have tea/coffee making facilities, all have bathroom en suite and some are on the ground floor.
There is a separate guests' sitting room with TV. Family room.
Dogs welcome by arrangement. No smoking. Most guests return!

Prices from £32.50 per person per night.

Mrs M. Codd, Highfield Farm, Tempsford Road, Sandy, Bedfordshire SG19 2AQ
Tel: 01767 682332; Fax: 01767 692503
e-mail: margaret@highfield-farm.co.uk
website: www.highfield-farm.co.uk

Other specialised holiday guides from FHG

Recommended **INNS & PUBS** OF BRITAIN

Recommended **COUNTRY HOTELS** OF BRITAIN

Recommended **SHORT BREAK HOLIDAYS** IN BRITAIN

The bestselling and original PETS WELCOME!

The GOLF GUIDE, *Where to Play, Where to Stay* IN BRITAIN & IRELAND

COAST & COUNTRY HOLIDAYS

SELF-CATERING HOLIDAYS IN BRITAIN

CARAVAN & CAMPING HOLIDAYS

CHILDREN WELCOME! Family Holiday & Days Out Guide

BRITAIN'S BEST **LEISURE & RELAXATION GUIDE**

Published annually: available in all good bookshops or direct from the publisher:
FHG Guides, Abbey Mill Business Centre, Seedhill, Paisley PA1 1TJ
Tel: 0141 887 0428 • Fax: 0141 889 7204
e-mail: admin@fhguides.co.uk • www.holidayguides.com

Berkshire

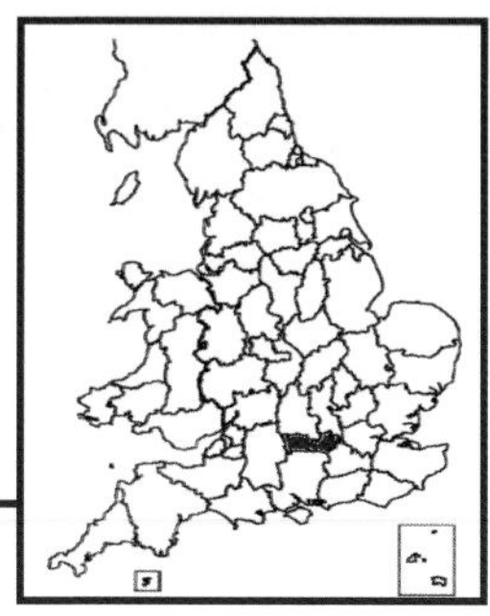

BLUEBELL HOUSE

LOVEL LANE, WINKFIELD,WINDSOR SL4 2DG

Tel & Fax: 01344 886828

Charming ex-coaching inn on the outskirts of Windsor and Ascot, and close to Bracknell and Maidenhead. Traditional rooms offering classic accommodation with an added touch of class. All rooms tastefully furnished and have TV, hairdryer, trouserpress, iron, mini-fridge and toaster/food warmer, one room has a four-poster bed. A very full Continental breakfast is taken in your room. . Private off-road parking.

e-mail: registrations@bluebellhousehotel.co.uk • www.bluebellhousehotel.co.uk

- Town centre location.
- Licensed bar and steam room.
- High quality accommodation at guest house prices.
- All rooms have en suite bathrooms, TV, tea/coffee making facilities, radio alarms, hairdryers, free wi-fi and internet.
- Heathrow Airport 25 minutes by car.
- Convenient for Legoland and trains to London.

Clarence Hotel

9 Clarence Road, Windsor, Berkshire SL4 5AE

Tel: 01753 864436 • Fax: 01753 857060 • www.clarence-hotel.co.uk

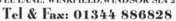

Donnington Castle
Image supplied by
West Berkshire Tourism Service
www.visitwestberkshire.org.uk

Cambridgeshire

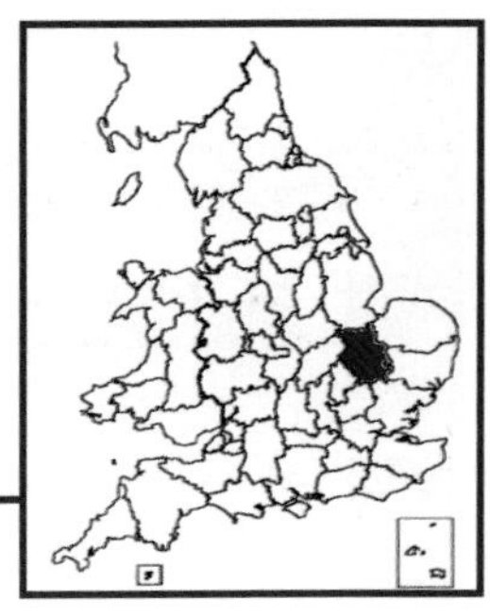

THE MEADOW HOUSE

2a High Street, Burwell,
Cambridge CB5 0HB
Tel: 01638 741926 • Fax: 01638 741861

e-mail: hilary@themeadowhouse.co.uk

The Meadow House is a magnificent modern house set in two acres of wooded grounds offering superior Bed and Breakfast accommodation in spacious rooms, some with king-size beds. The variety of en suite accommodation endeavours to cater for all requirements; a suite of rooms sleeping six complete with south-facing balcony; a triple room on the ground floor with three single beds and the Coach House, a spacious annexe with one double and one single bed; also one double and two twins sharing a well equipped bathroom. All rooms have TV, central heating and tea/coffee facilities.

Car parking. No smoking

Family rate available on request.

www.themeadowhouse.co.uk

CAMBRIDGE. Mr and Mrs Salt, Honeysuckle Cottage, 38 High Street, Grantchester, Cambridge CB3 9NF (01223 845977; Mobile: 0797 4767807).

Grantchester, the home of Jeffrey Archer, and former home to the poet Rupert Brooke, is a beautiful village one-and-a-half miles by car from Cambridge centre, or you can walk for about 30 minutes along the side of the River Cam, through the meadows whilst watching the punts. The house is recently renovated and is a mixture of Gothic and modern.

Rates: from £40 per person, all rooms en suite.

Dykelands Guest House

157 Mowbray Road,
Cambridge CB1 7SP
Tel: 01223 244300 • Fax: 01223 566746

Lovely detached guesthouse ideally situated for touring the city and countryside. Easy access from M11/J11 and only 1½ miles from city centre. Near Addenbrookes hospital. Colour TV, clock radio, tea/coffee making facilities. En suite and ground floor rooms available.

B&B from £40 single, from £46 to £56 double.

Car parking. No smoking.
Brochure on request.
Open all year.

AA ♦♦♦ Guest Accommodation

www.dykelands.com

DORSET HOUSE

35 Newton Road, Little Shelford,
Cambridge CB2 5HL • Tel: 01223 844440
E-mail: dorsethouse@msn.com
www.SmoothHound.co.uk

Just three miles from the historic city of Cambridge, ***DORSET HOUSE*** is situated in its own extensive grounds. The house has open fireplaces and wooden beams, and each luxury bedroom is individually decorated. Some rooms are en suite and all have colour TV and tea/coffee facilities. Breakfast is served in our lovely dining room.

If you are looking for the best:
Bed & Breakfast £38-£48 Single, £55-£65 Double, £69-£85 Family.

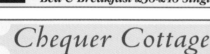

Chequer Cottage

Streetly End, Horseheath CB1 6RP
01223 891522

Set in a quiet hamlet of 15th Century thatched properties, our cottage offers a comfortable, peaceful stay in the countryside. Annexed, spacious accommodation with a king-sized bed and en suite facilities - loads of luxury and a warm welcome await you.

e-mail: stay@chequercottage.com
www.chequercottage.com

Manor Farm, Landbeach, Cambridge CB4 8ED • Tel: 01223 860165 • Fax: 01223 864748

Manor Farm is a lovely Georgian house with large spacious bedrooms, all with en suite or private bathroom, and a light airy sitting room that guests may use. Guests are welcome to relax in the large walled garden or take a walk on the farm. Landbeach is a small, pretty village about six miles north of Cambridge and ten miles south of Ely. There are many local pubs and restaurants, although none are within walking distance - why not bring a bicycle and cycle along the tow path into Cambridge? There is also a local bus service to the village and railway station at Waterbeach (the next village). Ample off road parking.

Terms from £35 per room single, £50 double and £65 triple.

e-mail: vhatley@btinternet.com
www.smoothhound.co.uk/hotels/manorfarm4

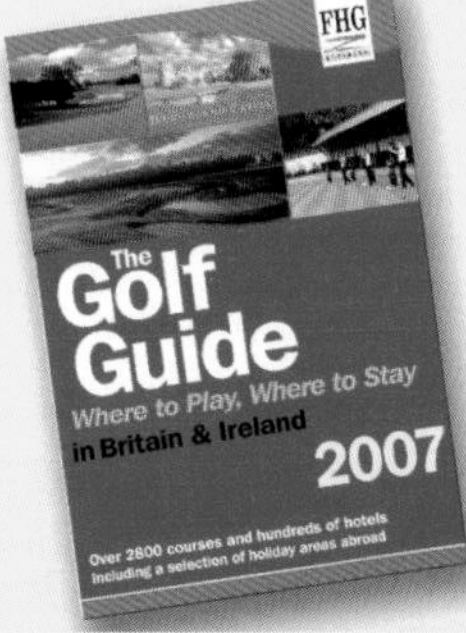

The Golf Guide · 2007

Where to Play, Where to Stay

Available from most booksellers, **The Golf Guide, Where to Play, Where to Stay** covers details of every UK golf course – well over 2800 entries – for holiday or business golf. Hundreds of hotel entries offer convenient accommodation, with accompanying details of the courses – the 'pro', par score, length and more. Including holiday golf in Ireland, France, Portugal, Spain, the USA, South Africa and Thailand.

Only £9.99 from booksellers or direct from the publishers:
FHG Guides, Abbey Mill Business Centre, Seedhill, Paisley PA1 1TJ **(postage charged outside UK)**

Stockyard Farm B&B

Wisbech Road, Welney, Wisbech, Cambs PE14 9RQ

Former fenland farmhouse, rurally situated between Ely and Wisbech. Ideal for touring, fishing and birdwatching - Ouse Washes Nature Reserves close by.

Mrs C. Bennett • Tel: 01354 610433

Two bedrooms, one double, one twin, both with handbasin, hot drinks facilities, radio and hairdryer • Guest lounge with colour TV and books • Conservatory breakfast room, garden and patio • Full central heating • Private parking • Vegetarians and vegans very welcome • Free-range produce • Pets welcome by arrangement - miles of riverside walks • Children over 10 years • Non-smoking throughout.

Sharps Farm *Bed & Breakfast*

Twentypence Road, Wilburton, Ely CB6 3PU

A charming tranquil setting awaits you along with friendly hospitality in our family home. Situated in open countryside and ideally placed to visit the surrounding historic sites of Cambridge, Ely and Newmarket. Two en suite ground floor rooms and one double on the first floor with private bathroom all have TV, radio alarm, tea/coffee making facilities and hairdryers. A delicious English breakfast is served in our garden room using eggs from our free range chickens. Evening meal by arrangement. Special diets catered for. Disabled facilities. Non-smoking. Ample parking. B&B from £27 per person.

Tel: 01353 740360 • e-mail: sharpsfarm@yahoo.com • www.sharpsfarm.co.uk

Cheshire

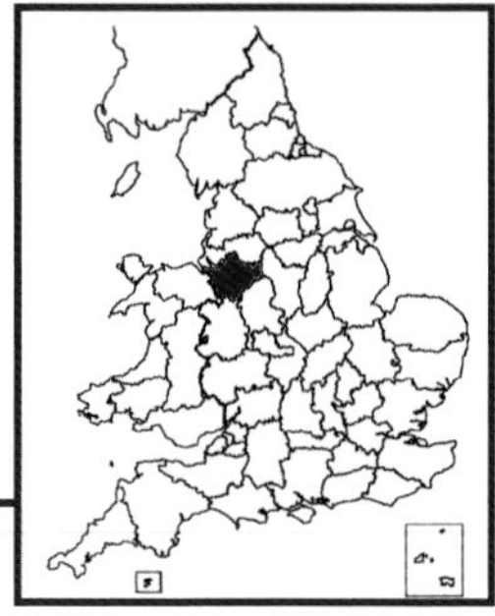

Cheshire - soak in the atmosphere of the historic city of Chester, created by an abundance of black-and-white buildings set in a circuit of glorious city walls, the most complete in the country. Chester's crowning glory is the 13th century Rows – two tiers of shops running along the main streets, offering a unique and sophisticated shopping experience. A leisurely walk along the finest city walls in Britain will take you past most of the city's delights like the stunning Eastgate Clock and the 1000-year-old Cathedral, a haven of reflective tranquillity in a lively, bustling, cosmopolitan centre. The biggest archaeological dig in Britain is currently underway at the 2000-year-old Roman Amphitheatre; there is architectural splendour to enjoy at every turn. The lush countryside surrounding Chester is peppered with stately homes, award-winning gardens and chic market towns featuring characteristic black-and-white half-timbered buildings. Tatton Park near Knutsford is one of Britain's finest Georgian manors, with acres of parklands and formal gardens, a perfect attraction to enjoy in every season, and the host of the RHS Flower Show in July. Or visit Arley Hall and Gardens near Northwich, with its stunning herbaceous borders and Country Fair and Horse Trials in May. For super chic in super villages and towns, breeze into Tarporley, Nantwich, Knutsford and Wilmslow where sophisticated shopping, fine cuisine and contemporary pleasures ensure an afternoon of indulgence and fine delights, with food and drink festivals being held throughout the year.

Balterley (near Crewe)

BALTERLEY (near Crewe). Mrs Joanne Hollins, Balterley Green Farm, Deans Lane, Balterley, Near Crewe CW2 5QJ (01270 820214).
Jo and Pete Hollins offer guests a friendly welcome to their home on a 145-acre working farm in quiet and peaceful surroundings. Green Farm is situated on the Cheshire/Staffordshire border and is within easy reach of Junction 16 on the M6. An excellent stop-over place for travellers journeying between north and south of the country. Two double en suite and two twin en suite in converted cottage can be either B&B or self-catering using the fully equipped kitchen in the cottage; all on ground floor. Tea-making facilities and TV in all rooms. Cot provided. This area offers many attractions; we are within easy reach of historic Chester, Alton Towers and the famous Potteries of Staffordshire.
Rates: Bed and Breakfast from £25 per person.
• Working farm, join in. • Children welcome. • Pets welcome. • Open all year. • Caravans and tents welcome.

• • • some fun days out in CHESHIRE

Cholmondeley Castle Gardens, Malpas • 01829 720383 • www.gardens-guide.com
Blue Planet Aquarium, Ellesmere Port • 0151 357 8804 • www.blueplanetaquarium.com
Chester Zoo, Upton-by-Chester • 01244 380280 • www.chesterzoo.org

Mitchell's of Chester Guest House

28 Hough Green, Chester CH4 8JQ

Tel: 01244 679004

Fax: 01244 659567

e-mail: mitoches@dialstart.net

www.mitchellsofchester.com

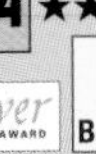

Visit Chester & Cheshire Annual Awards 2006 Best B&B - Commended

This elegantly restored Victorian family home is set on the south side of Chester, on a bus route to the city centre. Guest bedrooms have been furnished in period style, with fully equipped shower room and toilet, central heating, TV, refreshment tray and other thoughtful extras. An extensive breakfast menu is served in the elegant dining room, and the guest lounge overlooks the well-maintained garden.

The historic city of Chester is ideally placed for touring Wales and the many attractions of the North West of England.

HIGHER ELMS FARM

Brian and Mary Charlesworth, Higher Elms Farm, Minshull Vernon, Crewe CW1 4RG • Tel: 01270 522252

400-year old farmhouse situated on a working farm overlooking the Shropshire Union Canal. Oak-beamed comfort in dining and sitting rooms. Family, double, twin and single rooms available, all en suite with colour TV and tea/coffee making facilities. No dinners served, but there are four pubs within two miles. Convenient for M6, Jodrell Bank, Oulton Park, Bridgemere Garden World, Stapeley Water Gardens, Nantwich and Chester.

Bed and Breakfast from £26, half price for children under 12 years. Well behaved pets welcome.

Mill House

Higher Wych, Malpas, Cheshire SY14 7JR

Modernised mill house on the Cheshire/Clwyd border in a quiet valley, convenient for visiting Chester, Shrewsbury and North Wales. The house is centrally heated and has an open log fire in the TV lounge. Bedrooms have washbasins, radio and tea-making facilities. Two bedrooms have en suite shower and WC. Open January to November. Prices from £22 per person per night. Self-catering accommodation also available.

Tel: 01948 780362 • Fax: 01948 780566

email: angela@videoactive.co.uk • www.millhouseandgranary.co.uk

Publisher's note

While every effort is made to ensure accuracy, we regret that FHG Guides cannot accept responsibility for errors, misrepresentations or omissions in our entries or any consequences thereof. Prices in particular should be checked.

We will follow up complaints but cannot act as arbiters or agents for either party.

Cornwall

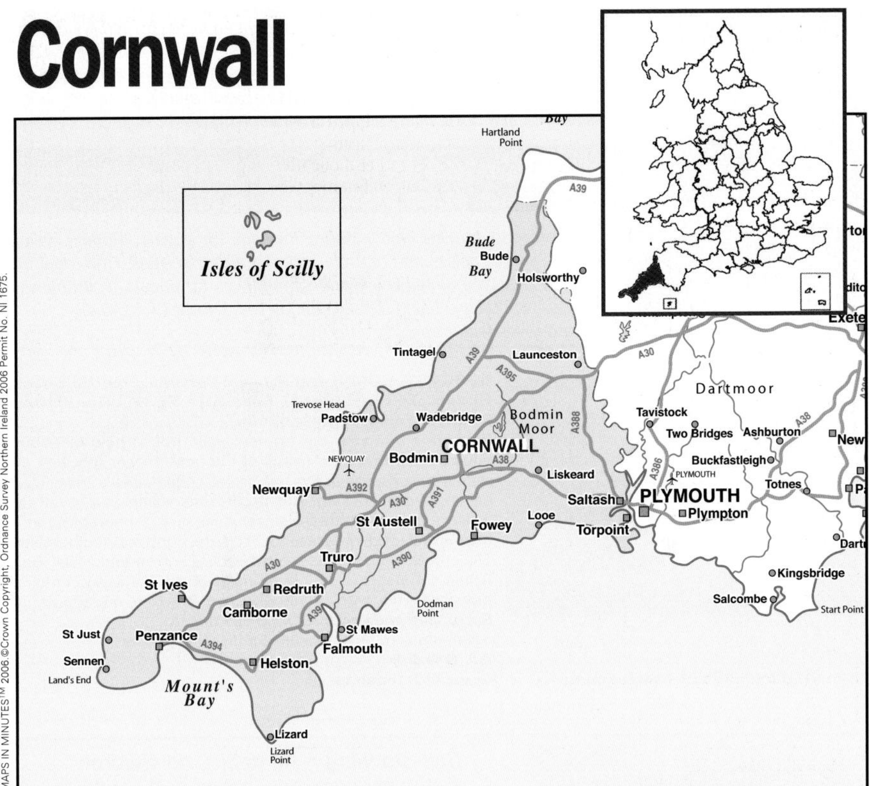

Cornwall receives most of its visitors over the summer months, exploring the beautiful beaches and indulging in the exceptional clotted cream teas - but the county has much to offer besides the Cornish pastie and the traditional bucket and spade holiday. The "shoulder" and winter months offer opportunities for the discerning visitor which may go unnoticed in the annual stampede to the beaches. There are villages boasting curious and ancient names - Come To Good, Ting Tang, London Apprentice and Indian Queens, often sporting parish churches, ancient graveyards and distinctive crosses which reveal their early Christian history. Wayside crosses, holy wells and Celtic stone circles are reminders that the Cornish are true Celts - it was they who embossed the headlands with cliff forts to repel marauders.

To discover more about life in the Iron Age there are numerous settlements to visit, for example Castle an Dinas, one of the largest preserved hill forts in Cornwall. Alternatively Chysauster Ancient Village is a deserted Roman village comprising eight well-preserved houses around an open court. More up-to-date is St Michael's Mount with its 14th century castle, or Prideaux Place, a stunning Elizabethan House, and Lanhydrock, the National Trust's most visited property in Cornwall, which was once the residence of a local family whose wealth came from tin mining.

A useful index of towns/counties appears on pages 9-42

Traditional Victorian granite farmhouse surrounded by fields on this working farm. Lanivet is the geographical centre of Cornwall and thereby central for touring the moor and the north and south coasts. The exciting Eden Project, Lost Gardens at Heligan and Lanhydrock House are close by. Fishing, cycling, golf and horse riding are available within the area. High Cross offers

High Cross Farm Lanivet, Near Bodmin PL30 5JR

Tel: 01208 831341 • Mrs Joy Rackham

ample off-road parking and modern facilities for guests. Rooms have hot/cold, shaver points and tea and coffee making facilities. One room is en suite. Separate dining room and sitting room for guests. Full English breakfast, optional evening meal. Open all year except Christmas.
Bed and Breakfast from £20.

BOSCASTLE. Ruth and Michael Parsons, The Old Coach House, Tintagel Road, Boscastle PL35 0AS (01840 250398; Fax: 01840 250346).
Relax in a 300 year old former coach house now tastefully equipped to meet the needs of the new millennium with all rooms en suite, colour TVs, radios, tea/coffee makers and central heating. Good cooking. This picturesque village is a haven for walkers with its dramatic coastal scenery, a photographer's dream, and an ideal base to tour both the north and south coasts. The area is famed for its sandy beaches and surfing whilst King Arthur's Tintagel is only three miles away. Come and enjoy a friendly holiday with people who care. Brochure on request.
Rates: Bed and Breakfast from £25 to £38.
•Non-smoking • Accessible for disabled guests.
AA ◆◆◆◆
e-mail: parsons@old-coach.co.uk
www.old-coach.co.uk

Non-smoking • No pets • No children
Set in own grounds (parking). En suite accommodation. Tea/coffee, TV in rooms. Overlooking Boscastle village, with views of coast and Lundy Island; close to sandy beaches, surfing. 3 miles Tintagel, King Arthur Country. Haven for walkers. Two minutes' walk to local 16th century inn, with real ales and good food. Open Easter to end October. Terms from £28pppn.

English Tourism Council ◆◆◆ GUEST ACCOMMODATION

Mrs P. E. Perfili, Trefoil Farm, Camelford Road, Boscastle PL35 0AD
Tel: 01840 250606
e-mail: trefoil.farm@tiscali.co.uk • www.thisisnorthcornwall.com

English Tourism Council ◆◆◆◆ GUEST ACCOMMODATION

Trehane Farmhouse

Our traditional farmhouse is in a magnificent position overlooking the sea and the wild rugged coastline of North Cornwall. It is in a peaceful and secluded position, yet close to the Coastal Path and hidden coves. Guests can enjoy plenty of wholesome, fresh, local food, home-made bread, and exciting vegetarian dishes. There are two pretty, en suite rooms with views over the fields to the sea. Sarah's interest in art is reflected in the original paintings, ceramics and art works around the house, and the area is a delight for artists and writers. Brochure available.

Sarah James, Trehane Farmhouse, Trevalga, Boscastle PL35 0EB

Tel: 01840 250510
james_sarah@btconnect.com

DOLSDON was once a 17th century coaching inn, now modernised, situated on the Launceston to Bude road within easy reach of sandy beaches, surfing, Tamar Otter Park, leisure centre with heated swimming pool, golf courses, fishing, tennis and horse riding and is ideal for touring Cornwall and Devon. Guests are welcome to wander around the 260 acre working farm. All bedrooms en suite with TV and tea making facilities. Comfortably furnished lounge has colour TV. Plenty of good home cooking assured - full English breakfast. Parking.

Bed and Breakfast from £22 • Reductions for children • Brochure available • Non-smoking

Mrs Christine Nancekivell, Dolsdon Farm, Boyton, Launceston PL15 8NT • Tel: 01288 341264

Situated on the Devon/Cornwall border six miles from the surfing beaches at Bude and Widemouth Bay, we are ideally placed for touring both Devon and Cornwall. Guests are welcome to wander on our 205 acre mixed farm. Three large and tastefully furnished family rooms sleeping up to four - two rooms en suite, all rooms are south facing and enjoy views of the surrounding farmland. Children are especially welcome - cot, highchair and free babysitting available. Full English breakfast served daily; ample four course meal available. Numerous sandy beaches nearby and the picturesque villages of Clovelly and Tintagel are within half an hour's drive.

Open from March to November. B&B from £22 per person.

Mrs Sylvia Lucas, Elm Park Farmhouse Bed & Breakfast, Bridgerule, Holsworthy, Devon EX22 7EL • 01288 381231

Sunrise offers something special... service with a smile, stylish en suite bedrooms, superb breakfasts and ideal location, close to beaches, shops, cafes and restaurants. An ideal place to stay at any time of the year

Beautifully refurbished Victorian house providing stylish and comfortable four diamond accommodation, overlooking golf course, moments' walk from the town and Blue Flag beaches. Excellent breakfast menu, including vegetarian. Special diets catered for. B&B from £25

Lesley & Bob Sharratt, Sunrise,
6 Burn View, Bude EX23 8BY
Tel: 01288 353214 • Fax: 01288 359911
e-mail: sunriseguest@btconnect.com
www.sunrise-bude.co.uk

Sunrise

• • • some fun days out in CORNWALL

Caerhays Castle Gardens, St Austell • 01872 501310 • www.caerhays.co.uk
National Maritime Museum, Falmouth • 01326 313388 • www.nmmc.co.uk
The Monkey Sanctuary, Looe • 01503 262532 • www.monkeysanctuary.org
Pendennis Castle, St Mawes • 0870 333 1181 • www.english-heritage.org.uk
Land's End, Sennen • 0870 458 0099 • www.landsend-landmark.co.uk
Goonhilly Satellite Earth Station, Lizard Peninsula • 0800 679593 • www.goonhilly.bt.com
King Arthur's Great Halls, Tintagel • 01840 770526 • www.kingarthursgreathalls.com
The Eden Project, St Austell • 01726 811911 • www.edenproject.com

Trencreek Farmhouse - 01840 230219

Comfortable farmhouse offering homely and relaxed family atmosphere. Situated in quiet and peaceful surroundings yet within easy reach of Crackington Haven. Well placed for easy access to coastal and countryside walks. Family, double and twin-bedded rooms, most en suite, all with tea/coffee making facilities. Two comfortable lounges. Games room. Separate diningroom. Generous portions of freshly prepared, home-cooked farmhouse food.

Children welcome, special rates for unders 12s.
Spring and Autumn breaks available. Non-smoking.

Margaret and Richard Heard,
Trencreek Farmhouse, St Gennys, Bude EX23 0AY

Highbre Crest, Whitstone, Holsworthy, Near Bude EX22 6UF

Stunning views to coasts and moors make this very spacious house a special destination for your holiday. With the added bonus of peace, tranquillity and delicious homemade country cooking, how can you resist paying us a visit? We are well situated for the coast and moors in Devon and Cornwall, including The Eden Project. Two double and one twin room - all en suite. Lounge with full size snooker table, dining room and comfortable large conservatory with spectacular coastal views. Garden for guests' use. Car parking space. Non-smoking establishment. Children over 12 welcome. Bed and Breakfast from £26. Open all year.

Mrs Cole • 01288 341002

West Nethercott Farm, North Cornwall

Personal attention and a warm welcome await you on this dairy and sheep farm. Watch the cows being milked, scenic farm walks. Short distance from sandy beaches, surfing and the rugged North Cornwall coast. Ideal base for visiting any part of Devon or Cornwall. We are located in Cornwall though our postal address is Devon. The traditional farmhouse has four bedrooms, two en suite; diningroom and separate lounge with TV. Plenty of excellent home cooking. Access to the house at anytime. Bed and Breakfast from £22-£27, Evening Meal available. Children under 12 years reduced rates. Weekly terms available.

Mrs Pearl Hopper, West Nethercott Farm, Whitstone, Holsworthy (Devon) EX22 6LD • 01288 341394
e-mail: pearl@westnethercott.fsnet.co.uk

Note

All the information in this guide is given in good faith in the belief that it is correct. However, the publishers cannot guarantee the facts given in these pages, neither are they responsible for changes in ownership or facilities that may take place after the date of going to press. Readers should always satisfy themselves that the facilities they require are available and that the terms, if quoted, still apply.

e-mail: family@parkyn.charitydays.co.uk

A warm welcome awaits you at our home, situated on the outskirts of a quiet village with easy access to Bodmin Moor and Dartmoor. Close to Callington, 3 miles; Launceston, Tavistock and Liskeard, all 9 miles. Convenient for Plymouth, Eden Project, or touring the coast. Locally there are opportunities for golf, swimming, cycling, horse riding or just a stroll in the quiet countryside.

En suite room available with TV, teamaking facilities and home-baking. Lounge for relaxation.

B&B from £22 per person per night. Non-smoking. Ideal for stop-over, mini breaks and holidays.

Come and let us spoil you

Roger and Geraldine Parkyn, 'Keadeen', Golberdon, Callington PL17 7LT • 01579 384197

Heritage House
1 Clifton Terrace, Falmouth TR11 3QG

We offer visitors a warm, friendly welcome at our comfortable family-run guesthouse. Centrally located for town and beaches. Single, twin, double and family bedrooms, all tastefully decorated, with colour TV, free tea/coffee, vanity basins and central heating. Access available at all times throughout the day. Children are welcome, with cot and highchair available. Bed and full English or vegetarian breakfast from £20 per person nightly. Reduced rates for longer stays. On-street parking available with no restrictions. Open all year (except Christmas).

Proprietor: Lynn Grimes
Tel: 01326 317834
e-mail: heritagehouse@tinyonline.co.uk
www.heritagehousefalmouth.co.uk

Rosemullion Hotel

Gyllyngvase Hill, Falmouth TR11 4DF • 01326 314690 • Fax: 01326 210098

Built as a gentleman's residence in the latter part of the 19th century, Rosemullion Hotel offers you a holiday that is every bit as distinctive as its Tudor appearance. Rosemullion is a house of great character and charm, appealing strongly to the discerning guest. The emphasis is very much on that rarest of commodities in today's world – peace. That is why we do not cater for children and do not have a bar of our own. A family-owned hotel continually being refurbished and updated to first class accommodation. Fully centrally heated with 13 bedrooms, some with glorious views over the bay. Large parking area.

Non-smoking • B&B £27.50 to £29.50pppn inclusive of VAT.

e-mail: gail@rosemullionhotel.demon.co.uk
www.SmoothHound.co.uk/hotels/rosemullion.html

A small, friendly, non-smoking guest house situated between the harbour and beach with views over Falmouth Bay. We are close to the railway station and within easy reach of the town. Wickham is the ideal base for exploring Falmouth and South Cornwall's gardens, castles, harbour, coastal footpath and much more. All rooms have television and beverage facilities, some have sea views. Open Easter to October.

Bed and Breakfast from £24 nightly, £161 weekly. Discount for children. Single overnight stays subject to availability.

e-mail: enquiries@wickhamhotel.freeserve.co.uk
www.wickham-hotel.co.uk
21 Gyllyngvase Terrace, Falmouth TR11 4DL
01326 311140

Hendra Farm, just off the main Helston/Falmouth road, is an ideal centre for touring Cornwall; three miles to Helston, eight to both Redruth and Falmouth. Safe sandy beaches within easy reach – five miles to the sea. Two double, one single, and one family bedrooms with washbasins and tea-making facilities; bathroom and toilets; sittingroom and two diningrooms. Cot, babysitting and reduced rates offered for children. No objection to pets. Car necessary, parking space. Open all year except Christmas. Evening Dinner optional. Tea and homemade cake before bed.

Bed and Breakfast only from £18 per night.

Mrs P. Roberts, Hendra Farm, Wendron, Helston TR13 0NR (01326 340470)

ROCKLANDS

"Rocklands" is situated overlooking part of Cornwall's superb coastline and enjoys uninterrupted sea views. The Lizard is well known for its lovely picturesque scenery, coastal walks and enchanting coves and beaches, as well as the famous Serpentine Stone which is quarried and sold locally. Open Easter to October. Generations of the Hill family have been catering for visitors on the Lizard since the 1850s. Three bedrooms with sea views, two en suite, tea/coffee making facilities and electric heaters; sittingroom with TV and video; sun lounge; diningroom with separate tables. Children and well trained pets welcome.

Bed and Breakfast £23pppn, en suite £25pppn; reductions for children under 10 years.

Mrs D. J. Hill, "Rocklands", The Lizard, Near Helston TR12 7NX • Tel: 01326 290339

Silver
SILVER AWARD

Trewint Farm

A Cornish Cream tea awaits your arrival; enjoy the peace and tranquillity of the countryside. Trewint is a working farm, well known for its prize-winning cattle. Enjoy walks around the area, or make use of the games room. All rooms are en suite, with matching decor, and TV and tea/coffee facilities. Have breakfast overlooking the garden, and watch the birds while you enjoy the farmhouse fare. Ideal for National Trust properties; Looe six miles.

Also available: self catering properties, sleep 4/5. Ideal for winter breaks.

Bed and Breakfast £28-£35 • Self-catering from £175.

Mrs Rowe, Trewint Farm, Menheniot, Liskeard PL14 3RE • 01579 347155
e-mail: holidays@trewintfarm.co.uk • www.trewintfarm.co.uk

Nebula Hotel

27 Higher Lux Street, Liskeard PL14 3JU 01579 343989

Relax in your home from home friendly hotel. Old English atmosphere in a Grade II Listed building. Unwind by our large granite fireplace in the lounge area with licensed bar. Six spacious comfortable en suite rooms, single, double, twin and family, all with TV and tea/coffee facilities. Large car park. Liskeard is ideally placed to tour Cornwall and Plymouth. Near the moors, coast, gardens, golf courses, Eden Project and museums. Enjoy! Book the whole hotel (sleeps 15) and use it as your home in a relaxing atmosphere. Terms from £30.

SOUTH WEST TOURISM, CORNWALL TOURIST BOARD

e-mail: info@nebula-hotel.com
www.nebula-hotel.com

• Bake Farm •

Pelynt, Looe, Cornwall PL13 2QQ
Tel: 01503 220244

This is an old farmhouse, bearing the Trelawney Coat of Arms (1610), situated midway between Looe and Fowey. Two double and one family bedroom, all en suite and decorated to a high standard, have tea/coffee making facilities and TV. Sorry, no pets, no smoking. Open from March to October. A car is essential for touring the area, ample parking. There is much to see and do here – horse riding, coastal walks, golf, National Trust properties, the Eden Project and Heligan Gardens are within easy reach. The sea is only five miles away and there is shark fishing at Looe.

Bed and Breakfast from £24 to £27. Brochure available on request.

Lancallan is a large 17th century farmhouse on a working 700-acre dairy and beef farm in a beautiful rural setting, one mile from Mevagissey. We are close to Heligan Gardens, lovely coastal walks and sandy beaches, and are well situated for day trips throughout Cornwall. Also six to eight miles from the Eden Project (20 minutes' drive). Enjoy a traditional farmhouse breakfast in a warm and friendly atmosphere.

Accommodation comprises one twin room and two double en suite rooms (all with colour TV and tea/coffee facilities); bathroom, lounge and diningroom.

Terms and brochure available on request. SAE please.

Mrs Dawn Rundle, Lancallan Farm, Mevagissey, St Austell PL26 6EW
Tel & Fax: 01726 842284
e-mail: dawn@lancallan.fsnet.co.uk • www.lancallanfarm.co.uk

B&B accommodation with magnificent views over the village and harbour, and only a short three/four minute walk to the harbour itself.

All rooms en suite or have private facilities with colour TV/tea and coffee making facilities. Centrally heated and double glazed. Sauna and a south-facing sun deck. Private off-road parking.

Ideal touring base. Special promotion for Heligan Gardens or Eden Project tickets (ring for details). For further information telephone **Helen Blamey**.

Tregorran, Cliff Street, Mevagissey PL26 6QW • Tel: 01726 842319
e-mail: patricia@parsloep.freeserve.co.uk • www.tregorran.homestead.com/home.html

Detached 10 bedroomed licensed hotel situated in one of Cornwall's most beautiful villages. Rooms have panoramic views of sea or countryside and most are en suite. Colour TV and tea/ coffee facilities in all rooms. Licensed bar. Short walk to one of Cornwall's finest beaches. Private car park. Mid-week bookings and short breaks early and late season. Ring for brochure or visit our website.

English Tourism Council ♦♦♦♦ GUEST ACCOMMODATION

Bed and Breakfast from £29 to £35 per night.

- Non-smoking Hotel. • Pets welcome.
- No children under 16. • Open Christmas and New Year.
- Self-catering flat also available.

Lisa Cooper and David Marsh, Highfield Lodge, Halwyn Road, Crantock TR8 5TR • 01637 830744
www.highfieldlodge.co.uk

St George's Hotel

The small hotel with a lot to offer. Fabulous sea views. Quality food and service. BIG BREAKFAST. Clean comfortable accommodation - en suite available. Colour TVs. Licensed bar and pool table. Two minutes from town centre and beaches. Large car park. Personal attention.

A warm welcome awaits friends old and new.

B&B from £168 per person per week.

e-mail: enquiries@stgeorgeshotel.free-online.co.uk
www.st-georges-newquay.co.uk

Mr and Mrs A Slater, St George's Hotel, 71 Mount Wise, Newquay TR7 2BP • 01637 873010

Take a break in the heart of Cornwall

A warm and friendly welcome awaits you at Pensalda. Situated on the main A3058 road, an ideal location from which to explore the finest coastline in Europe. Close to airport and the Eden Project. Double and family rooms available, all en suite, all with TV, tea/coffee making facilities, including two chalets set in a lovely garden. Fire certificate • Large car park • Licensed • Central heating • Non-smoking.

★★★ GUEST ACCOMMODATION

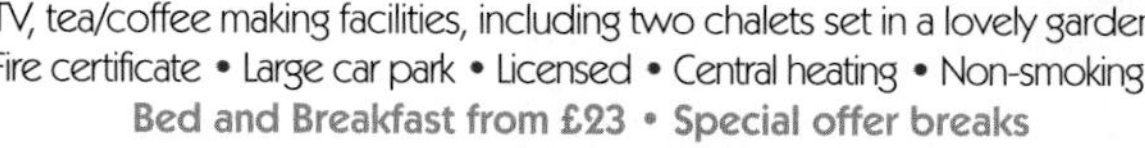

Bed and Breakfast from £23 • Special offer breaks November to March (excluding Christmas and New Year).

Karen and John, Pensalda Guest House, 98 Henver Road, Newquay TR7 3BL
Tel & Fax: 01637 874601 • e-mail: karen_pensalda@yahoo.co.uk
www.pensalda-guesthouse.co.uk

Publisher's note

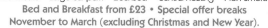

While every effort is made to ensure accuracy, we regret that FHG Guides cannot accept responsibility for errors, misrepresentations or omissions in our entries or any consequences thereof. Prices in particular should be checked.

We will follow up complaints but cannot act as arbiters or agents for either party.

Dewolf Guest House is situated on the A3058 into Newquay town centre. All the amenities of Newquay are close at hand with Porth Beach only a short walk from the guest house. We have double or family rooms including two chalets situated in the rear garden. All rooms are non-smoking and offer en suite facilities, colour TV and tea/coffee making facilities. Prices are from £22 per person. Special Christmas/New Year Breaks. Off-road car parking available. Some pets welcome by arrangement. Licensed. Open all year.

Meryl and Mark Dewolfreys • Dewolf Guest House
100 Henver Road, Newquay TR7 3BL
Tel: 01637 874746
e-mail: holidays@dewolfguesthouse.com
www.dewolfguesthouse.com

AA★★★★ NATC APPROVED
NATIONAL ACCESSIBLE SCHEME M1

Alicia

A warm welcome from your hosts Mike and Alison, who offer you a relaxed and friendly atmosphere in the comfort of their home. Traditional full English breakfast. Four en suite bedrooms, all tastefully furnished, with TV, clock/radio, hairdryer and refreshment tray; one standard with private facilities; iron provided. Relax in the conservatory or spacious lounge. Choose between the golden beaches along Newquay's coastline or a breathtaking coastal walk to Watergate Bay. The Eden Project, quaint fishing villages and the spectacular Cornish coastline, are all within 30 minutes' car ride. Open all year and fully centrally heated. Bed and Breakfast from £25 per person daily. Please telephone or write for brochure.

Mike and Alison Limer, Alicia, 136 Henver Road, Newquay TR7 3EQ • Tel: 01637 874328

web: www.alicia-guesthouse.co.uk
email: aliciaguesthouse@mlimer.fsnet.co.uk

Spring comes early this far west and an April walk is rewarded by a profusion of wild flowers. Cornwall coils out in to the warming Gulf Stream and so enjoys moist and mild conditions, which allow sub-tropical species to flourish. Visitors are drawn to the lush palms and ferns of Trebah and Glendurgan, the once dormant delight of the Lost Gardens of Heligan, the romantic terraces of St Michael's Mount and the many superb National Trust estates including Trelissick, Trengwainton, Lanhydrock and Cotehele.

Cornwall is also a story of artists and visionaries, both native and visiting, inspired by sights, colours and industries of this county. About a century ago, the painters Stanhope Forbes and Norman Garstin made the Newlyn School internationally famous. Ben Nicholson, Barbara Hepworth and Bernard Leach did the same for St Ives. The Tate Gallery St Ives and Barbara Hepworth Museum are a must for all art lovers, and Daphne Du Maurier's Smugglers Museum at Jamaica Inn will catapult anyone straight into Cornwall's smuggling heritage.

The FHG Directory of Website Addresses

on pages 313-346 is a useful quick reference guide for holiday accommodation with e-mail and/or website details

A 17th Century watermill which ground corn for the nearby Trerice Manor, now National Trust. Four miles from the north coast in the peaceful Gannel valley; very central for exploring Cornwall, convenient for Eden Project. In seven acres of beautiful grounds with river and wildlife pond. Enjoy Cornish cream teas in the tranquil gardens. The large, beamed mill-room is now the residents' lounge, with TV and bar. Non-smoking throughout.

Comfortable bedrooms: two double, one triple, one twin and two single. Some are en suite and all have washbasin and tea making facilities. Large car park. Bed and full Breakfast from £25.

Self-catering cottages also available. Please phone for colour brochure or view our website.

Terri and Dave Clark,
Trewerry Mill, Trerice,
St Newlyn East TR8 5GS
01872 510345
trewerry.mill@which.net
www.trewerrymill.co.uk

TREWITHEN FARMHOUSE is a renovated Cornish Roundhouse, set in a large garden and situated on a working farm enjoying country and coastal views. The picturesque town of Padstow with its pretty harbour and narrow streets with famous fish restaurants is only three miles away. St Merryn Parish boasts seven beautiful sandy beaches and bays. Also coastal walks, golf, fishing and horse riding on neighbouring farm. Hire a bike or walk along the Camel Trail cycle and footpath - winding for 18 miles along the River Camel. Eden Project 20 miles.

The accommodation has been tastefully decorated to complement the exposed beams and original features. All bedrooms are en suite or have private bathrooms, TVs and hot drink facilities.

- Parking • Full English breakfast • TV lounge.
- Bed and Breakfast from £25 to £30 per person per night.
- Winter weekend breaks available.
- Non-smoking.

Mrs Sandra May,
Trewithen Farm, St Merryn,
Near Padstow PL28 8JZ
01841 520420
www.trewithenfarmhouse.co.uk

Martin & Diane Miller, Beechwood, Alexandra Place, Penzance TR18 4NE • Tel: 01736 360380

Spacious and elegant Victorian villa ideally situated with easy access to both the sea and Penzance town centre. A short walk through the lovely Morrab gardens brings you within yards of the best pubs and restaurants in the area; set off in the other direction and the promenade is only a five minute walk away.

Three luxury en suite rooms on the first floor, one double, one family room and one twin bedded. All freshly decorated with colour TV and tea and coffee making facilities.

e-mail:dianemillera@aol.com • www.beechwoodpenzance.co.uk

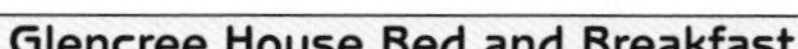

Glencree House Bed and Breakfast

An elegant, stylish and friendly Victorian Guesthouse at the heart of West Cornwall...
Relax, indulge yourself and enjoy....

- *Pamper*....stylish en suite rooms fully equipped for comfort and relaxation
- *Choice*...sea views, four-posters, king-size, twin, single and pet-friendly!
- *Indulge*...delicious breakfasts, real fires, cream teas and fresh flowers.
- *Peace*...quiet location near promenade, beautiful gardens and quiet coves.
- *Enjoy*...superb local cuisine and breathtaking scenery all year round!

Our philosophy is simple...we aim to make your stay special. We are friendly and welcoming, offer a high standard of service and pay particular attention to those little details you'll remember. It will make you want to return for years to come. Please call for a brochure or for further information.

Helen Cahalane, GLENCREE HOUSE, 2 MENNAYE ROAD, PENZANCE TR18 4NG
Tel/Fax: 01736 362026 • e-mail: stay@glencreehouse.co.uk • www.glencreehouse.co.uk

PENZANCE. "Tradewinds", 21 Regent Terrace, Penzance TR18 4DW (01736 330990).
Family-run guest house in seafront location, convenient for Isle of Scilly boat and parking. TV, tea/coffee making facilities. All rooms en suite. Family room for five. Full English breakfast, vegetarians welcome. Proprietor: **Mrs L. Matthews.**
Rates: terms from £25 per person. Reductions for children.
- Non-smoking.

Penalva Private Hotel
Alexandra Road, Penzance TR18 4LZ

The hotel is TOTALLY NON-SMOKING, offering full central heating, fresh immaculate interior, en suite facilities, excellent food and a real welcome with courteous service. Penalva is a well positioned, imposing, late Victorian hotel set in a wide tree-lined boulevard with ample parking, close to promenade and shops. Perfect centre for enjoying the wealth of beautiful sandy coves, historical remains and magnificent walks. Colour TV and tea/coffee making facilities in bedrooms. Special diets by prior arrangement. Sorry, no pets. Highly recommended. SAE, please, for brochure. *Open all year. Bed and Breakfast from £18 to £30. Weekly reductions. Children 6 to 12 half-price if sharing family rooms.*

Kate Owen • 01736 369060 • www.penalva.co.uk

Chy an Kerensa

Licensed Guest House situated by Coastal Path, directly overlooking miles of rolling surf, golden sands, rocks and heathland. Only 200 metres from beach and village centre, which has various restaurants, shops and pubs to suit all tastes and ages. Also tennis, bowls, wetsuit and surfboard hire, with golf and horse riding nearby. Our comfortable bedrooms, most en suite, have colour TV, central heating and tea/coffee making facilities. Many have panoramic sea views, as do our lounge/bar and dining room. Room only from £20 pppn, Bed and Breakfast from £25 to £30 pppn. A warm welcome assured.

Please write or telephone for further details -
Wendy Woodcock, Chy An Kerensa, Cliff Road, Perranporth TR6 0DR 01872 572470

Seaways is a small family guest house, 250 yards from safe, sandy beach. Surfing, riding, sailing, tennis, squash, golf all nearby. All bedrooms with en suite or private bathrooms, comprising one family, two double, two twin and a single room. Sittingroom; dining room. Children welcome (reduced price for under 10s). Cot, high chair available. Comfortable family holiday assured with plenty of good home cooking. Lovely cliff walks nearby. Padstow a short distance by ferry. Other places of interest include Tintagel, Boscastle and Port Isaac.

AA ♦♦♦

Non-smoking establishment. Open all year round.
Bed and Breakfast from £30.

Mrs P. White, Seaways, Polzeath PL27 6SU
Tel: 01208 862382
e-mail: pauline@seaways99.freeserve.co.uk • www.seawaysguesthouse.com

Picture courtesy Digital Presentations

B&B from £23 to £25 pppn

Situated on the Looe Bar side of Porthleven on the Lizard Peninsula. Sea views from bedrooms. Continental and English breakfast served with panoramic views over Mounts Bay. 264 yards from beach and coastal path. Five minutes' walk from harbour, shops, restaurants and inns. Guests are welcome to use the garden. Off-road parking on the property. Smoking in sun lounge only.

This house is also available to let and is equipped with all modern conveniences, including a wood-burning stove in the living room. Prices from £200 to £550 per week.

Mrs Neal, Tamarind, Shrubberies Hill, Porthleven, Helston TR13 9EA
01326 574303 or Tamsin on 07773 014169

LONG CROSS HOTEL & VICTORIAN GARDENS

TRELIGHTS, PORT ISAAC PL29 3TF • www.portisaac.com

Stay in one of Cornwall's most unusual hotels. Set in our own magnificent gardens in an Area of Outstanding Natural Beauty, and visited by thousands of garden lovers every year. Restaurant, Bar and Terraces with panoramic views. Spacious, newly refurbished, en suite rooms. Children's adventure play area.

Tel: 01208 880243
e-mail: longcross@portisaac.com

Set in a beautiful conservation village, local for hikers to Bodmin Moor (5 minutes), Sterts Theatre and famous Cornish Yarg cheese farm. Central for Eden Project, Looe and Trago Mills.

Come and try our candlelit three-course evening meals (£20) with complimentary bottle of wine, served in the conservatory overlooking the countryside and babbling brook. All rooms fully en suite; the Lilac Haven room also contains a four-poster antique pine bed.

Try our hot tub, summer house and gymnasium.

Our prices are from £28pppn; £38 single occupancy.

RAC ◆◆◆◆

Cornwall Tourism Awards Highly Commended 2002/3, Bronze Award 2005

Woodpeckers, Rilla Mill, Callington PL17 7NT • 01579 363717
e-mail: alison.merchant@virgin.net • www.woodpeckersguesthouse.co.uk

Pet-Friendly
Pubs, Inns & Hotels

on pages 298-311

Please note that these establishments may not feature in the main section of this book

Horizon Guest House .... St Ives

Do you want a holiday with first-class accommodation, and to feel at home instantly?

With beautiful sea view rooms overlooking Porthmeor Surf beach. We are close to the Coastal Footpath to Zennor, yet only five minutes from the Tate Gallery, Town Centre and beaches, and have some private parking. There is access to your rooms at any time; guests' lounge with colour TV, separate tables for dining and option of home-cooked dinner. All rooms en suite. Private parking.

Three-night breaks, early and late season £90.

Brochure and colour postcard available.

Julie Fitzgerald, Horizon Guest House, 5 Carthew Terrace, St Ives TR26 1EB • 01736 798069

FAIRFIELD HOUSE

Linda and Bob welcome you to their homely Edwardian Guest House with fabulous sea views. Ideally situated close to Carbis Bay beach in St Ives Bay, voted one of the most beautiful bays in the world. Two minutes' walk to the Coastal Path, beach and rail line (branch line to St Ives takes three minutes) or walk the beautiful Coastal Path to St Ives. Visit the galleries including the famous Tate, the cobbled streets and harbour, with its many restaurants/pubs.

Fairfield has been recently refurbished and new en suite facilities installed. Lovely airy rooms; all double/twin rooms have sea views across the bay to St Ives. Non-smoking guest house with emphasis on comfort, cleanliness and personal service. Cream teas served in our lovely garden.

Bed and Breakfast with varied menus from £29 per person per night.

Linda & Bob Gale, Fairfield House, Porthrepta Road, Carbis Bay, St Ives TR26 2NZ
01736 793771 • e-mail: info@fairfieldhouse.net • www.fairfieldhouse.net

Trewey Farm

Zennor, St Ives TR26 3DA

01736 796936

On the main St Ives to Land's End road, this attractive granite-built farmhouse stands among gorse and heather-clad hills, half-a-mile from the sea and five miles from St Ives. The mixed farm covers 300 acres, with Guernsey cattle and fine views of the sea; lovely cliff and hill walks. Guests will be warmly welcomed and find a friendly atmosphere.

Five double, one single and three family bedrooms (all with washbasin); bathroom, toilets; sittingroom, dining room. Cot, high chair and babysitting available.

Pets allowed • Car essential, parking
Open all year • Electric heating.
Bed and Breakfast only
SAE for terms, please.

Mrs N.I. Mann

Family-Friendly

Pubs, Inns & Hotels

See the Supplement on pages 293-297 for establishments which *really* welcome children.

Please note that these establishments may not feature in the main section of this book

TINTAGEL. Cate West, Chilcotts, Bossiney, Tintagel PL34 0AY (Tel & Fax: 01840 770324).

Without stepping onto a road, slip through the side gate of this 16th Century listed cottage into a landscape owned by the National Trust and designated as an Area of Outstanding Natural Beauty. Closest cottage to nearby Bossiney beach for rock pools, surfing, safe swimming and caves to explore. Walk the airy cliff path north to nearby Rocky Valley or on to picturesque Boscastle Harbour. Southwards takes you to the ruins of King Arthur's Castle and onwards to busy Trebarwith Strand. Notice you have not stepped onto a road yet? Detached traditional country cottage ideal for a small number of guests. Home cooking, warm informal atmosphere, large bright double/family bedrooms with beamed ceilings and olde worlde feel. All rooms have TV, tea/coffee makers. May I send you a brochure? Directions: Bossiney adjoins Tintagel on the B3263 (coast road), Chilcotts adjoins large lay-by with telephone box.

Rates: Bed and Breakfast from £20.

- Self-catering annexe available.

e-mail: cwest@tucansurf.com

Please note

All the information in this book is given in good faith in the belief that it is correct. However, the publishers cannot guarantee the facts given in these pages, neither are they responsible for changes in policy, ownership or terms that may take place after the date of going to press. Readers should always satisfy themselves that the facilities they require are available and that the terms, if quoted, still apply.

Cumbria

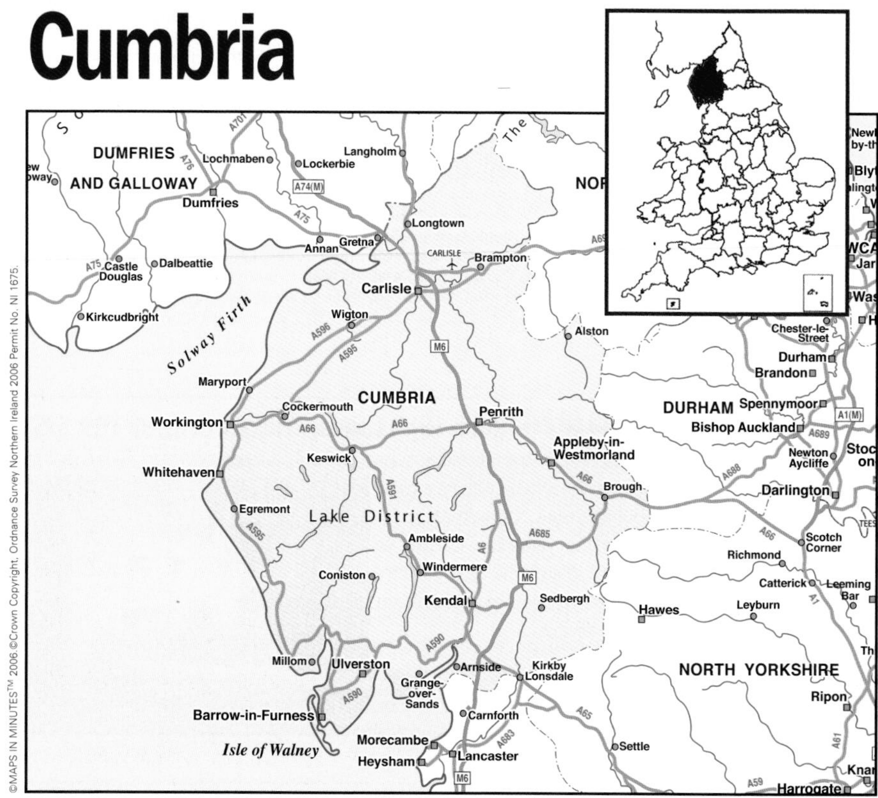

Cumbria - The Lake District is often described as the most beautiful corner of England, and it's easy to see why 15 million visitors head here every year. It is a place of unrivalled beauty, with crystal clear lakes, bracken-covered mountains, peaceful forests, quiet country roads and miles of stunning coastline.

At the heart of Cumbria is the Lake District National Park. Each of the lakes that make up the area has its own charm and personality: Windermere, England's longest lake, is surrounded by rolling hills; Derwentwater and Ullswater are circled by craggy fells; England's deepest lake, Wastwater, is dominated by high mountains including the country's highest, Scafell Pike. For those who want to tackle the great outdoors, Cumbria offers everything from rock climbing to fell walking and from canoeing to horse riding – all among stunning scenery.

Cumbria has many delightful market towns, historic houses and beautiful gardens such as Holker Hall with its 25 acres of award-winning grounds. There are many opportunities to sample local produce, such as Cumbrian fell-bred lamb, Cumberland Sausage, and trout and salmon plucked fresh from nearby lakes and rivers.

Cumbria is a county of contrasts with a rich depth of cultural and historical interest in addition to stunning scenery. Compact and accessible, it can offer something for every taste.

Ambleside Lodge

Heart of the English Lake District. This elegant Lakeland home, dating from the 19th century, has been sympathetically converted and now offers a high standard of accommodation. All bedrooms are en suite, with colour TV, tea/coffee making facilities and delightful views. The Premier suites and king-size four-poster rooms with jacuzzi spa baths offer relaxation and indulgence. Leisure facilities available at a private club just 5 minutes' drive away include swimming pool, sauna, steam room, squash, gym and beauty salon. Free parking.

AMBLESIDE LODGE, ROTHAY ROAD, AMBLESIDE, CUMBRIA LA22 0EJ
015394 31681 • Fax: 015394 34547 • www.ambleside-lodge.com

Ferndale Lodge

Lake Road, Ambleside, Cumbria LA22 0DB
Tel: 015394 32207
e-mail: stay@ferndalelodge.co.uk
website: www.ferndalelodge.co.uk

Ferndale Lodge is a small, family-run guesthouse where you will find a warm, friendly welcome and personal attention at all times. Offering excellent accommodation with good home cooked English or Vegetarian breakfast. Our 10 attractive bedrooms have all been individually decorated and furnished, each with full en suite facilities, colour television and tea/coffee making tray. Full central heating throughout, several rooms having views of the fells, and including ground floor bedrooms. The Ferndale is open all year round with a car park, offers packed lunches, hair dryer, clothes/boot drying and ironing facilities. A wide choice of places to dine, within minutes' walking distance, ranging from excellent pub food to superb restaurants of many varied cuisines will complete your day.

Bed and Breakfast £25.00 - £30.00 pppn. Weekly £175 - £196 pp. **Please phone for brochure.**

The Anchorage Guest House, Rydal Road, Ambleside LA22 9AY

Tel & Fax: 015394 32046

A warm welcome awaits you at the Anchorage in lovely Ambleside, the heart of the Lake District. Helen and Arthur, the resident owners, do their best to make your stay an enjoyable one. High quality accommodation in very comfortably furnished and decorated rooms. Open all year, with wonderful views of Loughrigg Fell and Wansfell Pike, yet only a few minutes' walk from the village centre. The house offers an ideal base from which to explore the Lake District with fell walking, climbing, mountain biking and water sports all nearby. For the less energetic, Ambleside village has a lot to offer, with The Bridge House, Museum and Cinema, not to mention all the traditional shops and cafes to explore. There are also plenty of restaurants and pubs for a great night out. Ample parking. Non-smoking.

e-mail: theanchorageguesthouse@hotmail.com • www.theanchorageguesthouse.co.uk

Broadview Guest House • Lake Road, Ambleside LA22 0DN

Broadview is a quality, friendly, non-smoking guest house in the heart of the Lake District. A short stroll from the centre of the village and Lake Windermere at Waterhead, Broadview is perfect for a holiday or a short break, whether as a base for touring or exploring the fells on foot. There are 6 comfortable guest rooms, (doubles, twins and a room that sleeps 3), most en suite or with private bathroom. All have TV, DVD, tea/coffee making facilities, mini-fridge, bathrobes, fluffy towels and hairdryer, along with the little extras to make your stay more comfortable. There is a king-size four-poster room for that extra special romantic break. The Broadview breakfast will set you up for the day, with local meats, free-range eggs and home-made breads. Vegetarian, vegan and most special diets catered for by prior arrangement. Drying facilities, maps, guides and packed lunches can be provided; free parking during your stay. Please visit our website, e-mail or phone for more information and details of our special offers. Rates £25-£40pppn. *We look forward to welcoming you to Broadview soon.*

www.broadviewguesthouse.co.uk • enquiries@broadviewguesthouse.co.uk • Tel: 015394 32431

Rothay House is an attractive modern detached guest house set in pleasant gardens with views of the surrounding fells.
All bedrooms are comfortable and well furnished, with en suite facilities, colour TV, tea and coffee trays.

Darren and Debra Hammond offer a friendly atmosphere in clean, attractive surroundings. The house is within easy walking distance of the village centre. Ambleside has a variety of interesting shops and restaurants and makes an ideal base for walking, touring or enjoying sailing, watersports and angling on Lake Windermere. Car not essential, but ample parking.

Open all year except January.
Children over 4 years welcome; sorry, no pets.
Strictly non-smoking

B&B from £29 to £35
Winter Weekend Breaks available.

ROTHAY HOUSE
Rothay Road, Ambleside LA22 0EE
Tel & Fax: 015394 32434
e-mail: email@rothay-house.com
www.rothay-house.com

The Dower House

Wray Castle, Ambleside
Cumbria LA22 0JA
Tel: 015394 33211

Lovely old house, quiet and peaceful, stands on an elevation overlooking Lake Windermere, with one of the most beautiful views in all Lakeland. Its setting within the 100-acre Wray Castle estate (National Trust), with direct access to the Lake, makes it an ideal base for walking and touring. Hawkshead and Ambleside are about ten minutes' drive and have numerous old inns and restaurants. Ample car parking; prefer dogs to sleep in the car. Children over five years welcome.

Bed and Breakfast from £31.00pp
Dinner, Bed & Breakfast from £46.00pp
Open all year round

Our 17th century former farmhouse is ideally located for exploring the Eden Valley, an area waiting to be discovered by those who seek tranquillity in an Area of Outstanding Natural Beauty. Very quiet location with outstanding views of the Pennines. Approximately one mile from the A66 and four miles west of Appleby, and very convenient for visits to the Lake District, Yorkshire Dales and Scottish Borders. Centrally heated accommodation includes two double (one en suite) and one twin room all with tea-making facilities. Hearty breakfasts are served, with special diets catered for. Children welcome. Non-smoking. Bed and Breakfast from £28.50 to £35; Evening Meal from £15 to £17.50. *Please send SAE for brochure.*

Barbara and Derick Cotton, Glebe House, Bolton,
Appleby-in-Westmorland CA16 6AW (017683 61125)
e-mail: derick.cotton@btinternet.com
www.glebeholidays.co.uk

• • • some fun days out in CUMBRIA

Museum of Lakeland Life, Kendal • 01539 722464 • www.lakelandmuseum.org.uk
Dove Cottage, Grasmere • 015394 35544 • www.wordsworth.org.uk
World of Beatrix Potter, Bowness-on-Windermere • 015394 88444 • www.hop-skip-jump.com
Honister Slate Mine, Borrowdale • 017687 77230 • www.honister-slate-mine.co.uk
Cumberland Pencil Museum, Keswick • 017687 73626 • www.pencils.co.uk
Trotters World of Animals, Bassenthwaite • 017687 76239 • www.trottersworld.com

Limnerslease, Bongate, Appleby CA16 6UE

Limnerslease is a family-run guest house five minutes' walk from the town centre. A good half-way stopping place on the way to Scotland. There is a good golf course and an indoor heated swimming pool. Many lovely walks are all part of the charm of Appleby. Two double and one twin bedrooms, all with washbasin, colour TV, tea/coffee making facilities at no extra charge; bathroom, toilet; dining room. Open January to November with gas heating. Ample parking. Bed and Breakfast from £22 to £25.

Mrs K.M. Coward • Tel & Fax: 017683 51578
e-mail: kathleen@limnerslease63.fsnet.co.uk
http://mysite.freeserve.com/limnerslease

Threapland Moss - 01697 322275

We offer Bed and Breakfast in our peaceful country house with accommodation for six guests, and a delightful self-catering cottage for four. Set in 80 acres of woodland near Bassenthwaite Lake, Cockermouth and Keswick on the edge of the National Park. Wake up to see the roaming deer and pheasant - a haven for wildlife, peace and tranquillity. Enjoy a delicious English, Continental or vegetarian breakfast in our dining room overlooking the garden and paddock. All rooms have TV and tea/coffee facilities. Private use of a luxurious leisure pool nearby. As members of "Horse Holidays in Cumbria" we can accommodate your horse, so you may enjoy exploring the local bridleways. An ideal location for exploring all the the Lake District has to offer and a warm welcome awaits. B&B from £25 to £35 pppn. Please telephone for brochure.

Andrena and Mike Hattersley, Threapland Moss, Bothel, Near Bassenthwaite CA7 2JW
e-mail: andrenahattersley@hotmail.co.uk
www.threaplandmoss.co.uk

Annisgarth B&B, 48 Craig Walk, Bowness-on-Windermere LA23 2JT

Tel: 015394 43866
www.annisgarth.co.uk

B&B from £20 to £35pppn

Exclusively non-smoking.

Sharron Moore welcomes you to her friendly and relaxed Victorian home, quietly situated only minutes' walk from Lake Windermere and all the cafes, pubs, restaurants, shops and attractions of Bowness village. Three double bedrooms, one twin, one family room and a deluxe room with a jacuzzi bath and lake view. All rooms have TV with DVD and a collection of movies and books to read. All diets are catered for including vegetarian and vegan. All produce is local with free range eggs. There is a real coal fire for those winter mornings.

Dalegarth Guest House, Hassness Estate, Buttermere CA13 9XA

Our guesthouse in the grounds of Hassness Estate on the shores of Buttermere is an ideal base for walkers or non-walkers.

The house has nine bedrooms, some en suite, a lounge and a breakfast room.

Standard rooms from £24 per person, en suite £30 per person. Evening meal from £5.

10% discount for three nights or more.

Tel: 017687 70233
e-mail: dalegarth-buttermere@supanet.com • www.dalegarthguesthouse.co.uk

Swaledale Watch, Whelpo, Caldbeck CA7 8HQ
Tel & Fax: 016974 78409

Mixed farm of 300 acres situated in beautiful countryside within the Lake District National Park. Central for Scottish Borders, Roman Wall, Eden Valley and the Lakes. Primarily a sheep farm (everyone loves lambing time). Visitors are welcome to see farm animals and activities. Many interesting walks nearby or roam the peaceful Northern fells. Enjoyed by many Cumbrian Way walkers. Very comfortable accommodation with excellent breakfasts. All rooms have private facilities. Central heating. Tea making facilities. We are a friendly Cumbrian family and make you very welcome. Bed and Breakfast from £22 to £28. Contact: **Mr and Mrs A. Savage**

e-mail: nan.savage@talk21.com
www.swaledale-watch.co.uk

Tel: 01228 521645

ABBERLEY HOUSE

33 Victoria Place, Carlisle CA1 1HP

An imposing town house offering informal, comfortable high standard en suite rooms with TV, tea and coffee facilities and private parking. We are only a short walk from the excellent town centre with its fine variety of shops, restaurants, pubs and of course the cathedral, castle and award-winning Tullie House museum. Also close by are Stoney Holme and Swift golf courses, the Sands sports and leisure centre and the splendid River Eden. A short drive takes you to historic Hadrian's Wall, the magnificent Lake District and romantic Gretna Green.

Our rates start from only £19 per person which includes English breakfast and taxes.

e-mail: bbs@abberleyhouse.co.uk • www.abberleyhouse.co.uk

English Tourism Council ♦♦♦♦ Guest Accommodation

~ Mrs Dorothy Nicholson, Gill Farm, Blackford, Carlisle, Cumbria CA6 4EL ~

In a delightful setting on a beef and sheep farm, this Georgian-style farmhouse, dated 1740, offers a friendly welcome to all guests.

Near Hadrian's Wall • Gretna Green • Lake District Golf • Fishing • Swimming • Large agricultural auction markets • Cycle path passes our entrance.

Accommodation is in one double room en suite, one double and one twin/single bedrooms. All rooms have washbasins, shaver points and tea/coffee making facilities. Two bathrooms, shower; lounge with colour TV; separate diningroom. Reductions for children. Central heating. Car essential, good parking.

GILL FARM

B&B from £23 to £27. Telephone for further details or directions. Tel: 01228 675326 • mobile: 07808 571586

The Shepherds

HOTEL & RESTAURANT

B&B £27.00 to £54.00

26 en suite rooms, single, double, twin and family, all furnished to a high standard. The restaurant is open throughout the day, serving a selection of bar meals and snacks, and the extensive evening menu is freshly and skilfully prepared by our chef. Enjoy a full English breakfast before exploring this breathtaking part of the Lake District.

Restaurant • Bar Meals • En suite facilities • Colour TV Trouser press & hair dryer • Direct-dial telephone • One wheel chair accessible room • Office services • Retail gifts & wool shop • Visitor centre • Live sheep show (Seasonal)

Egremont Road, Cockermouth, Cumbria CA13 0QX

Tel: 01900 822673 • Fax: 01900 820129
e-mail: reception@shepherdshotel.co.uk
www.shepherdshotel.co.uk

Cumbria - the Lake District also has strong literary connections. Visitors can see the sweeping landscapes that inspired the Lake poets, William Wordsworth and Samuel Taylor Coleridge, and the works of writers such as Arthur Ransome and Beatrix Potter. It is an area rich in heritage, with the beautiful ruins of Furness Abbey in the Lake District Peninsula, England's smallest cathedral in Carlisle, Birdoswald Roman Fort and Hadrian's Wall, where the Scots were kept out, and Carlisle Castle where Mary Queen of Scots was imprisoned. South from Carlisle runs the Eden Valley – an area of rolling green landscapes contrasting with the hump-backed open moors of the North Pennines. In the Western Lakes there are the lush and peaceful Ennerdale and Eskdale valleys and the sandstone cliffs of St Bees Head, part of a designated Heritage Coast. Cumbria has many delightful market towns, such as Alston, the highest market town in England, and Keswick, the jewel of the Northern Lakes. In the south, the cobbled streets of Ulverston have many claims to fame – the birthplace of Quakerism, Stan Laurel and pole vaulting. The Georgian town of Whitehaven was once Britain's third largest port, and further south, Barrow-in-Furness combines a Dock Museum with a modern centre. There are historic houses and beautiful gardens such as Holker Hall with its 25 acres of award-winning gardens and food hall selling succulent produce.

Rose Cottage

Lorton Road, Cockermouth CA13 9DX

Family-run guest house on the outskirts of Cockermouth. Warm, friendly atmosphere. Ample off-road parking. All rooms en suite with colour TV, tea/coffee, central heating and all have double glazing.

Pets most welcome in the house (excluding dining room), and there are short walks nearby. Ideal base for visiting both Lakes and coast.

Tel & Fax: 01900 822189 www.rosecottageguest.co.uk

Working farm situated in a peaceful part of Lorton Valley, the perfect base for your Lakeland holiday. Ideal for hill walking and touring around the Lake District. All rooms are en suite with central heating, tea/coffee making facilities and hairdryer. TV lounge with open fire. Magnificent views. Packed lunches available. A warm welcome awaits you.

Open all year.

B&B from £21.50 to £25 pppn, single £23 to £27

Mrs Nicholson, Swinside End Farm,
Scales, High Lorton, Near Cockermouth CA13 9UA
Tel: 01900 85134; mobile: 07913 337556; Fax: 01900 85410
e-mail: swinside@supanet.com

foresthow lake district guest house

Tucked away at the end of a quiet country lane lies Foresthow. It is a very special place surrounded by gardens and natural fellside. There is an amazing abundance of wildlife and excellent walks all from the doorstep. The views across the lovely Eskdale Valley are spectacular. All rooms, some en suite, have TV, tea/coffee making facilities and are warm and cosy. We are renowned for our hearty breakfasts and personal caring attention. Good eating places locally. Ample car parking. Narrow gauge steam railway five minutes' walk. Brochure available.

Mr & Mrs J. D. Bromage, Foresthow Guest House,
Eskdale, Holmrook CA19 1TR • 019467 23201
e-mail: info@foresthow.co.uk www.foresthow.co.uk

Paul and Fran Townsend

Pepper House

Satterthwaite LA12 8LS • Tel: 01229 860206

A warm welcome awaits in 16th century cruck-frame farmhouse with elevated position in tranquil valley on edge of Grizedale Forest (abundant wildlife), four miles from Hawkshead. Peaceful base for exploring the Lakes, close to Beatrix Potter's Hilltop and Ruskin's Brantwood. Miles of forest trails for walking and cycling. Sympathetically updated, all bedrooms have en suite facilities. Two comfortable lounges. Central heating, log fires; dining room and terraces with wonderful views. Licensed bar, generous home cooking. Non-smoking. Bed and Breakfast from £27 to £33; Dinner from £16. See all details at **www.pepper-house.co.uk** *Also ask us about two self-catering cottages, stunningly located on traditional Lakeland working farm, or go to* **www.hartsophallcottages.com**

Beckfoot Country House,

Helton, Penrith CA10 2QB

Tel: 01931 713241 • Fax: 01931 713391

e-mail: info@beckfoot.co.uk • www.beckfoot.co.uk

A beautiful Victorian country house set in three acres of gardens, with wonderful views of the Lowther valley, a tranquil and unspoilt corner of the Lake District National Park.

All rooms are en suite, spacious and well appointed with TV, hospitality tray and complimentary toiletries; luxurious executive suite with four-poster. Ironing facilities available. Cumbrian breakfast served in the oak-panelled diningroom.

Activities nearby include walking, cycling, horse riding, fishing, golf, swimming and paragliding, or visit Hadrian's Wall and the Scottish Borders, Eden Valley, historic Carlisle city, historic castles and gardens.

Special three-night breaks available. *AA* 

Russell Farm

Burton-in-Kendal, Carnforth, Lancs LA6 1NN

01524 781334• Fax: 01524 782511

Mrs A. Taylor

Why not spend a few days at Russell Farm?

The proprietors pride themselves on trying to give guests an enjoyable holiday with good food, friendly atmosphere, relaxing surroundings away from the hustle and bustle. The 150-acre dairy farm is set in a quiet hamlet one mile from the village of Burton-in-Kendal, and five miles from the old market town of Kirkby Lonsdale. An ideal centre for touring Lakes and Yorkshire Dales, or going to the coast. Ideal stopover for people travelling south or to Scotland, only five minutes from M6 Motorway.

One double, one single and one family bedrooms; bathroom, toilet; sittingroom and diningroom. Children welcome; cot, high chair and babysitting offered. Pets accepted, if well-behaved.

Evening Dinner, Bed and Breakfast or B&B. Reductions for children.

Car essential, parking. Send large SAE, please, for terms and brochure.

HOTEL & RESTAURANT Highfield, The Heads, Keswick CA12 5ER

www.highfieldkeswick.co.uk • info@highfieldkeswick.co.uk

Award-winning, non-smoking, Victorian town house hotel, quietly situated, with fantastic views of Derwentwater and the surrounding mountains, and only a few minutes' walk from the town centre, theatre and lake.

- 18 en suite bedrooms, with TV/DVD, tea/coffee making, hairdryers
- Family-owned and run, in an informal and relaxed atmosphere
- Award-winning restaurant • AA *Two Rosettes*
- 2 night breaks available from £110 D,B&B.

VisitBritain *Silver Award* • AA ★★ *Two Rosettes*

017687 72508

Please call for brochure, tariff and sample menu

Mrs S. Park, Langdale
14 Leonard Street, Keswick CA12 4EL
Tel: 017687 73977
website: www.langdaleguesthouse.co.uk

Victorian town house, quietly situated, yet close to town, park, lake and fells. All rooms furnished to a very high standard, having quality en suite facilities, central heating, colour TV, tea/coffee making facilities throughout. Family, double or twin available. Enjoy a good home cooked English or vegetarian breakfast or our popular Continental breakfast. We have a non-smoking policy throughout the house. We will ensure your stay is a pleasant one.
Bed and Breakfast from £25; Theatre Breaks.

KESWICK. Mrs Trafford, Bassenthwaite Hall Farm, Bassenthwaite Village, Near Keswick CA12 4QP (Tel & Fax: 017687 76393).
Bed and Breakfast - Good accommodation at sensible prices. A friendly welcome awaits you at our lovely 17th century farmhouse which is fully modernised whilst retaining its olde worlde character. A charming lounge/dining room furnished with antiques is available for guests' use any time. Delightful bedrooms with individual period furnishings. Hand basin in rooms, two bathrooms close by. Excellent Cumbrian breakfast, with healthy options. Switch off and unwind in this beautiful corner of England.
Rates: Bed and Breakfast from £25pppn.
• Small dogs welcome.

e-mail: stay@amtrafford.co.uk
www.bedandbreakfast-lakedistrict.co.uk

Lindisfarne Guest House
21 Church Street, Keswick CA12 4DX • Tel: 017687 73218

A cosy, friendly guest house with home cooking and hearty breakfasts. Situated within a residential area close to the town centre of Keswick and within easy walking distance of Lake Derwentwater and Fitz Park. We have some en suite rooms and all bedrooms have colour TV, tea/coffee facilities, central heating and washbasin.
Bed and Breakfast from £23; Evening Meal optional.
Chris and Alison Burns look forward to welcoming you.

e-mail: alison@burns1067.freeserve.co.uk
www.lindisfarnehouse.com

WYCK HOUSE - *KIRKBY LONSDALE*

Quality accommodation in Victorian town house, close to local pubs and restaurants. Double and twin rooms with en suite facilities; all rooms have TV and hospitality trays. The famous Ruskin's View and Devil's Bridge are only a short walk away. We are situated on the Cumbrian, Lancashire and Land's End to John O'Groats cycle ways. Safe storage for cycles. There are also two golf courses close by for keen golfers. Ideally situated between the Lakes and Dales. No smoking. B&B from £30 to £39pppn.

Pat & Brian Bradley, Wyck House,
4 Main Street, Kirkby Lonsdale LA6 2AE • Tel & Fax: 015242 71953
e-mail: wyckhouse@studioarts.co.uk • www.studioarts.co.uk/wyckhouse.htm

Cocklake House

MALLERSTANG CA17 4JT

017683 72080

Charming, High Pennine Country House B&B in unique position above Pendragon Castle in Upper Mallerstang Dale offering good food and exceptional comfort to a small number of guests. Two double rooms with large private bathrooms.
Three acres riverside grounds.
Dogs welcome.

Grizedale Lodge

Hawkshead, Ambleside LA22 0QL

Set in the heart of Grizedale Forest National Park, Grizedale Lodge is one of the most beautiful Bed and Breakfast locations. Within easy reach are the famous sculpture trails, sailing on Windermere or Coniston, Brantwood, Beatrix Potter country, trout fishing, and other attractions; Hawkshead five minutes. All rooms are en suite, centrally heated, and have colour TV, tea and coffee making facilities and hairdryers. Some have the added luxury of four-poster beds. Ample parking, TV lounge and sun terrace. Residential licence. Open all year, rates start from £30pppn.

Tel: 015394 36532 • Fax: 015394 36572
enquiries@grizedale-lodge.com • www.grizedale-lodge.com

ASKHILL FARM

Loweswater, Cockermouth CA13 0SU
01946 861640
e-mail: askhillfarm@aol.com
www.countrycaravans.co.uk/askhillfarm
Mrs M. Vickers • Telephone for a brochure

ASKHILL is a family-run farm which has beef and sheep, and is situated on the hillside overlooking Loweswater Lake. The area is ideal for fell-walkers; there are plenty of walks (high fells or low walks) to suit everyone's level of ability; we are handy for all the western lakes, Crummock Water, Buttermere, Ennerdale (with lots of woodland walks), Wast Water (the deepest lake). Loweswater is handy for Keswick (10 miles approx.), Cockermouth (8 miles), the city of Carlisle with Roman connections (30 miles approx.), Maryport, steeped in Roman history (12 miles), and we are roughly 12 miles from the Solway coast.

B & B from £25-£27pp; Dinner, B & B from £38pp.
Also 6 berth, self-catering caravan to let from £250 per week.

Riverside B&B

10 Selby Terrace, Maryport CA15 6NF
Tel: 01900 813595

Clean, welcoming Victorian townhouse, family-run. Many original features including stained glass entrance, staircase, fireplaces, coving etc. No smoking. Ideal base for the Lake District and Coastal Route. Cyclists and Walkers Welcome. Fishing available (sea and river). Delicious full English breakfast and towels provided. Colour TV and tea/coffee facilities in all rooms. Packed lunch available.

Standard rooms: one single, one double and one family(double and two single beds also used as a twin/double/triple), from £18pppn.
One double en suite room available from £22pppn. *Contact: Mrs L. Renac.*

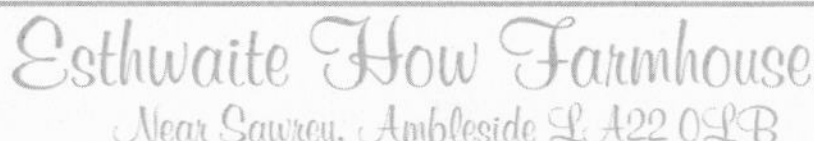

Near Sawrey, Ambleside LA22 0LB

A warm and friendly welcome awaits you in this lovely village where Beatrix Potter wrote her books. Beautiful views of the countryside and the lake can be seen from bedrooms and the diningroom. Ideal for walking, fishing and touring.

Two double rooms, one en suite, and one twin bedded room. Dining/sitting room with open log fire, central heating. Children welcome; babysitting can be arranged.

Open all year. Car essential, parking for three cars.

B&B from £20, en suite £25; D,B&B from £30, en suite £35.

Mrs Elizabeth Mallett - 015394 36450

Peter & Cynthia Barry, Blue Swallow Guest House, 11 Victoria Road, Penrith CA11 8HR • Tel: 01768 866335

A comfortable Victorian house set in the attractive market town of Penrith, ideally situated to explore the delightful Eden Valley, the wonderful scenery of the Lake District and the Yorkshire Dales National Parks. For golfing enthusiasts, Penrith boasts an 18 hole golf course and there are several more within easy driving distance. The resident proprietors look forward to welcoming you whether you are on holiday, just breaking a long journey or in the area for business - you'll be made to feel at home. Seven rooms, twin/double or family (four en suite), one private bathroom; two single en suite rooms. All rooms have colour TV, tea tray and central heating. Full English breakfast using local produce.Non-smoking throughout.

Bed and Breakfast from £27.50 to £35 pppn.

BLUE Swallow GUEST HOUSE

e-mail: blueswallow@tiscali.co.uk • www.blueswallow.co.uk

Family-Friendly
Pubs, Inns & Hotels

See the Supplement on pages 293-297 for establishments which *really* welcome children.

Please note that these establishments may not feature in the main section of this book

PENRITH. Mrs Ann Toppin, Gale Hall, Melmerby, Penrith CA10 1HN (01768 881254).

Mrs Ann Toppin welcomes guests to her home on a working beef/sheep farm 10 miles east of Penrith and the M6, a mile-and-a-half from the peaceful village of Melmerby. Beautiful setting at the foot of the Pennines and with extensive views of the Lakeland Fells. Ideal for walking, convenient for the Lake District. Single, double, twin or family rooms available; cot and babysitting. Residents' lounge. Special diets catered for. Full English or Vegetarian Breakfast served. Excellent bar meals available locally. ***Rates: Bed and Breakfast from £20; reduction for children under 12 years.***

• Working farm • Pets welcome by arrangement.

Albany House 5 Portland Place, Penrith CA11 7QN

e-mail: info@albany-house.org.uk • www.albany-house.org.uk

Close to the town centre, Albany House is a lovely mid-Victorian terraced property. Fine, spacious rooms (two double, two multi, one family), en suite facilities, central heating, colour TV, tea/coffee. Situated close to M6, A6 and A66, an ideal base for touring the Lake District, Eden Valley, Hadrian's Wall and Scottish Borders. An excellent stopover, with the warmest welcome and hearty breakfasts. B&B from £25pp.

Contact: Mrs Bell (01768 863072).

AA ★★★

Greenah Crag, Troutbeck, Penrith CA11 0SQ (017684 83233)

Enjoy a relaxing break at Greenah Crag, a 17th century former farmhouse peacefully located in the Lake District National Park, 10 miles Keswick, eight miles from M6. Ideal for exploring Northern Lakes and Western Pennines.

Two doubles en suite, and one twin with washbasin. Guests' sittingroom with woodburning stove • Full breakfast. Excellent choice of pubs within three miles • Regret no pets, no smoking.

Please telephone for brochure.
Bed and Breakfast from £23 per person.

e-mail: greenahcrag@lineone.net
www.greenahcrag.co.uk

Pallet Hill Farm is pleasantly situated two miles from Penrith, four miles from Ullswater, with easy access to the Lake District, Scottish Borders and Yorkshire Dales.

- Good farmhouse food and hospitality with personal attention.
- An ideal place to spend a relaxing break.
- Golf club, swimming pool, pony trekking in the area.
- Double, single and family rooms; Children welcome.
- Sorry, no pets. • Car essential, parking.
- Open Easter to November.

Bed and Breakfast £15 (reduced weekly rates), reduced rates for children.

Penrith, Cumbria CA11 0BY
Tel: 017684 83247

ULLSWATER. Knotts Mill Country Lodge, Watermillock, Penrith CA11 0JN (017684 86699).
Spacious guesthouse close to magical Ullswater, in peaceful, scenic surroundings. Ideal for walking, boating or touring the Lake District. Nine en suite bedrooms with stunning views, including family rooms. Our large dining room and lounge have picture windows that overlook the fells. Big breakfasts; fully licensed for wines, beer etc. 10 minutes from Junction 40 M6 with private grounds and parking. When the Lake District is at its most beautiful, with snow on the peaks, you can relax at Knotts Mill Country Lodge.
• Facilities for disabled guests.

ETC 

www.knottsmill.com

Brook House

30 Ellerthwaite Road, Windermere LA23 2AH

A friendly welcome awaits you at Brook House which is convenient for village and lake. Ideal touring centre. Personal service and excellent English cooking, under the personal supervision of the proprietors.
All rooms are decorated to a high standard; residents' lounge with colour TV; full central heating. All bedrooms have private showers/baths, colour TV, tea/coffee making facilities, and most have private toilets.
Access to rooms at all times. Guests' parking.
Full Fire Certificate. Open all year. Bed and Breakfast from £20 to £30.

Mrs J. Seal - 015394 44932
e-mail: stay@brookhouselakes.co.uk
www.brookhouselakes.co.uk

Elegant Victorian house on Windermere to Ambleside Road with a Lake viewpoint nearby. The front rooms overlook a tree-lined paddock, the rear rooms overlook Wynlass Beck where ducks, rabbits and the occasional deer can be seen. We have a private lounge for guests to relax in. All bedrooms have colour TV and tea/coffee making facilities. Non-smoking establishment. Ample private parking. A good selection of restaurants available nearby.

Rooms are available from £20.00 per person, all with en suite facilities.
Ring Gillian who will be happy to discuss your requirements.

Ambleside Road, Windermere LA23 1EU
Tel: 015394 46974 • Fax: 015394 42384
e-mail: enquiries@firgarth.com

Holly-Wood Guesthouse

Holly Road, Windermere, Cumbria LA23 2AF • Telephone 015394 42219

Holly-Wood is a beautiful, family-run Victorian house offering clean comfortable accommodation, set in a quiet position 3 minutes' walk from Windermere village amenities. It is the perfect place to unwind after a day exploring the Lakes.
• All rooms en suite • Private car park • Hearty traditional/vegetarian breakfasts • Non-smoking throughout • Help with walk planning available • All major credit cards accepted.

Bed & Breakfast from £25pppn.

Please contact Jo or Mark for more information

We look forward to welcoming you to Holly-Wood

e-mail: info@hollywoodguesthouse.co.uk • www.hollywoodguesthouse.co.uk

Pet-Friendly Pubs, Inns & Hotels

on pages 298-311

Please note that these establishments may not feature in the main section of this book

GREEN GABLES

37 Broad Street, Windermere LA23 2AB

AA ♦♦♦

A family-owned and run licensed guesthouse in Windermere centrally situated one-minute's walk from village centre with shops, banks and pubs and only five minutes from the station or bus stop. Accommodation comprises two doubles, one family triple/twin and one single room, all en suite; one family (four) and two family triple/twin rooms with private facilities; all with central heating, colour TV, hairdryers, kettles, tea & coffee. Comfortable lounge bar on the ground floor. No smoking in bedrooms. We can book tours and trips for guests and can advise on activities and special interests. B&B from £23 to £30 pppn. Special Winter offers available. Open just about all year round. Contact **Carole Vernon and Alex Tchumak**.

Tel: 015394 43886 • e-mail: greengables@FSBdial.co.uk • e-mail: info@greengablesguesthouse.co.uk

Meadow Cottage
Tel: 01539 821269
www.meadow-cottage.net

Sandra and David Lennon extend a warm welcome to guests who stay at Meadow Cottage. Set in one and a half acres, this old Lakeland cottage has spectacular views and is the ideal location when visiting this beautiful region. All bedrooms are en suite, have tea and coffee facilities and colour TV. We provide Aga-cooked vegetarian or English breakfasts. Some five miles from Lake Windermere, the popular heart of the Lake District, we are conveniently placed for touring, walking or cycling exploration. A flexible service is provided in this non-smoking guest house. Please enquire for details. Prices from £28 per person.

Mr and Mrs D. Lennon, Meadow Cottage, Ratherheath Lane, Crook, Kendal LA8 8JX

Derbyshire

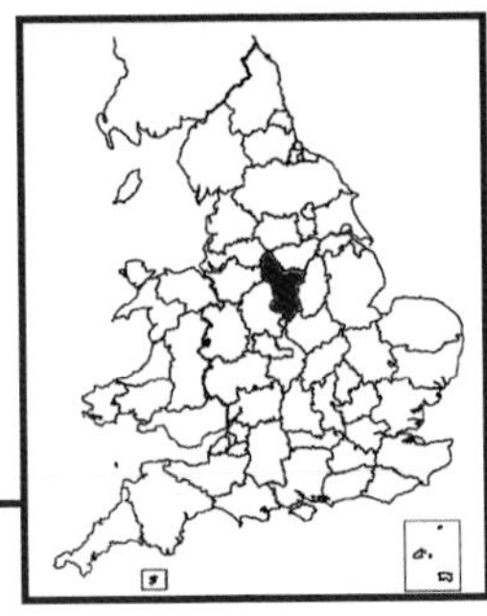

Turlow Bank

Hognaston, Ashbourne, Derbyshire DE6 1PW
Tel & Fax: 01335 370299
e-mail: turlowbank@w3z.co.uk
www.turlowbank.co.uk

AA ★★★★★ Guest Accommodation

Recently renovated early 19th century farmhouse in a quiet location, surrounded by glorious views. Spacious guest lounge with log fire; double bedroom with private bathroom, king-size bedroom en suite, central heating throughout. Full English breakfast, vegetarians catered for. Pub meals available locally, restaurant and cafe nearby. A step away from walking country and Carsington Water is only a short walk, where water sports, bird watching and cycling are available. Convenient for all attractions of the Peak District. *Bed and Breakfast from £35 to £55 pppn.*

Stone Cottage

A charming cottage in the quiet village of Clifton, one mile from the Georgian market town of Ashbourne.
Each bedroom is furnished to a high standard with all rooms en suite, with four-poster bed, TV and coffee making facilities.
A warm welcome is assured and a hearty breakfast in this delightful cottage.
There is a large garden to relax in.
Ideal for visiting Chatsworth House, Haddon Hall, Dovedale, Carsington Water and the theme park of Alton Towers.
B&B from £22.50 pp. Good country pubs nearby serving evening meals.
Enquiries to: ***Mrs A. M. Whittle, Stone Cottage, Green Lane, Clifton, Ashbourne, Derbyshire DE6 2BL • Telephone: 01335 343377 Fax: 01335 347117 • e-mail: info@stone-cottage.fsnet.co.uk***

AA ♦♦♦

Small family-run guest house with accent on good food, locally produced where possible, and quality accommodation in a warm and friendly atmosphere.

Originally three terraced cottages, now converted into one rather individual house which has been our home since 1986. Comfortable sitting room, five en suite bedrooms, all with colour TV and well-stocked tea tray. Safe parking in delightful garden at the rear of the house. No smoking.

Bed and Breakfast from £24 per person.

Compton House, 27-31 Compton, Ashbourne DE6 1BX
01335 343100 • e-mail: jane@comptonhouse.co.uk •
www.comptonhouse.co.uk

Victorian cowshed tastefully converted and furnished to a very high standard.Tranquil location, yet within easy reach of Alton Towers (8 miles), Chatsworth House, Calke Abbey and many other historic houses. The Potteries are close to hand, as is the American Adventure Theme Park.

Stay in one of our seven rooms – five double, one twin and a family suite, all with en suite facilities. Children welcome. Regret, no pets.

B&B from £26 double/twin, £35 single.

AA ◆◆◆◆, CLA BUILDING AWARD WINNER, NATIONAL ACCESSIBLE SCHEME LEVEL 3.

The Courtyard, Dairy House Farm,

Alkmonton, Longford, Ashbourne DE6 3DG

Tel: 01335 330187

e-mail: michael@dairyhousefarm.org.uk

www.dairyhousefarm.org.uk

MONA VILLAS

Church Lane
Middle Mayfield
Mayfield
Near Ashbourne
DE6 2JS

Tel: 01335 343773

A warm, friendly welcome to our home with purpose-built en suite accommodation. Beautiful views over open countryside. A local pub serves excellent food within a five minute walk. Situated near Alton Towers, Dove Dale, etc. Three en suite rooms available, single supplement applies. Family rooms available. Parking.

Bed and Breakfast from £22.50 to £25.00 per night.

e-mail: info@mona-villas.fsnet.co.uk

www.mona-villas.fsnet.co.uk

◆ At almost 1000ft above sea level, the village nestles at the head of Lathkill Dale, a National Nature Reserve, and is surrounded by the stunning scenery of the White Peak. Cycle hire and fantastic horse riding are available locally.

◆ Clean and comfortable accommodation awaits you. Rooms (single, double and twin) have en suite facilities, tea/coffee, colour TV, radio, and hairdryers and are centrally heated and double glazed. Freesat now being installed. Laundry facilities are also available to guests. A variety of Aga-cooked breakfasts are served daily

◆Children and pets welcome by arrangement.

◆ Ample private parking ◆ Drive and Hike service.

◆B&B from £25pppn

e-mail: rowsonfarm@btconnect.com

www.rowsonhousefarm.com

Rowson House Farm

Monyash, Bakewell DE45 1JH

Tel: 01629 813521

Looking for holiday accommodation?

for details of hundreds of properties throughout the UK including comprehensive coverage of all areas of Scotland try:

www.holidayguides.com

Relax in the warm and friendly atmosphere of our peaceful farmhouse situated on the edge of Lathkill Dale. Conveniently located for visiting the many attractions of the area. All rooms are en suite, colour TV and tea making facilities. Ground floor rooms available. A varied breakfast menu is offered, and packed lunches by arrangement. Excellent local inns and restaurants a short drive away.

Bed and Breakfast £25 - £27 per person sharing double/twin room. Single occupancy £35 per night. Discount for 3-night stays mid-week. No smoking in house.

Mrs Julia Finney, Mandale House, Haddon Grove, Bakewell DE45 1JF
Tel: 01629 812416
e-mail: julia.finney@virgin.net • www.mandalehouse.co.uk

Guests are warmly welcomed into the friendly atmosphere of Braemar, situated in a quiet residential part of this famous spa town. Within five minutes' walk of all the town's many and varied attractions i.e., Pavilion Gardens, Opera House, swimming pool; golf courses, horse riding, walking, fishing, etc are all within easy reach in this area renowned for its scenic beauty. Many of the Peak District's famous beauty spots including Chatsworth, Haddon Hall, Bakewell, Matlock, Dovedale and Castleton are nearby. Accommodation comprises comfortable double and twin bedded rooms fully en suite with colour TV and hospitality trays, etc. Full English Breakfast served and diets catered for. Non-smokers preferred.

Terms from £26.50 inclusive for Bed and Breakfast. Weekly terms available.

Roger and Maria Hyde, Braemar, 10 Compton Road, Buxton SK17 9DN
Tel: 01298 78050
e-mail: buxtonbraemar@supanet.com www.cressbrook.co.uk/buxton/braemar

Ye Olde Cheshire Cheese Inn

How Lane, Castleton, Hope Valley S33 8WJ
Telephone: 01433 620330 • Fax: 01433 621847
website: www.cheshirecheeseinn.co.uk • e-mail: kslack@btconnect.com

This delightful 17th century free house is situated in the heart of the Peak District and is an ideal base for walkers and climbers; other local attractions include cycling, swimming, gliding, horse riding and fishing. All bedrooms are en suite with colour TV and tea/coffee making facilities. A "Village Fayre" menu is available all day, all dishes home cooked in the traditional manner; there is also a selection of daily specials. Large car park. Full Fire Certificate. B&B from £25.00. All credit cards accepted.

SPECIAL GOLF PACKAGES ARRANGED.
PERSONAL TRAINING INSTRUCTOR AVAILABLE.

Please mention **FHG Guides** when making enquiries about accommodation featured in these pages

Free or reduced rate entry to Holiday Visits and Attractions – see our **READERS' OFFER VOUCHERS on pages 9-42**

This 120 acre mixed farm with Georgian farmhouse is set in peaceful rural surroundings, yet offers all the convenience of being only three miles west of Derby, on the A516 between Mickleover and Etwall. Within 10 miles there is a choice of historic houses to visit; Calke Abbey, Kedleston Hall, Sudbury Hall. Peak District 20 miles, Alton Towers 20 miles.

Accommodation in three bedrooms (one twin, one double en suite, one family room with en suite facilities), all with tea/coffee making facilities. Cot and high chair provided. Open all year. Croquet available. Bed and Breakfast from £26.

A warm and friendly welcome awaits you.

Mrs Catherine Dicken, Bonehill Farm, Etwall Road, Mickleover DE3 0DN

www.bonehillfarm.co.uk

Causeway House B&B, Back Street, Castleton, Hope Valley S33 8WE

01433 623291 • email: steynberg@btinternet.com

Causeway House is a 16th Century Cruck Cottage in the heart of Castleton in the beautiful Peak District. The area is renowned for its scenery, history and heritage with amazing walks, cycling and Blue John caves to visit

The accommodation has two en suite double rooms, a single and a twin room with shared bathroom, One of the rooms has a four-poster bed.

Nick and Janet Steynberg offer you a hearty Full English, Continental or Vegetarian Breakfast.

A piece of Heaven for you and your family.

MATLOCK. Mrs S. Elliott, "Glendon", Knowleston Place, Matlock DE4 3BU (01629 584732).

Warm hospitality and comfortable accommodation in this Grade II Listed building. Conveniently situated by the Hall Leys Park and River Derwent, it is only a short level walk to Matlock town centre. Large private car park. Rooms are centrally heated and have washbasin, colour TV and tea/coffee making facilities. En suite available. An ideal base for exploring the beautiful Peak District of Derbyshire, with easy access to many places of interest including Chatsworth House, Haddon Hall, Crich Tramway Village and Heights of Abraham cable car.

Rates: Bed and Breakfast from £25.50 per person.

• No smoking.

AA ◆◆◆◆

Ivy House Farm is a small arable working farm. The farmhouse, converted in 2000, has three double bedrooms and we have also converted our redundant cowsheds into three ground floor double/twin bedrooms, all of which are en suite, with tea/coffee making facilities and TV. The area has lots to do and see, such as Calke Abbey, ski slopes, Alton Towers, motor racing at Donington Park, not forgetting the National Forest. Children are welcome, but we are strictly non-smoking. Ample off-road parking. Bed and Breakfast from £32.

English Tourism Council ♦♦♦♦ GUEST ACCOMMODATION — Silver SILVER AWARD

Ivy House Farm Guesthouse, Stanton-by-Bridge, Derby DE73 7HT
Tel: 01332 863152
e-mail: mary@guesthouse.fsbusiness.co.uk www.ivy-house-farm.com

"Poppies"

Bank Square, Tideswell, Buxton SK17 8LA

"Poppies" is situated in the centre of an attractive Derbyshire village in the Peak District. Ideal walking country and within easy reach of Castleton, Bakewell, Matlock and Buxton. Accommodation comprises one family room and twin room with washbasins, one double room en suite, all with TV and tea/coffee making facilities. Bathroom and two toilets. Evening meals available by arrangement. Children welcome. Non smoking establishment.

Bed and Breakfast from £21; Evening Meal from £12.50.

Mr D.C. Pinnegar - 01298 871083
e-mail: poptidza@dialstart.net

Ample private parking • Non-smoking throughout
Bed and Breakfast from £23 per person

In one of the most picturesque villages in the Peak District National Park this 300-year-old cottage offers independent accommodation across the paved courtyard. Breakfast is served in the cottage. Rooms are furnished and equipped to a high standard; both having en suite shower rooms, tea/coffee making facilities, TV and heating. The village has two traditional pubs which provide food. Local attractions include village (National Trust) Market House, Chatsworth, Haddon Hall and many walks from the village in the hills and dales.

'WHICH?' GOOD BED & BREAKFAST GUIDE
'WHICH?' GUIDE TO GOOD HOTELS

Mrs Jane Ball, Brae Cottage,
East Bank, Winster DE4 2DT
Tel: 01629 650375

Devon

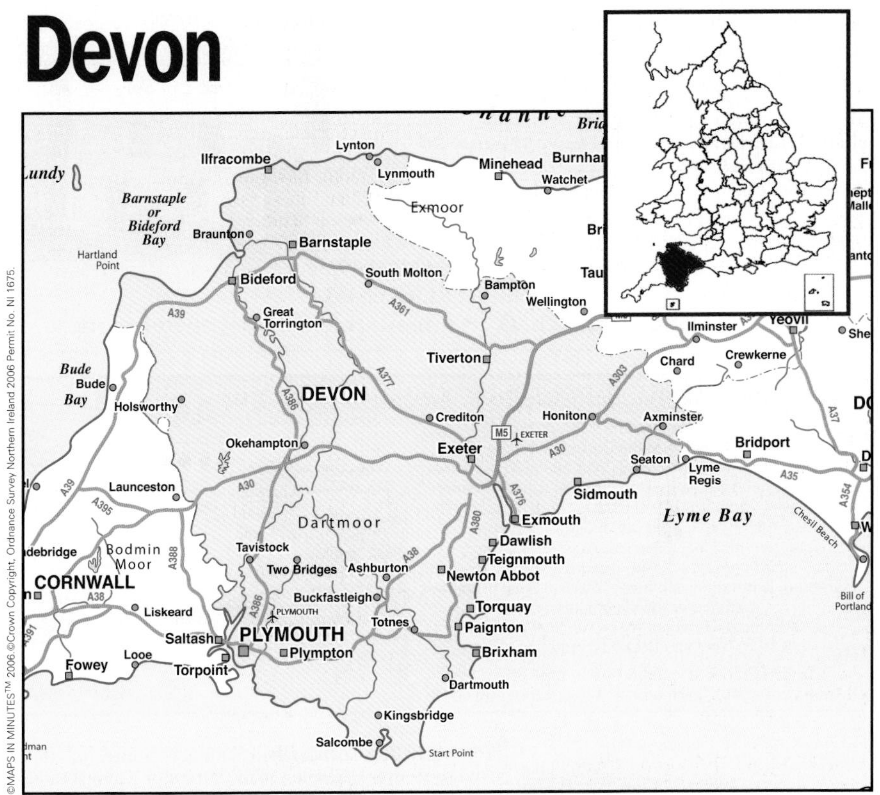

Devon is unique, with two different coastlines: bare rugged cliffs, white pebble beaches, stretches of golden sands, and the Jurassic Coast, England's first natural World Heritage Site. Glorious countryside: green rolling hills, bustling market towns and villages, thatched, white-washed cottages and traditional Devon longhouses. Wild and wonderful moorland: Dartmoor, in the south, embraces wild landscapes and picture-postcard villages; Exmoor in the north combines breathtaking, rugged coastline with wild heather moorland. Step back in time and discover historic cities, myths and legends, seafaring characters like Drake and Raleigh, and settings for novels by Agatha Christie and Conan Doyle.

Devon is home to an amazing and diverse range of birds. Enjoy special organised birdwatching trips, perhaps on board a RSPB Avocet Cruise or a vintage tram. Devon is the walking county of the South West – imagine drifts of bluebells lit by dappled sunlight, the smell of new mown hay, the sound of the sea, crisp country walks followed by a roaring fire and hot 'toddies'! If pedal power is your choice, you will discover exciting off-road cycling, leisurely afternoon rides, and challenging long distance routes such as the Granite Way along Dartmoor, the Grand Western Canal and the coastal Exmouth to Budleigh Circuit.

Please mention **Bed & Breakfast Stops**
when making enquiries about accommodation featured in these pages

Roborough House

85 East Street, Ashburton, Devon TQ13 7AL

Ideally located within easy walking distance of this popular Dartmoor town and perfect for exploring the nearby Moors. Buster, the friendly collie cross, and his family offer their guests a really welcoming atmosphere in their lovely Georgian house and large garden. There are excellent breakfasts to start the day and the spacious and comfortable bedrooms are fully en suite and include bathroom toiletries, hot-drink makers, colour TVs with DVD players and free films. There is easy access for the disabled and off-road parking can be arranged.

Telephone: 01364 654614

www.roboroughhouse.co.uk • e-mail: roborough@onetel.co.uk

Gages Mill Buckfastleigh Road, Ashburton TQ13 7JW

Lovely 14th century former wool mill, set in over an acre of gardens on the edge of the Dartmoor National Park. Seven delightful en suite rooms, one on the ground floor; all with tea and coffee making facilities, central heating, hairdryers, radio and alarm clocks. Large comfortable dining room with corner bar and granite archways. Cosy sitting room. Licensed. Ample car parking. Ideal base for touring South Devon or visiting Exeter, Plymouth, Dartmouth, the many National Trust properties and other places of interest.
Children over 12 years welcome. Sorry no pets.
Bed and Breakfast only.

Lynda Richards • Tel & Fax: 01364 652391
e-mail: gagesmill@aol.com • www.gagesmill.co.uk

Riversmead, a detached country house in the picturesque River Dart valley in the Dartmoor National Park, yet only three miles from Ashburton and the A38. Set in a one acre garden with stream and spinney, we offer quality en suite accommodation, two double and one twin room, with stunning views from all aspects. Ideally located for river walks, only two minutes from the house.

Guests' sittingroom with TV, full central heating, tea/coffee making facilities, comfortable dining room and ample parking. Drying room is available if required. Bed and Breakfast from £30pppn. Non-smoking. Children over 12. Dogs by arrangement. Open all year.

Mrs Joy Hasler, Riversmead, Newbridge, Near Ashburton TQ13 7NT
Tel: 01364 631224 • www.riversmead.net

The Durant Arms

Ashprington, Totnes, Devon TQ9 7UP

Nestling amidst the verdant beauty of the Dart Valley, this attractive inn has all the virtues of a traditional English country inn with the comforts of the contemporary holiday-maker in mind. The cuisine is worthy of special mention, with a wide range of main courses catering for all tastes, plus an interesting selection of imaginative desserts. Just three miles past the Elizabethan town of Totnes, this is a fine overnight stop and several beautifully appointed bedrooms suit the purpose admirably.

AA ♦♦♦♦♦

Tel: 01803 732240

e-mail: info@thedurantarms.com • www.thedurantarms.com

Near Barnstaple • Farmhouse B&B • Tel & Fax: 01271 858230

B&B from £20. Reduced rates for children under 12; weekly terms on request.

Our family working farm of 240 acres, with a pedigree herd of suckler cows and sheep, is situated in a small rural village between Barnstaple and Torrington, the Tarka Trail and Rosemoor Gardens. Six miles to the nearest beaches. Double room en suite, twin bedroom also available. Guest lounge with TV and tea/coffee making facilities. Good farmhouse cooking.

Ample parking • No pets • Non-smoking

Mrs J. Ley, West Barton, Alverdiscott, Near Barnstaple, Devon EX31 3PT

LEE HOUSE

Marwood, Barnstaple EX31 4DZ
Tel: 01271 374345

Stone-built Elizabethan Manor House dating back to 1256, standing in its own secluded gardens and grounds with magnificent views over rolling Devon countryside. James II ceilings, an Adam fireplace, antiques and the work of resident artist add interest. Easy access to coast and moor. Family-run, friendly and relaxing atmosphere. Walking distance to local pub with excellent food. Marwood Gardens one mile. Open April to October. One double, one twin room and one four-poster room, all en suite with colour TV and tea/coffee making facilities. Children over 12 years welcome. No smoking. Well-behaved pets welcome.

Bed and Breakfast from £25pppn.

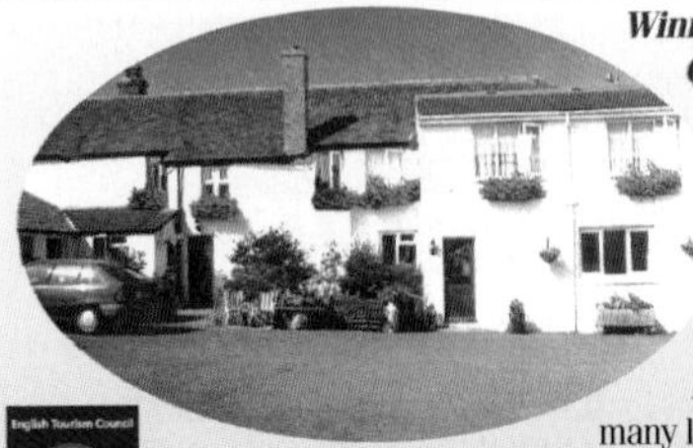

Winner of the 2002 Golden Achievement Award of Excellence for Quality and Service, this tastefully refurbished 16th century farmhouse is situated close to the road between Barnstaple and Bideford on the lovely Taw/Torridge estuary, immediately adjacent to the Tarka Trail. Open all year, the rooms are fully modernised, with colour TV and en suite facilities. With courtyard parking, this is an ideal base for touring Devon and Cornwall. It is within a mile of the sandy beach at Instow, and excellent pubs and restaurants. A self-catering cottage (**ETC ★★★**) is also available, and there are many leisure activities close at hand. For details contact:

2002 Golden Achievement Award of Excellence for Quality and Service

Peter Day, Lower Yelland Farm, Fremington, Barnstaple EX31 3EN
Tel: 01271 860101 / 07803 933642
e-mail: peterday@loweryellandfarm.co.uk
www.loweryellandfarm.co.uk

"Valley View"

Guineaford, Marwood, Barnstaple EX31 4EA

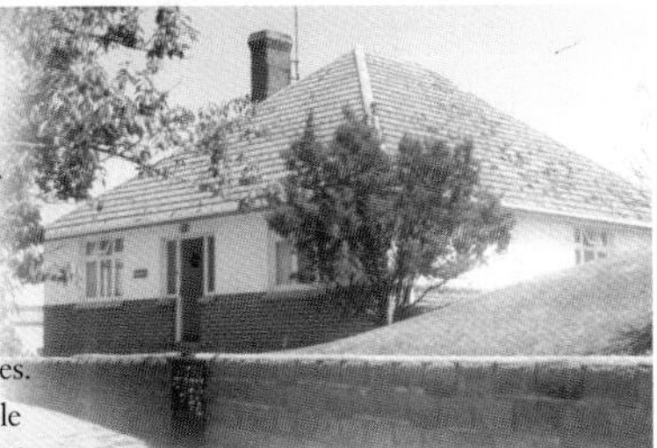

"Valley View" is a bungalow set in 320 acres of farmland which visitors are free to enjoy. The farm, situated 3½ miles from Barnstaple, near Marwood Hill Gardens and Arlington Court, produces lamb and is home to Helenbrie Miniature Shetland ponies. Accommodation comprises two bedrooms each containing a double and single bed. Bed and Breakfast from £20. Children are welcomed, half-price for those under 12 years. Babysitting free of charge. Pets by arrangement. Car essential – parking. Open all year.

Tel: 01271 343458
www.helenbriestud.co.uk

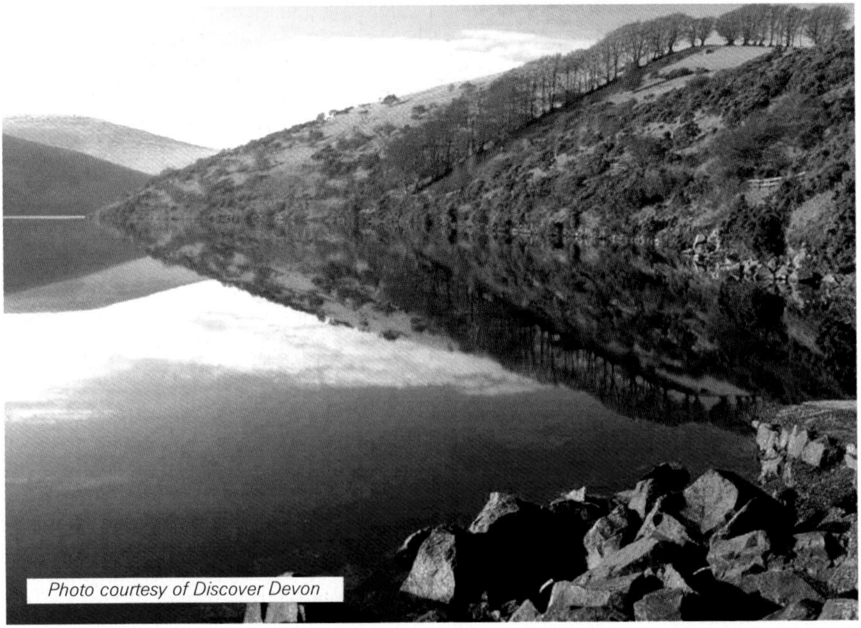

Photo courtesy of Discover Devon

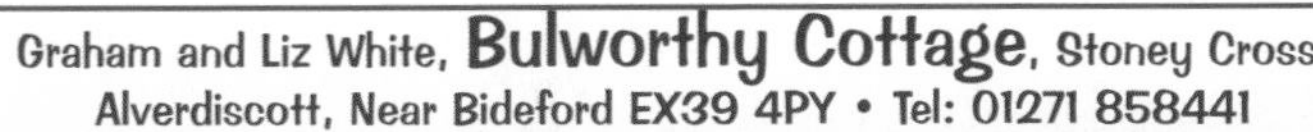

Graham and Liz White, **Bulworthy Cottage**, Stoney Cross, Alverdiscott, Near Bideford EX39 4PY • Tel: 01271 858441

Silver
SILVER AWARD

Once three 17th century miner's cottages, Bulworthy has been sympathetically renovated to modern standards whilst retaining many original features. Our twin and double guest rooms both offer en suite accommodation, with central heating, colour TV, and many other extras. Standing in quiet countryside, Bulworthy is within easy reach of the moors, Tarka Trail, South West Coastal Path, Rosemoor and numerous National Trust properties. We offer a choice of breakfasts and evening meals, using home grown and local produce whenever possible, with a wine list chosen to complement your meal.

e-mail: bulworthy@aol.com • www.bulworthycottage.co.uk

The Mount, Northdown Road, Bideford EX39 3LP Tel: 01237 473748

A warm welcome awaits you at The Mount in the historic riverside town of Bideford. This small, interesting Georgian building is full of character and charm and is set in its own semi-walled garden, with a beautiful Copper Beech, making it a peaceful haven so close to the town. Within five minutes easy walking, you can be in the centre of the Old Town, with its narrow streets, quay, medieval bridge and park. The Mount is also an ideal centre for exploring the coast, countryside, towns and villages of North Devon. The quiet, restful bedrooms, (single, double, twin and family) are all en suite. Tea and coffee making facilities are available. All rooms have TV. Non-smoking. Bed and Breakfast £30 to £33 per person per night.

Golfing breaks – discounted green fees.

English Tourism Council ♦♦♦♦ GUEST ACCOMMODATION

AA ♦♦♦♦

Devon • The English Riviera

WOODLANDS GUEST HOUSE

Parkham Road, Brixham, South Devon TQ5 9BU

Overlooking the beautiful Brixham Harbour

Victorian House with large car park at rear and unrestricted on-road parking to the front. All bedrooms en suite, with colour TV, tea/coffee making facilities, mini fridges etc. Four-Poster bedroom with panoramic views over Brixham Harbour and Torbay. Just a short walk away from the picturesque harbour, ancient fishing port with its quaint streets full of varied shops, pubs and restaurants. Ideal holiday base from which to explore the glorious South-West, romantic Dartmoor, boat trips, Paignton and Dartmouth Steam Railway.

Walkers can explore the marvellous Devon countryside. Fishing trips available from the harbour. Bed and Breakfast from £23pppn.

We hope to see you soon and make your stay a memorable one.

Phone 01803 852040, Paul and Rita Pope for free colour brochure and details

www.woodlandsdevon.co.uk • e-mail: woodlandsbrixham@btinternet.com

English Tourism Council ♦♦♦ GUEST ACCOMMODATION

GLEN COTTAGE

17th century thatched cottage idyllically set in secluded garden, with stream surrounded by woods. Adjoining a beauty spot with rocks, caves and waterfall. A haven for wildlife and birds; kingfishers and buzzards are a common sight. Outdoor swimming pool. Central for touring the moors or sea. Bed and Breakfast from £25. Tea/coffee all rooms.

Jill Shears, Glen Cottage, Rock Road, Chudleigh TQ13 0JJ (01626 852209)

The Oyster is a modern bungalow in the pretty, peaceful village of Colebrooke in the heart of Mid Devon. There is a spacious garden for children to play around or sit on the patio. Comfortable accommodation with tea/coffee making facilities, with TV in bedroom and lounge. Bedrooms en suite or with private bathroom - two double and one twin. Walking distance to the New Inn, Coleford, a lovely 13th century free house. Dartmoor and Exmoor are only a short drive away. Central heating. Open all year. Ample parking. Terms from £20 per person for Bed and Breakfast. Children and pets welcome. Smoking accepted.

To find us take the Barnstaple road (A377)out of Crediton, turn left after one-and-a-half miles at sign for Colebrooke and Coleford. In Coleford village turn left at the crossroads, then in Colebrooke village take the left hand turning before the church, the Oyster is the second on the right.

The Oyster
01363 84576

Pearl Hockridge, The Oyster, Colebrooke, Crediton EX17 5JQ

A warm welcome awaits you on our friendly working farm. Come and enjoy a relaxing holiday in our bungalow which is set in an Area of Outstanding Natural Beauty amongst the rolling hills of East Devon. Enjoy the views whilst dining and relaxing. Local attractions include the fishing village of Beer and picturesque Branscombe. If you enjoy walking, there are plenty of easily accessible country walks and we are close to the coastal footpaths. There is a full English Breakfast. Fresh and mainly homegrown produce is used to make excellent and varied Evening Meals. Sweets are all homemade. Early morning tea, evening drinks. Three bedrooms with washbasin, separate WC. TV in lounge, sun room. Children welcome. Please enquire for reasonable rates.

Mrs N. Rich, Sunnyacre, Rockerhayne Farm, Northleigh, Colyton EX24 6DA • 01404 871422

Hayne Farm, Cheriton Fitzpaine, Crediton EX17 4HR

Guests are welcome to our 17th century working beef and sheep farm, situated between Cadeleigh and Cheriton Fitzpaine. Exeter nine miles, Tiverton eight miles. South and North coast, Exmoor and Dartmoor within easy reach. Three local pubs nearby. Good farm fayre. Fishing lake; summer house overlooking duck pond.

Bed and Breakfast from £22, reduction for children.

Mrs M Reed - Tel: 01363 866392

Photo courtesy of Discover Devon

• • • some fun days out in DEVON

Chambercombe Manor, Ilfracombe • 01271 862624 • www.chambercombemanor.co.uk
Devon Railway Centre, Bickleigh • 01884 855671 • www.devonrailwaycentre.co.uk
National Marine Aquarium, Plymouth • 01752 600301 • www.national-aquarium.co.uk
Fursdon House & Gardens, Thorverton • 01392 860860 • www.fursdon.co.uk
Babbacombe Model Village, Torquay • 01803 315315 • www.babbacombemodelvillage.co.uk
Paignton Zoo, Paignton • 01803 697500 • www.paigntonzoo.org.uk
Quince Honey Farm, South Molton • 01769 572401 • www.quincehoney.co.uk
Watermouth Castle, Ilfracombe • 01271 867474 • www.watermouthcastle.com

WOODBINE GUESTHOUSE

1 Woodbine Terrace, Exeter, Devon EX4 4LJ
Tel: 01392 203302 Fax: 01392 254678

A small, friendly **non-smoking** guesthouse situated in quiet city centre location, within walking distance of shopping precincts, train/bus stations, University, museum and the historic Cathedral. Modern en suite rooms with hospitality tray, colour TV and shaver points. **Wireless internet access**, hairdryer, ironing facilities and some off-street parking available. Highly recommended. Please check website for up to date terms.

www.woodbineguesthouse.co.uk
e-mail: bookings@woodbineguesthouse.co.uk

Linda & Clive Aggett, **Braeside Guest House**

21 New North Road, Exeter EX4 4HF
Tel/Fax: 01392 256875

Family run Grade 11 Listed building in city centre, close to both stations, Exeter College and the University. All the bedrooms have washbasins, razor points, TV, tea/coffee making facilities. Standard or en suite rooms available. Cots available on request. Fire certificate. Varied breakfast menu, including vegetarian.

Terms from £25 to £28 per person per night.

e-mail: reception@braeside.biz • www.braeside.biz

Other specialised holiday guides from FHG

Recommended **INNS & PUBS** OF BRITAIN

Recommended **COUNTRY HOTELS** OF BRITAIN

Recommended **SHORT BREAK HOLIDAYS** IN BRITAIN

The bestselling and original **PETS WELCOME!**

The GOLF GUIDE, *Where to Play, Where to Stay* IN BRITAIN & IRELAND

COAST & COUNTRY HOLIDAYS

SELF-CATERING HOLIDAYS IN BRITAIN

BED & BREAKFAST STOPS

CARAVAN & CAMPING HOLIDAYS

CHILDREN WELCOME! Family Holiday & Days Out Guide

BRITAIN'S BEST LEISURE & RELAXATION GUIDE

Published annually: available in all good bookshops or direct from the publisher:
FHG Guides, Abbey Mill Business Centre, Seedhill, Paisley PA1 1TJ
Tel: 0141 887 0428 • Fax: 0141 889 7204
• E-mail: admin@fhguides.co.uk • Web: www.holidayguides.com

Pound House, Pound Lane, Exmouth EX8 4NP

Large Georgian house.
All rooms are en suite; tastefully furnished and decorated, with colour TV, tea/coffee making facilities.
Beautiful sandy beaches and natural beauty of Woodbury Common five minutes by car.
Attractions include golf, riding, hiking, swimming, National Trust and Heritage properties, coastal walks, Dartmoor and Exmoor National Parks, etc.
Large traditional English breakfast.
Visitors welcome to use garden.
Children and pets welcome.
Ample private parking. Details on request.
Terms from £25 pppn.

Tel: 01395 222684

Devoncourt Hotel

Douglas Avenue, Exmouth EX8 2EX

Tel: 01395 272277 • Fax: 01395 269315

Standing in four acres of mature subtropical gardens, overlooking two miles of sandy beach, yet within easy reach of Dartmoor and Exeter, Devoncourt provides an ideal base for a family holiday.

Single, double and family suites, all en suite, well furnished and well equipped; attractive lounge bar and restaurant.

indoor & outdoor heated pools * sauna * steam room spa & solarium * snooker room * putting * tennis & croquet * golf * sea fishing * horse riding nearby

B&B from £60 single, £90 double; self-catering /room only from £55 single, £85 double. Weekly rates available.

• WELCOMBE-IN •

Welcombe Cross, Hartland, Devon EX39 6HD

Telephone: 01288 331130 • Mobile: 07714 664547

- A pet-friendly, non-smoking, comfortable base for short or long stays in an Area of Outstanding Natural Beauty.
- Great breakfasts, with eggs from our own hens, local produce, and Julie's fabulous bread.
- Packed lunches and home-cooked evening meals can be provided by arrangement.
- Comfortable lounge where guests can relax, read (well stocked library), watch TV etc.
- Just two miles from spectacular Welcombe Mouth on the stunning North Devon coastline.
- Many great walks in the area, plus places of interest within easy travelling distance - Eden Project, Padstow, Newquay, Bude (10 miles), Clovelly (10 miles).
- Local sports include golf, horse riding, surfing and body boarding.

www.welcombe-in.co.uk

Pet-Friendly Pubs, Inns & Hotels

on pages 299-312

Please note that these establishments may not feature in the main section of this book

THE FOREST INN

Hexworthy, Dartmoor PL20 6SD

★★★ GUEST ACCOMMODATION

A haven for walkers, riders, fishermen, canoeists or anyone just looking for an opportunity to enjoy the natural beauty of Dartmoor. We specialise in home-made food using local produce wherever possible. With the emphasis on Devon beers and ciders, you have the opportunity to quench your thirst after the efforts of the day with a drink at the bar or relaxing on the chesterfields in the lounge area, complete with log fire for winter evenings. Muddy paws, booots and hooves welcome.

Tel: 01364 631211 • Fax: 01364 631515 • e-mail: info@theforestinn.co.uk

A most attractively situated working farm. The house is a very old traditional Devon farmhouse located just three miles east of Honiton and enjoying a superb outlook across the Otter Valley. Enjoy a stroll down by the River Otter which runs through the farmland. Try a spot of trout fishing. Children will love to make friends with our two horses. Lovely seaside resorts 12 miles, swimming pool, adventure parks and garden nearby. Traditional English breakfast, colour TV, washbasin, heating, tea/coffee facilities in all rooms.

Bed and Breakfast £18-£22 • Reductions for children.

Mrs June Tucker, Yard Farm, Upottery, Honiton EX14 9QP •• 01404 861680

Discover the real taste of Devon – freshly caught fish, scrumptious farmhouse cheeses, local ales, award-winning wines and traditional cream teas. From a bar meal in a local inn to a gourmet meal in a country house hotel, Devon is home to some superb, award-winning chefs who are more than a match for the competition, either at home or abroad. With so much to offer why not try one the South Hams or Tamar Valley Food Trails to discover the county's finest restaurants, as well as a few hidden gems!

Discover a vibrant Devon, with sailing regattas, walking, sporting, folk, food and garden festivals, not to mention surfing, rock climbing, hot air ballooning and fishing. Tavistock's Goose Fair, Flaming Tar Barrels, Widecombe Fair and the Blackawton Worm Charming Festival give just a flavour of the more traditional events that take place all year round. The county really is a mecca for golfers, and whether you are a scratch player or a beginner you will be sure to enjoy every minute! Play on a course amidst sand dunes, tread the heathery moorland or be side-tracked by stunning countryside or spectacular seascapes.

WENTWORTH HOUSE

Wentworth House, a friendly family-run private hotel built as a gentleman's residence in 1857, standing in lovely gardens only a stone's throw from the town and minutes from the sea, harbour and Torrs Walks. En suite rooms with colour TV and tea/coffee making facilities. Family rooms sleeping up to four persons. Home-cooked food with packed lunches on request. Spacious bar/ lounge. Secure storage for bicycles etc. Private parking in grounds. Open all year. No smoking.

Bed & Breakfast from £19.50. Bed, Breakfast & Evening Meal from £28.00. PRICES HELD FOR 2007. Discounted rates for weekly bookings.

Stay a few days or a week, Geoff & Sharon will make your visit a pleasant one.

2 Belmont Road, Ilfracombe EX34 8DR • Tel & Fax: 01271 863048

E-mail: wentworthhouse@tiscali.co.uk • www.hotelilfracombe.co.uk

Enjoy a rural retreat at Venn, which is only three miles from the dual carriageway. We are 20 minutes from beaches and South Dartmoor is visible from the farm. There are two family bedrooms, and a separate garden cottage which has two twin ground floor bedrooms overlooking a large pond. We also have self-catering for eight, four and two persons, again with ground floor bedrooms.

DISABLED CATEGORY 2 ACCESSIBILITY.

Mrs P. Stephens, Venn Farm, Ugborough, Ivybridge PL21 0PE • 01364 73240

www.SmoothHound.co.uk/hotels/vennfarm

The fully licensed Garden Room Restaurant provides tasty traditional home cooking with fresh quality produce. Large and small functions can be catered for in a friendly, relaxed atmosphere.

You and your family can be assured of a warm welcome from Anne Rossiter.

For B&B the farmhouse offers a choice of tastefully decorated family, double, twin or single rooms, all en suite, centrally heated and equipped with tea/coffee making facilities and TV. This is a non-smoking zone.

For Self-Catering there are two and three bedroomed cottages, with fully equipped kitchens, colour TV/video, night storage heaters and beautiful stone-built fireplaces. They have large gardens, perfect for children and parents alike.

BURTON FARMHOUSE Galmpton, Kingsbridge TQ7 3EY

Tel: 01548 561210 • Fax: 01548 562257

e-mail: anne@burtonfarm.co.uk • www.burtonfarmhouse.co.uk

AA ◆◆◆◆

www.glenvillelynmouth.co.uk

Glenville House, 2 Tors Road, Lynmouth EX35 6ET

Idyllic riverside setting for our delightful Victorian house built in local stone, full of character and lovingly refurbished, at the entrance to the Watersmeet Valley. Award-winning garden. Picturesque village, enchanting harbour and unique water-powered cliff railway nestled amidst wooded valleys. Beautiful area where Exmoor meets the sea. Breathtaking scenery, riverside, woodland and magnificent coastal walks with spectacular views to the heather-clad moorland. Peaceful, tranquil, romantic - a very special place.

Tastefully decorated bedrooms, most with pretty en suite facilities.
Elegant lounge overlooking river.
Enjoy a four-course breakfast in our attractive dining room.

Non-smoking. Licensed. B&B from £27 per person per night.

Tricia and Alan Francis • 01598 752202

e-mail: tricia@glenvillelynmouth.co.uk

LYNTON. The Sandrock Hotel & Bar, Longmead, Lynton EX35 6DH (01598 753307).

A fine example of Victorian architecture, retaining its original character. Located in a sunny, south-facing tranquil setting on the village edge close to the Valley of Rocks and the South West Coastal Path. Ideal for walkers and hikers or for those who just want to admire the beautiful scenery. Seven fully equipped large, en suite double/twin/family bedrooms. Also singles with private facilities. The Sandrock fully licensed bar and restaurant is also open to non-residents. There is a large car park for the use of residents and for bar/restaurant customers.

Rates: Bed and Breakfast £28 to £30pppn. Half board terms available. See website for details.

- This non-smoking hotel is open all year.

ETC ★★

e-mail: thesandrockhotel@talktalk.net

www.thesandrockhotel.co.uk

LYNTON. South View Guest House, 23 Lee Road, Lynton EX35 6BP (01598 752289).

South View is a small friendly guest house in the heart of the picturesque Exmoor village of Lynton. Open most of the year, our aim is to provide a comfortable base from which to explore this beautiful coastal region. We have five rooms, all fully en suite with colour TV, tea/coffee making facilities, hair dryer, alarm clock and individually controlled heating. We serve a full breakfast with a choice of menu. Our comfortable guests' lounge is always open. Private parking is available at the rear. Overnight guests welcome.

Rates: Bed and Breakfast from £25 to £30 per person per night.

ETC ★★★★ *GUEST HOUSE*

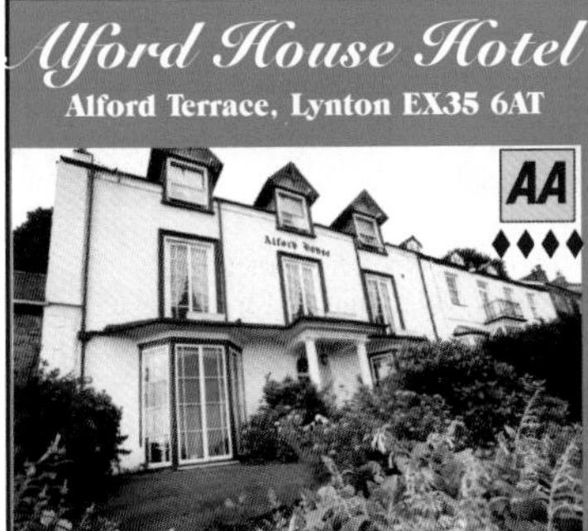

Alford House Hotel
Alford Terrace, Lynton EX35 6AT
AA
♦♦♦♦

Clare and David extend a warm welcome to you at their beautiful Georgian-style Grade II Listed private hotel, nestling on the slopes of Lynton, with stunning views of the sea and coastline. Individually decorated and furnished en suite rooms, elegant four-posters, all with colour TV and beverage making facilities.

Relax in our licensed bar, or quiet TV lounge with beautiful coastal views. Five minutes' walk to Lynton and the cliff railway to Lynmouth. You will enjoy a peaceful and relaxed holiday at Alford House, good food on the table and a genuine warm welcome, whatever the weather!! B&B from £28 per person.

e-mail: enquiries@alfordhouse.co.uk
www.alfordhouse.co.uk

A sunny, sheltered, traffic-free location set in landscaped gardens with uninterrupted views of the Watersmeet Estate. A short stroll along the Lynway takes you to Lynton village where you can ride the famous Cliff Railway to Lynmouth. We have spacious en suite rooms and comfortable lounge. All rooms with TV, hairdryer, hospitality tray and central heating.

Ground floor bedrooms • Level private car park
Children over 12 welcome • Non-smoking • Licensed
Bed and Breakfast from £25 to £28.

Pine Lodge, Lynway, Lynton EX35 6AX
01598 753230
e-mail: info@pinelodgelynton.co.uk

Moorlands

Woody Bay, Parracombe EX31 4RA • 01598 763224

Moorlands, formerly the Woody Bay Station Hotel, is a family-run establishment in a most beautiful part of North Devon, surrounded by Exmoor countryside and within two miles of the spectacular coastline. Very comfortable and quiet single, double or family suite accommodation, all en suite with bath or shower, colour TV and beverage making facilities. Moorlands has a licensed dining room and residents' lounge with open fire, a private outdoor swimming pool, all set in six acres of gardens. Open all year except Christmas. A perfect retreat for the country lover to relax in.

Bed and Breakfast £30 - £32pppn. Evening meals by arrangement £15.
3 nights Dinner, Bed & Breakfast £126pp.
Some ground floor rooms and self-catering apartments available.
Please see our website for special offers.

www.moorlandshotel.co.uk

Great Sloncombe Farm

Moretonhampstead Devon TQ13 8QF
Tel: 01647 440595

Share the magic of Dartmoor all year round while staying in our lovely 13th century farmhouse full of interesting historical features. A working mixed farm set amongst peaceful meadows and woodland abundant in wild flowers and animals, including badgers, foxes, deer and buzzards. A welcoming and informal place to relax and explore the moors and Devon countryside. Comfortable double and twin rooms with en suite facilities, TV, central heating and coffee/tea making facilities. Delicious Devonshire breakfasts with new baked bread.

Open all year~No smoking~Farm Stay UK
e-mail: hmerchant@sloncombe.freeserve.co.uk • www.greatsloncombefarm.co.uk

THE SMUGGLERS

Situated in the pretty village of Mortehoe, The Smugglers offers luxury accommodation from twin rooms to family suites. Treat yourselves and your pets to beautiful coastal walks and golden beaches, before you sample our delicious home-cooked meals, real ales and warm, year round hospitality.

The Smugglers Rest Inn, North Morte Road, Mortehoe, N. Devon EX34 7DR • Tel/Fax: 01271 870891
info@smugglersmortehoe.co.uk
www.smugglersmortehoe.co.uk

• • • some fun days out in DEVON

Chambercombe Manor, Ilfracombe • 01271 862624 • www.chambercombemanor.co.uk
Devon Railway Centre, Bickleigh • 01884 855671 • www.devonrailwaycentre.co.uk
National Marine Aquarium, Plymouth • 01752 600301 • www.national-aquarium.co.uk
Fursdon House & Gardens, Thorverton • 01392 860860 • www.fursdon.co.uk
Babbacombe Model Village, Torquay • 01803 315315 • www.babbacombemodelvillage.co.uk
Paignton Zoo, Paignton • 01803 697500 • www.paigntonzoo.org.uk
Quince Honey Farm, South Molton • 01769 572401 • www.quincehoney.co.uk
Watermouth Castle, Ilfracombe • 01271 867474 • www.watermouthcastle.com

the Ring of Bells inn

north bovey, devon tq13 8rb
tel: 01647 440375 • fax: 01647 440746
e-mail: info@ringofbellsinn.com • www.ringofbellsinn.com

For a real taste of Dartmoor, stay at the 13th century thatched Ring of Bells Inn in the delightfully unspoilt village of North Bovey. The Ring of Bells is surrounded by beautiful countryside, and is ideal as a base for exploring Dartmoor. The recently refurbished accommodation consists of five charming double/twin bedrooms, all with en suite bathrooms, tea and coffee facilities, and colour TV. Low beams and real fires add to the ambience, and as well as a variety of home-cooked bar meals, there is a cosy dining room where the chefs provide excellent fixed price and à la carte menus, which include local loin of venison, tender North Bovey steaks, Devon duckling, fresh Brixham fish, and some inspired vegetarian dishes. There is an interesting wine list, and a selection of well-kept local ales on tap. Featured as one of 'Devon's Finest', and awarded the 'Gold Seal' of excellence for quality and service, The Ring of Bells is simply enchanting.

AA ♦♦♦♦

Just off the A3072, five miles from Dartmoor, this 16th century farmhouse with barn conversions offers a total of twelve rooms, all en suite, family suites available. There is a non-smoking lounge with TV, games and books, to meet friends or to relax in, as well as a separate bar with a residential licence. You are assured of plenty of hearty Devonshire food and a warm welcome. Babies and well-behaved dogs are welcome by arrangement. We have farm walks, ponies, goats, rabbits, plus a working sheep flock and suckler cow herd. Walkers and cyclists on the Tarka Trail are catered for, with cycle sheds and packed lunches etc. *B&B from £30.00, Dinner from £12.50.*

Tel: 01837 851647

Higher Cadham Farm, Jacobstowe, Okehampton, Devon EX20 3RB • www.highercadham.co.uk

AMBER HOUSE HOTEL

6 Roundham Road, Paignton, Devon TQ4 6EZ • Tel: 01803 558372

✻ Family-run Hotel. ✻ Overlooks Goodrington Sands.
✻ All en suite. ✻ Ground floor rooms. ✻ Non-smoking.
✻ Good food; special diets catered for. ✻ Large car park.
✻ English Riviera climate ideal for Spring/Autumn breaks.
✻ Park and beach 5 minutes' walk. ✻ Walkers welcome.
✻ We pride ourselves on our high standards.

Contact: **Christine Clark & Lloyd Hastie.**

e-mail: enquiries@amberhousehotel.co.uk
www.amberhousehotel.co.uk

The No Smoking

Clifton Hotel Paignton,

9-10 Kernou Road, Paignton TQ4 6BA

Tel & Fax: 01803 556545

A licensed, "green" home from home in the heart of the English Riviera. Ideal level location just off the sea front and close to shops and stations.

On the SW Coastal Path. All rooms en suite with TV and beverages. Superb evening meals available using mostly organic produce - special diets catered for. Good public transport system for exploring locally and further afield - Exeter, Plymouth, Dartmoor, etc. Open Easter to late September. From £27 per person Bed and Breakfast. ***Steve and Freda Bamford Dwane.***

e-mail: b&b@cliftonhotelpaignton.co.uk • www.cliftonhotelpaignton.co.uk

Beaumont, Castle Hill, Seaton EX12 2QW

Spacious and gracious Victorian, seafront guesthouse in a quiet East Devon town on England's only World Heritage coastline. Shopping, restaurants and leisure facilities nearby. Unrivalled views over Lyme Bay and Beer Cliffs. Half-mile promenade just yards away. All five rooms en suite with TV, tea and coffee making facilities. Parking available. Bed and Breakfast from £30 per person per night. Special weekly rate. A warm welcome is assured.

Tony and Jane Hill • 01297 20832
e-mail: tony@lymebay.demon.co.uk
www.SmoothHound.co.uk/hotels/beaumon1.html

LOWER PINN FARM Peak Hill, Sidmouth EX10 0NN

Tel: 01395 513733

e-mail: liz@lowerpinnfarm.co.uk • www.lowerpinnfarm.co.uk

19th century built farmhouse on the World Heritage Jurassic Coast, two miles west of the unspoilt coastal resort of Sidmouth and one mile to the east of the pretty village of Otterton. Ideally situated for visiting many places, and for walking, with access to coastal path.

Comfortable, centrally heated en suite rooms with colour television and hot drink making facilities. Guests have their own keys and may return at all times throughout the day. Good hearty breakfast served in the dining room. Ample off-road parking. Children and pets welcome. Lower Pinn is a no smoking establishment. Open all year.

Bed and Breakfast from £25 to £30

Pinn Barton, Peak Hill, Sidmouth EX10 0NN

Peace, comfort and a warm welcome where we offer the little extras that attract guests back time and time again. Two miles from Sidmouth seafront. Lovely coastal walks and views from the farm. Warm and comfortable en suite bedrooms with TV, fridge, beverage trays and access at all times.

Open all year • No smoking • Children welcome

One twin, one double and one family room available.
Terms from £26 to £28 per person.

Mrs Betty S. Sage • Tel & Fax: 01395 514004
e-mail: betty@pinnbartonfarm.co.uk
www.pinnbartonfarm.co.uk

Partridge Arms Farm

Yeo Mill, West Anstey South Molton, North Devon EX36 3NU

Now a working farm of over 200 acres, four miles west of Dulverton, "Partridge Arms Farm" was once a coaching inn and has been in the same family since 1906. Genuine hospitality and traditional farmhouse fare await you. Comfortable accommodation in double, twin and single rooms, some of which have en suite facilities. There is also an original four-poster bedroom.

Children welcome • Animals by arrangement • Residential licence • Open all year
Fishing and riding available nearby • FARM HOLIDAY GUIDE DIPLOMA WINNER.

Bed and Breakfast from £22 to £27; Evening Meal from £11. **Hazel Milton • 01398 341217**
Fax: 01398 341569 • e-mail: bangermilton@hotmail.com
TOURIST ASSOCIATION

TIVERTON. Mrs L. Arnold, The Mill, Lower Washfield, Tiverton EX16 9PD (01884 255297).

A warm welcome awaits you at our converted mill, beautifully situated on the banks of the picturesque River Exe. Close to the National Trust's Knightshayes Court and on the route of the Exe Valley Way. Easy access to both the north and south coasts, Exmoor and Dartmoor. Only two miles from Tiverton. Relaxing and friendly atmosphere with delicious farmhouse fare. En suite bedrooms with TV and tea/coffee making facilities.

Rates: Bed and Breakfast from £26.

e-mail: arnold5@washfield.freeserve.co.uk

www.washfield.freeserve.co.uk

Fairmount House Hotel

Enjoy a taste of somewhere special in the tranquillity, warmth and informal atmosphere of our small hotel of character. Set above the picturesque Cockington Valley, Fairmount House, with its mature gardens and sun-filled terraces, is a haven for the discerning visitor seeking a peaceful setting for their holiday or short break. All our bedrooms are tastefully furnished, clean and comfortable, with en suite bathroom or shower, remote-control TV, tea and coffee making facilities. Relax with a drink in our conservatory bar, or choose from an extensive menu in our fully licensed restaurant. Bed and Breakfast from £24.

Herbert Road, Chelston, Torquay TQ2 6RW
Tel: 01803 605446

www.GROSVENORHOUSEHOTEL.co.uk
Wonderful company, excellent food
Mr & Mrs E, Wigan
Thanks for enjoyable stay and all your kindness
Mrs V, Cardiff
Lovely holiday well looked after, coming again
Mr & Mrs T Somerset
FALKLAND ROAD
TORQUAY
TQ2 5JP
Grosvenor House Hotel
Tel. 01803 294110
AA
Associate Guest Accommodation
GOOD SIZED ROOMS
ALL ENSUITE WITH
TEAMAKING & CTV
****
CAR PARK,
RAIL STATION 600m
****
SEAFRONT,THEATRE,
SHOPS 400m
fhg@grosvenorhousehotel.co.uk

Visit the FHG website
www.holidayguides.com
for details of the wide choice of accommodation featured in the full range of FHG titles

Aveland Hotel

A family run, licensed hotel in a quiet level location close to Cary Park. A short walk to St Marychurch Village and Babbacombe Downs with panoramic views across Lyme Bay. An ideal location for holidays, short breaks and many attractions in the area.

- AA 4 Star Guest Accommodation
- Licensed
- All rooms en-suite
- Evening meal optional
- Children welcome
- Car park and gardens
- Non Smoking Silver Award
- All major credit cards accepted

Aveland Road, Babbacombe, Torquay, Devon, TQ1 3PT
Tel/Minicom: 01803 326622 email: avelandhotel@aol.com
Website: www.avelandhotel.co.uk

HEATHCLIFF HOUSE HOTEL

16 Newton Road, Torquay, Devon TQ2 5BZ
Telephone: 01803 211580
e-mail: heathcliffhouse@btconnect.com • www. heathcliffhousehotel.co.uk

Owners: Adrian & Terri Bailey

This former vicarage is now a superbly appointed family-run hotel equipped for today yet retaining its Victorian charm. All the bedrooms have full en suite facilities, colour TV and drink making facilities. The elegant licensed bar boasts an extensive menu and unlike many hotels, the car park has sufficient space to accommodate all vehicles to eliminate roadside parking. Torquay's main beach, high street shops, entertainment and restaurants are all nearby and with full English breakfast included, it is easy to see why guests return time after time.

Tariff for B&B ranges between £21 and £32pppn. Four-poster & Family rooms available.
So, be it main holiday, touring or business, make the Heathcliff your 1st choice.

SEA POINT HOTEL

Lovely Grade II Listed building ideally situated in a quiet location just 10 minutes' walk to the harbour and the town's many other attractions. En suite rooms equipped with colour TV and beverage making facilities. Comfortable TV lounge, cosy residents' bar, outside decking area.

B&B from £17 to £25pppn. Children under 13 half price, under 2s free. Discount available on weekly bookings.

• Family-run • Open all year • Off-road parking •
• Children and pets welcome •

Please ring Kim or Dave for a brochure.

Old Torwood Road, Torquay • Tel: 01803 211808
e-mail: seapointhotel@hotmail.com • www.seapointhotel.co.uk

The Glenorleigh

26 Cleveland Road
Torquay
Devon TQ2 5BE
Tel: 01803 292135
Fax: 01803 213717

As featured on BBC Holiday programme

David & Pam Skelly
AA ★★★★

Situated in a quiet residential area, Glenorleigh is 10 minutes' walk from both the sea front and the town centre. •Delightful en suite rooms, with your comfort in mind. •Good home cooking, both English and Continental, plenty of choice, with vegetarian options available daily. •Bar leading onto terrace overlooking Mediterranean-style garden with feature palms and heated swimming pool. •Discounts for children and Senior Citizens. •Brochures and menus available on request. • B&B £30–£40; Dinner £14.

e-mail: glenorleighhotel@btinternet.com • www.glenorleigh.co.uk

Note

All the information in this guide is given in good faith in the belief that it is correct. However, the publishers cannot guarantee the facts given in these pages, neither are they responsible for changes in ownership or facilities that may take place after the date of going to press.

Readers should always satisfy themselves that the facilities they require are available and that the terms, if quoted, still apply.

Dorset

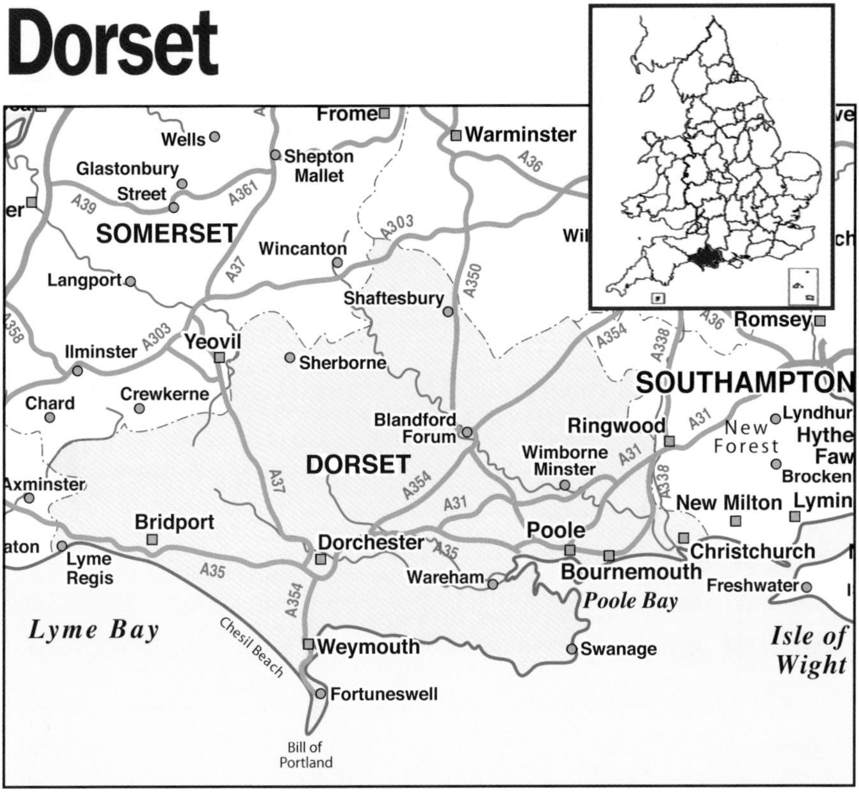

Frome
Warminster
Wells
Shepton Mallet
Glastonbury
Street
A39
A361
A36
A303
SOMERSET
Wincanton
A37
A350
Langport
Shaftesbury
Romsey
A303
Yeovil
Ilminster
Sherborne
A354
A338
A36
SOUTHAMPTON
Chard
Crewkerne
Blandford Forum
Ringwood
A31
Lyndhur
New Forest
Hythe
Faw
Brocken
Wimborne Minster
A31
DORSET
Axminster
A37
A354
A31
A338
New Milton
Lymin
Bridport
Poole
Dorchester
A35
Christchurch
Lyme Regis
A35
Wareham
Bournemouth
Freshwater
Poole Bay
A354
Lyme Bay
Chesil Beach
Weymouth
Swanage
Isle of Wight
Fortuneswell
Bill of Portland

Sandbanks, Dorset. Picture courtesy of Poole Tourism

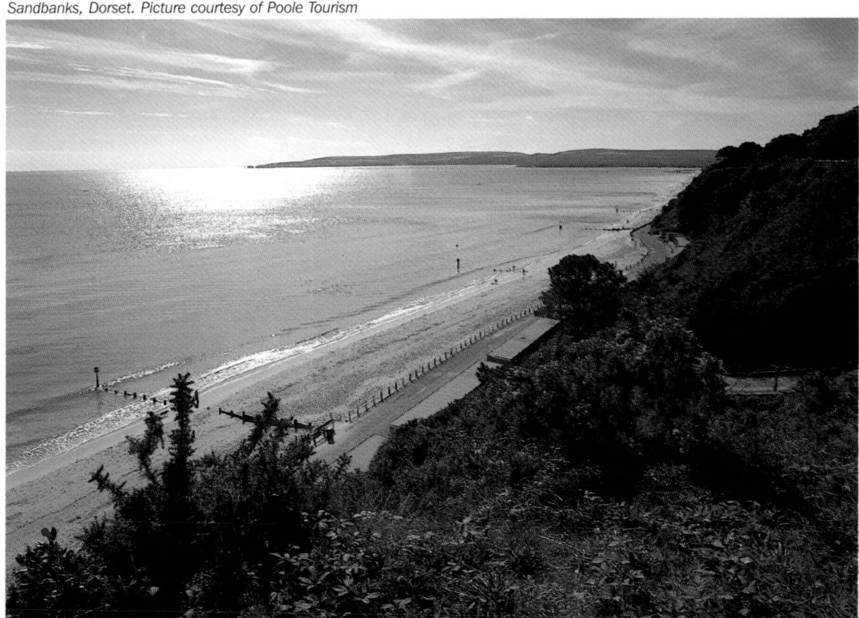

Watermeadow House

Tel & Fax: 01308 862619

Bridge Farm, Hooke, Beaminster, Dorset DT8 3PD

You are assured of a warm welcome at Watermeadow House, on the edge of the small village of Hooke, near Beaminster. We offer high quality accommodation in a friendly atmosphere. Two well furnished bedrooms with many facilities, and breakfast served in the attractive sunroom. A large lawned garden surrounds the house, where guests are welcome to enjoy the peace and tranquillity of the countryside. No smoking. Prices from £27 per person including full English breakfast. Children from £12.

e-mail: enquiries@watermeadowhouse.co.uk
www.watermeadowhouse.co.uk

Caroline and Vincent Pielesz, The Walnuts, 2 Prout Bridge, Beaminster DT8 3AY (01308 862211)
e-mail: caroline@thewalnuts.co.uk.

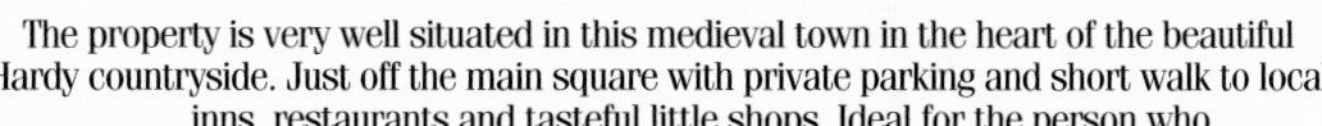

The property is very well situated in this medieval town in the heart of the beautiful Hardy countryside. Just off the main square with private parking and short walk to local inns, restaurants and tasteful little shops. Ideal for the person who enjoys coastal walks, exploring the countryside and visiting large country houses and gardens. The house has been very tastefully refurbished with en suite rooms, tea and coffee making facilities, all the comforts of home. Totally non-smoking.

Bed and full English breakfast from £45 per person.

The Country House Hotel in Bournemouth

Built by Edward VII as a Lovenest for Lillie Langtry. A rare gem of a hotel where the building, food, service and history blend to form something quite exceptional. Four posters, Jacuzzi's, complimentary leisure club and award-winning restaurant. Midweek and weekend breaks. As featured on BBC Holiday Show.

"Best Hotel in Bournemouth" - The Guardian

Derby Road, East Cliff, Bournemouth BH1 3QB
Tel: (01202) 553887 www.langtrymanor.com

• • • some fun days out in DORSET

Tank Museum, Bovington • 01929 405096 • www.tankmuseum.org
Alice in Wonderland Park, Christchurch • 01202 483444 • www.adventurewonderland.co.uk
Abbotsbury Swannery, Abbotsbury • 01305 871858 • www.abbotsbury-tourism.co.uk
Mapperton Gardens, Beaminster • 01308 862645 • www.mapperton.com

BOURNEMOUTH. Tony and Veronica Bulpitt, Sun Haven Guest House, 39 Southern Road, Southbourne, Bournemouth BH6 3SS (01202 427560).

The Sun Haven is in a superb position being only 150 yards from the cliff top, near the cliff lift and zigzag path to a beautiful sandy beach which is regularly awarded the European Blue Flag for superior water quality. Southbourne shopping area with its variety of cafes and restaurants is only a few minutes' walk away. A short drive or bus ride takes you to Bournemouth centre or Christchurch. All day access to rooms. All bedrooms have colour TV, shaver point, washbasin, tea/coffee making facilities and central heating. En suite available. A friendly welcome awaits you.

Rates: Bed and Breakfast from £20 per person per night.

- No smoking.

ETC ★★★

Comfortable private Edwardian house with stylish accommodation for the non-smoker. Situated on the cliff top with panoramic views of the bay, miles of sandy beach lie below with access by a zigzag path or cliff lift. Local shops, cafes and pubs are a short level walk away. All rooms en suite, with shower, toiletries, bathrobes; remote-control TV, clock radio, tea/coffee/chocolate facilities. Guests are assured of a warm welcome from the owners, who are responsible for producing thoroughly enjoyable meals served in our sea-facing diningroom. Private car park at rear for peace of mind.
Breathtaking views from our premier rooms.
Bed and Breakfast from £30pp. Regret no children under 10.

WESTCOTES HOUSE HOTEL 9 Southbourne Overcliff Drive, Bournemouth BH6 3TE • 01202 428512

Alum Dene Hotel

2 Burnaby Road, Alum Chine, Bournemouth BH4 8JF

• Tel: 01202 764011 •

Renowned for good old fashioned hospitality and friendly service. Come and be spoilt at our licensed hotel. All rooms en suite, with colour TV. Some have sea views. Only 200 metres from Alum Chine's sandy beach. Car Parking. Christmas House party. No charge for pets. Open all year.

Mayfield, 46 Frances Road, Knyveton Gardens, Bournemouth BH1 3SA

Sandra and Mike Barling make your comfort, food and relaxation their concern, offering a high standard of catering and comfort. Ideally situated overlooking Knyveton Gardens with bowls, petanque, tennis and sensory garden.
Handy for sea, shops, shows, rail and coach stations.
All rooms are en suite, with colour TV, teamaking, central heating, hairdryer, trouser press, fridge and radio alarm. Own keys. Parking.
Bed and Breakfast from £25 to £28 daily.
Bed, Breakfast and Evening Dinner from £155 to £185 weekly per person.
Bargain Breaks October/April.

Tel & Fax: 01202 551839 • www.hotelmayfield.co.uk

Registered with Bournemouth Quality Standards

Lynne and John welcome you to their family-run guest house. Comfortable lounge with colour television. Good home cooking. Tea and coffee making facilities in all rooms. En suite rooms available, full English Breakfast. Children welcome. Senior Citizens' reductions. Access 24 hours. Close to beach, shops and bus routes. Strictly no smoking. No stag or hen parties.

Terms £18 to £24 pppn.

Lynne and John Scott, Balmer Lodge,
23 Irving Road, Southbourne BH6 5BQ
Tel: 01202 428545
e-mail: balmer.lodge@ntlworld.com

DENEWOOD HOTEL

**40 Sea Road,
Bournemouth BH5 1BQ
Tel: 01202 309913
Fax: 01202 391155
www.denewood.co.uk**

Warm, friendly hotel in excellent central location, just 500 yards from the beach and close to the shops. Good parking. Single, twin, double and family rooms available, all en suite. Residential and restaurant licence. TV, tea/coffee and biscuits in rooms. Health salon and spa on site. Open all year. Children and pets welcome. Please check out our website.

**Bed and Breakfast from £22.50-£25.
Special weekly rates available
and Short Break discounts.**

A small, friendly, family-run, licensed, **NON-SMOKING** hotel, situated in one of the most pleasant parts of Southbourne, in a quiet tree-lined road. We are within two minutes of European award 'Blue Flag' beach, offering seven miles of sandy beaches and safe bathing. The promenade can be reached by either a zig-zag path or the popular cliff lift. The Woodside is in a wonderful position for cliff top walks, with panoramic views over the Isle of Wight and the Purbeck Hills. All rooms are en suite, with tea/coffee making facilities, colour TV and shaver points.

**Hazel & Keith Ingram,
Woodside Hotel,
29 Southern Road, Southbourne,
Bournemouth BH6 3SR
Tel: 01202 427213**

e-mail: enquiries@woodsidehotel.co.uk
www.woodsidehotel.co.uk

Looking for holiday accommodation?

for details of hundreds of properties
throughout the UK including
comprehensive coverage of all areas of Scotland try:

www.holidayguides.com

Situated ten minutes' walk from the market town of Bridport, two miles from the Jurassic Coast, ten miles from Lyme Regis and ten miles from the sub-tropical gardens at Abbotsbury, near Weymouth.

Bedrooms with TV, tea making facilities and washbasin. Parking space available.

Mrs K.E. Parsons

179 St Andrews Road, Bridport • 01308 422038

New House Farm

Stay in a modern, comfortable farmhouse on a small farm set in the rural Dorset hills and become one of the family. A large wild garden where you are welcome to sit or stroll round. Two large rooms available, both en suite, both with lovely views over the surrounding countryside, both with television, fridge and tea/coffee making facilities. We are near to Bridport and the seaside, golf courses, fossil hunting, beautiful gardens, wonderful walking, coarse fishing lake – lots to do.

Bed and Breakfast from £26.

English Tourism Council ♦♦♦ GUEST ACCOMMODATION

Jane Greening, New House Farm, Mangerton Lane, Bradpole, Bridport DT6 3SF
Tel & Fax: 01308 422884
e-mail: jane@mangertonlake.freeserve.co.uk • www.mangertonlake.co.uk

---

Old Dairy House

Relax in an Area of Outstanding Natural Beauty, one mile from Bridport town centre.

One twin, one double (non-smoking) bedrooms. Tea/coffee facilities. Guests' shared bathroom, also downstairs shower/cloakroom. Central heating throughout. Guests' TV lounge with open log fire. Hearty full English breakfast with home-made preserves. Gardens abundant with birds and wildlife. Off-road parking. Open all year for adults only. You will find an informal, friendly atmosphere and warm welcome.

Rural and coastal walks • Real tennis within short walk • 18 hole golf course two miles • Good selection of restaurants and pubs nearby.

Mrs Sally Long, Old Dairy House, Walditch, Bridport DT6 4LB • 01308 458021

Britmead House HOTEL

West Bay Road,
Bridport DT6 4EG
Tel: 01308 422941
Fax: 01308 422516

An elegant Edwardian house, family-run and ideally situated between Bridport and West Bay Harbour, with its beaches, golf course, Chesil Beach and Dorset Coastal Path.

We offer full en suite rooms (two ground floor), all with TV, tea/coffee making facilities, and hairdryer. South facing lounge and dining room overlooking the garden.

- Private parking.
- Non-smoking.

e-mail: britmead@talk21.com
www.britmeadhouse.co.uk

Frogmore Farm

Chideock, Bridport DT6 6HT

Set in the rolling hills of West Dorset, enjoying splendid sea views, our delightful 17th century farmhouse offers comfortable, friendly and relaxing accommodation. An ideal base from which to ramble the many coastal and country footpaths of the area (nearest beach Seatown one-and-a-half miles) or tour by car the interesting places of Dorset and Devon.

Bedrooms with en suite shower rooms, TV and tea making facilities. Guests' dining room and cosy lounge with woodburner. Well behaved dogs welcome. Open all year; car essential. Bed and Breakfast from £25. Brochure and terms free on request from Mrs Sue Norman.

Tel: 01308 456159

Kingfishers

Come to Kingfishers and relax on your large sunny balcony overlooking the river and gardens. Set in beautiful surroundings on the banks of the River Char, Kingfishers offers a secluded setting yet is only a short stroll to the beach and village amenities.

- 2 Miles Lyme Regis • Adjoining National Trust Land
- South Coast Path • Free Access • Ample Parking
- Home Cooked Food including clotted cream teas available throughout the day. *Open all year.*

Mr & Mrs Derham,
Kingfishers, Newlands Bridge,
Charmouth, Dorset DT6 6QZ
Tel: 01297 560232

ETC ◆◆◆◆

CHURCHVIEW GUEST HOUSE

Winterbourne Abbas, Dorchester, Dorset DT2 9LS Tel/Fax: 01305 889296

Our 17th century Guest House, noted for warm hospitality, delicious breakfasts and evening meals, makes an ideal base for touring beautiful West Dorset. Our character bedrooms are comfortable and well-appointed. Meals, served in our beautiful dining room, feature local produce, with relaxation provided by two attractive lounges and licensed bar. Hosts, Jane and Michael Deller, are pleased to give every assistance, with local information to ensure a memorable stay. Short breaks available. Non-smoking.

Terms: Bed and Breakfast: £30 – £38; Dinner, Bed and Breakfast: £46 – £57.

e-mail: stay@churchview.co.uk • www.churchview.co.uk

Visit the FHG website
www.holidayguides.com
for details of the wide choice of accommodation featured in the full range of FHG titles

This country house with its friendly and homely atmosphere welcomes you to the heart of Hardy's Wessex. Central for touring the many places of interest that Dorset has to offer, including Corfe Castle, Lyme Regis, Dorchester, Weymouth, Lulworth Cove, etc. Lovely country walks and many local attractions. Two double rooms, one single, en suite or separate bathroom. TV lounge, dining room. Large garden. Open all year. Central heating. Car essential, ample parking. Bed and Breakfast from £25. Take A35 from Dorchester, we are the last house at the western edge of the village.

Nethercroft

Winterbourne Abbas, Dorchester DT2 9LU

Mrs V.A. Bradbeer
Tel: 01305 889337
e-mail: v.bradbeer@ukonline.co.uk

Lulworth Cove, Dorset

Cromwell House Hotel

Catriona and Alistair Miller welcome guests to their comfortable family-run hotel, set in secluded gardens with spectacular sea views. Situated 200 yards from Lulworth Cove, with direct access to the Jurassic Coast. A heated swimming pool is available for guests' use from May to October. Accommodation is in 20 en suite bedrooms, with TV, direct-dial telephone, and tea/coffee making facilities; most have spectacular sea views. There is disabled access and a room suitable for disabled guests. Self-catering flat available. Restaurant, bar wine list.

B&B from £40. Two nights DB&B (fully en suite) from £114 per person. Off-peak mid week breaks all year except Christmas.

Cromwell House Hotel, Lulworth Cove, Dorset BH20 5RJ

Tel: 01929 400253/400332 • Fax: 01929 400566

www.lulworthcove.co.uk **ETC/AA/RAC ★★**

Applegrove,

West Road, West Lulworth, Wareham BH20 5RY

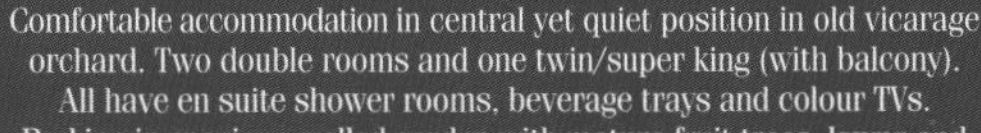

Comfortable accommodation in central yet quiet position in old vicarage orchard. Two double rooms and one twin/super king (with balcony). All have en suite shower rooms, beverage trays and colour TVs. Parking in spacious walled garden with mature fruit trees, lawns and garden furniture for guests' use. Generous traditional English, Vegetarian or Vegan breakfast using home grown produce and eggs. 10 minute stroll to Lulworth Cove. Coast path for other beaches, Durdle Door and Fossil Forest nearby. Central for South Dorset Coast.

B&B from £24 to £29 pppn, based on two sharing.

Open all year except Christmas and New Year.

English Tourism Council ♦♦♦ GUEST ACCOMMODATION

John and Jenny Aldridge (01929 400592)

e-mail: jennyandjohn@applegrove-lulworth.co.uk • www.applegrove-lulworth.co.uk

Family-Friendly

Pubs, Inns & Hotels

See the Supplement on pages 293-297 for establishments which *really* welcome children.

Please note that these establishments may not feature in the main section of this book

Comfortable accommodation on the edge of historic Lyme Regis in 200 year old character house with open beamed fireplace, raised gallery area and roof garden. 25 minutes' walk from the sea. Ideal for artists, fossil hunting, walking etc. Easy access by road. Axminster five miles with main line connection to Waterloo.

Accommodation comprises one single, one double, one double en suite; all with TV and tea/coffee making facilities. Full English Breakfast and vegetarian option. Secure courtyard area available for bikes/motor bikes, etc.

Rooms available from £22pppn.

Mrs L. Brown, Providence House,
Lyme Road, Uplyme DT7 3TH
Tel: 01297 445704

Providence House

Mrs Caroline Osmond, YEABRIDGE FARM, Whetley Cross, Mosterton, Near Beaminster DT8 3HE
Tel & Fax: 01308 868944

Caroline and family are looking to give all guests a warm welcome to this modern spacious thatched farmhouse with panoramic views of the West Dorset Downs. Accommodation available in one twin, one double, one family room en suite, all with tea/coffee making facilities. Large residents' lounge with colour TV. Children welcome. Ideal base for exploring - there are country footpaths within 100 yards. Coastal town and harbour eight miles away, and a golf course four miles. Post office, shop half-a-mile, various inns and public houses in the immediate area. A303 15 minutes, M5 30 minutes, A35 10 minutes.

Prices from £25 per person per night (reduced rates for children).
Evening Meals are available on request • Ample parking • Open all year • Non-smoking

e-mail: grahamosmond@btinternet.com • www.yeabridge.co.uk

Built in 1892, **HOLLY HEDGE FARM** is situated next to Bulbury Woods Golf Course, set in 11 acres of wood and grassland adjacent to lake. We are just 15 minutes away from the Purbecks, the beach and the forest. The area is ideal for walking or cycling and Poole Quay and Harbour are also nearby.

Accommodation comprises two double/family rooms, one twin and one single, all with en suite showers, colour TV, tea/coffee making facilities, radio alarms and central heating. Cottage available.

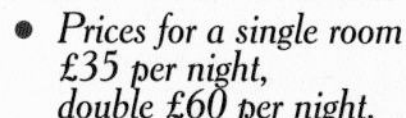

- *Open all year round for summer or winter breaks.*
- *Full English or Continental breakfast served.*

Mrs Stephenson

Holly Hedge Farm

Bulbury Lane, Lytchett Matravers,
Poole, Dorset BH16 6EP
Tel: 01929 459688

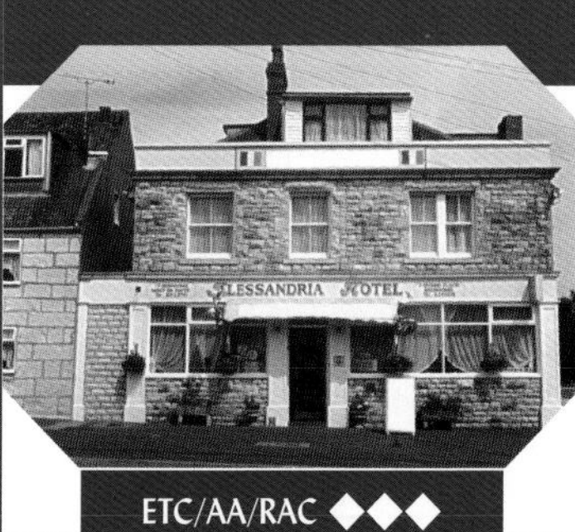

71 Wakeham, Easton, Portland DT5 1HW

This former 18th century inn is situated in a quiet location. Comfortable accommodation; 15 rooms, most en suite, some with sea view; colour TV; tea/coffee; free parking. Ground floor rooms. Children welcome. Four spacious en suite family rooms. Bed and Breakfast at reasonable prices. Vegetarians catered for. Warm and friendly hospitality. Same owner/manager for 16 years

Tel: 01305 822270/820108
Fax: 01305 820561
www.s-h-systems.co.uk/hotels/alessand.html

A 15th century former Manor House that has retained some lovely historical features. Now a farmhouse on a family-run dairy and beef farm. It is in a beautiful rural location yet only five miles from the A303, two miles from A30 and two hours by train from London. An ideal place to relax and unwind, enjoy traditional home baking and a warm friendly atmosphere. Close to the abbey town of Sherborne, National Trust Properties and many other places of interest to suit all people.

Accommodation – one twin room en suite, one double room with a private bathroom, and lounge with colour TV and log fires.

Bed and Breakfast from £27pppn, reductions for children under 10 years and weekly stays.

e-mail: kingman@stowell-farm.freeserve.co.uk

Stowell Farm

Stowell, Near Sherborne DT9 4PE
Tel: 01963 370200 • Mrs E. Kingman

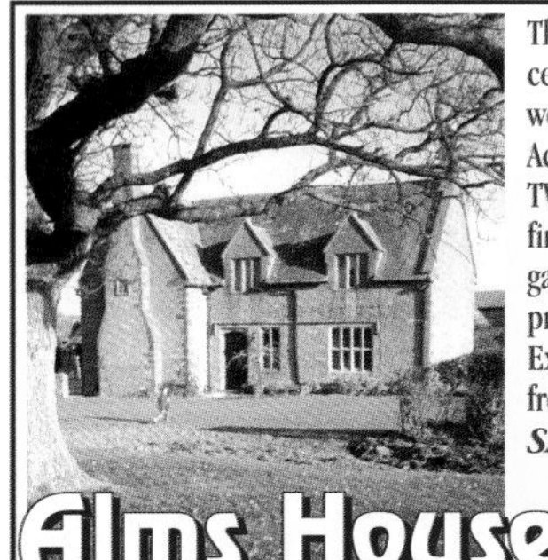

This charming old farmhouse was a monastery during the 16th century, restored in 1849 and is now a Listed building. A family-run working dairy farm, 140 acres overlooking the Blackmoor Vale. Accommodation is in three comfortable en suite rooms with colour TV and tea/coffee making facilities. Diningroom with inglenook fireplace, lounge with colour TV, for guests' use at all times. Also garden and lawn. Plenty of reading material and local information provided for this ideal touring area. Bed and Breakfast from £27. Excellent evening meals in all local inns nearby. Situated six miles from Sherborne with its beautiful Abbey and Castle.

Gold
GOLD AWARD

★★★★
GUEST ACCOMMODATION

SAE for further details. **Mrs Jenny Mayo**

Alms House Farm

Hermitage, Holnest, Sherborne, Dorset DT9 6HA
Tel and Fax: 01963 210296

STURMINSTER NEWTON. Mrs Jill Miller, Lower Fifehead Farm, Fifehead, St Quinton, Sturminster Newton DT10 2AP (01258 817335).
Come and have a relaxing holiday at Lower Fifehead Farm. Stay in our lovely listed 17th century farmhouse mentioned in Dorset books for its architectural interest, or Honeysuckle House, actually on the farm, and with outstanding views. Both offer excellent breakfasts and tea and coffee making. Honeysuckle House offers evening meals. We are within easy reach of all of Dorset's beauty spots. Excellent walking, and both riding and fishing can be arranged. Lower Fifehead Farm pictured here.
Rates: B&B from £22-£30pppn
Contact **Mrs Jessie Miller, Honeysuckle House (01258 817896)**
ETC ★★★★

• • • some fun days out in DORSET

Tank Museum, Bovington • 01929 405096 • www.tankmuseum.org
Alice in Wonderland Park, Christchurch • 01202 483444 • www.adventurewonderland.co.uk
Abbotsbury Swannery, Abbotsbury • 01305 871858 • www.abbotsbury-tourism.co.uk
Mapperton Gardens, Beaminster • 01308 862645 • www.mapperton.com

SWANAGE. Fairway Bed & Breakfast, 7a Demoulham Road, Swanage BH19 1NR (01929 423367).

Overlooking the bay with its sandy beaches,The Fairway offers a twin-bedded room, with its own access and pleasant garden views. Tea and coffee making facilities are provided, as well as TV and radio. A choice of Continental or cooked breakfast is offered, with home-made marmalade and jam. Car parking. Within easy reach of the town, countryside and coastal walks (Jurassic Coast); golf and tennis nearby. Bournemouth and Dorchester approx. 20 miles; nearest rail station Wareham. Ladies and couples preferred.

Rates: B&B from £25-£30pp

- Open May to October

e-mail: rita@ritawaller.plus.com
www.swanagefairway.co.uk

You can be sure of a warm welcome with good home-cooking whenever you stay at Sandhaven. We wish to make sure your stay is as relaxing and enjoyable as possible. All bedrooms are en suite and equipped with tea and coffee making facilities; all have colour TV. There is a residents' lounge, diningroom and conservatory for your comfort. The Purbeck Hills are visible from the guest house, as is the beach, which is only 100 metres away.

- *Bed and Breakfast is available from £26 to £31.*
- *Non-smoking bedrooms.*
- *Open all year except Christmas.*

Janet Foran, Sandhaven Guest House.
5 Ulwell Road, Swanage BH19 1LE • 01929 422322
e-mail: mail@sandhaven-guest-house.co.uk

Sandhaven
Guest House

TOLPUDDLE HALL
Tel: 01305 848986

Tolpuddle, Near Dorchester DT2 7EW

An historic house in village centre in an Area of Outstanding Natural Beauty, not far from the coast. Convenient for Bournemouth, Poole, Dorchester, Weymouth, Isle of Purbeck and many small market towns and villages. Centre for local interests e.g., birdwatching, walking, local history, Thomas Hardy, the Tolpuddle Martyrs, etc.

Two double, one family, one twin and two single bedrooms, all with TV • Full English breakfast
Tea/coffee making, TV sitting room
Small kitchen available to residents
Open all year • Pets welcome except high season

From £20pp. Weekly rate available.

Mary offers her guests a friendly welcome to her bungalow with a cup of tea. Situated in the quiet hamlet of Hyde, five miles west of Wareham, adjacent to East Dorset Golf Club; follow the sign from Wareham and we are the first bungalow past the golf club on the right. It is an ideal base for visiting Swanage, Poole and Bovington Tank Museum, with many interesting coastal walks, including Lulworth Cove.

Accommodation consists of three double bedrooms (one double, two twin beds), all with tea/coffee facilities, TV, central heating. Bathroom and separate shower room; two toilets. Visitors' lounge with colour TV and log fires in winter. Open all the year except Christmas. Car essential, ample parking. Bed and Breakfast from £20. No smoking.

Mrs Axford, Sunnyleigh, Hyde, Wareham BH20 7NT
Tel: 01929 471822

WEYMOUTH. Mrs Karina Hill, Pebble Villa, 13 Enkworth Road, Weymouth DT3 6JT (01305 837469).
Pebble Villa is a rather special Weymouth Bed and Breakfast. We have just one letting room where you will be treated as house guests, rather than visitors. Our non-smoking villa is situated about ten minutes walk from the beach and the South-West Coast Path in the heart of the Jurassic Coast. We are just over two miles from the centre of Weymouth, which can be reached on foot through the lovely Lodmoor Nature Reserve (RSPB). We have one double bedroom with a full en suite bathroom. There is a TV/video, tea/coffee facilities, hairdryer, radio/alarm and iron, and a silent mini-fridge will keep your drinks cool. There's free high-speed internet access for guests with wireless-enabled laptops. The bedroom overlooks the Mediterranean-style garden and is an oasis of peace and tranquillity. On fine warm days breakfast is served al fresco on the sea-view terrace.
Rates: £26 pppn with discount for stays of 3 nights or more.

GLENTHORNE

CASTLE COVE, 15 OLD CASTLE ROAD, WEYMOUTH DT4 8QB

Secluded beachfront B&B in elegant Victorian villa and well equipped apartments with panoramic sea views of Olympic sailing area. Extensive gardens, heated pool, play areas, dog friendly beach, coastal path. Parking.

Tel: 01305 777281 • Mobile: 07831 751526

e-mail: info@glenthorne-holidays.co.uk

www.glenthorne-holidays.co.uk

• Olivia Nurrish •

Old Harbour View

B&B from £35 to £40 pppn

Anna and Peter welcome you to their idyllic Georgian harbourside townhouse, offering two charming double bedrooms, both en suite. Old Harbour View enjoys Weymouth's historic harbour right outside the door, with harbourside restaurants, the ferries to Jersey, Guernsey and France, Weymouth beach and town centre just over the town bridge. From its position on the Jurassic Coastal Path, Old Harbour View gives you the base to explore the amazing prehistoric coast. Both rooms are beautifully decorated with deliciously comfortable beds, colour televisions with teletext and full tea/coffee facilities. A luxurious breakfast awaits you before you head out for the surrounding area.

Anna and Peter Vincent, Old Harbour View, 12 Trinity Road, Weymouth DT4 8TJ
01305 774633 • Fax: 01305 750828

A friendly welcome awaits you at FERNDOWN GUEST HOUSE

A welcoming place to stay, it is family-run by Mark and Jean. Situated just two minutes' walk to the seafront and five minutes into town, it is the ideal place to stay in Weymouth. All rooms have washbasins, colour TV and tea and coffee making facilities; some en suite available. Visitors are welcome to use the lounge with colour TV. **e-mail: odpjean@yahoo.co.uk**

FERNDOWN GUEST HOUSE

47 Walpole Street, Weymouth DT4 7HQ

Tel: 01305 775228

Mark and Jean Mitchell

Open from April to October. Bed and Breakfast from £18pppn.

Durham

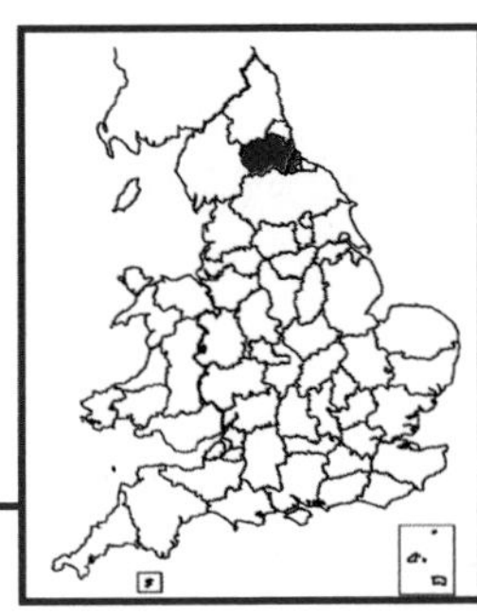

Please note

All the information in this book is given in good faith in the belief that it is correct. However, the publishers cannot guarantee the facts given in these pages, neither are they responsible for changes in policy, ownership or terms that may take place after the date of going to press. Readers should always satisfy themselves that the facilities they require are available and that the terms, if quoted, still apply.

Essex

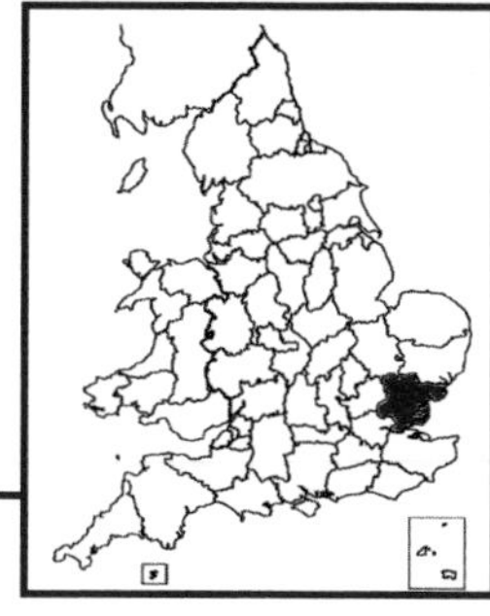

Essex - between London and England's East Coast lies the ancient county of Essex, a place of farms and forests, quiet villages and country towns, and also of seaside resorts offering traditional entertainments and exciting events. Thatched cottages and timber framed farmhouses are very characteristic as are the unmistakable outlines of windmills which still punctuate the horizon. Close to the European mainland, Essex has been influenced by many different cultures and historical events. The Normans left their mark in castles at Colchester, Castle Hedingham, Stansted and elsewhere, while Colchester's Roman walls remain to show the pedigree of Britain's oldest recorded town. Perhaps Essex is best known for its resorts. Southend, Clacton, Frinton, Walton and Dovercourt offer all the fun of the seaside but with much more besides. Down the centuries, Essex has been home to both the famous and the infamous. John Constable, England's greatest landscape painter, was inspired by the beauty of the Stour Valley; Hedingham Castle was once home to Edward de Vere, believed by many to be the true author of Shakespeare's works. Other famous names include the composers Gustav Holst and William Byrd, writers Dorothy L. Sayers, Sabine Baring-Gould and H.G. Wells, and the philosopher, John Locke.

Photo courtesy of Essex Development and Regeneration Agency

Seven Arches Farm

Georgian farmhouse set in large garden close to the ancient town of Colchester. The farm extends to 100 acres and supports both arable crops and cattle. Private fishing rights on the River Colne, which runs past the farmhouse. This is a good location for visits to North Essex, Dedham and the Stour Valley which have been immortalised in the works of John Constable, the landscape painter.

- Children and pets welcome.
- Open all year.
- Static caravan on caravan site also available.

◆ Bed and Breakfast from £30
◆ Evening Meal from £5
◆ Twin room £50
◆ Family room en suite

Mrs Jill Tod, Seven Arches Farm, Chitts Hill, Lexden, Colchester CO3 9SX
01206 574896

Peveril Hotel

51 North Hill, Colchester CO1 1PY
Tel & Fax: 01206 574001

Town centre hotel with unrestricted parking all weekend and evenings (6pm to 8.30am).

Comfortable lounge bar and excellent restaurant providing a comprehensive range of English, Continental and Asian foods, all home cooking.

Our hotel is within easy reach of all amenities and only seven miles from Constable Country and six miles from the North Sea.

www.peverilhotel.co.uk

THE OLD MANSE, 15 Roman Road, Colchester CO1 1UR • 01206 545154

e-mail: wendyanderson15@hotmail.com • www.doveuk.com/oldmanse

Award-winning spacious Victorian family home situated in a quiet square beside the Castle Park. Only three minutes' walk from bus/coach station or through the Park to town centre.

We promise a warm welcome and a friendly, informal atmosphere. All rooms have central heating, TV and tea/coffee making facilities. One twin and one double room, both en suite, and one twin with private facilities. Full, varied English Breakfast.

B&B from £35 single, £62 double.

Only 30 minutes' drive from Harwich and Felixstowe. Within easy reach of Constable country and one hour's train journey from London.
Sorry, no smoking.

Mrs Wendy Anderson

RETREAT GUEST HOUSE

12 Canewdon Road, Westcliff-on-Sea, Essex SS0 7NE
Mr & Mrs Bartholomew
Tel: 01702 348217/337413 • Fax: 01702 391179

Quality accommodation ideally situated in the quieter more picturesque side of Southend. Close to the Cliffs Pavilion and beautiful gardens. Conveniently by Westcliff station and near to the seafront leading to Southend's main attractions.

• All remote-control colour TV • Most rooms with DVD or video • Tea/Coffee making facilities • Choice of English Breakfast • Private secure parking.

Most bedrooms en suite, some on ground floor.
En suite rooms also available with own kitchen.

B&B from £25 per person • Major debit/credit cards accepted
e-mail: retreatguesthouse.co.uk@tinyworld.co.uk

Gloucestershire

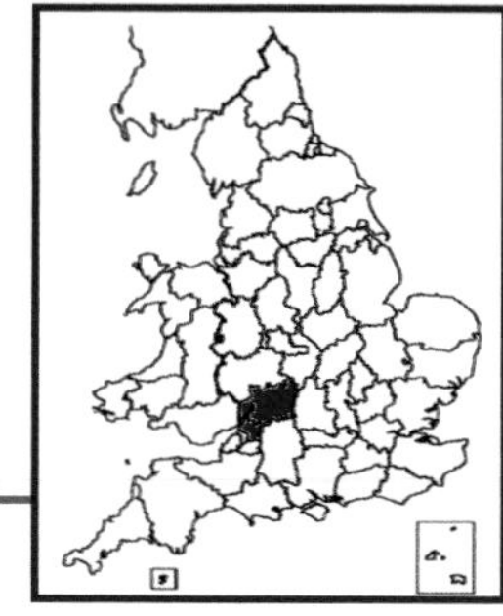

Gloucestershire, in an enviable position west of London between Bath, Oxford and Stratford-on-Avon, has style, elegance, charm.....and cheese rolling. The funkiest Farmers' Markets, happening hotels and, once a year, a mad scramble down the steepest slope to catch a cheese or two.

The county is best known for the Cotswolds, but the area includes The Royal Forest of Dean, Cheltenham, Tewkesbury and Gloucester.

In recent years the Cotswolds area has reinvented itself. Forget twee B&Bs and chintzy hotels, the Cotswolds is now a hotspot of chic hotels, award-winning designer farm shops and entertaining farmers' markets. Liz Hurley, Hugh Grant, Kate Moss, Kate Winslet and Sam Mendes have recently moved to the area and it's easy to see why. The Cotswolds offer space and escape in a beautiful environment and that's exactly what's on offer to visitors too.

Nearby, the Royal Forest of Dean is the last great English broadleaf forest, formerly a hunting ground for the kings of England. Nowadays it's emerging as a great destination for adrenaline sports and activity breaks, all against the backdrop of acres of woodland and nature reserves. It's one of the most colourful corners of England - daffodils, green shoots and bluebells in spring, and gold in Autumn.

Bath

POOL FARM

Bath Road, Wick, Bristol BS30 5RL

Tel: 0117 937 2284

Welcome to our 350 year old Grade II Listed farmhouse on a working farm. On A420 between Bath and Bristol and a few miles from Exit 18 of M4, we are on the edge of the village, overlooking fields, but within easy reach of pub, shops and golf club. We offer traditional Bed and Breakfast in one family and one twin room with tea/coffee facilities and TV; guest lounge. Central heating. Ample parking. Open all year except Christmas. Terms from £22pppn.

Box Hedge Farm is set in 200 acres of beautiful rural countryside on the edge of the Cotswolds. Local to M4/M5, central for Bristol and Bath and the many tourist attractions in this area. An ideal stopping point for the South West and Wales. We offer a warm, friendly atmosphere with traditional farmhouse cooking. All bedrooms have colour TV and tea/coffee making facilities. Full details on our website.

B&B from £26 single standard, from £31 single en suite, £48 double standard, £55 double en suite. Family rooms - prices on application. All prices include VAT.

• Self-catering accommodation also available •

www.bed-breakfast-bristol.com

Marilyn and Bob Downes
Box Hedge Farm, Coalpit Heath, Bristol BS36 2UW
01454 250786

Thornbury Golf Centre

Golf Lodge AA ★★ lodge with spacious twin and single rooms, all en suite, individually designed and traditionally furnished. Ideal accommodation for visiting golfers, family and friends, business travellers, mid-journey breaks or as a holiday base. The adjacent clubhouse features a welcoming bar and dining area serving a wide range of hot and cold food from 7.30am to 9,.00pm. Prices from £51.95 per night (room only).

Call: 01454 281144

Thornbury Golf Centre, Bristol Road, Thornbury, Bristol BS35 3XL

AA ★★

www.thornburygc.co.uk

Located just 10 minutes from Junction 16 of the M5 on the A38

Roylands Farm Cottage Bed & Breakfast

Fernhill, Almondsbury, Bristol, Gloucs BS32 4LU • Tel: 07791 221102 • 07768 286924

ROYLANDS FARM COTTAGE is a comfortable home-from- home situated within a working farm, with classic styling to blend in with its rural surroundings. Rooms are spacious, bright and welcoming with all usual en suite and private facilities, lounge and kitchen. One single, one twin and a double bedroom, all with full English breakfast, towels, TV and tea and coffee making facilities. Uniquely guests can take advantage of their own lounge, or relax and take in the beautiful views of the Severn estuary and the surrounding countryside from the adjoining conservatory or large country garden. Ample secure and secluded off-road parking.

e-mail: jane@roylandfarmcottage.co.uk
www.roylandfarmcottage.co.uk

FHG Guides

publish a large range of well-known accommodation guides.
We will be happy to send you details or you can use the order form at the back of this book.

Dove House

**128 Cheltenham Road,
Bishops Cleeve,
Cheltenham GL52 4LZ**

Dove House is situated on the outskirts of Cheltenham, close to the Racecourse and is ideal as a base for touring/ walking the Cotswolds, Forest of Dean, Tewkesbury, Evesham. Golf courses and private fishing lakes close by. All rooms are furnished to a high standard and have central heating, colour TV and tea/coffee making facilities. Ample parking and garden for guests' use. Bed and Breakfast from £20pppn; en suite available. Open all year.

Tel/Fax: 01242 679600
Mobile: 07973 424358
e-mail: eric.howells@googlemail.com

'Brymbo' ETC ◆◆◆◆

Honeybourne Lane, Mickleton, Chipping Campden, Gloucestershire GL55 6PU

Tel: 01386 438890 • Fax: 01386 438113

e-mail: enquiries@brymbo.com • www.brymbo.com

A warm and welcoming farm building conversion with large garden in beautiful Cotswold countryside, ideal for walking and touring.

All rooms are on the ground floor, with full central heating. The comfortable bedrooms all have colour TV and tea/coffee making facilities. Sitting room with open log fire. Breakfast room. Children and dogs welcome. Parking. Two double, two twin, one family. Bathrooms: three en suite, two private or shared. Bed and Breakfast: single £27 to £42; double £45 to £60. Brochure available. Credit Cards accepted.

Close to Stratford-upon-Avon, Broadway, Chipping Campden and with easy access to Oxford and Cheltenham.

Holly House is set in the centre of the picturesque thatched Cotswold village of Ebrington. Ideally situated for touring the Cotswolds and Shakespeare's country. Two miles Chipping Campden and Hidcote Gardens, five miles Broadway, 11 miles Stratford-upon-Avon, 19 miles Warwick. Double, twin and family rooms available, all beautifully appointed with en suite facilities, TV and tea and coffee. Laundry facility available. Private parking. Non-smoking. Lovely garden room at guests' disposal. Village pub serves meals. Bike hire available locally.

AA ★★★★ Guest Accommodation

Directions: from Chipping Campden take B4035 towards Shipston on Stour, after half-a-mile turn left to Ebrington, we are in the centre of the village.

Double/Twin: £60-£70 • Single: £45-£60
Family: £70-£90 • Child reductions.

Mr J. Hutsby, Holly House, Ebrington,
Chipping Campden GL55 6NL • 01386 593213 • Fax: 01386 593181
e-mail: hutsbybandb@aol.com • www.hollyhousebandb.co.uk

Spacious en suite accommodation in a converted barn in the middle of the countryside. Friendly and tranquil with beautiful views across the Cotswold hills, yet only five minutes from picturesque Bourton-on-the-Water with its many attractions.

Single rooms from £30 per night, double/twin £22 pppn and family room £22 per adult/£10 for children under 10.

Self-catering also available. Sorry, no smoking or pets. For photos and extra information please visit our website.

www.hillbarnholidays.co.uk
e-mail: ali.lane@ukonline.co.uk

Alison Lane, Hill Barn, Clapton Road, Bourton-on-the-Water GL54 2LF
01451 810472

Quality all ground floor accommodation. "Kilmorie" is Grade II Listed (c1848) within conservation area in a lovely part of Gloucestershire. Double, twin, family or single bedrooms, all having tea tray, colour TV, radio, mostly en suite. Very comfortable guests' lounge, traditional home cooking is served in the separate diningroom overlooking large garden. Perhaps walk waymarked farmland footpaths which start here. Children may "help" with our pony, and "free range" hens. Rural yet perfectly situated to visit Cotswolds, Royal Forest of Dean, Wye Valley and Malvern Hills. Children over five years welcome. No smoking, please. Ample parking.

Bed and full English Breakfast from £21 per person

S.J. Barnfield, "Kilmorie Smallholding", Gloucester Road, Corse, Staunton, Gloucester GL19 3RQ
e-mail: sheila-barnfield@supanet.com

AA ♦♦♦♦

Silver SILVER AWARD

Situated in an attractive village on the River Thames, this family-run guest house is only eight miles from Burford and 12 miles from Swindon. Ideal base for touring the Cotswolds, with Kemscott Manor and Buscot House and Gardens nearby. We are close to the river and guests can make use of our lovely garden.

One family, two double (en suite), one twin (en suite) and two single rooms available. One room has a Victorian four-poster bed and one room is on the ground floor. Breakfast is served in our airy conservatory overlooking the garden.

Non-smoking • Pets by arrangement • Open all year.

Bed and Breakfast from £30 to £40 single; £50 to £65 double.

A warm and friendly welcome is assured at Cambrai Lodge.

Mr and Mrs J. Titchener, Cambrai Lodge, Oak Street,
Lechlade on Thames GL7 3AY • 01367 253173 • Mobile: 07860 150467
e-mail: cambrailodge@btconnect.com

THE FOUNTAIN INN & LODGE

Parkend, Royal Forest of Dean, Gloucestershire GL15 4JD.

Traditional village inn, well known locally for its excellent meals and real ales. A Forest Fayre menu offers such delicious main courses as Lamb Steak In Woodland Berry Sauce and Gloucester Sausage in Onion Gravy, together with a large selection of curries, vegetarian dishes, and other daily specials.

Centrally situated in one of England's foremost wooded areas, the inn makes an ideal base for sightseeing, or for exploring some of the many peaceful forest walks nearby.

All bedrooms (including one specially adapted for the less able) are en suite, decorated and furnished to an excellent standard, and have television and tea/coffee making facilities. Various half-board breaks are available throughout the year.

Tel: 01594 562189 • Fax: 01594 564438 • e-mail: thefountaininn@aol.com • www.thefountaininnandlodge.com

---

• • • some fun days out in GLOUCESTERSHIRE

Cinderbury Iron Age Experience, Coleford • 01594 833 073 • www.cinderbury.co.uk
Woodchester Mansion, Stonehouse • 01453 861541 • www.woodchester.ruthani.co.uk
Berkeley Castle, Berkeley • 01453 810332 • www.berkeley-castle.com

STONEHOUSE. Mrs D.A. Hodge, Merton Lodge, 8 Ebley Road, Stonehouse GL10 2LQ (01453 822018). A former gentleman's residence situated about three miles from Stroudwater interchange on the M5 (Junction 13), on B4008 (keep going on old road) just outside Stonehouse towards Stroud. Opposite side to Wyevale Garden Centre, 300 yards from the Cotswold Way. Full central heating and washbasins in all bedrooms; one en suite. Only cotton or linen sheets used. Two bathrooms with showers. Large sittingroom with panoramic views of Selsey Common. Well placed for Cotswold villages, Wildfowl Trust, Berkeley Castle, Westonbirt Arboretum, Bath/Bristol, Cheltenham and Gloucester ski slope and Forest of Dean. Satisfaction guaranteed. Excellent cuisine. Carvery/pub 200 yards away. Friendly welcome.

Rates: Bed and Breakfast from £23 per person, en suite from £25 per person. Children half price.

• Sorry, no smoking or dogs.

ETC ◆◆

STOW-ON-THE-WOLD. Robert Smith and Julie-Anne, Corsham Field Farmhouse, Bledington Road, Stow-on-the-Wold GL54 1JH (01451 831750; Fax: 01451 832247). A traditional farmhouse with spectacular views of Cotswold countryside. Quiet location one mile from Stow, ideally situated for exploring all Cotswold villages including Bourton-on-the-Water, Broadway, Burford and Chipping Campden. Within easy reach of Cheltenham, Oxford and Stratford-upon-Avon; also places of interest such as Blenheim Palace, Warwick Castle and many National Trust houses and gardens. Family, twin and double bedrooms, mostly en suite. TV, tea tray and hairdryer in all rooms. Relaxing guest lounge/ dining room. Excellent pub food five minutes' walk. ***Rates: Bed and Breakfast from £24 (reductions for children).***

- Open all year.

ETC/AA ◆◆◆

e-mail: farmhouse@corshamfield.co.uk **www.corshamfield.co.uk**

The Withyholt Guest House

Paul Mead, Edge, near Stroud, Gloucestershire GL6 6PG

Modern guesthouse in Gloucestershire close to Gloucester Cathedral, Tetbury, Stroud. Many lovely country walks. Pets welcome. En suite bedrooms, large lounge. Large garden.

Telephone: 01452 813618

Fax: 01452 812375

The Cotswolds area is hugely enjoyable at any time of year. Winter can be enjoyed in some of the finest hotels in Britain – and if you can't manage a full stay, why not book a tea or dinner? A pre-dinner drink in front of an open fire in an elegant and relaxing country house hotel must be one of the joys of life. The area also has an impressive collection of pubs – such as The Trouble House near Cirencester and The Plough at Ford. Spring and summer bring the great gardens of the area, such as Hidcote, to the fore, and there are many smaller private gardens open under the charitable "National Gardens Scheme". There are some delightful attractions in this area, farm parks, high quality museums, and artists and craftspeople. Autumn has its own glories, including autumnal colours at two arboretums, Westonbirt and Batsford. Activities include cycling, walking, riding and campsites.

Treasured towns and villages include Stow-on-the-Wold, the Slaughters, Bibury, Chipping Campden, Cirencester, Winchcombe and Painswick. In his English Journey in 1933, J.B Priestley described the Cotswolds as "the most English and the least spoiled of all our countrysides" and today it is still regarded as quintessentially English. Much of the landscape is a designated Area of Outstanding Natural Beauty. The famous drystone walls of the area represent not only the history of the area but are an important conservation feature. The construction of the walls is a matter of skill, with no mortar involved to hold them together, thus the name.

Abbots Court
Church End, Twyning
Tewkesbury
GL20 6DA

A large, quiet farmhouse on a working farm set in 350 acres, built on the site of monastery between the Malverns and Cotswolds, half a mile M5-M50 junction.

Six en suite bedrooms with colour TV and tea making facilities. Centrally heated. Open all year except Christmas. Large lounge with open fire and colour TV. Lawn. Cot and high chair available. Laundry facilities.

Coarse fishing available on the farm

Ideally situated for touring with numerous places to visit • Swimming, tennis, sauna, golf within three miles

Bed and Breakfast from £21 to £25.
Reduced rates for children and Senior Citizens.

Mrs Bernadette Williams • Tel & Fax: 01684 292515
e-mail: abbotscourt@aol.com

Ireley is an 18th century farmhouse located in the heart of gentle countryside, one-and-a-half miles from Winchcombe and within easy reach of Cheltenham, Gloucester, Stratford-upon-Avon and Worcester.

The cosy yet spacious guest rooms (one double and two twin) offer either en suite or private bathroom. Relax in the evening beside a traditional open fire and in the morning enjoy a delicious English breakfast. Families are welcome, to enjoy the unique atmosphere of this working farm.

Mrs Margaret Warmington, Ireley Farm,
Broadway Road, Winchcombe GL54 5PA
Tel: 01242 602445 • e-mail: warmingtonmaggot@aol.com

B&B from £25 per person.

WOODCHESTER. Mrs Wendy Swait, Inschdene, Atcombe Road, South Woodchester, Stroud GL5 5EW (01453 873254). Inschdene is a comfortable family house with magnificent views across the valley, set in an acre of garden near the centre of a quiet village. A double room with private bathroom and a twin-bedded room are available, both being spacious with washbasin and tea/coffee making facilities. Colour TV available in the rooms. Woodchester is an attractive village with excellent local pubs renowned for their food, and all within easy walking distance. An ideal centre for the Cotswolds and close to Slimbridge, Berkeley Castle and Westonbirt Arboretum and more, including Badminton and Gatcombe Horse Trials.
Rates: Bed and Breakfast from £22.50 per person.
- Guests are requested not to smoke in the house.

Publisher's note

While every effort is made to ensure accuracy, we regret that FHG Guides cannot accept responsibility for errors, misrepresentations or omissions in our entries or any consequences thereof. Prices in particular should be checked.

We will follow up complaints but cannot act as arbiters or agents for either party.

Hampshire

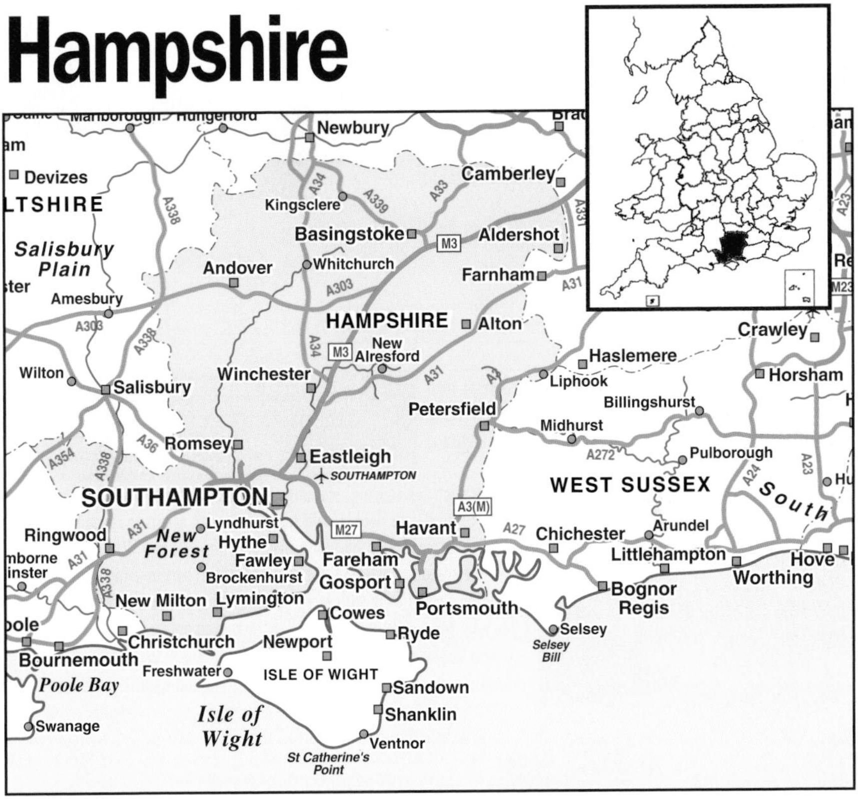

Newbury
Devizes
LTSHIRE
Camberley
Kingsclere
Salisbury Plain
Basingstoke
Aldershot
Andover
Whitchurch
Farnham
Amesbury
HAMPSHIRE
Alton
New Alresford
Crawley
Haslemere
Wilton
Salisbury
Winchester
Liphook
Horsham
Billingshurst
Petersfield
Midhurst
Romsey
Eastleigh
Pulborough
SOUTHAMPTON
WEST SUSSEX
South
Ringwood
New Forest
Lyndhurst
Hythe
Havant
Chichester
Arundel
Fawley
Fareham
Littlehampton
Hove
Brockenhurst
Gosport
Worthing
New Milton
Lymington
Bognor Regis
Cowes
Portsmouth
Christchurch
Newport
Ryde
Selsey
Selsey Bill
Bournemouth
Freshwater
ISLE OF WIGHT
Poole Bay
Sandown
Shanklin
Swanage
Isle of Wight
Ventnor
St Catherine's Point
A338
A34
A339
A33
A331
M3
A303
A31
A3
A272
A23
A24
A36
A354
A27
A3(M)
M27
M23

New Forest Ponies. Photo: Joe Low

Ideally situated for the delights of the New Forest, scenic cliff top walks, local beaches, pleasure cruises to the Isle of Wight, the Needles and historic Hurst Castle, horse riding, cycling, golf and a whole host of indoor and outdoor pursuits. Laurel Lodge is a comfortable, centrally heated, converted bungalow, offering twin, double & family rooms. All rooms are fully en suite with tea and coffee making facilities, comfortable chairs, colour TV and alarm clock radio. Ground floor rooms available. Breakfast is served in our conservatory/diningroom with views over the garden.

Bed and Breakfast from £25 per person • Special deals for longer breaks • Children welcome, cot and high chair supplied by prior arrangement • Off-road parking for all rooms • Strictly no smoking • Open all year • Please phone for further details.

Lee & Melanie Snook, Laurel Lodge,
48 Western Avenue, Barton-on-Sea, New Milton BH25 7PZ • 01425 618309

Maria and John offer a warm and friendly welcome at their spacious bungalow in a quiet location on the outskirts of Brockenhurst within easy walking distance of the village and just a few minutes' walk from open forest.

Mrs Maria Delstanche, LITTLE HEATHERS
Whitemoor Road, Brockenhurst SO42 7QG
Tel: 01590 623512
e-mail: littleheathers@msn.com
www.newforest.demon.co.uk/littleheathers.htm

Ideal location for touring, walking, cycling and horse riding. Golf courses nearby. Ground floor double/twin rooms, one with access to the garden and a small private patio. All rooms have their own facilities and TV, radio, hairdryer, tea/coffee and other extras. Full English breakfast served using local produce. Lymington Yacht Haven with ferry to Isle of Wight, Beaulieu Motor Museum, Exbury Gardens, Bournemouth and Southampton only a short drive away.

• Guests are welcome to relax in our lovely garden. • We are a non-smoking establishment. • From £60 per room to include full English Breakfast.

BROCKENHURST (New Forest). Hilden, Southampton Road, Boldre, Brockenhurst (New Forest) SO41 8PT (01590 623682; Fax: 01590 624444).

Hilden is a friendly Edwardian home in two-and-a-half acres of gardens and paddock, 50 yards from the open New Forest, offering wonderful cycling, riding and walking. Both the pretty Georgian sailing town of Lymington and the New Forest village of Brockenhurst (80 minutes to Waterloo by train) are about two miles away. There are numerous very good pubs and restaurants nearby, including The Hobler Inn, which serves excellent food, under 200 yards away. Stabling can be arranged, as can cycle hire, and riding from various local stables within five minutes' drive.

• Children and dogs welcome.

www.newforestbandb-hilden.co.uk

Photo courtesy
Hampshire County Council

OAKLEA GUEST HOUSE

London Road, Hook RG27 9LA
Tel: 01256 762673 • Fax: 01256 762150

Friendly, family-run Guest House. All bedrooms en suite and non-smoking. Guest lounge with SKY TV, licensed bar. Evening meals available on request. Easy access from J5 M3, London 55 mins by train.

AA ♦♦♦

GOLF: Many excellent courses within 10-mile radius.
HORSE RACING at Sandown, Ascot and Goodwood.
SHOPPING at The Oracle, Reading and Festival Place, Basingstoke.
DAYS OUT: Thorpe Park, Chessington, Legoland, Windsor Castle, Hampton Court, RHS Wisley, Milestones.

e-mail: reception@oakleaguesthouse.co.uk • www.oakleaguesthouse.co.uk

Set in its own grounds in a quiet location, this delightful 1912 period house offers a friendly and relaxed atmosphere, a high standard of accommodation and ample parking.

A delicious choice of breakfasts is served in the spacious residents' dining room.

Only five minutes' walk from the High Street and Quay area, ideal for mariners and for travellers catching Isle of Wight ferries.

Delightful forest and coastal walks.
Open all year.

The Rowans, 76 Southampton Road, Lymington SO41 3GZ
Tel: 01590 672276 • Fax: 01590 688610 • e-mail: therowans@totalise.co.uk

Harts Lodge

AA ★★★★ Guest Accommodation

Bungalow (non-smoking), set in three acres. Large garden with small lake. Quiet location. Three miles west of Lymington. Friendly welcome. Double, twin and family en suite rooms, each with tea/coffee making facilities and colour TV. Delicious four-course English breakfast. The sea and forest are five minutes away by car. Horse riding, golf and fishing are nearby.
The village pub, ½ mile serves excellent meals. Sorry, no pets.
Bed and Breakfast from £27.50 per person.

242 Everton Road, Everton, Lymington, Hampshire SO41 OHE

Tel: 01590 645902

B&B from £29 to £36 per person per night.
Three-night short breaks for two people sharing, including breakfast from £186

Ha'Penny House

A delightful character house with a warm, friendly atmosphere. Set in a quiet area of the unspoilt village of Milford-on-Sea and just a few minutes' walk to both sea and village, it is ideally situated for visiting the New Forest, Bournemouth, Salisbury and the Isle of Wight. The comfortable bedrooms are all en suite, with TV, hospitality tray and many extra touches. Award-winning breakfast menu with many choices. Large sunny diningroom and cosy guest lounge. Attractive gardens and summer house. Ample private parking. Non-smoking. Self-catering apartment also available. Open all year.

Carolyn and Roy Plummer, Ha'penny House, 16 Whitby Road, Milford-on-Sea, Lymington SO41 OND • 01590 641210
e-mail: info@hapennyhouse.co.uk • www.hapennyhouse.co.uk

VB ★★★★★ *SILVER AWARD* • **AA** ★★★★★ *BREAKFAST AWARD*

NEW FOREST. Mrs J. Pearce, "St Ursula", 30 Hobart Road, New Milton BH25 6EG (01425 613515).
Large detached family home offering every comfort in a friendly relaxed atmosphere. Off Old Milton Road, New Milton. Ideal base for visiting New Forest with its ponies and beautiful walks; Salisbury, Bournemouth easily accessible. Sea one mile. Leisure centre with swimming pool etc, town centre and mainline railway to London minutes away. Twin (en suite), double, family, single rooms, all with handbasin, TV and tea-making facilities. High standards maintained throughout; excellent beds. Two bathrooms/showers, four toilets. Cot etc, available. Pretty garden with barbecue which guests are welcome to use. Lounge with large colour TV. Two diningrooms. Smoke detectors installed. Full central heating.
Rates: Bed and Breakfast from £25.
• Downstairs twin bedroom suitable for disabled persons. • Children and pets welcome. • Open all year.
ETC ◆◆◆◆, *NATIONAL ACCESSIBLE SCHEME LEVEL 1.*

This late 17th century farmhouse, with its large garden, is open to guests throughout most of the year. Located quarter-of-a-mile west of the B2146 Petersfield to Chichester road, one-and-a-half-miles south of Petersfield, the house makes an ideal base for touring the scenic Hampshire and West Sussex countryside. Queen Elizabeth Country Park two miles adjoining picturesque village of Buriton at the western end of South Downs Way.

Accommodation consists of three twin-bedded rooms (two with washbasin), one bathroom/toilet; sittingroom/ breakfast room. Full central heating. Children welcome, cot provided. Sorry, no pets. Car essential, ample parking adjoining the house. Non- smoking.

B&B only from £22 per adult, reductions for children under 12 years. Open all year except Christmas, March and April.

Mrs Mary Bray, Nursted Farm, Buriton, Petersfield GU31 5RW • 01730 264278

PORTSMOUTH. Graham & Sandra Tubb, "Hamilton House", 95 Victoria Road North, Portsmouth PO5 1PS (Tel & Fax: 023 928 23502).
Delightful Victorian townhouse B&B, centrally located five minutes by car from Continental and Isle of Wight Ferry Terminals, M27/A27, Stations, City Centres, University, Sea-front, Historic Ships/Museums and all the tourist attractions that Portsmouth, and its resort of Southsea, has to offer. Bright, modern, centrally heated rooms with remote-control colour TV, hairdryer, clock, cooler fan and generous tea/coffee making facilities. Some rooms have en suite facilities. Ideal touring base for Southern England. Full English, Vegetarian and Continental breakfasts are served in lovely Spanish-style dining room. Also Continental breakfasts served from 6am (for early morning travellers). Nightly/weekly stays welcome all year.
Rates: Bed and Breakfast £26 to £28pp nightly in standard rooms and £29 to £31pp in en suite rooms.
• TOTALLY NON-SMOKING.
ETC/AA ◆◆◆◆
e-mail: sandra@hamiltonhouse.co.uk **www.hamiltonhouse.co.uk**

• • • some fun days out in HAMPSHIRE

The Spinnaker Tower, Portsmouth • 023 9285 7520 • www.spinnakertower.co.uk
Broadlands, Romsey • 01794 505010 • www.broadlands.net
Blue Reef Aquarium, Portsmouth • 023 9287 5222 • www.bluereefaquarium.co.uk
Exbury Gardens & Steam Railway, Beaulieu • 023 8089 1203 • www.exbury.co.uk
New Forest Museum, Lyndhurst • 023 8028 3444 • www.newforestmuseum.org.uk

Fraser House is situated one mile from the market town of Ringwood, overlooking the Avon Valley. This comfortable family house is on the edge of the New Forest, famous for its ponies, deer and pleasant walks. It is ten miles from Bournemouth and the South Coast, and is convenient for visiting Southampton, Stonehenge and the cathedral city of Salisbury. All rooms have en suite bath or shower facilities, central heating, comfortable beds, colour TV, tea/coffee making facilities, hairdryer. Guest lounge with colour TV. Fishing and water sports available nearby.

Tel: 01425 473958

Ample parking space • Most major credit cards accepted

Bed and Breakfast from £30 per person per night • Non-smoking • Open all year

e-mail: mail@fraserhouse.net • www.fraserhouse.net

Mr & Mrs M. Burt, Fraser House, Salisbury Road, Blashford, Ringwood BH24 3PB

Dormy House Hotel *21 Barnes Lane, Sarisbury Green / Warsash, Southampton SO31 7DA*

Tel: 01489 572626 • Fax: 01489 573370

e-mail: dormyhousehotel@warsash.globalnet.co.uk • www.dormyhousehotel.net

AA ♦♦♦♦ Guest Accommodation

Tranquil Victorian House set in a quiet residential area, fully modernised and located within half a mile of the River Hamble and Warsash, perfect for all activities on the river.

Accommodation consists of a charming dining room, comfortable lounge, twelve tastefully decorated, en suite bedrooms, each with tea/coffee making facilities, direct-dial telephones and remote-control TV. Ground floor bedrooms have access to the attractive and peaceful garden.

Fully licensed. Local restaurants offer a broad range of traditional, light or ethnic menus. Easy access to the many attractions along the South Coast, Isle of Wight and the New Forest and within easy reach of Business Parks at Whitely, Segensworth and Hedge End.

VERULAM HOUSE Guests are warmly welcomed to this comfortable, warm, roomy Edwardian establishment, in a nice residential area. Good cuisine. Two twin and one double room (used as singles when necessary) all with TV and tea/coffee making facilities; two bathrooms - plenty of hot water. Car parking space.

Five minutes by car to historic Southampton city noted for its parks; railway station 10 minutes. Airport, Cross Channel ferries and Isle of Wight within easy reach and not far from M27, M3, Portsmouth, Winchester, Bournemouth, New Forest and coast.

Bed and Breakfast from £28 per person per night. Non-smokers only.

Mrs Rose Pell, Verulam House, 181 Wilton Road, Shirley, Southampton SO15 5HY
Tel: 023 8077 3293 or 07790 537729

Photo courtesy Hampshire County Council

WINCHESTER. Lang House, 27 Chilbolton Avenue, Winchester SO22 5HE (Tel & Fax: 01962 860620). Winchester is one of the most beautiful cities in Britain and somewhere that demands exploration. Good accommodation is a must, and that is to be found at Lang House. Built at the beginning of the 20th century it has all the graciousness of buildings of that time. You will be warm in winter and enjoy the cool airy rooms in summer. Ample parking in the grounds and the house overlooks the Royal Winchester Golf Course. All bedrooms have en suite facilities and are comfortable and well furnished with colour TV and tea/coffee making facilities. You can be assured of a warm and friendly welcome and Winchester has a plethora of good eateries.
Rates: single from £45, double from £60.
www.langhouse.co.uk

MAYS FARM

Twelve minutes' drive from Winchester, (the 11th century capital city of England), Mays Farm is set in rolling countryside on a lane which leads from nowhere to nowhere. The house is timber framed, originally built in the 16th century and has been thoroughly renovated and extended by its present owners, James and Rosalie Ashby.

Longwood Dean,
Near Winchester SO21 1JS
www.englishbandb.com

There are three guest bedrooms, (one double, one twin and one either), each with a private bathroom or shower room. Dining room with open log fire and views over terrace and garden. Ducks, geese, chickens and goats make up the two-acre "farm". Booking is essential. Please phone or fax for details.

Tel: 01962 777486
Fax: 01962 777777 (office hours)

Useful Guidance for Guests and Hosts

Every year literally thousands of holidays, short breaks and ovemight stops are arranged through our guides, the vast majority without any problems at all. In a handful of cases, however, difficulties do arise about bookings, which often could have been prevented from the outset.

It is important to remember that when accommodation has been booked, both parties – guests and hosts – have entered into a form of contract. We hope that the following points will provide helpful guidance.

Guests

- **When enquiring about accommodation, be as precise as possible. Give exact dates, numbers in your party and the ages of any children.**
- **State the number and type of rooms wanted and also what catering you require – bed and breakfast, full board etc. Make sure that the position about evening meals is clear – and about pets, reductions for children or any other special points.**
- **Read our reviews carefully to ensure that the proprietors you are going to contact can supply what you want. Ask for a letter confirming all arrangements, if possible.**
- **If you have to cancel, do so as soon as possible. Proprietors do have the right to retain deposits and under certain circumstances to charge for cancelled holidays if adequate notice is not given and they cannot re-let the accommodation.**

Hosts

- **Give details about your facilities and about any special conditions. Explain your deposit system clearly and arrangements for cancellations, charges etc. and whether or not your terms include VAT.**
- **If for any reason you are unable to fulfil an agreed booking without adequate notice, you may be under an obligation to arrange suitable alternative accommodation or to make some form of compensation.**

Herefordshire

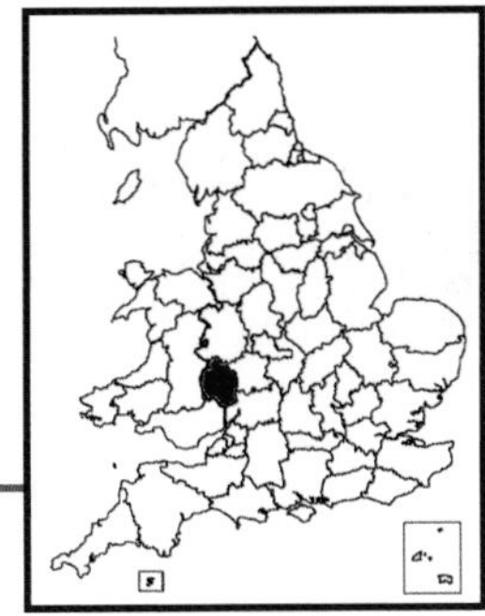

Herefordshire lies on the border with Wales, but is merely a stone's throw from Birmingham, Bristol, the Cotswolds and Cardiff. Green countryside, meandering rivers and acres of traditional cider orchards make up the landscape of this most rural of counties. It is home to the Hereford breed of cattle and has since become recognised for the standard of its local food and drink.

Hereford, a traditional Cathedral City but with the feel of a market town, offers visitors an interesting array of shops, cafes and bistros. The Norman Cathedral is home to the world famous Mappa Mundi, the oldest map of the world, and to the largest Chained Library in the world. The five market towns (Bromyard, Kington, Ledbury, Leominster and Ross-on-Wye) all offer something different to delight the visitor, and the 'Black and White Village' Trail explores a group of villages with beautiful half-timbered houses, cottages and country inns.

There is something for everyone – tranquil gardens, inviting tea-rooms, castles and historic houses, and of course, plenty of fresh country air in which to try canoeing, cycling, pony trekking, or maybe a good walk along one of the many long distance trails that intersect the county, including the recently opened Herefordshire Trail.

Hereford

Sink Green Farm

Rotherwas, Hereford HR2 6LE • Tel: 01432 870223
e-mail: enquiries@sinkgreenfarm.co.uk
www.sinkgreenfarm.co.uk

A friendly welcome awaits you at this our 16th century farmhouse overlooking the picturesque Wye Valley, yet only three miles from Hereford. Our individually decorated en suite rooms, one four-poster, all have tea/coffee making facilities, colour TV and central heating. Relax in our extensive garden, complete with summer house and hot tub, or enjoy a stroll by the river. Fishing by arrangement.

Prices from £28 per person • Children welcome • Pets by arrangement

The Coach House

The Coach House is an 18th century coaching stable providing unique Bed & Breakfast accommodation near Ledbury. All around is wonderful walking country, from the Malvern Hills to the Black Mountains. In the main house, guests have sole use of a lounge and kitchen, with a choice of single, double and twin rooms, all en suite. Newly converted for 2006, the Tower Suite of private lounge and en suite double bedroom.

Tariffs for 2007: £25pppn double and twin, £30 single. Reduced by £1.50pppn for 3 nights and more. **Tower Suite:**, £150 for two nights, and £60 per night thereafter.

Mrs S.W. Born, The Coach House, Putley, Near Ledbury HR8 2QP (01531 670684).
e-mail: wendyborn@putley-coachhouse.co.uk www.putley-coachhouse.co.uk

Hill Farm, Eastnor, Ledbury

HILL FARM is a 300-year-old stone and brick farmhouse surrounded by woodland at the foot of the Malvern Hills, one mile from Ledbury and one mile from Eastnor Castle. Accommodation comprises one twin room and two family rooms also used as twin/double rooms, all with washbasin, TV and tea/coffee making facilities. Guests' own sittingroom with log fire and the dining room look out onto a large garden and rural views.

Bed and Breakfast from £20-£25. Evening Meal by arrangement from £12.

Mrs C. Gladwin, Hill Farm, Eastnor, Ledbury HR8 1EF (01531 632827)

Publisher's note

While every effort is made to ensure accuracy, we regret that FHG Guides cannot accept responsibility for errors, misrepresentations or omissions in our entries or any consequences thereof. Prices in particular should be checked.

We will follow up complaints but cannot act as arbiters or agents for either party.

Rossendale House, 46 Broad Street, Leominster HR6 8BS • 01568 612464

ROSSENDALE HOUSE is a 17th century town house in the centre of historic Leominster. Restaurants, taverns and places of interest are on our doorstep. Railway and bus stations are conveniently close. A perfect base for visiting Hereford, Ludlow, Bromyard, Kington, The Marches, Black & White villages and the glorious surrounding countryside. Our en suite double rooms are each unique and extremely comfortable, they are exceptional value at £50 per night (£35 single occupancy). Room rates include breakfast and we are delighted to offer vegetarian and special diet options. We have secure private parking facilities for all guest vehicles and covered overnight storage for cycles, fishing tackle, etc. The house has spacious secluded gardens. ROSSENDALE HOUSE IS A NO SMOKING ESTABLISHMENT.

e-mail: enquiries@rossendalehouse.co.uk • www.rossendalehouse.co.uk

OLD KILNS Tel & Fax 01989 562051

Howle Hill, Ross-on-Wye HR9 5SP

A high quality bed and breakfast establishment in picturesque, quiet village location. Central for touring Cotswolds, Malvern, Stratford-upon-Avon, Wye Valley and Royal Forest of Dean.

Centrally heated, private parking. Some rooms with super king-size bed plus en suite shower, toilet; also brass king-size four-poster bed with private bathroom and jacuzzi. Colour TV and tea/coffee making facilities in bedrooms. Lounge with log fire. Full English breakfast. Open all year. Children and pets welcome (high chair, cots and babysitting service provided).

AA ♦♦♦♦ Guest Accommodation

Bed and Breakfast from £20 per person. Please telephone for free brochure.

Self-catering cottages also available, sleeping 2–14, with four-poster beds and jacuzzi.

BROOKFIELD HOUSE

A detached, Grade II Listed building, dating from the 18th century, which has been refurbished to a high standard by the present owners. Accommodation comprises large, tastefully decorated en suite rooms with king-size bed, TV and hospitality tray.

Within an easy stroll of the centre of Ross-on-Wye and with the advantage of a large private car park.

- Price includes a Full English Breakfast with a vegetarian option.
- Please note we are a non-smoking establishment.
- Bed & Breakfast from £29pppn.

AA ★★★★ Guest Accommodation

www.brookfield-house.co.uk

Mrs Maggie Adams, Brookfield House, Over Ross Street, Ross-on-Wye HR9 7AT • 01989 562188

A 16th century former coaching inn, Lea House has been beautifully refurbished, with exposed oak beams, an inglenook fireplace, antiques and imaginative decor. The spacious bedrooms have kingsize or twin beds and full en suite or private bathrooms. AA award-winning breakfasts are a real treat, with home-made breads and jams, fresh fruit and juice, local butcher's sausages and locally smoked fish. Dinner is also available on request.

On the Hereford/Gloucester border, adjacent to the Royal Forest of Dean and the spectacular Wye Valley, there is a wealth of activities and wonderful walking.

We accept dogs and children • Non-smoking • Bed and Breakfast from £29 - £33 pppn.

Lea House, Lea, Ross-on-Wye HR9 7JZ
Tel: 01989 750652

enquiries@leahouse.co.uk
www.leahouse.co.uk

Hertfordshire

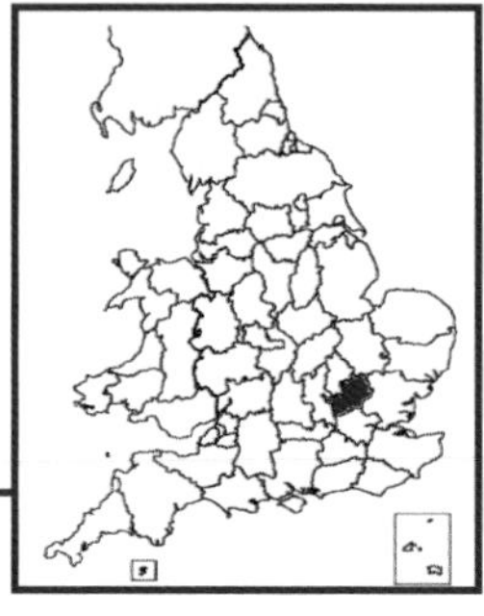

Tall Trees

6 Swallow Close, Nightingale Road, Rickmansworth WD3 7DZ

Large detached house situated in a quiet cul-de-sac with the centre of Rickmansworth only a short walk away. It is a small picturesque old town where there are many places to eat. We are five minutes' walk from the Underground station, half-an-hour to central London. Full breakfast served with homemade bread and preserves. Vegetarians and coeliacs catered for. Tea and coffee making facilities in rooms. Off-street parking. Convenient for M25 and Watford. No pets. This is a non-smoking household. Bed and Breakfast from £29.

Mrs Elizabeth Childerhouse - 01923 720069

WATFORD. Grove End Hotel, 73 Bushey Hall Road, Bushey, Watford WD23 2EN (01923 226798; Fax: 01923 210877). Situated in an acre of lovely gardens, this small, welcoming, family-run establishment has been in business for the past 35 years. It has 29 rooms to suit most people's pockets and taste, from basic single rooms to family rooms through to en suite. All rooms have satellite TV, washhand basin, and tea making facilities. En suite rooms also have shower, toilet, hairdryer, direct-dial phone and radio alarm. All rooms include a full English cooked buffet breakfast. There is a small bar, open from Monday to Thursday, which serves bar food from a varied menu. Weekend stays on a Bed and Breakfast basis only.
e-mail: grove.end@ntlworld.com
www.groveendhotel.co.uk

Isle of Wight

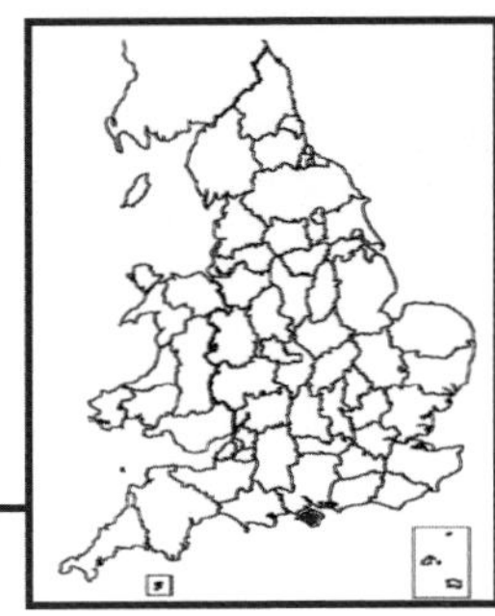

The Isle of Wight has several award-winning beaches, including Blue Flag winners, all of which are managed and maintained to the highest standard. Sandown, Shanklin and Ryde offer all the traditional delights; or head for Compton Bay where surfers brave the waves, fossil hunters admire the casts of dinosaur footprints at low tide, kitesurfers leap and soar across the sea and paragliders hurl themselves off the cliffs

Newport is the commercial centre of the Island with many famous high street stores and plenty of places to eat and drink. Ryde has a lovely Victorian Arcade lined with shops selling books and antiques. Cowes is great for sailing garb and Godshill is a treasure chest for the craft enthusiast. Lovers of fine food will enjoy the weekly farmers' markets selling home-grown produce and also the Garlic Festival held annually in August.

Many attractions are out of doors to take advantage of the Island's milder than average temperatures. However, if it should rain, there's plenty to choose from. There are vineyards offering wine tasting, cinemas, theatres and nightclubs as well as sports and leisure centres, a bowling alley and an ice skating rink, home to the Island's very own ice hockey team – the Wight Raiders.

The Island's diverse terrain makes it an ideal landscape for walkers and cyclists of all ages and abilities. Pony trekking and beach rides are also popular holiday pursuits and the Island's superb golf courses, beautiful scenery and temperate climate combine to make it the perfect choice for a golfing break.

Sandown

30 Station Avenue, Sandown, Isle of Wight PO36 9BW
Tel: 01983 402356 •• Fax: 01983 403647
e-mail: enquiries@fernsidehotel.co.uk •• www.fernsidehotel.co.uk

This family-run hotel is ideally situated within walking distance of sandy beaches, town centre and visitor attractions - the perfect location for a relaxing and enjoyable holiday or short break.

- Bed & Breakfast accommodation
- 11 comfortable en suite rooms (all non-smoking). Ground floor and family rooms (cots available).
- Remote-control colour TV and tea/coffee in all rooms, comfortable lounge with books, magazines and games
- Traditional full English breakfasts served in our dining room.

SANDHILL HOTEL

6 Hill Street, Sandown, Isle of Wight PO36 9DB
Tel: 01983 403635 • Fax: 01983 403695

Trevor Sawtell and family welcome you to a friendly family hotel five minutes' walk from the beach and train station. All rooms are en suite, with colour TV, tea/coffee and telephone with internet ports. We have a reputation for quality food served in our comfortable dining room, and after dinner, why not take a stroll in nearby Los Altos Park. Bed and Breakfast from £37. Bed, Breakfast and Evening Meal (five courses) from £42 per night. Special rates for children. Disabled friendly. Please call for brochure.

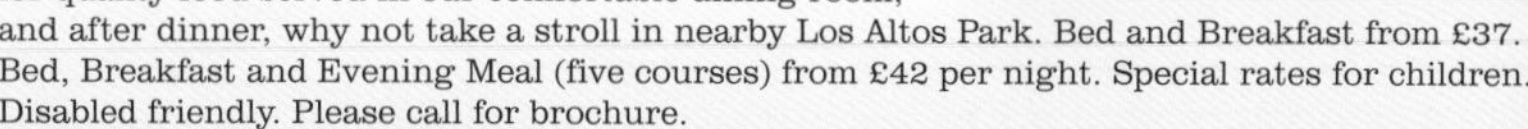

e-mail: sandhillhotel@btconnect.com • www.sandhill-hotel.com

Strang Hall

Uplands Road, Totland, Isle of Wight PO39 0DZ

Strang Hall was built in 1924 to an Arts and Crafts design for an American millionaire. Set in its gardens overlooking Totland Bay, surrounded by an Area of Outstanding Natural Beauty, there are long westerly views to the Dorset coast. The landscape, coast, light and air quality are fantastic. With just four guests here at any one time, it's a real opportunity to unwind. The excellent double or king-sized bedrooms with private bathrooms have panoramic sea, village and downland views. The guest sitting room opens onto the terrace; the breakfast room overlooks the top lawn. Breakfast choices include traditional English or Continental dishes, home-made bread and preserves. We have a big, friendly flatcoated retriever and an elderly cat. We are non smoking.

Tel: Mrs Val Hudson • 01983 753189
e-mail: Strang_hall@hotmail.com • www.strang-hall.co.uk

Sandy Lane Guest House, Colwell Common Road,

Totland Bay PO39 0DD • Tel & Fax: 01983 752240
e-mail: louise@sandylane-iow.co.uk

Sandy Lane is a relaxed, welcoming family-run bed & breakfast. Bedrooms are spacious, comfortably furnished and fully equipped, with en suite or private facilities. Wireless internet access, great breakfast and high standards. Four minutes' walk to beautiful Colwell Bay with its picturesque surrounding countryside. Walkers and cyclists are welcome. Previous visitors' comments include: *'A little gem'*, *'excellent discovery'* and *'A man of few words, all I can say is first class'*.

All non-smoking. Open all year.

• • • some fun days out in THE ISLE OF WIGHT

Calbourne Water Mill, Calbourne • 01983 531227 • www.calbournewatermill.co.uk
Fort Victoria, Yarmouth • 01983 760283 • www.fortvictoria.co.uk
Dinosaur Farm Museum, Brighstone • 01983 740844 • www.dinosaur-farm.co.uk
The Needles Park, Alum Bay • 0870 458 0022 • www.theneedles.co.uk

Kent

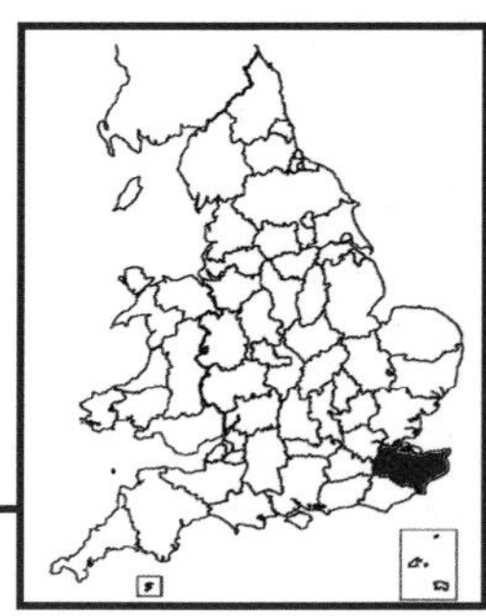

Bolden's Wood Fiddling Lane, Stowting, Near Ashford, Kent TN25 6AP

Between Ashford/Folkestone. Friendly atmosphere – modern accommodation (one double/twin, two singles) on our Smallholding, set in unspoilt countryside. No smoking throughout. Log-burning stove in TV lounge. Full English breakfast. Country pubs (meals) nearby. Children love the old-fashioned farmyard, free range chickens, friendly sheep and... Llamas, Alpacas and Rheas. Treat yourself to a Llama-led Picnic Trek to our private secluded woodland and downland and enjoy watching the bird life, rabbits, foxes, badgers and occasionally deer. Easy access to Channel Tunnel and Ferry Ports.

Bed and Breakfast £25.00 per person.
Contact: Jim and Alison Taylor

e-mail: StayoverNight@aol.com
www.countrypicnics.com

e-mail: platham@tesco.net

CANTERBURY. Mrs Prudence Latham, Tenterden House, The Street, Boughton, Faversham ME13 9BL (01227 751593).

Stay in one of the en suite bedrooms (one double, one twin) in this delightful gardener's cottage and stroll through the shrubbery to the 16th century diningroom, in the main house, for a traditional English breakfast, beneath the Dragon Beam. Close to Canterbury, Whitstable and the Channel Ports. It makes an ideal base for exploring Kent, then walk to one of the historic inns in the village for your evening meal. Tea/coffee making facilities. Off-road parking.

Rates: Bed and Breakfast from £23 per person.

- Open all year.

ETC ◆◆◆

www.faversham.org/tenterdenhouse

AA ♦♦♦ Guest Accommodation

Upper Ansdore

Beautiful secluded Listed Tudor farmhouse with various livestock, situated in an elevated position with far-reaching views of the wooded countryside of the North Downs. The property overlooks a Kent Trust Nature Reserve, is five miles south of the cathedral city of Canterbury and only 30 minutes' drive to the ports of Dover and Folkestone. The accommodation comprises one family, three double and one twin-bedded rooms. All have shower and WC en suite and tea making facilities. Dining/sitting room, heavily beamed with large inglenook. Pets welcome. Car essential.

Tel: 01227 700672

Bed and Breakfast from £27.50 per person. Credit cards accepted.

Mr and Mrs R. Linch, Upper Ansdore, Duckpit Lane, Petham, Canterbury CT4 5QB
e-mail: rogerd@talktalk.net • www.upperansdore.co.uk

English Tourism Council ♦♦♦ Guest Accommodation

South Wootton House

Capel Road, Petham, Canterbury CT4 5RG

A beautiful farmhouse with conservatory set in extensive garden, surrounded by fields and woodland. Fully co-ordinated bedroom with private bathroom. Tea/coffee facilities, colour TV. Children welcome. Canterbury four miles. Non-smoking. Bed and Breakfast from £30. Open all year.

Frances Mount

Tel: 01227 700643 • Fax: 01227 700613

Bleriot's • • • Dover

This non-smoking Victorian residence is set in a tree-lined avenue, in the lee of Dover Castle, within easy reach of trains, bus station, town centre, ferries and cruise terminal. Channel Tunnel approximately 10 minutes' drive. Off-road parking. We specialise in one night 'stop-overs' and mini-breaks. Single, double, twin and family rooms with full en suite. All rooms have colour TV, tea and coffee making facilities, and are fully centrally heated. Full English breakfast served from 7am. Reduced rates for room only. Open all year. MasterCard and Visa accepted.

English Tourism Council ♦♦♦ Guest Accommodation

Bed and Breakfast £24 to £28 per person per night.
Mini-Breaks January to April and October to December £21 per person per night.

Bleriot's, 47 Park Avenue, Dover CT16 1HE • Tel: 01304 211394
e-mail: info@bleriots.net • www.bleriots.net

Family-Friendly
Pubs, Inns & Hotels

See the Supplement on pages 293-297 for establishments which *really* welcome children.

Please note that these establishments may not feature in the main section of this book

FOLKESTONE. Mr & Mrs M. Sapsford, Wycliffe Hotel, 63 Bouverie Road West, Folkestone CT20 2RN (Tel & Fax: 01303 252186).
However long, or short, your stay, a warm welcome is guaranteed at our friendly, family hotel offering clean, comfortable and affordable accommodation. We are based centrally and are close to all amenities. Our menu is interesting and varied, and guests have their own keys for freedom of access at all times. If you are travelling to or from the Continent we can offer an ideal stopover as we are conveniently situated just 10 minutes from the Channel Tunnel and an easy drive from the port of Dover. Off-street parking. All major credit cards accepted. Please write or call for our brochure.

Rates: Bed and Breakfast from £25, Evening Meal from £8.50.
• Pets welcome • Children welcome - family rooms available
e-mail: sapsford@wycliffhotel.freeserve.co.uk **www.wycliffehotel.com**

Waterkant is a small guest house situated in a tranquil Kent Wealdon Village of olde worlde charm. A warm and friendly welcome is assured and the relaxed and informal atmosphere is complemented by excellent service and comfortable surroundings. Bedrooms have private or en suite bathrooms, four-poster beds, tea/coffee making facilities, colour TV and are centrally heated and double glazed. Lounge with colour TV. The beautifully landscaped Mediterranean-style gardens bounded by a stream provides a large pond, summerhouse for visitors' use and ample parking. Fast trains to London and a wealth of historic places to visit nearby. Open all year.
Visitors return year after year. Bed and Breakfast from £20, with reduced rates for children, Senior Citizens, midweek and winter season bookings, and referrals from FHG. Participants in ETC's Quality Assurance schemes.

Mrs Dorothy Burbridge, Waterkant Guest House, Moat Road, Headcorn, Ashford TN27 9NT
Tel: 01622 890154 • e-mail: colin@waterkant.freeserve.co.uk • www.headcornbb.co.uk

Heron Cottage

Peacefully situated in own grounds of six acres amidst acres of arable farmland, boasting many wild animals and birds, a stream and pond for coarse fishing. Within easy reach of Leeds Castle and many National Trust Properties including Sissinghurst Castle. You can choose between six tastefully furnished rooms with en suite and TV, or one room with separate bathroom. All rooms are centrally heated and have tea/coffee making facilities. There is a residents' lounge with log fire. Evening meals by arrangement.

Bed and Breakfast from £25 to £30 per person per night.

Mrs Susan Twort, Heron Cottage, Biddenden, Ashford TN27 8HH
Tel: 01580 291358

Pet-Friendly
Pubs, Inns & Hotels
on pages 298-311

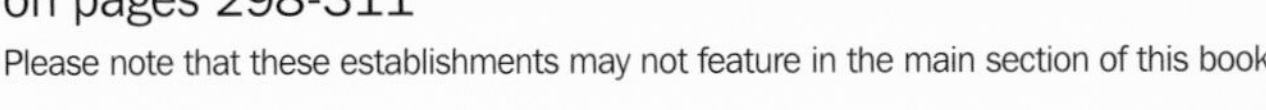

Please note that these establishments may not feature in the main section of this book

Lancashire

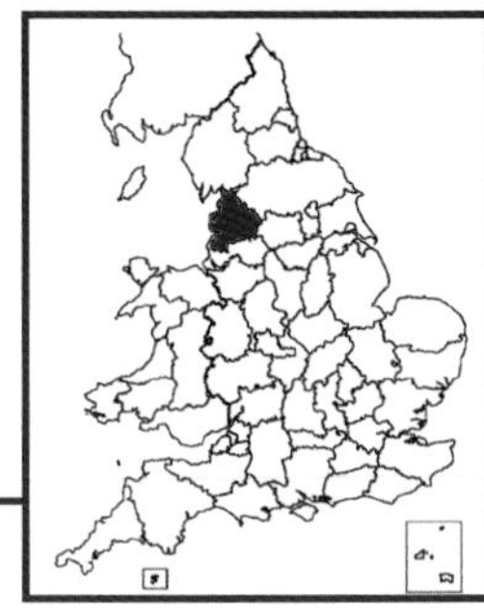

Sunnyside & Holmsdale Hotel

25-27 High Street, North Shore, Blackpool FY1 2BN

Two minutes from North Station, five minutes from Promenade, all shows and amenities. Colour TV lounge. Central heating. No smoking. Children welcome. Reductions for children sharing. Senior Citizens' reductions May and June, always welcome.

Special diets catered for, good food and warm friendly atmosphere awaits you. Bed and Breakfast from £20. Overnight guests welcome when available. Small parties catered for.

Elsie and Ron Platt
Tel: 01253 623781
e-mail: elsieandron@amserve.com

SUSSEX HOTEL

14-16 Pleasant Street, Blackpool FY1 2JA
Tel/Fax: 01253 627824

The Sussex Hotel offers all the amenities associated with larger hotels without the disadvantages – masses of other residents, noisy bars and of course, price. Children not accepted. Each of the 20 bedrooms is either twin or double, and has en suite shower and WC, colour TV, tea making facilities, silent refrigerator, room safe and full central heating. Excellent food is beautifully served, with ample portions and choice of menu. Ideally situated towards the North Shore, the hotel is minutes away from the rail and bus station, town centre, theatres and sea front. Proprietor: **Mr S. Griffin**

e-mail: sussexhotel.blackpool@virgin.net
www.sussexhotelblackpool.com

Parr Hall Farm

Within an hour of the Lake District, Yorkshire Dales, Peak District, Chester and North Wales, Parr Hall Farm is an ideal base for touring the local area. Attractions nearby include Camelot Theme Park, Martin Mere, Southport, Blackpool and antiques at Bygone Times, Heskin Hall, Park Hall and Botany Bay. All rooms are en suite, with central heating. Children are welcome, regret no pets. No smoking. **ETC/AA ★★★★**

From M6 take A5209 for Parbold, then immediately take B5250 right turn for Eccleston. After five miles, Parr Lane is on the right, the house is first on the left.

B&B from £30 per person, reductions for children.

e-mail: parrhall@talk21.com
www.thedelph.com/parr.html

Parr Hall Farm, Eccleston, Chorley PR7 5SL • 01257 451917 • Fax: 01257 453749

• • • some fun days out in LANCASHIRE

Leighton Hall, Carnforth • 01524 734474 • www.leightonhall.co.uk
RSPB Leighton Moss, Near Carnforth • 01524 701601 • www.rspb.org.uk
Sea Life, Blackpool • 01253 622445 • www.sealifeeurope.com
Blackpool Zoo, Blackpool • 01253 830830 • www.blackpoolzoo.org.uk
National Football Museum, Preston • 01772 908442 • www.nationalfootballmuseum.com
British Commercial Vehicle Museum • 01772 451011 • www.commercialvehiclemuseum.co.uk

Rakefoot Farm

Chaigley, Near Clitheroe BB7 3LY

VisitBritain ★★★★
VisitBritain ★★★/★★★★

Tel: (Chipping) 01995 61332 or 07889 279063 • Fax: 01995 61296
e-mail: info@rakefootfarm.co.uk • website: www.rakefootfarm.co.uk

Family farm in the beautiful countryside of the Ribble Valley in the peaceful Forest of Bowland, with panoramic views. Ideally placed for touring Coast, Dales and Lakes. 9 miles M6 Junction 31a. Superb walks, golf and horse riding nearby, or visit pretty villages and factory shops. Warm welcome whether on holiday or business, refreshments on arrival.

BED AND BREAKFAST or SELF-CATERING in 17th century farmhouse and traditional stone barn conversion. Wood-burning stoves, central heating, exposed beams and stonework. Most bedrooms en suite, some ground floor. Excellent home cooked meals, pubs/restaurants nearby. Indoor games room, garden and patios. Dogs by arrangement. Laundry. **Past winner of NWTB Silver Award for Self-catering Holiday of the Year.**

B&B £20 - £32.50pppn sharing, £20 - £37.50pn single
S/C four properties (3 can be internally interlinked)
£100 - £595 per property per week. Short breaks available.

• ROSE COTTAGE •

Tel: 01254 813223 • Fax: 01254 813831

LONGSIGHT ROAD (A59), CLAYTON-LE-DALE, NEAR MELLOR, RIBBLE VALLEY, LANCS BB1 9EX

A warm welcome awaits in our exclusively non-smoking 200-year-old cottage. At the gateway to the Ribble Valley, an ideal stop when visiting Scotland, only 30 minutes' drive to Blackpool and the Yorkshire Dales. Rural location, only 5 miles from the M6 J31, ideal for walkers and cyclists, also business persons wanting a friendly, homely environment. Each well equipped room offers guests a comfortable, relaxing stay; all have private facilities, welcome tray, TV, electric fan and fridge for guests' use.

Off-road parking, including covered parking for motorbikes and cycle lock. Pets welcome.

e-mail: bbrose.cott@talk21.com www.SmoothHound.co.uk/hotels/rosecott.html

LANCASTER. Roy and Helen Domville, Three Gables, Chapel Lane, Galgate, Lancaster LA2 0PN (01524 752222).
A large detached bungalow, three miles south of Lancaster and 400 yards from Lancaster University. Access from M6 Junction 33 and A6 in Galgate village. Two double bedrooms each with shower, toilet, colour TV and tea/coffee making facilities. One bedroom also has a private TV lounge. Full central heating. Spacious parking. A good location for visiting Blackpool, Morecambe, the Lake District and Yorkshire Dales. You will be sure of a friendly welcome and a homely atmosphere.
Rates: Bed and Breakfast from £25 per person.
• Sorry, no pets. • Non-smokers only please. • Open all year.

Photo courtesy of Blackpool Tourism

Broadwater House

The Broadwater is a small friendly guest house, situated on the select East Promenade with glorious views of Morecambe Bay and Lakeland Mountains. Only five minutes' walk from the town centre, shops and amusements. We offer every comfort and the very best of foods, varied and plentiful with choice of menu. All rooms en suite with heating, colour TV and tea making facilities. A perfect base for touring, the Broadwater is only 45 minutes' drive away from Blackpool, Yorkshire Dales and the Lake District, and 10 minutes from the historic city of Lancaster.

Bed and Breakfast from £22
Dinner available

Mrs R. Holdsworth, Broadwater House, 356 Marine Road, East Promenade, Morecambe LA4 5AQ • 01524 411333

Tel: 01253 790324
www.bellfarm.co.uk

BELL FARM

Beryl and Peter welcome you to their 18th century farmhouse in the quiet village of Pilling. The area has many footpaths and is ideal for cycling. Easy access to Blackpool, Lancaster, the Forest of Bowland and the Lake District. One family room, one double and one twin. All en suite. Tea and coffee making facilities. Lounge and dining room. All centrally heated. Full English breakfast.

Children and pets welcome.
Open all year except Christmas and New Year.
Bed and Breakfast from £27.50 - £50.

Peter Richardson, Bell Farm, Bradshaw Lane, Scronkey, Pilling, Preston PR3 6SN

WILLOW COTTAGE B&B

Thropps Lane West, Longton, Preston PR4 5SW

This award-winning olde worlde cottage is set in the lovely Lancashire countryside, with beautiful views from every window. The cottage dates back to the 16th century and still retains beams and wood burners. Rooms are tastefully decorated and have TV, radio, dressing gowns and hairdryers. A warm welcome awaits you, and home cooked, locally produced food is served. You can relax in the gardens, or visit the many attractions in the area. Safe parking. We are around 12 minutes from the M6, M62 and M65.

Mrs A. Caunce • 01772 617570

Leicestershire & Rutland

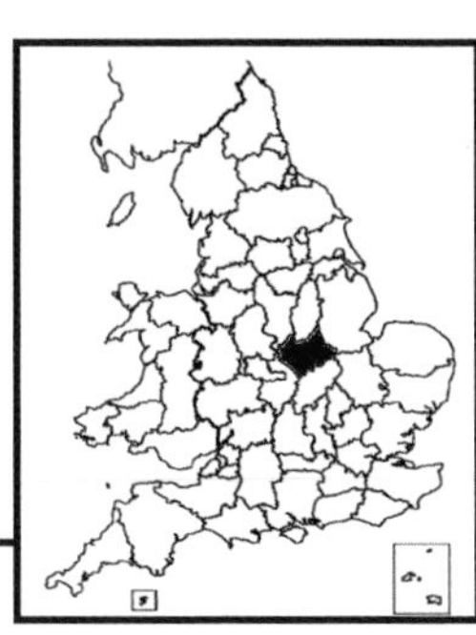

THE Old Rectory

Belton-in-Rutland, Oakham LE15 9LE
Tel: 01572 717279 • Fax: 01572 717343

Guest accommodation. Victorian country house and guest annexe in charming village overlooking Eyebrook valley and rolling Rutland countryside. Comfortable and varied selection of rooms, mostly en suite, with direct outside access. Prices from £25 per person per night including breakfast. Small farm environment (horses and sheep) with excellent farmhouse breakfast. Public House 100 yards. Lots to see and do: Rutland Water, castles, stately homes, country parks, forestry and Barnsdale Gardens. Non-smoking. Self catering also available.

e-mail: bb@iepuk.com www.theoldrectorybelton.co.uk

Abinger Guest House

Situated ¾ mile west of Leicester city centre, Abinger Guest House offers exceptional standards of comfort, cleanliness, cuisine and configuration at bargain basement prices. Refurbished and redecorated to demanding standards, all eight guest rooms offer TV with Freeview, designer glass washbasins, complimentary beverages, luxury sprung mattresses, hairdryers and mini-refrigerators. Ample parking is available, and regular buses to the city stop just outside, with easy access to many attractions. Breakfast fare is regularly complimented by guests, and the best produce available is offered.

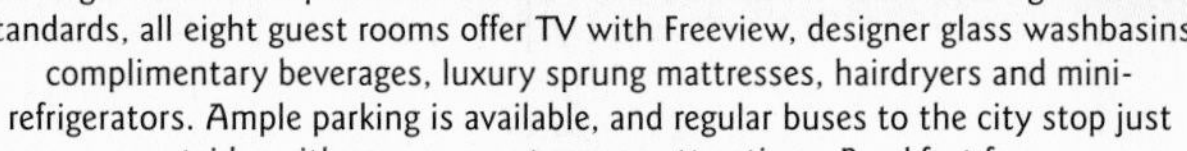

Bob, Teresa and Mel will be delighted to welcome you.

175 Hinckley Road, Leicester LE3 0TF • 0116 255 4674
www.leicesterguest.co.uk

MELTON MOWBRAY. Hillside House, 27 Melton Road, Burton Lazars, Melton Mowbray LE14 2UR (01664 566312; Fax: 01664 501819).

Situated on the edge of the village with views over rolling countryside, Hillside House is a comfortable, converted old farm building, offering one double and one twin room both en suite, and one twin with private bathroom. All have colour TV and tea/coffee making facilities. There is a guests' lounge; Rutland Water, Geoff Hamilton's Garden and Belvoir Castle are close by. Melton Mowbray with its bustling market is one and a half miles away. ***Rates: Bed and Breakfast from £23 to £25; 10% reduction for 3-night stay (except during special events).Single supplement.***

• Children over ten only. • Closed Christmas and New Year.

ETC ◆◆◆◆

e-mail: hillhs27@aol.com
www.hillside-house.co.uk

Lincolnshire

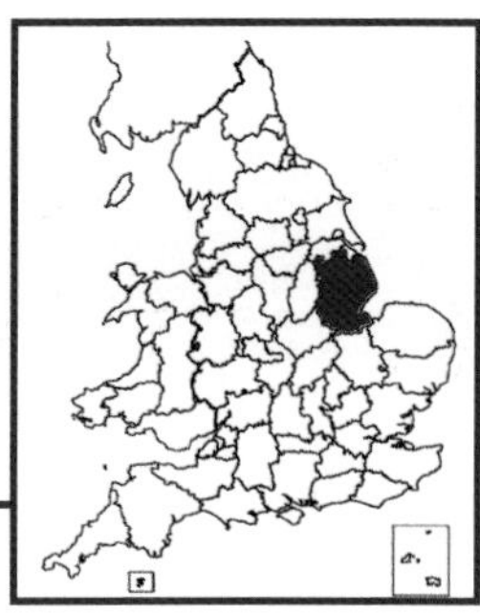

An early 18th century Listed farmhouse with spacious en suite bedrooms and original beamed ceilings. Enjoy a generous farmhouse breakfast using fresh local produce. Centrally located for five 'Bomber Country' museums, championship golf at Woodhall Spa, antiques at Horncastle and local fishing. Historic pubs nearby serving excellent evening meals. Within easy reach of the east coast and the Lincolnshire Wolds. One double and one twin bedroom. Central heating, tea and coffee facilities and colour TV.

Open all year except Christmas • No smoking
Children welcome • B&B from £20pp;
reductions for three days or more.

Mrs C. Whittington, High House Farm, Tumby Moorside, Near Coningsby, Boston PE22 7ST • Tel: 01526 345408 • e-mail: HighHousefarm@aol.com

We offer a warm and friendly stay at our delightfully converted 18th century coaching inn, so get away from the 'hurly burly' of modern life, and escape to the peace and quiet, although Lincoln is only 12 miles away and many other attractions are nearby.

The Black Swan Guest House

21 High Street, Marton, Gainsborough, Lincs DN21 5AH
Tel & Fax: 01427 718878
info@blackswanguesthouse.co.uk
www.blackswanguesthouse.co.uk

All rooms en suite, with full facilities; Comfortable guest lounge. Breakfasts are made with the best quality local produce and should set you up for the day. We are a non-smoking establishment.

Single from £40, double/twin from £65.

Baumber Park

Spacious elegant farmhouse in quiet parkland setting, on a mixed farm. Large plantsman's garden, wildlife pond and grass tennis court. Fine bedrooms with lovely views, period furniture, log fires and books. Central in the county and close to the Lincolnshire Wolds, this rolling countryside is little known, quite unspoilt, and ideal for walking, cycling or riding. Championship golf courses at Woodhall Spa. Well located for historic Lincoln, interesting market towns and many antique shops. Enjoy a relaxing break, excellent breakfasts, and a comfortable, homely atmosphere.

Two double, one twin,all en suite or private bathroom.
Bed and Breakfast from £29.

Mrs C.E. Harrison, Baumber Park, Baumber, Near Horncastle LN9 5NE
01507 578235 • Fax: 01507 578417 • mobile: 07977 722776
http://uk.geocities.com/baumberpark/thehouse

KEDDINGTON HOUSE Host Home

5 Keddington Road, Louth LN11 0AA
Tel: 01507 603973 • Mobile: 0781 8290990

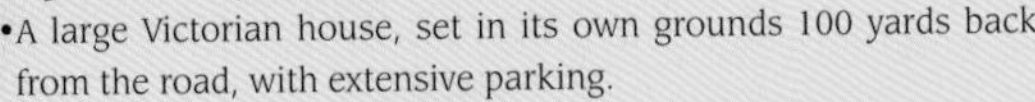

Tony and Beverly Moss offer:

- A large Victorian house, set in its own grounds 100 yards back from the road, with extensive parking.
- Double/twin/single and family en suite rooms
- Separate lounges with tea/coffee/biscuits always available
- Heated outdoor swimming pool (summer months only)
- Easy access to Louth town centre – Lincolnshire Wolds

Ideally placed for Lincoln, Grimsby and Market Rasen Racecourse. Within half-an-hour of the seaside at Mablethorpe and Skegness. Cadwell Park 10 minutes away - early breakfasts if required.

e-mail: beverly@keddingtonhouse.co.uk • www.keddingtonhouse.co.uk

Bed & Breakfast at No. 19 West Street

Kings Cliffe, Near Stamford, Peterborough PE8 6XB
Tel: 01780 470365 • Fax 01780 470623

A beautifully restored 500-year-old Listed stone house, reputedly one of King John's Hunting Lodges, situated in the heart of the stone village of Kings Cliffe on the edge of Rockingham Forest. Both the double and twin rooms have their own private bathrooms, and there is colour TV and a welcome tray in each. In the summer breakfast can be served on the terrace overlooking a beautiful walled garden. Off-street parking is behind secure gates. Within 10 miles there are seven stately homes, including Burghley House famous for the Horse Trials, Rutland Water, and the beautiful old towns of Stamford and Oundle. Open all year.

A non-smoking house • Bed and Breakfast from £25 per person • Proprietor: Jenny Dixon
e-mail: kjhl_dixon@hotmail.com • www.kingjohnhuntinglodge.co.uk

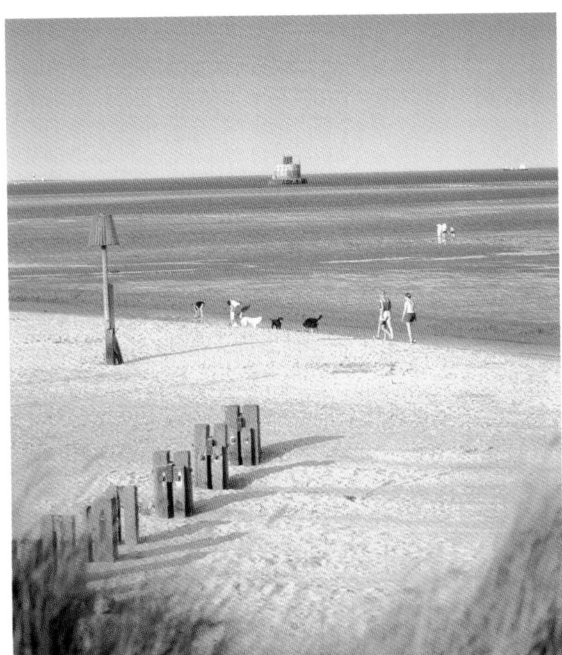

Photo courtesy North East Lincolnshire Council

Mrs S. Evans, Willow Farm,
Thorpe Fendykes, Wainfleet,
Skegness PE24 4QH
Tel: 01754 830316
Email: willowfarmhols@aol.com
Website: www.willowfarmholidays.co.uk

In the heart of the Lincolnshire Fens, Willow Farm is a working smallholding with free range hens, goats, horses and ponies. Situated in a peaceful hamlet with abundant wildlife, ideal for a quiet retreat – yet only 15 minutes from the Skegness coast, shops, amusements and beaches.

Bed and Breakfast is provided in comfortable en suite rooms from £20 per person per night, reductions for children (suppers and sandwiches can be provided in the evening on request). Rooms have tea and coffee making facilities and a colour TV and are accessible to disabled guests. Friendly hosts! Ring for brochure.

WOODHALL SPA. Barbara and Tony Hodgkinson, Kirkstead Old Mill Cottage, Tattershall Road, Woodhall Spa LN10 6UQ (01526 353637; mobile: 07970 040401). A warm welcome awaits you at this peaceful, sunny, detached house, which is set beside the River Witham on the outskirts of Woodhall Spa, a village which is noted for its 'old world' charm, park with open-air heated swimming pool, Kinema in the woods and championship golf course. A new garden, three-acre woodland garden, rowing boat, riverbank walks and membership of a local leisure club are also yours to enjoy, plus seasonal coarse fishing. There are numerous pubs and restaurants locally, or you are welcome to bring back a takeaway. We have a telephone, e-mail, fridge, iron and hairdryer for guests to use, and each of our three guest bedrooms (two en suite) has a TV, clock radio and hot drinks tray. A video, piano and open fire help to make the lounge a relaxing area. A cooked, typical English breakfast is served or you can choose a lighter, healthy option.

Rates: From £27 per person

- Non-smoking.

www.woodhallspa.com

• • • some fun days out in LINCOLNSHIRE

Rand Farm Park, Near Wragby • 01673 858904 • www.randfarmpark.com
National Fishing Heritage Centre, Grimsby • 01472 313131 • www.nelincs.gov.uk

Family-Friendly
Pubs, Inns & Hotels

See the Supplement on pages 293-297 for establishments which *really* welcome children

Pet-Friendly
Pubs, Inns & Hotels

on pages 298-312

Please note that these establishments may not feature in the main section of this book

Merseyside

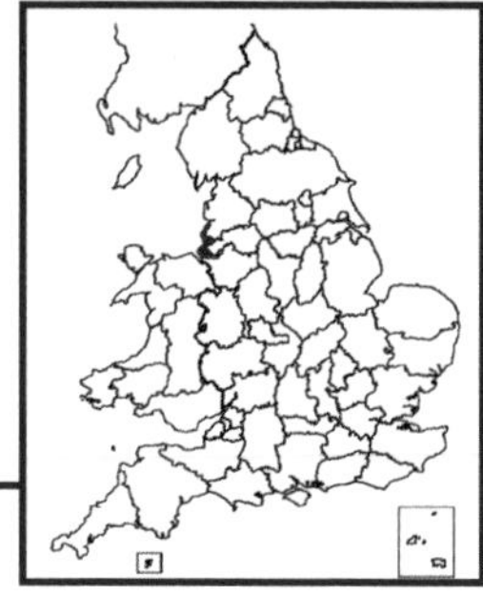

BEBINGTON. The Bebington Hotel, 24 Town Lane, Bebington, Wirral CH63 5JG (0151-645 0608).
A family business which guarantees a warm and friendly welcome within a professional atmosphere. Close to Bebington station and within easy reach of Birkenhead, Liverpool and Chester. All rooms en suite, colour TV, tea/coffee facilities. Car park. Residents' licence. Family rooms available.
• Residential licence. • Children welcome
e-mail: vaghena@aol.com

Tel: 0151-734 2216
e-mail: info@holmeleigh.com
www.holmeleigh.com

Holme Leigh Guest House

93 Woodcroft Road, Wavertree, Liverpool L15 2HG

Recently fully refurbished • All rooms comfortably furnished complete with TV, tea and coffee and en suite facilities • Full central heating • Award-winning breakfast room • Close to Sefton Park, just two miles from the M62 and 20 minutes from the airport, 2½ miles from city centre.

Single rooms available from £22 per night, doubles and twins from £44. Family rooms also available. All rates include VAT and Continental breakfast.

English Tourism Council ♦♦♦ GUEST ACCOMMODATION

Rosedale Hotel
ETC/AA/RAC ♦♦♦♦

One of Southport's most centrally situated hotels, ideally placed for the beach, parks, entertainment, golf courses and the famous Lord Street. The perfect location whether you are on holiday or on business. The resident proprietors make every effort to ensure that all their guests have a happy and comfortable stay. Full central heating and private parking. All rooms have tea/coffee making facilities and colour TV. Residents' bar and separate TV lounge. We are a small, family-run hotel offering a warm and friendly atmosphere. Children welcome. Sorry, no pets. Bed and Breakfast from £30

11 Talbot Street, Southport PR8 1HP
Tel & Fax: 01704 530604
e-mail: info@rosedalehotelsouthport.co.uk
www.rosedalehotelsouthport.co.uk

Norfolk

Aylsham

THE OLD PUMP HOUSE, Holman Road, Aylsham, Norwich NR11 6BY

01263 733789 • theoldpumphouse@btconnect.com • www.theoldpumphouse.com

This comfortable 1750s house, owned by Marc James and Charles Kirkman, faces the old thatched pump and is a minute from Aylsham's church and historic marketplace. It offers five bedrooms (including one four-poster) in a relaxed and elegant setting, with colour TV, tea/coffee making facilities and hair dryers in all rooms. English breakfast with free-range eggs and local produce (or vegetarian breakfast) is served in the pine-shuttered sitting room overlooking the peaceful garden. Aylsham is central for Norwich, the coast, the Broads, National Trust houses, steam railways and unspoilt countryside. Well behaved children and dogs welcome.

Bed and Breakfast from £45.00 to £65.00. Dinner by prior arrangement from October to May. Non-smoking. Off road parking for six cars.

Please mention **FHG Guides** when making enquiries about accommodation featured in these pages

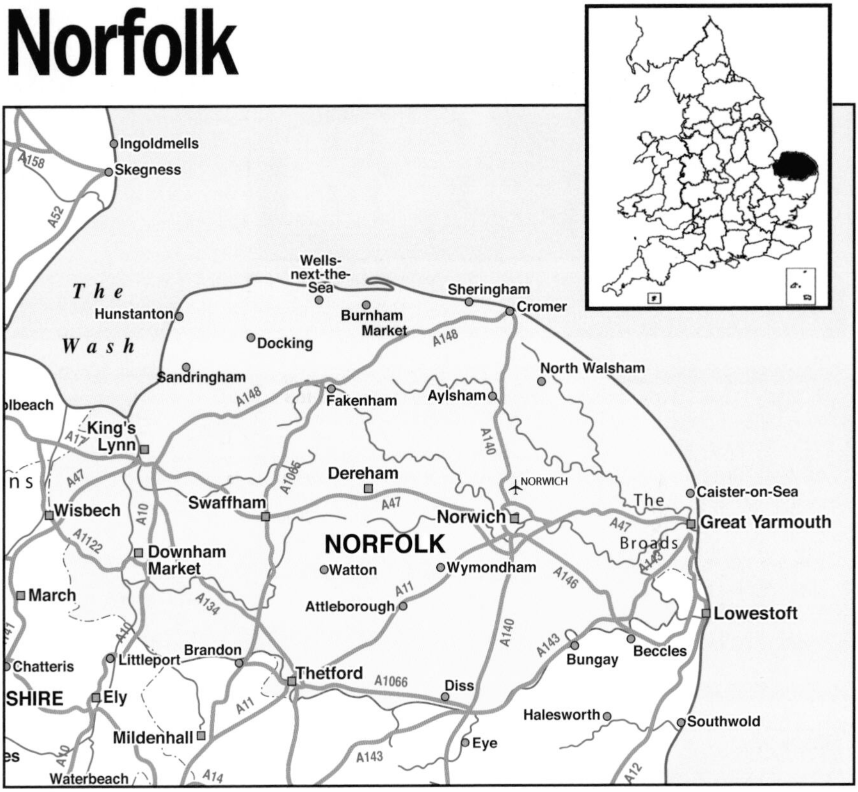

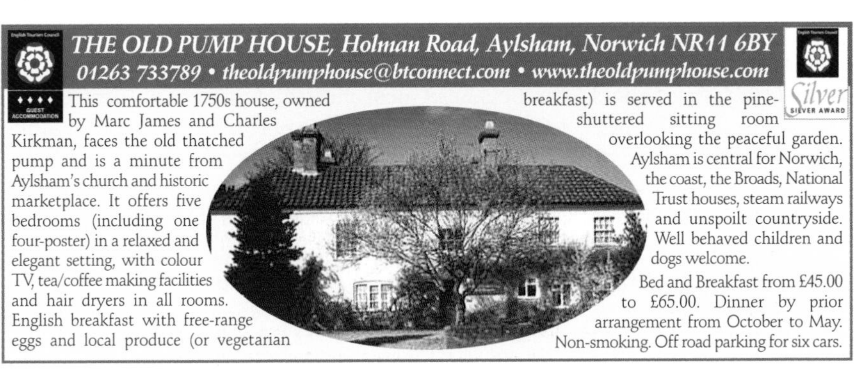

Peacock House

Old Tudor farmhouse with original beams and antique furniture, surrounded by paddocks and orchard, with a wildlife pond to the rear. Lovely countryside with good walks, 3½ miles from Dereham; close to Norwich, National Trust houses, Sandringham, beaches.

- All rooms en suite, tea/coffee facilities and TV.
- Guest lounge.
- Evening meals available in the long dining room.
- Very warm welcome.
- B&B from £26pp.
- Open all year

★★★★ GUEST ACCOMMODATION

Silver SILVER AWARD

Mark & Linda Stuckey, Peacock House, Peacock Lane, Old Beetley, Dereham NR20 4DG
Tel: 01362 860371 • e-mail: peacockhouse2006@aol.com • www.peacock-house.co.uk

---

Homely guest house with own keys and access at all times. Centrally situated, it is only two/three minutes from the seafront and five minutes from shopping centre.

Every amenity provided - tea making facilities in all rooms, comfortable accommodation and an ideal location.

Bed and Breakfast terms from £16 to £18 nightly, room only available. Children catered for (half-price rates sharing with two adults).

Dogs accepted on enquiry.

Mrs E. Dack, `Dacona',
120 Wellesley Road,
Great Yarmouth NR30 2AP

01493 856863 or 855305

The Beeches Guest House

The Beeches is an established, family-run guest house located in historic King's Lynn.
All bedrooms are en suite or have a private bathroom, and are equipped with colour TV, hairdryer, and tea/coffee making facilities.
We offer a superb breakfast menu, and evening meals by arrangement.

Mrs Hilary Sellers, The Beeches Guest House, 2 Guanock Terrace, King's Lynn PE30 5QT • 01553 766577 • www.beechesguesthouse.co.uk

---

Harbour View Barns, Eastbank Farm,

Garners Lane, Sutton Bridge, Spalding, Lincs PE12 9YP

Beautifully restored, turn-of-the-century, traditional barns, adjacent to traditional farmhouse on the borders of Lincolnshire, Norfolk and Cambridgeshire. Within a short distance of the coast, with enjoyable walks and birdwatching. Situated beside the River Nene, and close to other good inland fishing rivers. Close to market towns in the direction of both King's Lynn and Spalding. 10 rooms, all en suite and decorated to a high standard. Themed breakfast and evening restaurant area, lounge area, ample parking, relaxing garden with large pond.
B&B from £30 per person per night.

Tel: 01406 351333

Greenacres Farmhouse

Woodgreen, Long Stratton, Norwich NR15 2RR

Period 17th century farmhouse on 30 acre common with ponds and natural wildlife, 10 miles south of Norwich (A140). The beamed sittingroom with inglenook fireplace invites you to relax. A large sunny dining room encourages you to enjoy a leisurely traditional breakfast. All en suite bedrooms (two double/twin) are tastefully furnished to complement the oak beams and period furniture, with tea/coffee facilities and TV. Full-size snooker table and all-weather tennis court for guests' use. Jo is trained in therapeutic massage, aromatherapy and reflexology, and is able to offer this to guests who feel it would be of benefit. Come and enjoy the peace and tranquillity of our home.Bed and Breakfast from £25. Reductions for two nights or more. Non-smoking.

Tel: 01508 530261 • www.abreakwithtradition.co.uk

The ideal base to explore East Anglia & The Norfolk Broads

Simon and Heather welcome you to this former village school, fully refurbished in 2005, with views over the quiet Tas Valley, south of Norwich. Oakbrook House is the ideal touring base for East Anglia for work or leisure, centrally situated in the region. Nine warm comfortable rooms of various sizes and prices to match individual budget and comfort, each with en suite wc and basin, colour TV, clock radio and hospitality tray, en suite or private shower. All diets catered for, central heating, smoke-free, pets by arrangement. Evening meals and daytime use of the facilities available.

Contact us for brochure. Long stay discounts. B&B from £19 pppn.

OAKBROOK HOUSE

Oakbrook Guest House, Frith Way, Great Moulton, Norwich NR15 2HE

Tel: 01379 677359 • mobile: 07885 351212

e-mail: oakbrookhouse@btinternet.com • www.oakbrookhouse.co.uk

Freehouse & Restaurant

SEA PALLING. Tony and Liza Etheridge, The Old Hall Inn, Sea Palling NR12 0TZ (01692 598323; Fax: 01692 598822).
The Old Hall Inn is an old world character freehouse/restaurant situated on the coast road between Cromer and Great Yarmouth. It is in the middle of the village and just five minutes' walk from one of the best beaches along the Norfolk coast. There are six letting rooms, three of which are en suite, all have tea/coffee making facilities and TV. There is a non-smoking à la carte restaurant and bar meals are also available. Wireless internet available.
Rates: prices start at £35 for a single room, inclusive of full English breakfast, and £50 for a double room (two persons) per night.
- Well behaved children and pets are welcome.

A warm welcome awaits you at this attractive barn conversion. Set in quarter-of-an-acre in quiet location close to the shops and picturesque harbour of Wells.

Three en suite guest bedrooms (two twin and one double) at ground floor level overlook their own patio and garden area.

Ample car parking. Sorry no smoking in the bedrooms.

Ideal for the bird watching sanctuaries at Cley, Salthouse and Titchwell. Close to Sandringham, Holkham and the Shrines at Walsingham.

Prices from £32 to £36 daily; £215 to £225 weekly. 10% reduction three nights or more.

Mrs Dorothy MacCallum, Machrimore, Burnt Street, Wells-next-the-Sea NR23 1HS • 01328 711653
e-mail: dottiemac39@hotmail.com • www.machrimore.co.uk

WEST RUNTON (near Cromer). Homefield Guest House, 48 Cromer Road, West Runton, Cromer NR27 9AD (01263 837337).
A warm welcome awaits you at Homefield, a large Victorian house which is only five minutes' walk from the beach, and is ideal for a relaxing break, or as a base for exploring the treasures of North Norfolk. Beautifully restored, it has six fully en suite bedrooms with power showers, TV and tea/coffee making facilities; rooms enjoy sea or woodland views. There is also a lovely four-poster suite with private balcony. There is a good breakfast selection, including vegetarian and lighter options. Good selection of restaurants in the village for evening meals. Ample car parking.
Rates: B&B from £30pppn.
- All rooms non-smoking. • No children. • No pets.

AA 

e-mail: homefield@hotmail.co.uk
www.homefieldguesthouse.co.uk

Friendly Bed and Breakfast in an elegant Victorian house, in Wroxham 'Capital of Norfolk Broads'. Ideal for touring, day boats and boat trips on the beautiful Broads, fishing, steam railways, National Trust Houses, Wroxham Barns. Near north Norfolk coast, Great Yarmouth and Norwich. Good local restaurants and pubs. Guests arriving by train will be met. All rooms en suite, tea/coffee, colour TV. Hearty breakfasts. Conservatory, garden, car park, central heating and public telephone. Ring for brochure

Bed and Breakfast from £25 per person.

- All bedrooms non-smoking • Open all year

Tel: 01603 782991
www.wroxhamparklodge.com

Wroxham Park Lodge
142 Norwich Road,
Wroxham NR12 8SA

Northamptonshire

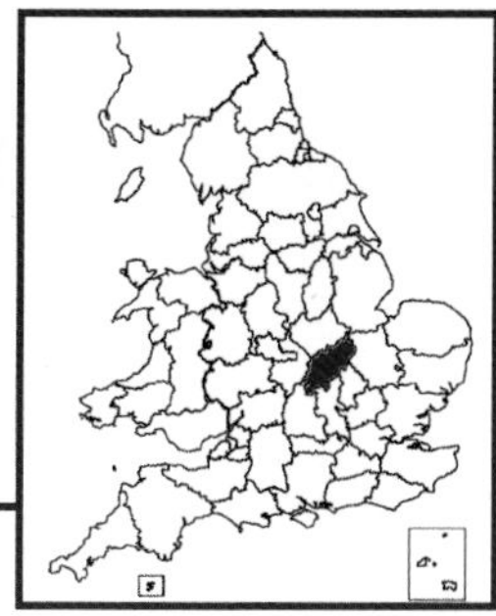

Murcott Mill, Long Buckby NN6 7QR

Tel: 01327 842236; Fax: 01327 844524
e-mail: carrie.murcottmill@virgin.net
www.murcottmill.com

Imposing Georgian mill house set within a working farm. Large garden and lovely outlook over open countryside. All rooms are en suite with colour TV. Central heating throughout and visitors have their own lounge and dining room with open log fires. An ideal stopover, close to M1, and good location for touring.

Children and pets welcome.

Bed and Breakfast from £28 single; double £50. Open all year.

ENJOY A HOLIDAY in our comfortable 17th century farmhouse with oak beams and inglenook fireplaces. Four-poster bed now available. Peaceful surroundings, large garden containing ancient circular dovecote. Dairy Farm is a working farm situated in a beautiful Northamptonshire village just off the A14, within easy reach of many places of interest or ideal for a restful holiday. Good farmhouse food and friendly atmosphere. Open all year, except Christmas. Bed and Breakfast from £25 to £35 (children under 10 half price); Evening Meal £17.

Mrs A. Clarke, Dairy Farm, Cranford St Andrew, Kettering NN14 4AQ
Telephone: 01536 330273

Peartree Farm

ALDWINCLE, KETTERING NN14 3EL

Peartree Farm is situated in the Nene Valley in the picturesque village of Aldwincle. We are a working farm of about 500 acres, with beef cattle and arable land. There are a lot of lovely walks around the farm and surrounding area, including a nature reserve and fishing lakes nearby. Beverley runs six rooms (five double, one twin) all en suite with TV and hospitality tray. There is a guests' lounge to relax in. Evening meals are by prior arrangement. We welcome both business visitors and holidaymakers to our home.

01832 720614

Northumberland

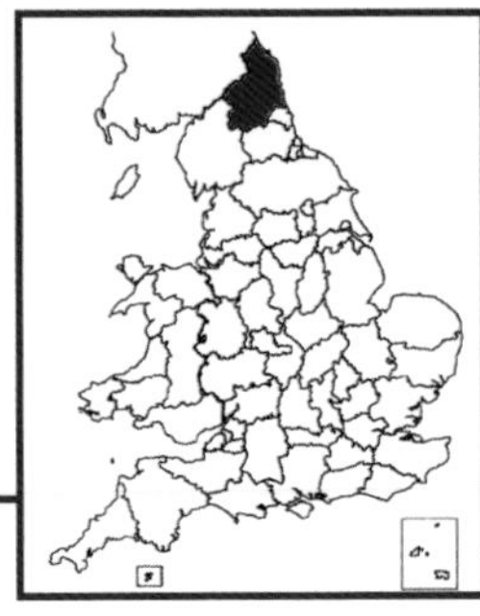

ALNWICK. K. and J. Bateman, Charlton House, 2 Aydon Gardens, South Road, Alnwick NE66 2NT (01665 605185). Charlton House is a very special guest house, where our guests are always welcomed in a friendly, relaxed atmosphere. All rooms are beautifully decorated, some with original fireplaces and patchwork quilts. All bedrooms have private facilities, alarm clock radio, hair dryer, hospitality trays and colour TV. There is also a comfortable guest lounge. Choose from Traditional English, vegetarian or Continental breakfasts. Private and off-street parking. We think you will remember Charlton House fondly, long after your stay has ended.

Rates: tariff from £28pppn (includes Breakfast).

ETC ★★★★. *WHICH?' 'GOOD BED AND BREAKFAST' GUIDE, PRIDE OF NORTHUMBRIA FOOD HYGIENE AWARD.*

www.SmoothHound.co.uk/hotels/charlt2.html

e-mail: sed@hazelrigg.fsnet.co.uk
www.farmhousebandb.co.uk

South Hazelrigg is situated between the market town of Wooler and the coastal village of Belford, approx. 10 minutes off the A1 road, ideally placed for trips to the beach, Farne Islands, Holy Island, the Cheviot Hills and the many castles. Rooms are spacious and comfortable with hospitality trays and colour TV. Breakfast is served in the elegant dining room and the local village inns provide an extensive menu. Local activities include birdwatching, fishing, horse riding and golf, Bamburgh being the most scenic English course.

Silver
SILVER AWARD

Sheila Dodds, South Hazelrigg, Chatton, Alnwick NE66 5RZ

01668 215216 • mobile: 07710 346076

Comfortable farmhouse accommodation on working mixed farm situated on the Heritage Coast between the villages of Craster and Howick. Ideal base for walking, golfing, bird-watching or exploring the coast, moors and historic castles. The Farne Islands, famous for their colonies of seals and seabirds, and Lindisfarne (Holy Island) are within easy driving distance. Accommodation is in two double rooms with washbasins. Guests have their own TV lounge/dining room with full central heating. Bed and Breakfast from £25. Open April to October. Non-smoking.

Howick Scar Farm House
Craster, Alnwick NE66 3SU
Tel & Fax: 01665 576665
e-mail: stay@howickscar.co.uk
www.howickscar.co.uk

farm STAY UK

Low Fotherley is an impressive Victorian farmhouse built around 1895 situated on the A68 south of Riding Mill in the beautiful Northumbrian countryside with outstanding views. The market towns of Hexham and Corbridge are nearby. Explore Hadrian's Wall, Durham, Beamish, Kielder, the Scottish Borders, Northumberland's coastline, Bamburgh and the Farne Islands. The farmhouse has lots of character, with open fireplaces and beams. The house is spacious and comfortable.

Our rooms are of a high standard. One twin en suite, one double en suite and one double with private facilities, all with full central heating, TV, tea/coffee making facilities, hairdryer and radio. Farmhouse breakfast is cooked on the Aga with toast, home-made jams and marmalade. Families welcome. No smoking. £27.50 per person, discounts for children.

ETC ◆◆◆◆ • FARM STAY UK MEMBER.

Mrs L. Adamson, Low Fotherley Farm, Riding Mill, Corbridge NE44 6BB Tel: 01434 682277
e-mail: hugh@lowfotherley.fsnet.co.uk
www.westfarm.freeserve.co.uk

❖ Struthers Farm ❖

Catton, Allendale, Hexham NE47 9LP

Struthers Farm offers a warm welcome in the heart of England, with many splendid local walks from the farm itself. Panoramic views. Situated in an area of outstanding beauty. Double/twin rooms, en suite bathrooms, central heating. Good farmhouse cooking. Ample safe parking. Come and share our home and enjoy beautiful countryside. Near Hadrians Wall (½ hour's drive). Children welcome, pets by prior arrangement. Open all year. Bed and Breakfast from £25; Optional Evening Meal from £12.50.

Contact Mrs Ruby Keenleyside

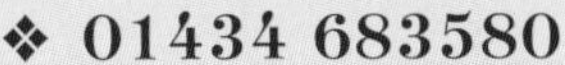

West Wharmley

Hexham, Northumberland NE46 2PL

Tel & Fax: 01434 674227

Set on a 550 acre working farm, we offer a warm welcome to our well appointed accommodation which has outstanding views over the South Tyne Valley. The self-contained wing of the 18th century farmhouse is traditionally decorated to a high standard, with full central heating. A large private sittingroom, complete with wood-burning stove, oak beams and colour TV, provides a homely retreat for the evenings. Two large, comfortable bedrooms, both en suite, have colour TVs and tea/coffee making facilities. Aga-cooked breakfast using local produce. Close to Hadrian's Wall and very accessible to Northumberland's many attractions. Bed and Breakfast from £27.50 to £35pppn.

Dating from 1747, this stone-built Inn and restaurant features excellent bar meals and a la carte menus, good choice of wines and cask and bottle conditioned beers.

A friendly, family run hotel, with 14 en-suite bedrooms, including ground floor rooms with disabled access, it is ideally placed for exploring Hadrian's Wall, Kielder and Border Reiver country. Pets are very welcome.

PPPN £40.00 min £45.00 max

BATTLESTEADS
HOTEL & RESTAURANT
Wark, Hexham, Northumberland
NE48 3LS. TEL: (01434) 230 209
Email: info@battlesteads.com
www.battlesteads.com

Katerina's Guest House

High Street, Rothbury NE65 7TQ • 01669 620691

Charming old guest house, ideally situated for the amenities of pretty Rothbury village, and to explore Northumberland's hills, coast, Alnwick Castle and gardens. Beautiful bedrooms, each decorated and colour co-ordinated to enhance its individual character; some with original stone fireplaces/beamed ceilings, all en suite, with four-poster beds, TV, and superbly stocked tea tray (with home-made scones!). Wide, interesting choice of breakfasts; licensed evening meals also available – sample Cath's bread, 'whisky porridge', vegetarian nutballs, or Steak Katerina. Bed and Breakfast from £28.

e-mail: cath@katerinasguesthouse.co.uk
www.katerinasguesthouse.co.uk

Wyndgrove House

A warm and friendly welcome awaits you at Wyndgrove House. Quietly situated within short walking distance of the sea front. Newly refurbished, comfortable rooms all with en suite facilities. Four poster, double, family and ground floor twin rooms available. *No smoking*. Vegetarian breakfast on request. Perfectly located for the beautiful coast and countryside with its many historic castles. Ideally based for birdwatching, walking, golfing, diving, horse riding and cycling. By boat you can visit Holy Island and the Farne Islands, with colonies of seals and seabirds. Short drive to Bamburgh and Alnwick. B&B from £30 pppn.

Paul and Donna, Wyndgrove House, 156 Main Street, Seahouses NE68 7UA • 01665 722855

This traditional country cottage is set in beautiful terraced gardens with a stream, and is only five minutes' walk from the village, castle, river walks and sandy beaches. The accommodation is comfortably furnished and includes two double rooms and one family room. All on ground floor with washbasins, shaver points, colour TV, tea/coffee making facilities and heating; en suite available. Residents' lounge. Warkworth makes an ideal base from which to explore rural Northumberland and the Borders with their unspoilt beauty and historic interest.

★★★★ GUEST ACCOMMODATION

Children welcome, reduced rates • Non-smokers
Private parking • Colour brochure available • Open all year
• Terms from £26pppn; en suite from £28pppn.
e-mail: beck-n-call@lineone.net
www.beck-n-call.co.uk
Tel: 01665 711653

Beck'N'Call
Birling West Cottage
Warkworth NE65 0XS

• • • some fun days out in NORTHUMBERLAND

Alnwick Castle, Alnwick • 01665 510777 • www.alnwickcastle.com
Grace Darling Museum, Bamburgh • 01668 214465 • www.rnli.org.uk

Nottinghamshire

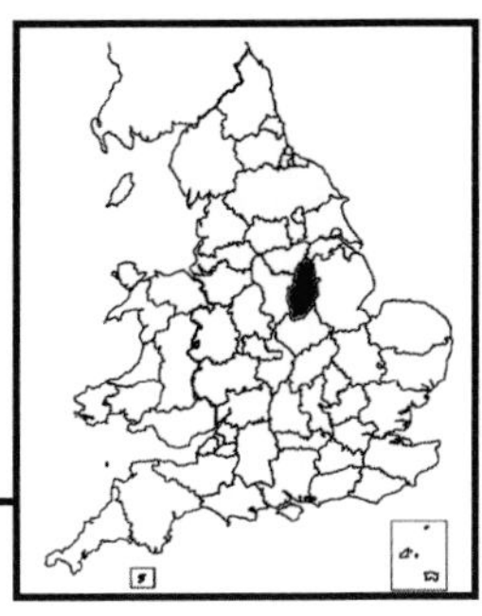

EDWINSTOWE (near Mansfield). Robin Hood Farmhouse B&B, Rufford Road, Edwinstowe NG21 9JA (Tel & Fax: 01623 824367).

Traditional Olde English farmhouse in Robin Hood's village in the middle of Sherwood Forest. We are in close proximity of Clumber and Rufford Country Parks and adjacent to Center Parcs and South Forest Leisure Complex. Easy access to Nottingham and Lincoln. The farmhouse, which is set in extensive gardens, is open and centrally heated all year round. Accommodation comprises double/family and twin room, colour TV, tea/coffee making facilities in all rooms. Ample secure parking.

Rates: from £22.50 per person per night. Reductions for children and extra nights.

• Pets and special requirements available on request.

e-mail: robinhoodfarm@aol.com

This is a stone-built farmhouse, standing 300 yards back from A632 on edge of village. It is on a 155-acre mixed farm with dogs, cats, goats, chicks, calves. Situated on the edge of Sherwood Forest, six miles from Visitors' Centre, eight miles from M1, 10 miles from A1. Chatsworth House, Newstead Abbey, Hardwick Hall and Creswell Crags all within easy reach. One double en suite, one double and one twin with shared bathroom; toilet; fitted carpets throughout. Open fires. Background central heating for comfort all year round. Large sittingroom/diningroom with colour TV.

Children welcome; babysitting • No pets • Car essential – parking. Tea/coffee making facilities • B&B from £18 per night, Evening Meal available nearby • Non-smokers only. Rates reduced for children • Open March to October inclusive.

Mrs L. Palmer, Boon Hills Farm, Nether Langwith, Mansfield NG20 9JQ • 01623 743862
e-mail: palmers@boonhills.wanadoo.co.uk
www.bedandbreakfast-nottinghamshire.com

Boon Hills

Dalestorth Guest House is an 18th century Georgian family home converted in the 19th century to become a school for young ladies of the local gentry and a boarding school until the 1930s. In 1976 it was bought by the present owners and has been modernised and converted into a comfortable, clean and pleasant guest house serving the areas of Mansfield and Sutton-in-Ashfield, offering overnight accommodation of Bed and Breakfast or longer stays to businessmen, holidaymakers or friends and relations visiting the area. Please send for further information.

Mr P. Jordan, Dalestorth Guest House,
Skegby Lane, Skegby,
Sutton-in-Ashfield NG17 3DH
01623 551110

Oxfordshire

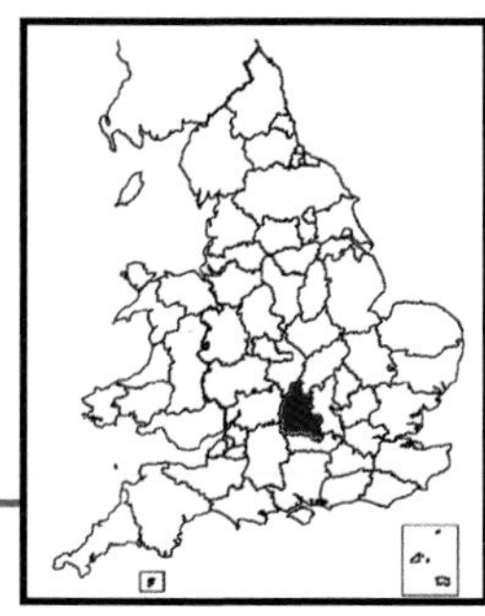

Oxfordshire is a fascinating blend of rolling countryside, bustling market towns and over 6000 years of history. Whether you are looking for a relaxing stay in the country, a cruise on the Oxford Canal or the shoppers' paradise of Bicester Village, there is something for everyone.

The Oxfordshire Cotswolds is a designated Area of Outstanding Natural Beauty, ideal for an activity break, whether walking, cycling or horse riding. There are miles of way-marked routes for whole day expeditions or gentle afternoon strolls.

For a touch of cosmopolitan city culture, visit Oxford, city of dreaming spires. The streets, houses, colleges, churches and chapels of the city represent a carefully documented catalogue of English history, with over 900 buildings of architectural or historic interest, including the Bodleian Library, one of the world's greatest collections of books, with over 5 million volumes. Opera, ballet, pantomime, musicals and major concerts are among a wide variety of performing arts taking place, often in historic settings such as the Sheldonian Theatre, Christ Church Cathedral, and the Holywell Music Room.

Market towns such as Banbury, famous for its landmark Cross, and Bicester are an exciting blend of traditional history and heritage and lively shopping and entertainment. Antique centres, local artists' studios and farm shops mix with quality high street shopping - and don't miss the traditional markets offering a range of produce and products unique to the area.

Banbury

Bed and Breakfast from £25
Child under 10 sharing family room £12
A warm welcome awaits you

NEW FARMHOUSE situated on edge of village off A423 Southam Road, three miles north of Banbury overlooking the beautiful Cherwell Valley. Ideally situated for touring Cotswolds, Stratford, Warwick, Oxford, Blenheim Palace. Local pubs serving evening meals Tuesdays to Saturdays.

Very comfortable accommodation comprising one twin room, one family room (one double and one single bed). Tea/coffee making facilities, hair dryers; central heating; shower room with electric shower; guests' sittingroom with colour TV. All rooms fully carpeted. Non-smoking. Parking.

Sorry, no pets.

Mrs Rosemary Cannon
High Acres Farm
Great Bourton
Banbury OX17 1RL
Tel & Fax: 01295 750217

THE OLD BAKERY

Skirmett, Near Henley-on-Thames RG9 6TD

This welcoming family house is situated on the site of an old bakery, seven miles from Henley-on-Thames and Marlow; half-an-hour from Heathrow and Oxford; one hour from London. It is in the Hambleden Valley in the beautiful Chilterns, with many excellent pubs selling good food nearby. Excellent village pub in Skirmett within easy walking distance. One double en suite, one twin-bedded room and one double with use of own bathroom. All with TV and tea making facilities. Open all year. Parking for five cars (car essential). Children and pets welcome.

Bed and Breakfast from £30 single; £60 double, £75 en suite.

e-mail: lizzroach@aol.com
Tel: 01491 638309 • Office: 01491 410716
Fax: 01491 638086

A large comfortable house in a quiet location near town and River Thames. Very good for short breaks and visits to Oxford, Windsor and London, and river trips along the famous Henley Regatta course. Plenty of places to eat. Good area for walking. Easy to get to Heathrow. All rooms have colour TV, tea/coffee making facilities, washbasin, most en suite. Full central heating. Full English breakfast. Regret no dogs. Good parking, some off-road. Open all year.

Single room from £38, double/twin £60 to £70. Single occupancy in double room £40 to £50.

e-mail: abbottsleigh@hotmail.com
Tel & Fax: 01491 572982
Mobile: 07958 424337

Mrs K. Bridekirk, Abbottsleigh, 107 St Marks Road, Henley-on-Thames RG9 1LP

The Close

Guest House

Witney Road
Long Hanborough
Oxfordshire
OX29 8HF

We offer comfortable accommodation in house set in own grounds of one-and-a-half acres. Three family rooms, four double rooms; all en suite; one double and one single.

All have colour TV and tea/coffee making facilities. Full central heating. Use of garden and car parking for eight cars. Please mention FHG when booking.

Close to Woodstock, Oxford and the Cotswolds.
Open all year except Christmas. Bed and Breakfast from £20.
Mrs I.J. Warwick (01993 882485).

Hill Grove Farm

Crawley Road, Minster Lovell, Witney
Oxon OX29 0NA • 01993 703120

HILL GROVE is a mixed 300-acre working farm situated in an attractive setting with rural views overlooking the River Windrush Valley. Good walking area and easy access to Oxford, Woodstock (Blenheim Palace), Witney, and Burford (Gateway to the Cotswolds) and renowned for its Wildlife Park).

Our animals include 2 gorgeous donkeys fostered from the Devon Donkey Sanctuary.

Hearty breakfasts and a warm welcome.

Open all year except Christmas. Non-smoking.

B&B: one double room with private shower £28-£29pp • one double en suite £31-£32 • one double/twin en suite £31-£32.

Mrs Katharine Brown

e-mail: katharinemcbrown@btinternet.com
www.countryaccom.co.uk/hill-grove-farm

OXFORD. Mr Stratford, The Bungalow, Cherwell Farm, Mill Lane, Old Marston, Oxford OX3 0QF (01865 557171). Modern bungalow on five acres set in countryside but only three miles from the city centre. Offering comfortable accommodation and serving traditional breakfast. Colour TV, tea/coffee facilities in all rooms. Private parking. Not on bus route.

Rates: Bed and Breakfast from £25 to £28 per person.

- Non-smoking.

ETC ◆◆◆

e-mail: ros.bungalowbb@btinternet.com
www.cherwellfarm-oxford-accom.co.uk

Arden Lodge

Modern detached house in select part of Oxford, within easy reach of Oxford Centre. Excellent position for Blenheim Palace and for touring Cotswolds, Stratford, Warwick etc. Close to river, parks, country inns and golf course. Easy access to London. All rooms have tea/coffee making and private facilities. Parking. Bed and Breakfast from £25 per person per night.

Mr and Mrs L. Price, Arden Lodge, 34 Sunderland Avenue (off Banbury Road), Oxford OX2 8DX
Tel: 01865 552076 • Fax: 01865 512265 • mobile: 07702 068697

Conifer Lodge

New, luxury stone house on the outskirts of Oxford, only 2 miles frequent bus service to the city centre, yet situated in the peace and quiet of the countryside.

Central heating in all rooms • Double glazed throughout • Colour TV • Large garden and patio • Parking

B&B from £35 per person - business persons welcome. No cancellations accepted within 7 days of occupancy.

Conifer Lodge, 159 Eynsham Road, Oxford OX2 9NE
Tel: 01865 862280 • www.smoothhound.co.uk/oxford

A peaceful setting and a warm, friendly atmosphere await you

Witney is famous for blankets, made here for over 300 years. Our house was built in 1959, of Cotswold stone. Set in two acres and situated on picturesque Wood Green, with football and cricket pitches to the rear, yet only 10 minutes' walk from the centre of this lively, bustling market town. An ideal touring centre for Oxford University (12 miles), Blenheim Palace (eight miles), Cotswold Wildlife Park (eight miles) and country walks. Ample parking.

Silver
SILVER AWARD

Three delightful en suite bedrooms with central heating, tea/coffee making facilities, hairdryer and colour TV. Non- smoking. Bed and full English Breakfast from £29.

Mrs Elizabeth Simpson, Field View, Wood Green, Witney OX28 1DE
01993 705485 • Mobile: 07768 614347
e-mail: bandb@fieldview-witney.co.uk

Shropshire

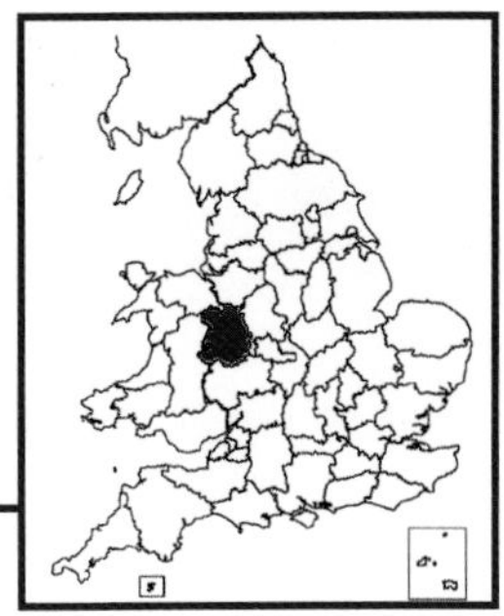

Shropshire is perhaps less well-known than other English counties. This is despite being the birthplace of Charles Darwin, home to the world's first iron bridge (now a World Heritage Site), having not one, but two of the finest medieval towns in England, inspiring the creation of the modern Olympics, and being the kingdom of the real King Arthur. After all, Shropshire is easy enough to find and get to from almost anywhere. (Hint: just north of Birmingham or south of Manchester depending on your direction of travel, and sitting snugly on the Welsh borders).

It may also come as a surprise to find out just how much is on offer. There are plenty of indoor and outdoor attractions, so the weather isn't a problem either. In Ironbridge, you can step into the past at the Ironbridge Gorge Museums where you'll find 10 museums to visit, all following the history of the Industrial Revolution. For retail therapy at its best, small independent shops can be found in all its market towns, full of those special 'somethings' you were looking for and even some things you weren't.

Shrewsbury is the beautiful county town, and home (naturally enough) to the Shrewsbury Summer Season – packed with over 200 events including the Shrewsbury Flower Show and the Cartoon Festival. There is also the Darwin Festival to celebrate the town's most famous son, and the foot-tapping Folk Festival. Ludlow, a medieval town, once the seat of the Welsh parliament, and now famed equally for its events and food, is also full of surprises. The Ludlow Festival is an annual two week gathering of actors, musicians, singers, entertainers, and generally some blooming interesting people to keep you rather amused.

All in all, Shropshire has a surprising amount to offer. So take the Shropshire option – for a great day out, fresh clean air and no jams (except those the W.I. make!)

An Edwardian house offers a warm welcome and comfortable en suite rooms with great views of the Stretton Hills. For the walker, the area is a delight in all seasons, right from the doorstep. Many National Trust and other historic properties are within easy reach.

Family-run B&B with 7 en suite bedrooms
Comfortable guest lounge • Residential licensed bar

Mynd House, Ludlow Road, Little Stretton, Church Stretton, Shropshire SY6 6RB
Tel: 01694 722212 • www.myndhouse.co.uk • e-mail: info@myndhouse.co.uk

Rooms with a view...

North Hill Farm

Cardington, Church Stretton SY6 7LL
Tel: 01694 771532

Farmhouse guest accommodation in the beautiful Shropshire hills, one mile from Cardington village. Quiet, rural setting with plenty of wildlife. Ideal walking and riding country. Rooms have wonderful views with TV & hot drinks tray. Great local pubs. Well behaved dogs and horses welcome. Bed and full English breakfast from £24 per person. En suite courtyard room £30 per person. Dogs £2 per night. Non-Smoking.

Mrs Chris Brandon-Lodge
e-mail: cbrandon@btinternet.com • www.virtual-shropshire.co.uk/northhill/

Lovely 17th century farmhouse in peaceful village amidst the beautiful South Shropshire Hills, an Area of Outstanding Natural Beauty. The farmhouse is full of character and all rooms have heating and are comfortable and spacious. The bedrooms are either en suite or private bathroom with hairdryers, tea/coffee making facilities, patchwork quilts and colour TV. There is a lounge with colour TV and inglenook fireplace. Children welcome. We are a working farm, centrally situated for visiting Ironbridge, Shrewsbury and Ludlow, each being easily reached within half an hour. Touring and walking information is available for visitors. Bed and full English Breakfast from £24pppn. Non-smoking. Open all year excluding November, December and January.

Mrs Mary Jones, Acton Scott Farm, Acton Scott, Church Stretton SY6 6QN • Tel: 01694 781260

Fax: 0870-129 4591 • e-mail: fhg@actonscottfarm.co.uk • www.actonscottfarm.co.uk

Put your feet up and relax in the recliners as the beauty of the garden and the views of Clun and its surrounding hills provide solace from the stress of modern day life. Receive a warm welcome at this traditional oak-beamed farmhouse set back from the working farm. Three bedrooms, double en suite, tea/coffee facilities and good home cooking. Visitors' lounge with inglenook fireplace; separate dining room. Walks, history and attractions all close by.

Llanhedric

Bed and Breakfast from £25. Reductions for children.
Non-smoking household. Regret no dogs in house.
Open April to October.

Mrs M. Jones, Llanhedric, Clun, Craven Arms SY7 8NG • 01588 640203

Ron and Jenny Repath, Meadowlands,
Lodge Lane, Frodesley, Dorrington
SY5 7HD
Tel & Fax: 01694 731350
e-mail: meadowlands@talk21.com
www.meadowlands.co.uk

Meadowlands

Former farmhouse, set in eight acres of gardens, paddocks and woodland, with pleasant woodland trail for guests' use. Quiet location in a delightful hamlet seven miles south of Shrewsbury. The guest house lies on a no-through road to a forested hill rising to 1000ft. Meadowlands features panoramic views over open countryside to the Stretton Hills.

Guest accommodation includes en suite facilities and every bedroom has a colour TV, drink-making facilities and a silent fridge. Guests' lounge with maps and guides for loan. Central heating. Plenty of parking space. Strictly no smoking.

Bed and Breakfast from £25 • Brochure available

LUDLOW. M.A. and E. Purnell, Ravenscourt Manor, Woofferton, Ludlow SY8 4AL (Tel & Fax: 01584 711905). Ravenscourt is a superb, recently renovated Tudor Manor set in two acres of lovely gardens. Beautifully furnished and equipped bedrooms. Wonderful area for walking or touring. Two miles from Ludlow, famous for its restaurants and architecture, eight miles from Leominster, famous for antiques, and 15 miles from Hereford and Worcester with their historic cathedrals. Close to National Trust properties and only 40 minutes from Ironbridge and Stratford. Excellent home cooked food. All rooms are en suite with remote-control colour TV, tea/coffee facilities and central heating. Warm welcome assured.

Rates: Bed and Breakfast from £32.50 per person based on two sharing; £5 per night discount for three nights or more. Self-catering cottages available, £140 to £330 per week, 10% discount for two weeks.

ETC ◆◆◆◆◆ *GOLD AWARD.*

e-mail: elizabeth@ravenscourtmanor.plus.com **www.smoothhound.co.uk or www.cottagesdirect.com**

The Four Alls Inn & Motel

Newport Rd, Woodeaves, Market Drayton TF9 2AG

A warm welcome is assured at the Four Alls, situated in a quiet location of Woodeaves yet only a mile from the town of Market Drayton, and within easy reach of Shropshire's premier attractions.

Relax in our spacious bar, sample our home-cooked food and excellent traditional beers, then enjoy a good night's sleep in one of our nine en suite chalet-style rooms with central heating, TV and tea/coffee making facilities. The function room is available for weddings, celebrations or as a conference venue and can accommodate 50-100. Large car park.

AA ◆◆◆

Tel: 01630 652995 • Fax: 01630 653930

e-mail: inn@thefouralls.com • www.thefouralls.com

Sambrook Manor

Sambrook, Newport TF10 8AL

Sambrook is a quiet, pretty village set in picturesque countryside close to the Shrops/Staffs border and within easy reach of Lilleshall sports centre, H.A.A.C., Ironbridge, Shrewsbury, Stafford and the Potteries. The charming historic Listed manor house (1702 AD) offers comfortable bedrooms, all en suite with TV and tea tray, and a relaxing lounge and conservatory, which opens on to a large garden. Full English breakfast cooked to your individual taste. Close to the Shropshire Union Canal and the national cycle network and with easy access to the Midlands motorway network. Local pub/restaurant within walking distance, also local fishing and horse riding. Stabling available and many accessible bridle paths. Private on-site parking. Boot room and cycle shelter. B&B Double/Twin £25, Single £30, reduction for children.

www.sambrookmanor.com

Tel: 01952 550256 • mobile: 07811 915535

TOP FARM HOUSE Knockin, Near Oswestry SY10 8HN

Full of charm and character, this beautiful 16th century Grade 1 Listed black and white house is set in the delightful village of Knockin. Enjoy the relaxed atmosphere and elegant surroundings of this special house with its abundance of beams. Sit in the comfortable drawing room where you can read, listen to music, or just relax with a glass of wine (please feel free to bring your own tipple). Hearty breakfasts from our extensive menu are served in the lovely dining room which looks out over the garden. The large bedrooms are all en suite, attractively decorated and furnished. All have tea/coffee making facilities, colour TV, etc. Convenient for the Welsh Border, Shrewsbury, Chester and Oswestry. Friendly hosts and great atmosphere. Bed and Breakfast from £27.50 to £35.

TELEPHONE: 01691 682582

E-MAIL: p.a.m@knockin.freeserve.co.uk

Visiting Shropshire?

Why not enjoy the warm welcome and home-from-home atmosphere at Oakfields, which is in a quiet, idyllic setting located in the picturesque village of Myddle made famous by Gough's "History of Myddle" written in 1700. All ground floor bedrooms, each tastefully decorated and equipped with colour TV, tea-making facilities, washbasin, hairdryer and shaver point; cot and high chair also available; guests' TV lounge. Central heating throughout. Large and pleasant garden for guests to enjoy. 15 minutes from Shrewsbury and Hawkstone Park and convenient for Ironbridge, Wales, Chester, etc. Golf and riding nearby. Extensive car park. Non-smoking.

B&B: Single £28 per night, Double or Twin £25pppn.

Nearest main road A528, also straight road from A5.

Mrs Gwen Frost, Oakfields, Baschurch Road, Myddle, Shrewsbury SY4 3RX
Tel: 01939 290823 • Mobile: 07952 058945

The Mill House Shrewsbury Road, High Ercall, Telford TF6 6BE

Judy and Chris Yates welcome you to The Mill House, an 18th century converted water mill situated beside the River Roden on a 9 acre working small holding. Located in the village of High Ercall, halfway between the historic county town of Shrewsbury and the new town of Telford.

Luxury B&B accommodation in three beautifully decorated, en suite bedrooms. Perfect for exploring Shropshire and the Welsh borderlands. A short distance from the World Heritage Site of the Ironbridge Gorge and the surrounding area offers a wide range of attractions and activities to suit all tastes.

Children welcome. Dogs by prior arrangement. Non-smoking.
Single £35 pppn, Double/Twin £24pppn,
Family room (sleeps 4) from £24 pppn.

01952 770394 • e-mail: cjpy@lineone.net • www.ercallmill.co.uk

Pet-Friendly
Pubs, Inns & Hotels

on pages 298-311

Please note that these establishments may not feature in the main section of this book

Somerset

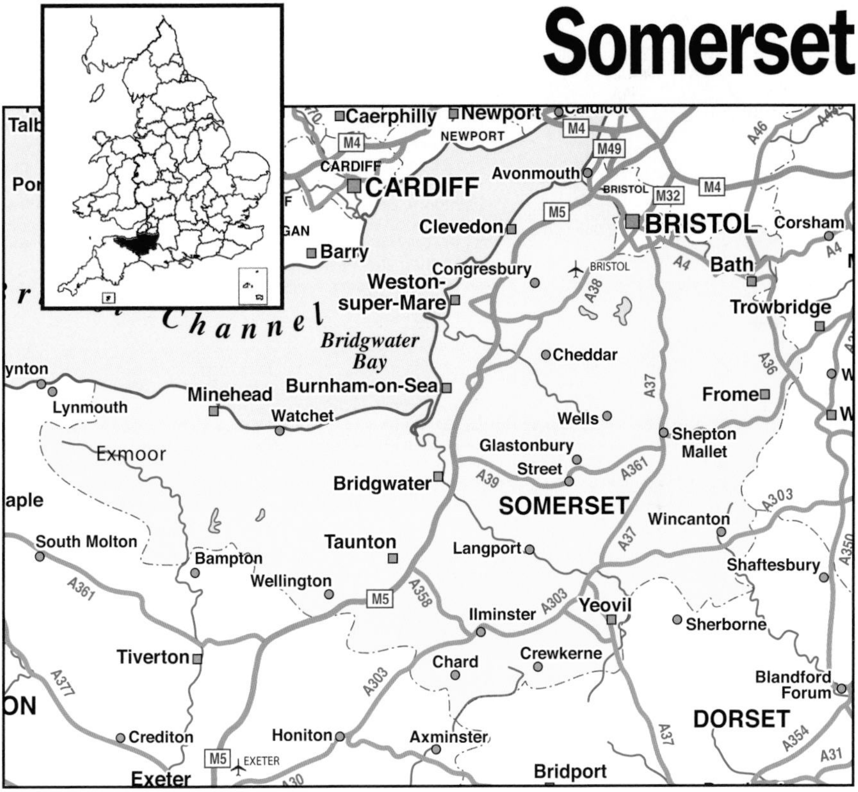

Bath

Free or reduced rate entry to
Holiday Visits and Attractions – see our
READERS' OFFER VOUCHERS on pages 9-42

BATH. Mrs Chrissie Besley, The Old Red House, 37 Newbridge Road, Bath BA1 3HE (01225 330464; Fax: 01225 331661).
Welcome to our romantic Victorian "Gingerbread" house which is colourful, comfortable and warm; full of unexpected touches and intriguing little curiosities. The leaded and stained glass windows are now double glazed to ensure a peaceful night's stay. Each bedroom is individually furnished, some with antiques and a king-size bed. All have colour TV, complimentary beverages, radio alarm clock, hairdryer and either en suite shower or private bathroom. Generous four-course breakfasts are served. Waffles, pancakes or kippers are just a few alternatives to our famous hearty English grill. Dinner is available at the local riverside pub, just a short stroll away. We have private parking.

Rates: Prices range from £27.50 to £35 per person in double rooms. Single occupancy from £38 B&B.

- Non-smoking

AA ◆◆◆◆

e-mail: orh@amserve.com **www.oldredhouse.co.uk**

BATH. Mrs D. Strong, Wellsway Guest House, 51 Wellsway, Bath BA2 4RS (01225 423434).
A comfortable Edwardian house with all bedrooms centrally heated; washbasin and colour television in the rooms. On bus route with buses to and from the city centre every few minutes or an eight minute walk down the hill. Alexandra Park, with magnificent views of the city, is five minutes' walk. Bath is ideal for a short or long holiday with many attractions in and around the city; Longleat, Wells and Bristol are all nearby. Parking available.

Rates: Bed and Breakfast from £25 single, £50 double, with a pot of tea to welcome you on arrival.

ETC ◆◆

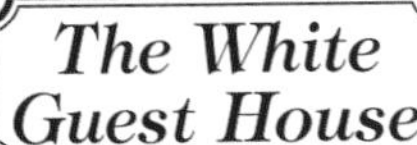

Steve and Anna Wynne welcome you to their guest house. Very conveniently located five minutes' walk to the city and all of Bath's famous attractions.

AA ◆◆◆ Guest Accommodation

Close to the Kennet and Avon canal (Bath in Bloom winners.) All rooms en suite, with central heating, TV, tea/coffee facilities. Traditional cooked breakfast or Continental breakfasts. Sorry, no pets and no smoking.

B&B single from £35, double/twin from £25pp. Min. 2 nights stay.

Free bottle of wine when you mention 'FHG'

23 Pulteney Gardens, Bath BA2 4HG • 01225 426075
e-mail: thewhiteguesthouse@zoom.co.uk
www.thewhiteguesthouse.co.uk

Enjoy the friendly atmosphere of this delightful Victorian House. Each bedroom is individually furnished. All have colour TV, complimentary beverages, radio alarm clock and en suite shower. All rooms are non- smoking. Traditional English breakfast is served in the breakfast room. There is ample off-road car parking and a baby-listening service is available. There is a pleasant river walk into Bath, or alternatively, through the Royal Victoria Park, past the world famous Royal Crescent and Circus.

Mrs Mary Cooper

Flaxley Villa

9 Newbridge Hill,
Bath BA1 3PW
01225 313237
e-mail:
Flaxleyvilla@fsmail.net

Prices start from £25pppn

Waltons Guest House

17 Crescent Gardens, Upper Bristol Road, Bath BA1 2NA
Tel: 01225 426528 Fax: 01225 420350

A warm welcome is assured in this gracious family-run Victorian home which offers an excellent base, minutes' walk from all the major attractions in the heart of Georgian Bath. There are 10 double/twin room, three single and two family rooms, five of which are en suite. Delicious full English Breakfast. Open all year. Group bookings catered for. Public car park at rear.

AA ♦♦

B&B £35-£50 single, £50-£85 double/twin, £50-£100 family room.

Bath - Toghill House Farm B&B and Cottages

Stay at Toghill in one of our tastefully decorated rooms offering a high level of comfort. Combine this with a traditional English breakfast and you will soon understand why many guests return time after time. All rooms have en suite bathrooms, television and tea/coffee making facilities.

Lovingly restored self-catering cottages also available

David and Jackie Bishop, Toghill House Farm, Freezing Hill, Wick, Near Bath BS30 5RT
Brochure - Tel: 01225 891261 • Fax: 01225 892128
www.toghillhousefarm.co.uk

Leigh Farm

200-year old, comfy, warm farmhouse on working livestock farm, with open log fire in the guest lounge during the winter months. Central heating, TV, video. Bedrooms with TV and beverage trays. Double en suite, family room with private bathroom. Menu available, breakfasts cooked to order. B&B from £27, discounts for 3 days or more. Credit cards accepted. Regret no pets. Self catering also available.

For brochure contact: Josephine Smart
Leigh Farm, Pensford, Near Bristol BS39 4BA • Tel & Fax: 01761 490281

Bristol International Airport 10 miles approx.

Visit the FHG website
www.holidayguides.com
for details of the wide choice of accommodation featured in the full range of FHG titles

BRISTOL. Downs View Guest House, 38 Upper Belgrave Road, Clifton, Bristol BS8 2XN (0117 9737046; Fax: 0117 9738169).
A well established, family-run Victorian guest house situated on the edge of Durdham Downs. All rooms have panoramic views over the city or the Downs. We are one-and-a-half miles north of the city centre, just off Whiteladies Road where there are plenty of restaurants, shops and buses. We are within walking distance of Bristol Zoo and Clifton Suspension Bridge. There are nine en suite rooms, all with tea/coffee making facilities, washbasin, colour TV and central heating. Full English breakfast.
Rates: Bed and Breakfast from £45 single, £60 double.
- All rooms non-smoking.

ETC ◆◆◆

The Model Farm

Model Farm is situated two miles off the A37 in a hamlet nestling under the Dundry Hills. A working arable and beef farm in easy reach of Bristol, Bath, Cheddar and many other interesting places. The spacious accommodation is in two en suite rooms, one family and one double, with tea/coffee facilities. Separate dining room and lounge with colour TV for visitors. Private parking. Open all year (except Christmas and New Year). Bed and Breakfast from £25.

Mrs M. Hasell, The Model Farm, Norton Hawkfield, Pensford, Bristol BS39 4HA • 01275 832144
e-mail: margarethasell@hotmail.com • www.themodelfarm.co.uk

Brinsea Green Farm

Brinsea Green is a Period farmhouse surrounded by open countryside. Set in 500 acres of farmland, it has easy access from the M5, (J21), A38 and Bristol Airport. Close to the Mendip Hills, the historic towns of Bath, Bristol and Wells, plus the wonders of Cheddar Gorge and Wookey Hole. Beautifully furnished en suite/shower bedrooms offer lovely views, comfortable beds, complimentary hot drinks and biscuits, radio, alarm, toiletries, sewing kit and hairdryer for your convenience. Both guest lounge (with TV) and dining room have inglenook fireplaces providing a warm, home from home atmosphere. Choose from our wide range of books and enjoy real peace and tranquillity.

SINGLE FROM £24 -£30 **DOUBLE FROM £38 - £48**

Mrs Delia Edwards, Brinsea Green Farm
Brinsea Lane, Congresbury, Near Bristol BS49 5JN
Tel: Churchill (01934) 852278 • Fax: (01934) 852861
e-mail: delia@brinseagreenfarm.co.uk
www.brinseagreenfarm.co.uk

Honeydown Farm

Situated in quiet countryside one-and-a-half miles from Crewkerne, we offer friendly and comfortable accommodation in our modern farmhouse on a working dairy farm with panoramic views. Ideal for a short break or holiday, with many National Trust properties and private gardens locally. The Dorset coast is only 14 miles. One double en suite, one double and one twin, both with washbasin; hospitality trays and TV in rooms. Enjoy the patio and garden or relax in the lounge or conservatory.

Non-smoking • Brochure available.

Bed and Breakfast from £52 double, £31 single.

**Mrs Catherine Bacon,
Honeydown Farm, Seaborough Hill,
Crewkerne TA18 8PL
Tel & Fax: 01460 72665
e-mail: c.bacon@honeydown.co.uk
www.honeydown.co.uk**

Marsh Bridge Cottage. This superb accommodation has been made possible by the refurbishment of this Victorian former gamekeeper's cottage on the banks of the River Barle. The friendly welcome, lovely rooms, delicious (optional) evening meals using local produce, and clotted cream sweets are hard to resist! Open all year, and in autumn the trees that line the river either side of Marsh Bridge turn to a beautiful golden backdrop. Just off the B3223 Dulverton to Exford road, it is easy to find and, once discovered, rarely forgotten. From outside the front door footpaths lead in both directions alongside the river. Fishing available.

Terms from £25 per person Bed and Breakfast or £41 per person Dinner, Bed and Breakfast.

Mrs Carole Nurcombe, Marsh Bridge Cottage, Dulverton TA22 9QG • 01398 323197

Higher Langridge Farm

Find our 17th century farmhouse hidden amid picturesque countryside two miles south-west of Dulverton - off the beaten track.

Welcome to Higher Langridge Farm - Farmhouse Bed & Breakfast near Dulverton, the southern gateway to Exmoor. On a family-run working farm on the Devon/Somerset border, our 17th century farmhouse is secluded in peaceful, quiet countryside and enjoys spectacular views. Just two miles off the A396 at Exebridge, very accessible, and a short drive from Dulverton, a small, friendly Exmoor town with an interesting selection of gift shops, tea rooms, pubs and restaurants. The surrounding landscape is home to many wild animals, including red deer, often seen from the farmhouse.

Prices from £25 to £30 based on two sharing

**Mrs Gill Summers, Higher Langridge Farm,
Exbridge, Dulverton TA22 9RR • 01398 323999
e-mail: info@langridgefarm.co.uk
www.langridgefarm.co.uk**

Attractive private house set in pretty gardens on the edge of Dulverton, 10 minute walk from the centre and a short drive to Tarr Steps and the moors. Comfortable, tastefully decorated rooms with lovely country views and a friendly informal atmosphere. One double, one twin, both en suite, plus one double/single with private bathroom. Superb full English breakfast.

Cyclists welcome. Route Three West Country Way on doorstep. Ample private parking and lock-up cycle shed.

No dogs • Non-smoking • Children welcome aged 8 or over. • Excellent location for touring Exmoor, West Somerset and North Devon.

Open all year (except Christmas and New Year). Terms: £20 to £25pppn (single £25).

**Mrs M. Rawle, Winsbere House, Dulverton, Exmoor TA22 9HU (01398 323278).
e-mail: info@winsbere.co.uk
www.winsbere.co.uk**

In the centre of quaint English village, an ideal location for walking and exploring Exmoor, the surrounding coastline and the many local attractions, The Yarn Market Hotel is a comfortable, family-run hotel which provides a friendly, relaxed atmosphere. All rooms are en suite, with tea and coffee making facilities, and colour TV. Some have four-poster beds, and some have views over the spectacular surrounding countryside. Family rooms are also available. The restaurant offers a mouth-watering selection of dishes featuring local produce whenever possible. Packed lunches available. Drying facilities. Non-smoking. Well-behaved pets are welcome. Party bookings and midweek breaks a speciality. B&B from £35.

THE YARN MARKET HOTEL
High Street, Dunster TA24 6SF

Tel: 01643 821425 Fax: 01643 821475
e-mail: yarnmarket.hotel@virgin.net
web: www.yarnmarkethotel.co.uk

Meare Manor

200 year old Manor House set in own grounds with beautiful gardens and views over Mendip Hills. Peaceful setting in the heart of King Arthur country. Ideal base for tourist attractions including Glastonbury Abbey, Chalice Well, Wells Cathedral, Cheddar Gorge and Clarks Shopping Village. Warm welcome assured with friendly help and advice. Family rooms available. Hospitality trays, colour TV. Ample car parking.
Open all year. From M5, Junction 23 follow A39 Glastonbury - Street, take B3151 Glastonbury to Wedmore, approximately three miles from Glastonbury. Bed and Breakfast from £50 double occupancy per night.

VisitBritain ★★★★

Sue Chapman, Meare Manor, 60 St Mary's Road, Meare, Glastonbury BA6 9SR • Tel 01458 860449 • Fax: 01458 860855
e-mail: reception@mearemanor.com • www.mearemanor.com

Barrow is a dairy farm of 146 acres. The house is 15th century and of much character, situated between Wells, Glastonbury and Shepton Mallet. It makes an excellent touring centre for visiting Somerset's beauty spots and historic places.

Two double rooms, one family room, one single room and one twin-bedded room, each with washbasin, TV and tea/coffee making facilities. Guests can enjoy farmhouse fare in generous variety, home baking a speciality. Bed and Breakfast, with optional four-course Dinner available. Children welcome. Open all year except Christmas. Sorry, no pets.

B&B single £26 per room, double/twin £50 per room, family £68-£70 per room. Dinner £14 each.

Mrs M. White, Barrow Farm, North Wootton, Near Glastonbury BA4 4HL
Tel & Fax: 01749 890245

• • • some fun days out in SOMERSET

Jane Austen Centre, Bath • 01225 443000 • www.janeausten.co.uk
Tropiquaria, Watchet • 01984 640688 • www.tropiquaria.co.uk
West Somerset Railway, Minehead • 01643 704996 • www.west-somerset-railway.co.uk
Westonbirt Arboretum, Tetbury • 01666 880220 • www.forestry.gov.uk/westonbirt
Wookey Hole, Wells • 01749 672243 • www.wookey.co.uk
Dyrham Park, Near Bath • 01179 372501 • www.nationaltrust.org.uk
Cheddar Caves & Gorge, Cheddar • 01934 742343 • www.cheddarcaves.co.uk

Imposing country house in Exmoor National Park on the wooded slopes of West Porlock commanding exceptional sea views of Porlock Bay and countryside. Set in five acres of beautiful woodland gardens unique for its variety and size of unusual trees and shrubs and offering a haven of rural tranquillity. The house has large spacious rooms with fine and beautiful furnishings throughout. Two double, two twin and one family bedrooms, all with en suite or private bathrooms, TV, tea/coffee making facilities, radio-alarm clock and shaver point. Non-smoking. Private car park. Bed and Breakfast from £30 to £32.50 per person. Credit cards accepted. Sorry, no pets.

West Porlock House
01643 862880

Margery and Henry Dyer, West Porlock House, West Porlock, Near Minehead TA24 8NX
E-mail: westporlockhouse@amserve.com

THATCHED COUNTRY COTTAGE & GARDEN B&B

An old thatched country cottage halfway between Taunton and Honiton, set in the idyllic Blackdown Hills, a designated Area of Outstanding Natural Beauty. Picturesque countryside with plenty of flowers and wildlife. Central for north/south coasts of Somerset, Dorset and Devon. Double/single and family suite with own facilities, TV, tea/coffee. Conservatory/Garden Room. Evening Meals also available. Open all year. B&B from £20pppn.

Mrs Pam Parry, Pear Tree Cottage,
Stapley, Churchstanton, Taunton TA3 7QA
Tel & Fax: 01823 601224
e-mail: colvin.parry@virgin.net
www.SmoothHound.co.uk/hotels/thatch.html OR **www.best-hotel.com/peartreecottage**

TAUNTON. Mr and Mrs P.J. Painter, Blorenge House, 57 Staplegrove Road, Taunton TA1 1DG (Tel & Fax: 01823 283005). Spacious Victorian residence set in large gardens with a swimming pool and large car park. Situated just five minutes' walking distance from Taunton town centre, railway, bus station and Records Office. 24 comfortable bedrooms with washbasin, central heating, colour TV and tea making facilities. Five of the bedrooms have traditional four-poster beds, ideal for weekends away and honeymoon couples. Family and twin rooms are available. The majority of rooms have en suite facilities. Large dining room traditionally furnished; full English breakfast/ Continental breakfast included in the price. Please send for our colour brochure.

ETC/AA ◆◆◆◆

www.blorengehouse.co.uk

TAUNTON. James and Katie Hawthorne, Pound Farm, Bishops Lydeard, Taunton TA4 3DN (01823 433443). Set at the foot of the Quantock Hills, Pound Farm offers a warm family welcome. A working farm of sheep, horses and arable, we will offer you a peaceful and friendly stay. Home-made cake and tea on arrival, pleasantly decorated bedrooms with bath and shower en suite facilities in all rooms. Guests have their own sitting room where breakfast is served in front of an open log fire. We are five minutes' drive from the West Somerset Railway and half an hour from Exmoor and the West Somerset coast. We look forward to welcoming you to our home.

Rates: £25pppn.

- Open all year round.

ETC 

e-mail: hawthorne@poundfarmsomerset.wanadoo.co.uk **www.poundfarm.co.uk**

Bishop's Hull, Taunton TA1 5AB
Tel & Fax: 01823 289732

Grade II Listed former Corn Mill, situated on the edge of a conservation village just two miles from Taunton. We have two lovely double bedrooms, The Mill Room with en suite facilities overlooking the weir pool, and The Cottage Suite with its own private bathroom, again with views over the river. Both rooms are centrally heated, with TV, generous beverage tray and thoughtful extras. Guests have their own lounge and dining area overlooking the river, where breakfast may be taken from our extensive breakfast menu amidst machinery of a bygone era. We are a non-smoking establishment.

Double en suite £27.50 pppn, double with private bathroom £25 pppn, single occupancy from £35 pn.

You can always expect a warm welcome at this historic villa, with just the right blend of comfortable, spacious accommodation, friendly efficient staff and the personal attention of its family owners. Located one mile from the M5 motorway, it makes an ideal base for business stays, or as a touring centre for this attractive corner of the West Country. Facilities include ten en suite bedrooms with colour TV, tea/coffee making facilities, direct dial telephone, etc. Honeymoon suite, conference facilities, restaurant and ample parking. Superbly accessible to Quantock, Blackdown Hills, Exmoor, North and South Devon coasts. Our tariff is inclusive of a Full English Breakfast.

Tel: 01823 442502 • Fax: 01823 442670
www.hotelfalcon.co.uk
mail@hotelfalcon.co.uk

The Falcon Hotel
Henlade, Taunton
TA3 5DH

Hungerford Farm is an attractive 13th century farmhouse on a family-run 350 acre farm with cattle, horses, free range chickens and ducks. We are situated in beautiful countryside on the edge of the Exmoor National Park. Ideal country for walking, riding or cycling. The medieval village of Dunster with its spectacular castle, mentioned in the Domesday Book, and the numerous attractions of Exmoor are all a short distance away. There is a good choice of local pubs within easy reach. Double and twin bedrooms with TV. Children welcome. Stabling available for visitors' horses. Dogs by arrangement.
From £22 per person. Open February to November.

Hungerford Farm, Washford, Somerset TA23 0JZ
Tel: 01984 640285 • e-mail: sarah.richmond@virgin.net

Family-Friendly
Pubs, Inns & Hotels

See the Supplement on pages 293-297 for establishments which *really* welcome children.

Please note that these establishments may not feature in the main section of this book

WELLS. Mrs Sue Crane, Birdwood House, Bath Road, Wells BA5 3EW (01749 679250).

Imposing Victorian house situated on the edge of the Mendip Hills but only one and a half miles from Wells town centre. Accommodation consists of two double en suite rooms, one double and one single room, all with TV and tea/coffee making facilities. Off-road secure parking. Located close to a walking trail and cycling route; facilities available for cycle storage. Groups and parties welcome.

Rates: Bed and Breakfast from £25 per person.

• Children welcome. • Pets by arrangement. • No smoking. • Open all year.

AA ◆◆◆

www.birdwood-bandb.co.uk

'LANA'

Hollow Farm, Westbury-sub-Mendip,
Near Wells, Somerset BA5 1HH
Tel & Fax: 01749 870635
Mrs Sheila Stott
e-mail: Sheila@stott2366.freeserve.co.uk

Modern farmhouse on working farm. Comfortable family home in beautiful gardens with views of Somerset Levels and Mendips. Quiet location. Breakfast room for sole use of guests. Full English breakfast. Meals available at local pub five minutes' walk away. En suite rooms with fridge, hairdryer, tea/coffee making facilities, shaver point, colour TV and central heating. Non-smoking.

Terms £28pppn, reduced rates for 3 nights or more.

Double-Gate Farm

Godney, Near Wells BA5 1RX

An award-winning B&B on the banks of the River Sheppey. All bedrooms are en suite, attractively decorated and thoughtfully equipped. Breakfast in the farmhouse dining room or in the garden, the extensive menu offering local and home grown produce accompanied with home-made bread. An ideal base for exploring this pretty and interesting county. Children welcome. No smoking or pets. Self-catering also available. B&B from £30 to £32.50 per person.

Tel: 01458 832217 • Fax: 01458 835612
e-mail: doublegatefarm@aol.com
www.doublegatefarm.com

Please note

All the information in this book is given in good faith in the belief that it is correct. However, the publishers cannot guarantee the facts given in these pages, neither are they responsible for changes in policy, ownership or terms that may take place after the date of going to press. Readers should always satisfy themselves that the facilities they require are available and that the terms, if quoted, still apply.

Sunset Bay Hotel 53 Beach Road,

Weston-Super-Mare BS23 1BH • 01934 623519

Small, family-run hotel enjoying an unrivalled position on the seafront, with superb views to Weston Bay and the Welsh coastline. A guest lounge on the first floor overlooks the bay, with games and books for the enjoyment of our guests.

Breakfast is served in the dining room/bar overlooking the beach and lawns, and though we do not provide evening meals, there is a menu of hot and cold snacks. Packed lunches can be supplied on request.

All rooms en suite, or with private bathroom, and TV, tea/coffee making facilities, hairdryers and towels are supplied in all rooms. Complimentary tray of tea and cakes on arrival.

Ideal for family holidays, weekend breaks, short breaks and holidays at any time of year. **Non-smoking.**

e-mail: relax@sunsetbayhotel.co.uk
www.sunsetbayhotel.co.uk

Resident host: Mrs Margaret Holt

"MOORLANDS"

Hutton, Near Weston-super-Mare,
Somerset BS24 9QH
Tel and Fax: 01934 812283
e-mail: margaret-holt@hotmail.co.uk
www.guestaccom.co.uk/35

Enjoy fine food and warm hospitality at this impressive late Georgian house set in landscaped gardens below the slopes of the Western Mendips. A wonderful touring centre, perfectly placed for visits to beaches, sites of special interest and historic buildings. Families with children particularly welcome; reduced terms and pony rides. Full central heating, open fire in comfortable lounge. Open all year. Bed and Breakfast from £23 per person.

North Down Farm

In tranquil, secluded surroundings on the Somerset/ Devon Border. Traditional working farm set in 150 acres of natural beauty with panoramic views of over 40 miles. M5 7 miles, Taunton 10 miles. All rooms tastefully furnished to high standard include en suite, TV, and tea/coffee facilities. Double, twin or single rooms available. Dining room and lounge with log fires for our guests' comfort; centrally heated and double glazed. Drying facilities. Delicious home produced food a speciality. Fishing, golf, horse riding and country sports nearby. Dogs welcome.

Bed and Breakfast from £29 pppn,
B&B and Evening Meal £225 weekly.
North Down Break: three nights B&B and Evening Meal £109 per person.
Jenny Cope, North Down Farm, Pyncombe Lane, Wiveliscombe, Taunton TA4 2BL • Tel & Fax: 01984 623730
e-mail: jennycope@btinternet.com • www.north-down-farm.co.uk

English Tourism Council ◆◆◆◆ GUEST ACCOMMODATION

Silver SILVER AWARD

Staffordshire

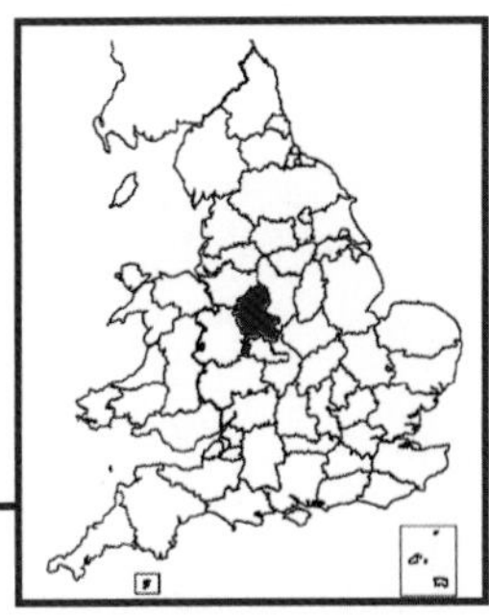

OFFLEY GROVE FARM Adbaston, Eccleshall, Staffs ST20 0QB • Tel/Fax: 01785 280205

You'll consider this a good find! Quality accommodation and excellent breakfasts. Small traditional mixed farm surrounded by beautiful countryside. The house is tastefully furnished and provides all home comforts. Whether you are planning to book here for a break in your journey, stay for a weekend or take your holidays here, you will find something to suit all tastes among the many local attractions. Situated on the Staffordshire/ Shropshire borders we are convenient for Alton Towers, Stoke-on-Trent, Ironbridge, etc. Reductions for children. Play area for children. Open all year. Many guests return.

Bed and Breakfast all en suite from £26pp • Self-catering cottages available • Brochure on request.

e-mail: enquiries@offleygrovefarm.co.uk • www.offleygrovefarm.co.uk

200-year-old working family farm overlooking the Churnet Valley offering very comfortably furnished accommodation in four en suite bedrooms and family rooms in a converted barn. Within easy reach of the Potteries, Peak District and Alton Towers (less than 3 miles). Non-smoking. Own entrance with access at any time.

Bed and Breakfast from £24. Special short breaks available.

Mrs D. Bickle, Crowtrees Farm, Oakamoor, Stoke-on-Trent ST10 3DY
Tel & Fax: 01538 702260
e-mail: dianne@crowtreesfarm.co.uk
www.crowtreesfarm.co.uk

FHG Guides

publish a large range of well-known accommodation guides. We will be happy to send you details or you can use the order form at the back of this book.

Sam and Joan would like to invite you to stay in their 17th century stone-built farmhouse nestling in the Staffordshire Moorlands. Hollinhurst Farm is a working farm offering our visitors the opportunity of seeing a variety of free-ranging animals in a beautiful location.

A high standard of facilities is available for the discerning traveller - we offer a selection of rooms to cater to your needs including ground floor accommodation. Twin, double and family rooms available, all equipped with TV and tea/coffee making facilities, most of our rooms are en suite and have panoramic views. Within easy reach of the M6 and A50.

English Tourism Council ♦♦♦ GUEST ACCOMMODATION

Hollinhurst Farm Bed & Breakfast
Park Lane, Endon, Stoke-on-Trent ST9 9JB
Tel: 01782 502633 • e-mail: joan.hollinhurst@btconnect.com
www.smoothhound.co.uk/hotels/hollinhurst

TAMWORTH. Mrs Jane Davies, Middleton House Farm, Middleton, Near Tamworth B78 2BD (01827 873474; Fax: 01827 872246).

Middleton House Farm is a family-run arable farm of 400 acres. The farmhouse dates back to the 18th century and, after extensive refurbishment, consists of six bedrooms, all individually and tastefully furnished to a very high standard with locally crafted old pine furniture. Situated just two miles from J9 of M42 opposite the Belfry Golf Course, 15 minutes from Birmingham and NEC, 10 minutes from Tamworth (Castle, Snowdome and Drayton Manor). Guests' own lounge and diningroom with individual tables. Bedrooms all with colour TV, hospitality tray, hairdryer and extras; full central heating. Ample car parking.

Rates: Bed and Breakfast from £30 per person.

- Non-smoking.

ETC ◆◆◆◆ *SILVER AWARD.*

e-mail: rob.jane@tinyonline.co.uk

www.middletonhousefarm.co.uk

Useful Guidance for Guests and Hosts

Every year literally thousands of holidays, short breaks and overnight stops are arranged through our guides, the vast majority without any problems at all. In a handful of cases, however, difficulties do arise about bookings, which often could have been prevented from the outset.

It is important to remember that when accommodation has been booked, both parties – guests and hosts – have entered into a form of contract. We hope that the following points will provide helpful guidance.

Guests

- **When enquiring about accommodation, be as precise as possible. Give exact dates, numbers in your party and the ages of any children.**
- **State the number and type of rooms wanted and also what catering you require – bed and breakfast, full board etc. Make sure that the position about evening meals is clear – and about pets, reductions for children or any other special points.**
- **Read our reviews carefully to ensure that the proprietors you are going to contact can supply what you want. Ask for a letter confirming all arrangements, if possible.**
- **If you have to cancel, do so as soon as possible. Proprietors do have the right to retain deposits and under certain circumstances to charge for cancelled holidays if adequate notice is not given and they cannot re-let the accommodation.**

Hosts

- **Give details about your facilities and about any special conditions. Explain your deposit system clearly and arrangements for cancellations, charges etc. and whether or not your terms include VAT.**
- **If for any reason you are unable to fulfil an agreed booking without adequate notice, you may be under an obligation to arrange suitable alternative accommodation or to make some form of compensation.**

Suffolk

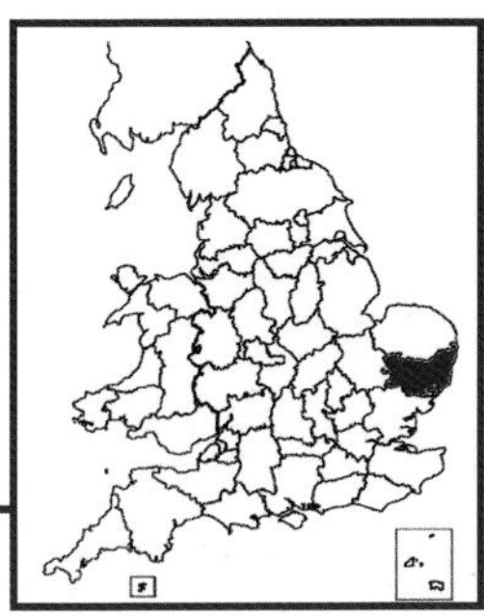

Signposted on B1119, Fiddlers Hall is a 14th century, moated, oak-beamed farmhouse set in a beautiful and secluded position. It is two miles from Framlingham Castle, 20 minutes' drive from Aldeburgh, Snape Maltings, Woodbridge and Southwold. A Grade II Listed building, it has lots of history and character. The bedrooms are spacious; one has en suite shower room, the other has a private bathroom. Use of lounge and colour TV. Plenty of parking space. Lots of farm animals kept. Traditional farmhouse cooking. Bed and Breakfast terms from £65 per room.

Mrs Jennie Mann, Fiddlers Hall, Cransford, Near Framlingham, Woodbridge IP13 9PQ • 01728 663729 • www.fiddlershall.co.uk

---

High House Farm ETC ◆◆◆

Cransford, Framlingham, Woodbridge, Suffolk IP13 9PD

Tel: 01728 663461 * Fax: 01728 663409
e-mail: b&b@highhousefarm.co.uk
website: www.highhousefarm.co.uk

Exposed oak beams ✦ inglenook fireplaces ✦ one double room, en suite and one large family room with double and twin beds and private adjacent bathroom ✦ children's cots ✦ high chairs ✦ books ✦ toys ✦ outside play equipment ✦ attractive semi-moated gardens ✦ farm and woodland walks

Explore the heart of rural Suffolk, local vineyards, Easton Farm Park, Framlingham and Orford Castles, Parham Air Museum, Saxtead Windmill, Minsmere, Snape Maltings, Woodland Trust and the Heritage Coast.

Bed and Breakfast from £25. Reductions for children and stays of three nights or more.

A comfortable modernised Edwardian house set in a large secluded garden located four miles south of Ipswich. Ideally situated to explore the Suffolk heritage coast and countryside, within easy reach of "Constable Country", Lavenham, Kersey, the historic market town of Bury St Edmunds plus many other picturesque locations.

Twin, double and single bedrooms; guests' bathroom with shower and toilet, lounge with TV. Good pub meals available in the village. Double and Twin from £26 per person per night. No smoking.

Mrs Rosanna Steward, High View, Back Lane, Washbrook, Ipswich IP8 3JA

Tel: 01473 730494

e-mail: rosanna3@suffolkholidays.com
www.suffolkholidays.com

A warm welcome awaits you at our exceptional moated farmhouse dating from the 13th Century, and set in extensive grounds including Ace all weather tennis court, in a superb spot two and a half miles north of Dennington, 13 miles from Woodbridge. A comfortable base with log fires in winter and plenty of beams. Close to Snape Maltings, the coast, Minsmere and many places of interest.

Accommodation comprises one double and one twin bedroom, or two twins let as singles; guests' own bathroom and sitting room. Good pubs nearby. Bread and marmalade home made.

Parking available • Children welcome • Non-smoking.
B&B from £25 single, £50 double/twin. ETC ◆◆◆

Grange Farm, Dennington, Woodbridge IP13 8BT

Tel: 01986 798388 • mobile: 07774 182835 • www.grangefarm.biz

Surrey

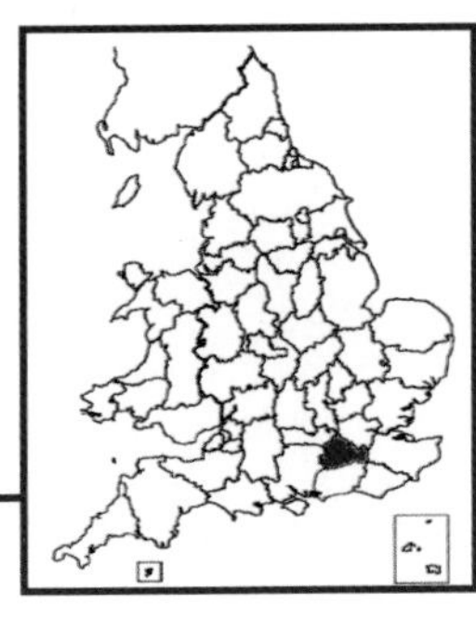

GATWICK. Carole and Adrian Grinsted, The Lawn Guest House, 30 Massetts Road, Horley RH6 7DF (01293 775751; Fax: 01293 821803).

The Lawn is a lovely Victorian house in a pleasant garden, two minutes from the centre of Horley and one-and-a-half miles from Gatwick. All rooms are en suite with colour TV, hairdryers, tea/coffee/chocolate trays and direct dial telephones. Horley, with its restaurants, shops and pubs is 150 yards away. The mainline railway station (300 yards) has services to London (Victoria 40 minutes) and Brighton (45 minutes). The Lawn is ideal for those 'overnighting' before or after a flight from Gatwick Airport. On site holiday parking by arrangement.

Rates: B&B from £58 per en suite double/twin room.

• A totally non-smoking establishment

ETC/AA/RAC ◆◆◆◆, *ETC SILVER AWARD, RAC SPARKLING DIAMOND AWARD.*

e-mail: info@lawnguesthouse.co.uk **www.lawnguesthouse.co.uk**

HASLEMERE (near). Mrs Langdale, Heath Hall Farm, Bowlhead Green, Godalming GU8 6NW (01428 682808).

Converted stable courtyard surrounded by its own farmland on edge of village of Bowlhead Green. Countryside charming with outstanding walking. Ideal base for many famous historic attractions - Losely House, Petworth House, Wisley RHS Garden, Arundel Castle, Midhurst (Cowdray Castle), historic Portsmouth. Plenty in locality to visit with children. Central for golf courses; polo at Midhurst. Close to South and North Downs. Relaxed atmosphere in house, domestic pets, cattle, sheep, ducks and chooks. All rooms have en suite bathrooms, TV, tea/coffee making facilities. Wire-free computer access, security encrypted. Three rooms on ground floor. Ample car parking. Warm welcome with friendly help and advice.

Rates: £30 per person per night, £10 per child (up to 14 years). Cot provided on application (£10 per night)

• Dogs welcome if kept under control and with prior arrangement • Children welcome • Open all year

e-mail: heathhallfarm@btinternet.co.uk **www.heathhallfarm.co.uk**

The Gables Guest House

50 Bonehurst Road, Horley RH6 8QJ

Tel: 01293 774553 • Fax: 01293 430006

The Gables Guest House is a family-run business and has 17 letting rooms of various sizes from single through to family accommodation (some en suite). Situated on the Sussex/Surrey border, we are not only convenient for Gatwick Airport and central London but also ideally placed for visits to local tourist attractions. Trains to Brighton are frequent and travel by road is quick and easy. Horley has a good selection of restaurants where you can enjoy a good quality evening meal.

Terms from £35 single room, £70 family room.
Airport parking available. Please enquire for further details.

e-mail: info@thegablesguesthousegatwick.co.uk • www.thegablesguesthousegatwick.co.uk

Gorse Cottage,

66 Balcombe Road,
Horley RH6 9AY • 01293 784402

Friendly, welcoming accommodation, two miles from Gatwick Airport in residential area with pubs and restaurants within walking distance. Five minutes from railway station serving London (45 minutes) and the South East. Early breakfast catered for, light breakfast served after 7.30am - cereal, scrambled eggs (free-range), toast, coffee, tea and juice. Centrally heated, pleasant room with tea and coffee making facilities. Terms £42 double/twin, £30 single. Long or short term accommodation offered for business people, terms to be negotiated.

OXTED. Pinehurst Grange Guest House, East Hill (A25), Oxted RH8 9AE (01883 716413).
Victorian ex-farmhouse offers one double, one twin and one single bedroom. All with washbasin, tea/coffee making facilities, colour TV; residents' dining room. Private parking. Close to all local amenities. Only 20 minutes' drive from Gatwick Airport and seven minutes' walk to the station with good trains to London/ Croydon. Also close to local bus and taxi service. There are many famous historic houses nearby including "Chartwell", "Knole", "Hever Castle", and "Penshurst Place". Very handy for Lingfield Park racecourse. WALKERS NOTE: only one mile from North Downs Way.

- No smoking

e-mail: laurie.rodgers@ntlworld.com

SURBITON. Mrs Menzies, Villiers Lodge, 1 Cranes Park, Surbiton KT5 8AB (020 8399 6000).
Excellent accommodation in small Guest House. Tea/coffee making facilities in all rooms. Close to trains and buses for London, Hampton Court, Kew, Windsor and coast. Ham House is a favourite visiting place and Merton Abbey Mills is a wonderful place for a day shopping and exploring.
Rates: £20 per person per night

Free or reduced rate entry to
Holiday Visits and Attractions – see our
READERS' OFFER VOUCHERS on pages 9-42

Sussex

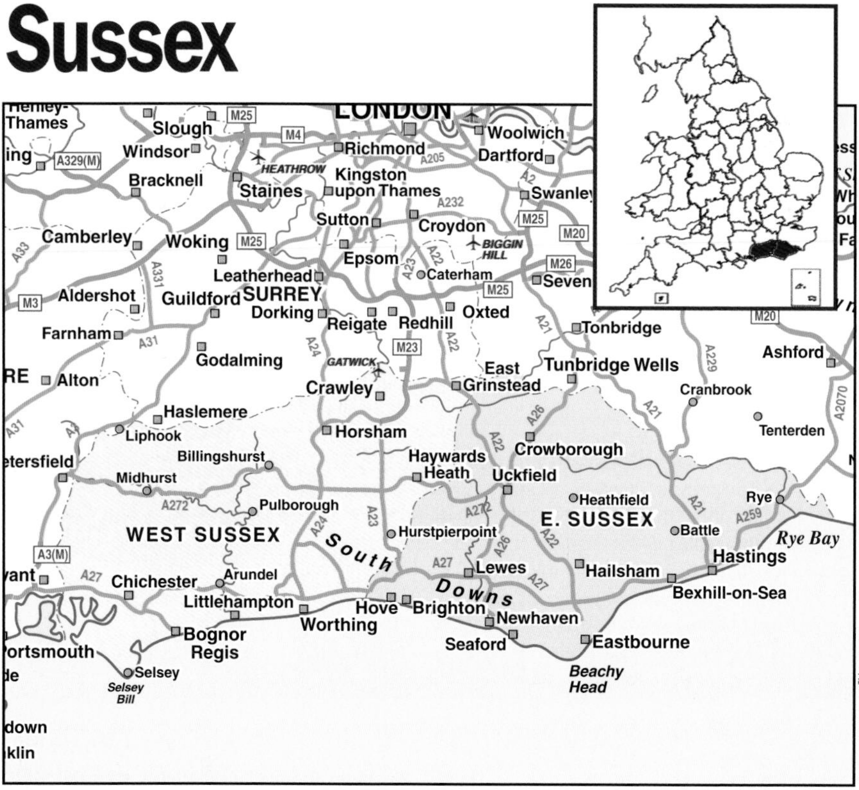

East Sussex

Brighton

Woodlands Farm

Burwash, Etchingham TN19 7LF

Woodlands Farm stands one third of a mile off the road, surrounded by fields and woods. This peaceful and beautifully modernised 16th century farmhouse offers comfortable and friendly accommodation. Sitting/dining room; two bathrooms, one en suite, double or twin-bedded rooms (one has four-poster bed) together with excellent farm fresh food. This is a farm of 108 acres with a variety of animals and is situated within easy reach of 20 or more places of interest to visit and half an hour from the coast.

Open all year • Central heating • Literature provided to help guests. Children welcome • Dogs allowed if sleeping in owner's car. Parking • Evening Meal optional • Non-smoking.

Bed and Breakfast from £35 single to £60 double.

Telephone or SAE please • Mrs E. Sirrell • Tel & Fax: 01435 882794

e-mail: liz_sir@lineone.net
www.SmoothHound.co.uk/hotels/woodlands.html

The Cherry Tree B&B

15 Silverdale Road, Lower Meads, Eastbourne BN20 7AJ

A small, charming Edwardian Guesthouse with a friendly and relaxed atmosphere. Named 'Small Business of the Year' in the Eastbournbe Business Awards, judges praised the attention paid to guests, making it feel like a 'home from home'. Elegantly furnished with stylish decor, all nine guest rooms are en suite, with TV, radio, wireless internet, hospitality tray with complimentary cookies, and English toiletries. The lounge is furnished with paintings and antiques, with a large variety of books and films, newspapers. magazines, board games, and chocolates. Ideal location, 5 minutes from major conference and theatre venues, restaurants, seafront, Beachy Head and the Downs.

On offer: reflexology treatments, theatre ticket booking, holiday planning service, buffet lunches, individual hampers, and 'breakout' meeting rooms. Totally non-smoking.

Tel: +44 (0)1323 722406
e-mail: lynda@cherrytree-eastbourne.co.uk
www.cherrytree-eastbourne.co.uk

Far End

139 Royal Parade, Eastbourne, East Sussex BN22 7LH
www.farendhotel.co.uk

From the moment you arrive you are assured of a warm welcome and real "home from home" atmosphere. Our centrally heated bedrooms with colour TV and tea/coffee making facilities are tastefully decorated, most have en suite facilities and sea views. Residents have their own lounge and private car park. Enjoy freshly prepared traditional home cooking. Special diets can be catered for. Credit cards accepted.

Tel: 01323 725666
Tim and Karen Camp

We are adjacent to the popular Princes Park with boating lake, lawns, bowling greens and pitch'n'putt, close by you can enjoy sailing, fishing, bowling, tennis and swimming. We are in easy reach of Beachy Head, the South Downs and Newhaven. We will be delighted to provide information on the many local attractions and services, and shall do our best to make your stay as memorable and pleasant as possible.

Bed and Breakfast from £23
Evening Meal available.
Low season short breaks.
Please call or write for colour brochure.

AA

• • • some fun days out in EAST SUSSEX

Drusillas Park, Alfriston • 01323 874100 • www.drusillas.co.uk
Michelham Priory, Hailsham • 01323 844224 • www.sussexpast.co.uk
Ashdown Forest Llama Park, Forest Row • 01825 712040 • www.llamapark.co.uk

Situated in quiet private country lane one mile north of the market town of Hailsham with its excellent amenities including modern sports centre and leisure pool, surrounded by footpaths across open farmland. Ideal for country lovers. Dogs and children welcome. The coast at Eastbourne, South Downs, Ashdown Forest and 1066 country are all within easy access.

The non-smoking accommodation comprises one twin room, double room en suite; family room en suite and tea/coffee making facilities. Bed and Breakfast from £22. Reductions for children.

Tel & Fax: 01323 841227
www.longleysfarmcottage.co.uk

David and Jill Hook, Longleys Farm Cottage, Harebeating Lane, Hailsham BN27 1ER

Bolebroke Castle

Henry VIII's hunting lodge, Bolebroke Castle is set on a beautiful 30 acre estate with lakes, woodlands and views to Ashdown Forest, where you will find 'Pooh Bridge'. Antiques and beamed ceilings add to the atmosphere. Four-poster suite available. B&B or Self-Catering options. Please call for our brochure.

In the heart of "Winnie the Pooh" country.

AA ◆◆◆◆ www.bolebrokecastle.co.uk

Bolebroke Castle, Hartfield, East Sussex TN7 4JJ
Tel: 01892 770061

Westwood Farm

Farm with pigs, sheep, chickens, etc. Quiet rural location off country lane half-a-mile from B2093 approximately two miles from seafront and town centre. Golf course nearby. Central position for visiting places of interest to suit all ages. Elevated situation with outstanding views over Brede Valley.
Double, twin, family rooms with en suite and private facilities. Colour TV, tea/coffee in all rooms, two bedrooms on ground floor. Full English breakfast. Off-road parking.
Bed and Breakfast from £22.50 to £32.50pp for two persons sharing. Reduced rates for weekly booking. Also available six-berth self-catering caravan – details on request.

Mr & Mrs S. York
Westwood Farm
Stonestile Lane
Hastings
TN35 4PG

• Tel & Fax: 01424 751038 • mobile: 07837 271797
• e-mail: york@westwood-farm.fsnet.co.uk
• www.SmoothHound.co.uk/hotels/westwoodf.html

English Tourism Council ◆◆◆ GUEST ACCOMMODATION

Seafront family-run hotel, half-a-mile west of Hastings Pier. Spacious lounge, licensed bar, central heating throughout. Radio/room-call/baby-listening. En suite rooms with TV also available. Free access at all times. Unrestricted/disabled parking. In the heart of 1066 country close to Battle Abbey, Bodiam and Hever Castles, Kipling's Batemans and historic Cinque Ports plus Hastings Castle, Caves, Sealife Aquarium, local golf courses and leisure centres.

Wi-fi broadband access throughout • Non-smoking throughout hotel
Children welcome, half price when sharing room • Open all year

GRAND HOTEL, GRAND PARADE, ST LEONARDS, HASTINGS TN38 0DD
Tel & Fax: 01424 428510/0870 2257025
e-mail: petermann@grandhotelhastings.co.uk
www.grandhotelhastings.co.uk

B& B from £15
Evening Meal from £15

e-mail: info@littlesaltcote.co.uk

RYE. Barbara and Denys Martin, Little Saltcote, 22 Military Road, Rye TN31 7NY (01797 223210; Fax: 01797 224474). Situated in a quiet road, just ten minutes' walk from the centre of medieval Rye, Little Saltcote is an Edwardian family home which offers off-road parking and five comfortable rooms (one at ground floor), all with TV/DVD, radio and beverage tray. We welcome families and are pleased to offer tourist advice or arrange bike hire. Ideally located for touring Sussex and Kent's varied attractions, including everything from sandy beaches to castles, historic houses and gardens. Rates include acclaimed full English or vegetarian breakfast.

Rates: from £30 per person.

• Pets welcome by arrangement • No smoking

AA ◆◆◆◆

www.littlesaltcote.co.uk

West Sussex

Arundel

Woodacre offers Bed and Breakfast in a traditional family home with accommodation for up to 10-12 guests. The house is set in a beautiful garden surrounded by woodland. We are well positioned for Chichester, Arundel, Goodwood and the seaside and easily accessible from the A27. Our rooms are clean and spacious and two are on the ground floor. We serve a full English breakfast in our conservatory or diningroom overlooking the garden. Plenty of parking space. Everyone is very welcome. Bed and Breakfast from £27.50 per person. Credit cards accepted. Pets welcome.

Mrs Vicki Richards, Woodacre, Arundel Road, Fontwell,
Arundel BN18 0QP • 01243 814301
e-mail: wacrebb@aol.com • www.woodacre.co.uk

A charming 17th century Priory restored to its former glory with a blend of historic charm. Situated in a picturesque rural village close to Bognor Regis, Chichester, Arundel, Goodwood, Fontwell and within easy access of Portsmouth, Brighton, Continental ferry port and all major commuting routes. Facilities include superb en suite rooms equipped to 4 star standard, four-poster water bed with jacuzzi bath, secluded outdoor swimming pool, Cordon Bleu cuisine, homemade bread and jams. Residential licence. Open all year.

Single £35, doubles from £27.50 to £35 per person per night inclusive of full English Breakfast

Deborah S. Collinson, The Old Priory, 80 North Bersted Street, Bognor Regis PO22 9AQ
01243 863580 • Fax: 01243 826597 • e-mail: old.priory@btconnect.com

Broxmead Paddock

A warm welcome awaits you at this country-style B&B set in 2½ acres of land in an Area of Outstanding Natural Beauty in the Sussex Downs. Relax in our garden with a cream tea, listen to the birds, walk through the woods and along the numerous footpaths and take time out to recharge your batteries. Alternatively we are close to several National Trust properties, only 15 minutes from Brighton, 20 minutes from Gatwick Airport and only 50 minutes from London.

Single, twin, double and family rooms available, all rooms have private bathroom, TV, tea/coffee facilities and central heating. Children welcome - cot and high chair available. Open all year with the exception of Christmas and New Year.

Bed and full English breakfast from £20.

Broxmead Paddock, Broxmead Lane, Bolney, Haywards Heath RH17 5RG • 01444 881458 • Fax: 01444 881491
e-mail: broxmeadpaddock@hotmail.com
www.broxmeadpaddock.eclipse.co.uk

"Meadowhills"

Stedham, Midhurst, West Sussex GU29 0PT
Tel: 01730 812609 or Mobile: 07776 262147

Built in 1908 this small, comfortable, country estate is set in its own grounds of 25 acres with magnificent views over the South Downs.

Activities include Fishing Rights • Walkers' Paradise • Riding Stables nearby • 20 miles to South Coast • Golf • Polo • Leisure Centres • Horse Racing at Fontwell and Goodwood.

Places of interest include Uppark • The Weald & Downland Open Air Museum • Petworth House and other National Trust Properties • Chichester Festival Theatre.

Call or write for further information and tariff • www.meadowhills.co.uk

• • • some fun days out in WEST SUSSEX

Weald & Downland Museum, Chichester • 01243 811363 • www.wealddown.co.uk
Arundel Castle, Arundel • 01903 882173 • www.arundelcastle.org
Knockhatch Adventure Park, Hailsham • 01323 442051 • www.knockhatch.com

Tyne & Wear

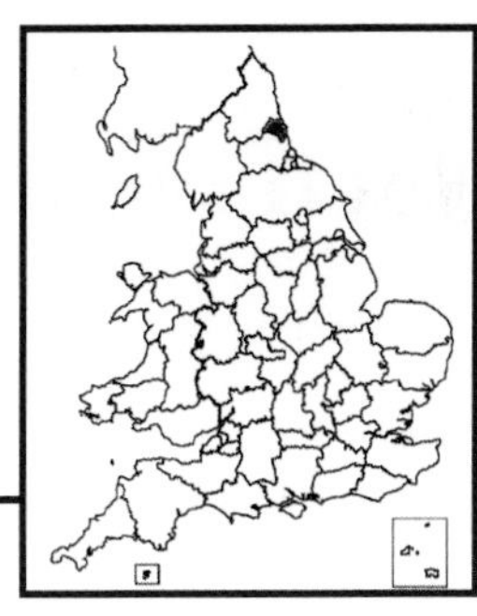

Warwickshire

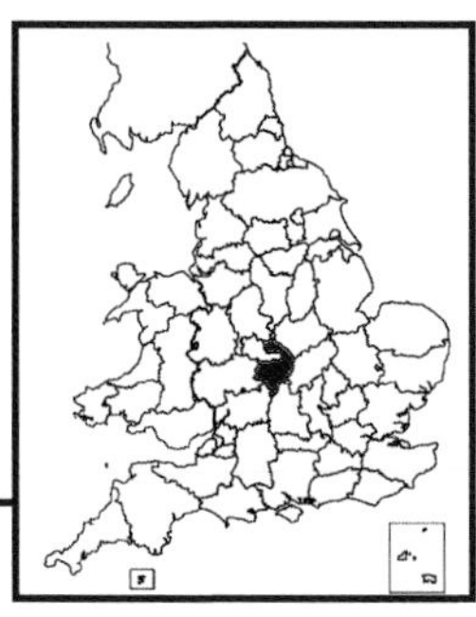

The Globe Hotel

54 Birmingham Road, Alcester B49 5EG
Tel & Fax: 01789 763287

A warm and friendly hotel in the historic market town of Alcester (seven miles from Stratford-upon-Avon). Stylish and spacious en suite bedrooms with remote-control TV, radio alarm clock, direct dial telephones, modem connection and hospitality trays. Ideally placed for Stratford-upon-Avon, motorways M40/42 and M5, Airport/NEC (30 minutes) and touring the Cotswolds.

AA ♦♦♦♦ Guest Accommodation

English Tourism Council ♦♦♦♦ Guest Accommodation

Single room from £49.50 • Double/twin room £62.50 • Family suite £79.50 .
Rates include breakfast • Totally refurbished in 2000.

www.theglobehotel.com

Sambourne Hall Farm

Beautiful 16th Century Farmhouse set in 500 acres of farmland in picturesque village. Large comfortable bedrooms, own sitting room. Walled garden. Excellent local pubs nearby. Coughton Court one mile. Ragley Hall five miles and Stratford-upon-Avon 10 miles. Ideal for business or vacation. National Exhibition Centre and Cotswolds easy access.

Terms from £40 single, £50-£55 double.

Mrs Hammersley, Sambourne Hall Farm, Sambourne, Alcester B96 6NZ • 01527 852151

Hollyhurst GUEST HOUSE

A comfortable Victorian house close to the town centre and a pleasant stroll from Kenilworth Castle. A market town with excellent restaurants, located in the heart of the Warwickshire countryside, Kenilworth is well connected by road and convenient for the NEC, Stoneleigh Park and the University of Warwick. You'll find the Hollyhurst perfect as a business base or holiday stopover. In either case we offer real hospitality and home comforts in our seven-bedroom guest house. Four rooms have en suite/private facilities and there is private parking for up to seven vehicles.

AA ♦♦♦ Guest Accommodation

No smoking • No pets
Bed and Breakfast from £25 per person

Trudi and Ken Wheat, The Hollyhurst Guest House,
47 Priory Road, Kenilworth CV8 1LL
Tel: 01926 853882 • Fax: 01926 853882
e-mail: admin@hollyhurstguesthouse.co.uk
www.hollyhurstguesthouse.co.uk

Hill Farm

Guests are welcome all year round to this comfortable, centrally heated farmhouse on a 350 acre mixed working farm. Ideally situated for Warwick, Coventry, Stratford-upon-Avon, Leamington Spa, Royal Showground, Birmingham, NEC and the Cotswolds.

Three pretty double bedrooms and two twin rooms with washbasins, tea and coffee facilities and TV. Some are en suite. Guests' sittingroom with colour TV; lovely conservatory for breakfast dining and excellent Breakfast Menu. Car preferable, ample parking.

Farm Stay UK member. FHG past Diploma Winner. Bed and Breakfast from £25-£35pp

Mrs R. Gibbs, Hill Farm, Lewis Road, Radford Semele, Leamington Spa CV31 1UX

www. hillfarm.info Tel: 01926 337571

Comfortable family Guest House situated at the town end of Evesham Road on the B439 (Bidford). 10 minutes' walk to River Avon, Shakespearean properties, theatre. One hour's drive to Cotswolds. Tea-making facilities and TV in bedrooms; centrally heated. Pets in room. Parking, though car not essential. Lift from bus or train station by arrangement.

Bed and Breakfast: room with shower, washbasin £20pp
en suite toilet, shower, washbasin £22.50pp.
Weekly terms £120-£140. Evening Meals £10.00 extra.
Single person supplement £10 pppn.

Mrs Hazel Mellor, ARRANDALE, 208 Evesham Road, Stratford-upon-Avon CV37 9AS
Tel: (01789) 267112 • www.arrandale.netfirms.com

Holly Tree Cottage

Birmingham Road, Pathlow, Stratford-upon-Avon CV37 0ES
Tel & Fax: 01789 204461

Period cottage dating from 17th Century, with antiques, paintings, collection of porcelain, fresh flowers, tasteful furnishings and friendly atmosphere. Picturesque gardens, orchard, paddock and pasture with wildlife and extensive views over open countryside. Situated 3 miles north of Stratford-upon-Avon towards Henley-in-Arden on A3400. Rooms have television, radio/alarm, hospitality trays and hairdryers. Breakfasts are a speciality. Pubs and restaurants nearby. Ideally located for Theatre, Shakespeare Country, Heart of England, Cotswolds, Warwick Castle, Blenheim Palace and National Trust Properties. Well situated for National Exhibition Centre, Birmingham and National Agricultural Centre, Stoneleigh. Children welcome, pets by arrangement. Non-smoking. Bed and Breakfast from £30 per person.

e-mail: john@hollytree-cottage.co.uk • www.hollytree-cottage.co.uk

Visit the FHG website
www.holidayguides.com
for details of the wide choice of accommodation featured in the full range of FHG titles

West Midlands

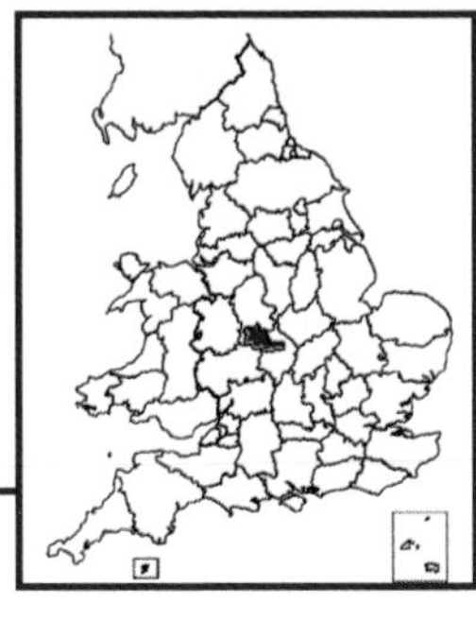

The Hollies Guest House

Kenilworth Road, Hampton-in-Arden, Solihull B92 0LW
01675 442941/442681
e-mail: info@theholliesguesthouse.co.uk
www.theholliesguesthouse.co.uk

Just a short drive from the NEC, The Hollies provides excellent Bed & Breakfast accommodation in 10 en suite bedrooms, all with colour TV and tea/coffee making facilities. Our friendly hospitality makes guests feel relaxed and at home, and there is a visitors' lounge and 'honesty' bar.

THE KINFAYRE B&B

41 High Street, Kinver, Stourbridge, West Midlands DY7 6HF
Tel: 01384 872565 • Mobile: 07714 105325.
e-mail: saxanjax@hotmail.co.uk

The Kinfayre B&B merges enthusiasm with experience to produce a high level of service for all its guests.

All our rooms are clean and comfortable, and a pleasant breakfast is assured, following a good nights sleep!

B&B: Single £38.50, Double/Twin £48.50
Double/twin and single rooms available.

ETC ◆◆◆◆ *SILVER AWARD.*

TANWORTH-IN-ARDEN. Grange Farm, Forde Hall Lane, Tanworth-in-Arden, Solihull B94 5AX (01564 742911; Mobile: 07771 704157).

A warm welcome awaits you at this peaceful 17th century farmhouse, set in 200 acres of beautiful countryside with footpaths and wildlife pools. Grange Farm has sloping floors, beams and log fires. There are three tastefully furnished bedrooms, two en suite, and all with colour TV, tea/coffee making facilities, radio/clock alarms, and hairdryers. The house is centrally located for easy access to the NEC, NAC, Stratford-upon-Avon, the Cotswolds, Warwick and Worcester.

Rates: Bed and Breakfast from £35 per person double/twin, £45 single.

www.grange-farm.com

WOLVERHAMPTON. Featherstone Farm Hotel, New Road, Featherstone, Wolverhampton WV10 7NW (01902 725371; Fax: 01902 731741; mobile: 07836 315258).

This is a small, high-class country house hotel set in five acres of unspoiled countryside, only one mile from Junction 11 on the M6 or Junction 1 on the M54. The main house has eight en suite bedrooms with all the facilities one would expect in a hotel of distinction. Kings Repose Indian Restaurant, serving freshly prepared dishes, and licensed bar. Secure car park.

• Children and pets welcome. • Self-contained fully furnished cottages with maid service are also available.

ETC ★★★

e-mail: info@featherstonefarm.co.uk
www.featherstonefarm.co.uk

Wiltshire

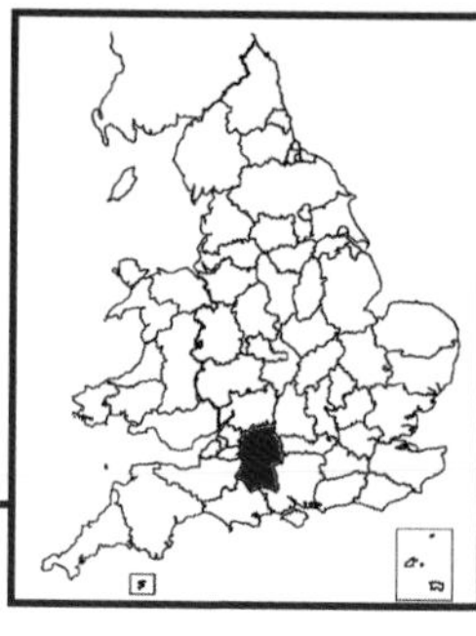

Park Farm Barn, Westrop, Corsham SN13 9QF

Converted 18th century tithe barn with newly constructed Cotswold-style B&B accommodation close by. Park Farm Barn has three en suite bedrooms which are light and spacious with apex ceilings and beams. Ideal base for the many interesting and historic places in and around Corsham, situated in the delightful hamlet of Westrop, one mile from Corsham and seven miles from Junction 17 on the M4. The National Trust village of Lacock is only a short drive away with a number of excellent pubs for evening meals. Castle Combe and Bradford-upon-Avon only 20 minutes, Bath ten miles.

Children welcome, cot and highchair available. No smoking. Parking.
Terms from £35 pppn single, £30 pppn double/twin.

ETC ◆◆◆◆, FARM STAY UK MEMBER.

Kate Waldron • Tel: 01249 715911 • Mobile: 07976 827083 • Fax: 01249 701107
e-mail: parkfarmbarn@btinternet.com • www.parkfarmbarn.co.uk

Littleton Lodge

Littleton Panell (A360), West Lavington, Devizes SN10 4ES
Tel: 01380 813131

AA ◆◆◆◆ Guest Accommodation

Superb Victorian family house set in one acre of private grounds, overlooking vineyard within pretty conservation village. Five minutes' drive from historic Devizes. All rooms en suite with beverage tray, TV and radio/alarms. Choice of scrumptious breakfast. Excellent meals are available at two pubs within five/ten minutes' walk. Stonehenge is only 15 minutes' drive and Littleton Lodge is an ideal base to explore the Wiltshire White Horses, prehistoric Avebury, Georgian Bath (40 mins), Salisbury (20 mins), the National Trust village of Lacock, as well as numerous country houses and gardens, including Longleat. Private parking.

Mastercard, Visa and Switch accepted.
Single occupancy from £45, Double from £60.

e-mail: stay@littletonlodge.co.uk
www.littletonlodge.co.uk

Lovett Farm • www.lovettfarm.co.uk

Enjoy traditional hospitality at our delightful farmhouse on a working farm just three miles from the historic town of Malmesbury with its wonderful Norman abbey and gardens and central for Cotswolds, Bath, Stratford, Avebury and Stonehenge.

Two attractive en suite bedrooms with delightful views, each with tea/coffee making facilities, colour TV and radio. Delicious full English breakfast served in our cosy dining room/lounge. Central heating throughout. Bed and Breakfast from £27.50. Credit cards accepted. Non-smoking accommodation. Open all year.

Mrs Susan Barnes

Lovett Farm, Little Somerford, Near Malmesbury SN15 5BP

Tel & Fax: 01666 823268 • Mobile: 07808 858612 • e-mail: sue@lovettfarm.co.uk

WERNHAM FARM

Clench Common, Marlborough, Wiltshire SN8 4DR

Tel: 01672 512236

e-mail: margglvsf@aol.com

This working farm is set in picturesque countryside on Wansdyke, off the A345. It is close to Marlborough, Avebury, Pewsey and the Kennet & Avon Canal.

Accommodation is available in two family bedrooms, one en suite and one with private bathroom.

Terms: £40 single, £55 double.

Five caravan and camping pitches are also available.

Jackie & James Macbeth

Manor Farm

Collingbourne Kingston, Marlborough, Wiltshire SN8 3SD

Tel: 01264 850859

e-mail: stay@manorfm.com

www.manorfm.com

Manor Farm B&B

- Attractive Grade II Listed farmhouse on working family farm, very easy to find, 12 minutes south of Marlborough on the A338 Salisbury Road.
- Our comfortable, spacious and well equipped rooms are all en suite or private, and include double, twin and family (for four).
- Sumptuous traditional, vegetarian, and other special diet breakfasts.
- Beautiful countryside with superb walking and cycling from the farm.
- Pleasure flights by helicopter from our private airstrip.
- Horses and pets welcome • Ample private parking
- Non-smoking • Credit cards welcome

B&B from £27 pppn

SALISBURY. Dawn and Alan Curnow, Hayburn Wyke Guest House, 72 Castle Road, Salisbury SP1 3RL (Tel & Fax: 01722 412627).

Hayburn Wyke is a Victorian house, situated adjacent to Victoria Park, and a ten minute riverside walk from the city centre. Salisbury and surrounding area have many places of interest to visit, including Salisbury Cathedral, Old Sarum, Wilton House and Stonehenge. Most bedrooms have en suite facilities, all have washbasin, television, and tea/coffee making equipment. Private car parking for guests. Credit cards and Switch accepted.

Rates: Bed and full English Breakfast from £24.

• Children are welcome at reduced rates. • Sorry, no pets (guide dogs an exception). • Open all year.

AA ◆◆◆

e-mail: hayburn.wyke@tinyonline.co.uk **www.hayburnwykeguesthouse.co.uk**

Spinney Farmhouse ~ Thoulstone, Chapmanslade, Westbury BA13 4AQ

Off A36, three miles west of Warminster; 16 miles from historic city of Bath. Close to Longleat, Cheddar and Stourhead. Reasonable driving distance to Bristol, Stonehenge, Glastonbury and the cathedral cities of Wells and Salisbury. Pony trekking and fishing available locally.

• Washbasins, tea/coffee-making facilities and shaver points in all rooms.
• Family room available. • Guests' lounge with colour TV.
• Central heating. • Children and pets welcome.
• Ample parking. • Open all year. • No smoking

Enjoy farm fresh food in a warm, friendly family atmosphere.
Bed and Breakfast from £23 per night. Reduction after 2 nights.
Evening Meal £12.

Telephone 01373 832412 • Madeline Hoskins & Family

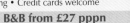

Worcestershire

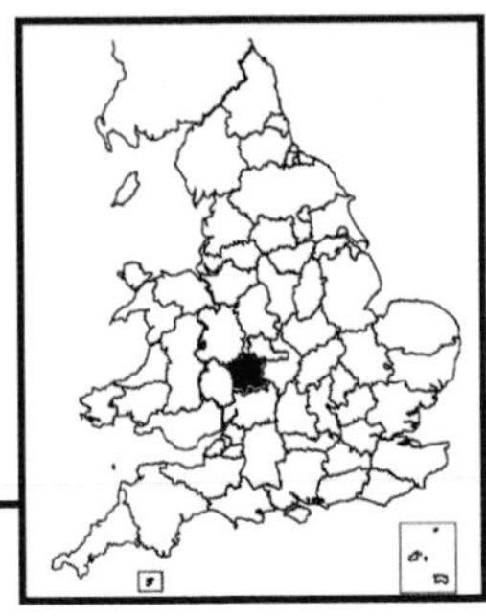

B&B from £26 to £35 single
£44 to £60 double

Croft Guest House, Bransford, Worcester WR6 5JD

16th-18th century part black-and-white cottage-style country house situated in the Teme Valley, four miles from Worcester and Malvern. Croft House is central for visiting numerous attractions in Worcester, Hereford, the Severn Valley and surrounding countryside. River and lake fishing are close by, and an 18-hole golf course is opposite. Three en suite guest rooms (two double, one family) and two with washbasins are available. All bedrooms are non-smoking. Rooms are double glazed and have colour TV, radio alarm and courtesy tray. TV lounge, residential licence. Dogs welcome by arrangement.

Full English breakfast and evening meals are prepared from home-grown/made or locally sourced produce.

Ann & Brian Porter • Tel: 01886 832227 • Fax: 01886 830037
e-mail: hols@crofthousewr6.fsnet.co.uk • www.croftguesthouse.com

BRICKBARNS, a 200-acre mixed farm, is situated two miles from Great Malvern at the foot of the Malvern Hills, 300 yards from the bus service and one-and-a half miles from the train. The house, which is 300 years old, commands excellent views of the Malvern Hills and guests are accommodated in one double, one single and one family bedrooms with washbasins; two bathrooms, shower room, two toilets; sittingroom and diningroom. Children welcome and cot and babysitting offered. Central heating. Car essential, parking. Open Easter to October for Bed and Breakfast from £20 nightly per person. Reductions for children and Senior Citizens. Birmingham 40 miles, Hereford 20, Gloucester 17, Stratford 35 and the Wye Valley is just 30 miles.

Mrs J.L. Morris, Brickbarns Farm, Hanley Road, Malvern Wells WR14 4HY
Tel: 016845 61775 • Fax: 01886 830037

Yorkshire

Note

All the information in this guide is given in good faith in the belief that it is correct. However, the publishers cannot guarantee the facts given in these pages, neither are they responsible for changes in ownership or facilities that may take place after the date of going to press.

Readers should always satisfy themselves that the facilities they require are available and that the terms, if quoted, still apply.

East Yorkshire

Rosebery House

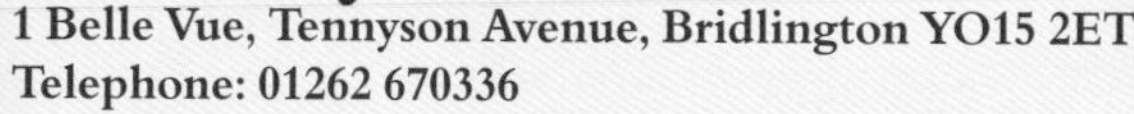

1 Belle Vue, Tennyson Avenue, Bridlington YO15 2ET
Telephone: 01262 670336

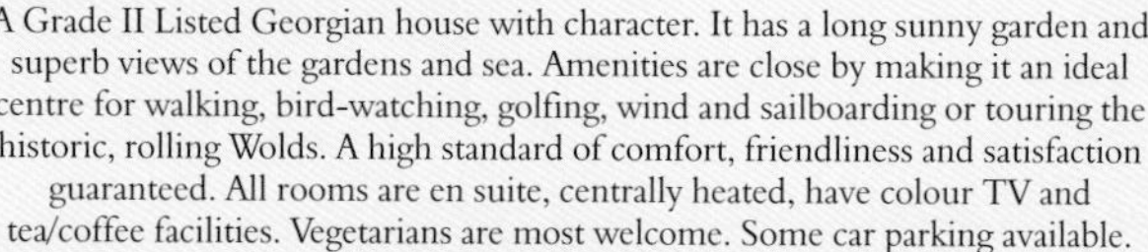

A Grade II Listed Georgian house with character. It has a long sunny garden and superb views of the gardens and sea. Amenities are close by making it an ideal centre for walking, bird-watching, golfing, wind and sailboarding or touring the historic, rolling Wolds. A high standard of comfort, friendliness and satisfaction guaranteed. All rooms are en suite, centrally heated, have colour TV and tea/coffee facilities. Vegetarians are most welcome. Some car parking available. Open all year except Christmas and New Year.

Bed and Breakfast from £22.50 per person.

Senior Supersaver October to June

Kelleythorpe Farm

Lovely Georgian farmhouse with large garden in idyllic setting overlooking a small lake, the source of the River Hull. Friendly atmosphere, attractive bedrooms with pretty chintzes. Centrally situated for York, the coast or the moors.

Mrs Tiffy Hopper
Kelleythorpe Farm
Driffield YO25 9DW

200-acre farm with pedigree Aberdeen Angus herd. Beef for sale in shop.

Bed and Breakfast from £22.
Children welcome.

01377 252297

North Yorkshire

THE BUCK INN

Chop Gate, Bilsdale, Middlesbrough TS9 7JL
Tel: 01642 778334 • www.buck-inn.co.uk

You are assured of a warm welcome at the Buck Inn, situated in a small, unspoilt village on the edge of the North York Moors, on the B1257 between Stokesley and Helmsley. The fully stocked bar offers well-kept ales and lagers, spirits and fine wines, and an excellent bar snack menu is served in a friendly atmosphere. An à la carte menu is available lunchtimes and evenings in the more formal, yet peaceful, surroundings of the dining area, and the freshly prepared dishes can be followed by a tempting choice of mouth-watering desserts.

Bed and Breakfast accommodation is available in comfortably furnished double and twin en suite rooms, all with colour television and refreshment tray.

ROWANTREE FARM is a family-run dairy farm situated in the heart of the North York Moors. Ideal walking and mountain biking area, with panoramic moorland views. Coast easily accessible. Our non-smoking home comprises one family room and one twin-bedded room, with private bathroom and private shower room, also full central heating, beverage tray, clock radio and hairdryer. Relax in our residents' lounge with colour TV/video. Ample car parking.

- *Children welcome; cot and high chair available.*
- *Good home cooking (vegetarians catered for), served in our separate dining room. Packed lunches available.*
- *B&B from £23; Evening Meal by prior arrangement.*

Mrs L. Tindall, Rowantree Farm, Ainthorpe, Whitby YO21 2LE • 01287 660396
e-mail: krbsatindall@aol.com • www.rowantreefarm.co.uk

Beautiful old farmhouse (pre 1750) situated in a lovely valley close to quiet roadside. Working farm set in 120 acres of pastureland and woods. Centre of National Park. Warm and friendly atmosphere. Diningroom/Lounge for guests with TV and books. Close to river, one mile from Glaisdale village and mainline railway, eight miles to Whitby, four miles steam railway and Heartbeat country. Both bedrooms have pretty decor and TV. One double/twin and one family room, both en suite. Full Yorkshire Breakfast. Packed lunches. All diets catered for. B&B from £23-£27. No pets, no smoking.

e-mail: egtonbanksfarm@agriplus.net
website: www.egtonbanksfarm.agriplus.net

EGTON BANKS FARM

✦Glaisdale, Whitby YO21 2QP✦
Tel: 01947 897289

Red House Farm

Listed Georgian farmhouse featured in "Houses of the North York Moors". Completely refurbished to the highest standards, retaining all original features. Bedrooms have bath/shower/toilet, central heating, TV and tea making facilities. Excellent walks straight from the doorstep. Friendly farm animals – a few cows, horses, geese and pretty free-roaming hens. One-and-a-half acres of gardens, sitting-out areas. Magnificent views. Interesting buildings – Listed barns now converted to 3 holiday cottages. Games room with snooker table. Eight miles from seaside/Whitby. Village pub within walking distance. Stabling available for horses/dogs. Non-smoking.

Tom and Sandra Spashett, Red House Farm, Glaisdale, Near Whitby YO21 2PZ • Tel & Fax: 01947 897242
e-mail: spashettredhouse@aol.com
www.redhousefarm.com

Homely, comfortable, Christian accommodation. Spacious stone built bungalow in beautiful Nidderdale which is very central for touring the Yorkshire Dales; Pateley Bridge two miles, Harrogate 14 miles, Ripon nine miles. Museums, rocks, caves, fishing, bird watching, beautiful quiet walks, etc all nearby. En suite rooms (one twin, two double), TV. Private lounge. Tea making facilities available. Choice of breakfast. Evening meals available one mile away. Ample parking space on this working farm. Open Easter to end of October.

English Tourism Council ♦♦♦ GUEST ACCOMMODATION

Mrs C.E. Nelson, Nidderdale Lodge Farm, Fellbeck, Pateley Bridge, Harrogate HG3 5DR • Tel: 01423 711677

A high standard of comfortable accommodation awaits you at The Coppice, with a reputation for excellent food and a warm friendly welcome. All rooms en suite with telephones. Quietly located off Kings Road, five minutes' walk from the elegant shops and gardens of the town centre. Just three minutes' walk from the Conference Centre. Ideal location to explore the natural beauty of the Yorkshire Dales. Midway stop Edinburgh–London.

Free Yorkshire touring map - ask for details.

Bed and Breakfast £38 single, £58 double, twin from £60, family from £68; Evening Meal £18.50.

The Coppice

9 Studley Road, Harrogate HG1 5JU
Tel: 01423 569626 • Fax: 01423 569005
e-mail: coppice@harrogate.com • www.harrogate.com/coppice

A beautifully situated 400 acre working stock farm with extensive views over Ryedale. We offer a friendly, family welcome with home made scones on arrival. A ground floor double en suite room is available and includes hospitality tray with home-made biscuits. Sittingroom with TV and open fire on chilly evenings, diningroom with patio doors to conservatory. You will be the only guests so the breakfast time is up to you. Full English Breakfast includes home-made bread and preserves.

Terms from £25 per person.

Excellent eating places in Helmsley and the nearby villages. York, Castle Howard and the North York Moors within half-an-hour drive.

Barn Close Farm

Rievaulx, Helmsley, North Yorkshire YO62 5LH

01439 798321

Mrs J. Milburn

BARN CLOSE FARM is nicely situated in the North York Moors National Park. This family farm in beautiful surroundings offers homely accommodation to holidaymakers all year round. Within easy reach of Rievaulx Abbey and many other places of interest, it is an ideal centre for tourists.

Pony trekking nearby.

Good walking terrain!

Highly commended for good food.

Two double rooms, one en suite; bathroom; toilets; sitting room and dining room.

Bed and Breakfast from £25 to £35, Evening Dinner £15.

"WHICH?" RECOMMENDED. "DAILY TELEGRAPH" RECOMMENDED.

THE NEW INN MOTEL

Main Street
Huby
York YO61 1HQ
Tel: 01347 810219
AA ◆◆◆

Nestling behind the New Inn, this modern, motel-style accommodation has a quiet location in the village of Huby, 9 miles north of York. Comfortable bedrooms are spacious and neatly furnished, and breakfast, which makes use of locally sourced produce, is served in the cosy

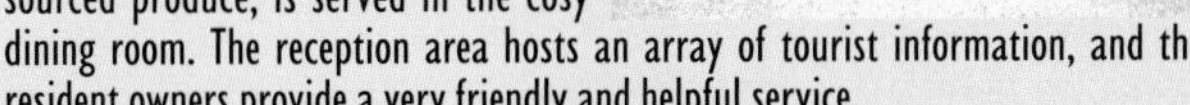

dining room. The reception area hosts an array of tourist information, and the resident owners provide a very friendly and helpful service.

8 en suite non-smoking ground floor rooms of which 3 are family rooms • Parking available
Prices from £35-£45 (single) and £60 (double) • Tea/coffee, central heating and TV

www.newinnmotel.co.uk • enquiries@newinnmotel.freeserve.co.uk

NEWTON HOUSE, KNARESBOROUGH

Spacious, delightful accommodation and wonderful, freshly cooked breakfast. This 18th century building is complemented by newly refurbished and individually decorated en suite bedrooms which are exceptionally well equipped, some with king-size or four-poster beds. Family rooms available. Private parking. Ideally situated for Harrogate, York and the Yorkshire Dales. Winner of the AA Pet Friendly Award.

Tel: 01423 863539

AA 4 Red Diamonds, VisitBritain Gold Award

e-mail: newtonhouse@btinternet.com
www.newtonhouseyorkshire.com

• • • some fun days out in NORTH YORKSHIRE

RHS Garden - Harlow Carr, Harrogate • 01423 565418 • www.rhs.org.uk
Ripley Castle & Gardens, Harrogate • 01423 770152 • www.ripleycastle.co.uk
Yorkshire Air Museum, Elvington • 01904 608595 • www.yorkshireairmuseum.co.uk
Ingleton Waterfalls Walk, Ingleton • 01756 795621 • www.ingletonwaterfallswalk.co.uk
Kinderland Fun, Play & Activity Park, Scarborough • 01723 354555 • wwww.kinderland.co.uk

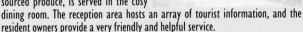

Sunnyridge •• ARGILL FARM

Harmby, Leyburn DL8 5HQ • Tel: 01969 622478
Mrs Hilary Richardson • richah@freenet.co.uk

Situated on a small sheep farm in Wensleydale, Sunnyridge is a spacious bungalow in an outstanding position. Magnificent views are enjoyed from every room. In the heart of the Yorkshire Dales and the midst of Herriot country, it is an ideal centre for exploring the wide variety of activities and attractions; or a restful stop-over for travellers. Sample Yorkshire hospitality and relax in comfortable ground floor accommodation comprising one double or twin bedroom and one family/double/twin-bedded room, both en suite, each with colour TV, tea/coffee facilities and hairdryer.

Non-smoking • Guest lounge • Children welcome • Pets by arrangement • B&B from £24

Golden Lion HOTEL

Market Place, Leyburn, North Yorkshire DL8 5AS

At the gateway to Wensleydale, this splendid hotel dates from 1765, although it has been tastefully modernised. Light meals and afternoon teas are served in the bars, and the restaurant with its picture windows and colourful murals is a popular venue. Excellent accommodation is available in rooms with bathrooms en suite, television, telephone, radio and tea and coffee-makers. A lift operates to all floors and many rooms are specially adapted to the needs of disabled guests. Within easy walking distance is the little town of Middleham on the River Ure which is well known as a racehorse training centre.

Tel: 01969 622161
Fax: 01969 623836
info@goldenlionleyburn.co.uk

One twin and one double en suite rooms, one single; all with tea/coffee making facilities and TV; alarm clock/radio and hairdryer also provided; diningroom; central heating.

Tangalwood

Roxby Road,
Thornton-le-Dale,
Pickering
YO18 7SX

ETC ★★★★

Very clean and comfortable accommodation with good food. Situated in a quiet part of this picturesque village, which is in a good position for Moors, "Heartbeat" country, coast, North York Moors Railway, Flamingo Park Zoo and forest drives, mountain biking and walking. Good facilities for meals provided in the village. Open Easter to October for Bed and Breakfast from £24 each. Private car park. Secure motorbike and cycle storage.

TELEPHONE: 01751 474688 • www.accommodation.uk.net/tangalwood

Banavie is a large semi-detached house set in a quiet part of the picturesque village of Thornton-le-Dale, one of the prettiest villages in Yorkshire with its famous thatched cottage and bubbling stream flowing through the centre. We offer our guests a quiet night's sleep and rest away from the main road, yet only four minutes' walk from the village centre. One large double or twin bedroom and two double bedrooms, all tastefully decorated with en suite facilities, colour TV, hairdryer, shaver point etc. and tea/coffee making facilities. There is a large guest lounge, tea tray on arrival. A real Yorkshire breakfast is served in the dining room. Places to visit include Castle Howard, Eden Camp, North Yorkshire Moors Railway, Goathland ("Heartbeat"), York etc. There are three pubs, a bistro and a fish and chip shop for meals. Children and dogs welcome. Own keys. Car parking at back of house.

B&B from £24 - £29 pppn • SAE please for brochure • Welcome Host • Hygiene Certificate held • No Smoking • Mrs Ella Bowes

BANAVIE, ROXBY ROAD, THORNTON-LE-DALE, PICKERING YO18 7SX
Tel: 01751 474616 • e-mail: info@banavie.co.uk • www.banavie.uk.com

RICHMOND. Mrs S. Lawson, Stonesthrow, Dalton, Near Richmond DL11 7HS (01833 621493; mobile: 07970 655726). With a welcoming fire, private garden and conservatory, Stonesthrow offers you a friendly, family atmosphere. Unmistakable Yorkshire hospitality from the moment you arrive – we greet you with a tea or coffee and home made cakes. Situated midway between the towns of Richmond and Barnard Castle, it offers you an ideal base for exploring the Yorkshire Dales, Teesdale, and York. Stonesthrow, has well appointed bedrooms with TV, tea/coffee facilities and full central heating. Off-road parking.

Rates: B&B £20pppn double, £25 single.

- Non-smoking • Sorry, no pets
- Children eight and over are welcome.

Whashton Springs Farm

Mrs Jane Turnbull

★★★★ GUEST ACCOMMODATION

Silver SILVER AWARD

Richmond, North Yorkshire DL11 7JS • Tel: 01748 822884 • Fax: 01748 826265

Family working farm in the heart of Herriot Country. Delightful Georgian farmhouse with unusual bay windows, overlooking lawn and stream.

Yorkshire breakfasts using local produce.
All bedrooms en suite (one romantic four-poster).
Historic Richmond 3 miles.
Open all year except Christmas.
Children over 5 welcome. No smoking.

whashtonsprings@btconnect.com
www.whashtonsprings.co.uk

Browson Bank Farmhouse Accommodation

A newly converted granary set in 300 acres of farmland. The accommodation consists of three very tastefully furnished double/twin rooms all en suite, tea and coffee making facilities, colour TV and central heating. A large, comfortable lounge is available to relax in. Full English breakfast served. Situated six miles West of Scotch Corner (A1). Ideal location to explore the scenic countryside of Teesdale and the Yorkshire Dales and close to the scenic towns of Barnard Castle and Richmond. Terms from £22.50 per night.

Browson Bank Farmhouse, Browson Bank, Dalton, Richmond DL11 7HE
Tel: (01325) 718504 or (01325) 718246

Holmedale

A warm and friendly welcome awaits you at Holmedale, our Georgian home. Dalton is a lovely, peaceful village midway between Richmond and Barnard Castle, seven miles west of Scotch Corner, an ideal stop between the South and Scotland.

Let your holiday start here

Full central heating • Comfortable sitting room with open fire when chilly • Personal attention • Good home cooking
One double en suite • One twin with bathroom
Tea/coffee making facilities
From £21 per person

Mrs L. Brooks, Holmedale, Dalton, Richmond DL11 7HX
Tel: 01833 621236

The most beautifully situated accommodation

Five ground floor en suite rooms round a pretty courtyard. All our rooms are full of character - oak beams etc., with modern facilities, all with views of the countryside. Private fishing lake. Terms from £60 to £75.

Details from

Mrs L. Hitchen, St George's Court, Old Home Farm, High Grantley, Ripon HG4 3PJ

Tel: 01765 620618

♦♦♦♦

RIPON near. Mrs Julie Bailes, Cherry Croft, Bedale Lane, Wath, Ripon HG4 5ER (01765 640318).
Cherry Croft is situated in the quiet village of Wath, approx. three miles north of the historic market town of Ripon; two miles from A1(M). Accommodation comprises two double rooms with TV and tea making facilities. All rooms are on the ground floor. Ideal location for touring the Dales and Herriot Country.
Rates: £20 per person, Bed & Breakfast.

ROBIN HOOD'S BAY. Mrs B. Reynolds, 'South View', Sledgates, Fylingthorpe, Whitby YO22 4TZ (01947 880025).
Pleasantly situated, comfortable accommodation in own garden with sea and country views. Ideal for walking and touring. Close to the moors, within easy reach of Whitby, Scarborough and many more places of interest. There are two double rooms, lounge and diningroom. Parking spaces. Phone for further details.
Rates: Bed and Breakfast from £22, including bedtime drink.

Photo courtesy Scarborough Borough Council

Brinka House, 2 Station Square, Ravenscar, Scarborough YO13 0LU • 01723 871470

Situated in Ravenscar – midway between Scarborough and Whitby with stunning views across to Robin Hood's Bay and surrounded by the moors. The village boasts a variety of walks, cycle tracks, golf course, pony and llama trekking and a bus service that runs from the front door into town.

A warm welcome and tasty breakfast awaits everyone, vegetarians and special diets are catered for. We have a romantic double room with a large corner bath en suite, and a twin/family room en suite. All rooms have TV, drinks facilities and sea views.

Rates: £22.50 per person per night, £25 for single room.

www.brinkahousebedandbreakfast.co.uk

SCARBOROUGH. Mrs L.M. Coates, Howdale, 121 Queens Parade, Scarborough YO12 7HU (Freephone: 0800 056 6622; Tel & Fax: 01723 372696).
Overlooks beautiful North Bay. Close to town. Licensed. Excellent food. Clean, comfortable rooms with colour TV, tea/coffee making facilities and hairdryer. Most en suite.
Rates: from £23 per person.
ETC ◆◆◆◆
e-mail: mail@howdalehotel.co.uk
www.howdalehotel.co.uk

Simon and Val extend a warm Yorkshire welcome and invite you to share their charming farmhouse in the pleasant countryside between Scarborough and Filey. All our bedrooms are tastefully decorated and have en suite facilities, colour TV, and well-stocked beverage trays. Hearty breakfasts that will keep you going all day are served in the conservatory overlooking the lovely garden. Our 350-acre farm has diversified and we now have the Stained Glass Centre and tearoom which are open to visitors. Cayton offers easy access to Scarborough, Filey, Whitby, the North York Moors, and York.

Killerby Cottage Farm

Simon and Val Green, Killerby Cottage Farm, Killerby Lane, Cayton, Scarborough YO11 3TP
Tel: 01723 581236 • Fax: 01723 585146
e-mail: val@stainedglasscentre.co.uk
www.smoothhound.co.uk/hotels/killerby

Angela & Roland Thompson, THE WINDMILL BED AND BREAKFAST
Mill Street, Off Victoria Road, Scarborough YO11 1SZ • 01723 372735

18th Century Windmill Non-Smoking establishment offering quality accommodation 5 minutes from town centre, station and Stephen Joseph Theatre. We have 9 en suite rooms, with a mix of double, family, twin and four-poster rooms at varying prices. All our rooms have tea/coffee facilities and remote-control colour TV, and are centrally heated. We also have 2 lovely apartments in the Windmill itself where you can stay on a bed and breakfast or self-catering basis. There is private parking in the courtyard for up to 7 cars.

Bed and Breakfast from £30.00 per person per night.

Children aged 2-14 £10; children under 2 £5.00 when sharing with two adults.

www.windmill-hotel.co.uk • • • • • e-mail: info@windmill-hotel.co.uk

Distinctively Different Peaceful and relaxing retreat, octagonal in design and set in two acres of private grounds with 360° panoramic views of the National Park and sea. An ideal centre for walking or touring. Two miles from Scarborough and within easy reach of Whitby, York and the beautiful North Yorkshire countryside. Tastefully decorated en suite centrally heated rooms with colour TV and all with superb views. Attractive dining room, guest lounge and relaxing conservatory. Traditional English breakfast, including vegetarian. Licensed. Private parking facilities. Personal service and warm, friendly Yorkshire hospitality. Bed and Breakfast from £25 to £36. Christmas packages.

Non-smoking • Children over 7 years welcome • Spacious 5-berth caravan also available for self-catering holidays.

Sue and Tony Hewitt, Harmony Country Lodge, Limestone Road, Burniston, Scarborough YO13 0DG • 0800 2985840 • Tel & Fax: 01723 870276
e-mail: tony@harmonylodge.net • www.harmonylodge.net

Detached 16th century farmhouse in private grounds. Quiet, with safe parking. One mile east of Skipton, Gateway to the Dales, and close to many places of beauty and interest. Luxury B&B with fireside treats in the lounge. All rooms are quiet and spacious, with panoramic views, washbasin and toilet (some full en suite), tea/coffee facilities and electric overblankets. Sorry, no smoking, no pets, no children.
Terms: £26-£36pppn; single occupancy £36-£50.
Opn all year. Credit cards accepted.
Farm cottage sometimes available.

Tel: 01756 793849
www.yorkshirenet.co.uk/accgde/lowskibeden

LOW SKIBEDEN FARMHOUSE, HARROGATE ROAD, SKIPTON BD23 6AB

Gamekeeper's Inn

Long Ashes Park, Threshfield, Near Skipton, North Yorkshire BD23 5PN • Tel: 01756 752434

Our friendly freehouse inn is located in the heart of Wharfedale, perfect for exploring the beautiful Yorkshire Dales. The bar and restaurant have a light, modern, airy feel and you can enjoy fine cask ales, beers and wines in a relaxing non-smoking environment. Our superb restaurant serves only fresh food, cooked to order. Vegetarian meals are available. The comfortable rooms are all of the highest standard with crisp white linen, en suite bathrooms, tea and coffee makers, TV and a DVD library. Guests have free use of the facilities at the adjacent Leisure Club including gym and swimming pool.

e-mail: info@gamekeeperinn.co.uk • www.gamekeeperinn.co.uk

BROOKLYN B&B

Sea captain's house in quiet location in old part of this picturesque, historic fishing village.
Views across rooftops to Cowbar cliffs.
Pets and children welcome.

MS M.J. HEALD, BROOKLYN B&B, BROWN'S TERRACE, STAITHES, SALTBURN-BY-THE-SEA TS13 5BG
Tel: 01947 841396 • m.heald@tesco.net

Glen Free is an old Lodge Bungalow set in a very peaceful situation, but still only one mile from A1 motorway (off the B6267 Masham/Thirsk road). Approx. seven miles from Ripon, Thirsk, Bedale. York and Harrogate 40 minutes approx. One double room and one double with single bed with washbasin. Central heating, tea making facilities and TV. All rooms ground floor. Golf, fishing, swimming and riding available locally. Ideal for touring the Dales and Herriot country.

Mr A. Bowyer, Glen Free,
Holme-on-Swale, Sinderby, Near Thirsk
YO7 4JE • 01845 567331

Glen Free
B&B from £18pppn

WHITBY. Jill & Brian McNeil, Long Leas Farm, Hawsker, Whitby YO22 4LA (01947 603790).
Discover historic Whitby, pretty fishing villages, way-marked walks. A Grade II Listed farm house for B&B with limited accommodation for dogs.

- Dogs welcome.

"Come as a Guest - Leave as a Friend"

ASHFORD NON-SMOKING GUEST HOUSE

The Ashford is a family-run guest house providing a relaxed, informal atmosphere and friendly service. Situated on Whitby's West Cliff, the Ashford occupies a superb position in Royal Crescent, overlooking Crescent Gardens and the sea. It is ideally situated for coastal and country walks, and makes an excellent base for exploring the North York Moors. Take a short drive inland and visit "Heartbeat Country", the North York Moors Railway, Rievaulx Abbey, Pickering and a myriad of pretty moorland villages, or take the coast road to discover the attractions of Scarborough, Bridlington and Filey. A little further afield you will find the historic city of York and Harrogate.

• Full central heating • Comfortable lounge • All bedrooms have en suite facilities, courtesy tray and colour TV • Good home cooking • Access at all times • ETC ◆◆◆

Bed and Breakfast from £23.50

Janice and Donna Hillier
ASHFORD NON-SMOKING GUEST HOUSE
8 Royal Crescent, Whitby YO21 3EJ
Tel: 01947 602138
e-mail: info@ashfordguesthouse.co.uk
www.ashfordguesthouse.co.uk

Ryedale House Exclusive to non-smokers, welcoming Yorkshire house of character at the foot of the moors, National Park "Heartbeat" country. Three-and-a-half-miles from Whitby. Magnificent scenery, moors, dales, picturesque harbours, cliffs, beaches, scenic railways, superb walking - it's all here! Highly commended, beautifully appointed rooms with private facilities, many extras. Guest lounge; breakfast room with views over Esk Valley. Enjoy the large south-facing terrace and landscaped gardens. Extensive traditional and vegetarian breakfast choice. Local inns and restaurants - two within a short walk. Parking available, also public transport

English Tourism Council ♦♦♦♦ GUEST ACCOMMODATION

Bed and Breakfast: double £27-£28, single £30, minimum stay two nights • Weekly reductions all season. Monday-Friday 4 night offers available (not high season) • Regret, no pets or children.

Mrs Pat Beale, Ryedale House, Coach Road, Sleights, Near Whitby YO22 5EQ
Tel & Fax: 01947 810534 • www.ryedalehouse.co.uk

WELLGARTH HOUSE ETC ★★★

Wetherby Road, Rufforth, York YO23 3QB

A warm welcome awaits you at Wellgarth House.....

Ideally situated in Rufforth (B1224), three miles from York, one mile from the ring road (A1237) and convenient for Park & Ride. Bed & Breakfast from £28pppn. All rooms are en suite and have tea and coffee making facilities and colour TV. Excellent local pub two minutes' walk away. Large private car park.

TEL: 01904 738592
MOBILE: 07711 252577

www.wellgarthhouse.co.uk

Newton House

Diana and John offer all their guests a friendly and warm welcome to their Victorian end town house a few minutes' walk from the city centre, York's beautiful Minster, medieval walls and museums. We are only a 40 mile drive from coastal resorts, the lovely Yorkshire Moors and Dales. Three double/twin en suite rooms, colour TV, tea/coffee tray, central heating. Breakfast menu. Car park. Non-smoking. Fire Certificate. Terms from £26pp.

Newton House, Neville Street, Haxby Road, York YO31 8NP • 01904 635627

York House

62 Heworth Green, York YO31 7TQ

Receive a warm welcome at this family-run guesthouse. Enjoy breakfast in our attractive conservatory or outside on our beautiful patio. York House is approximately 10 minutes' walk from York Minster and is the perfect base for a visit to York or the surrounding areas. Rooms offer all the conveniences you could need for a relaxing and enjoyable stay.

Some of the facilities offered:

en suite shower or bath facilities • four-poster • double, twin, family and single rooms • tea/coffee making facilities • off-street parking • full English/vegetarian breakfast. • *No smoking establishment* • *Prices from £28pppn.* • *Children welcome*

Tel & Fax: 01904 427070 • David and Katherine Leedham
e-mail: yorkhouse.bandb@tiscali.co.uk
www.yorkhouseyork.com

• • • some fun days out in NORTH YORKSHIRE

RHS Garden - Harlow Carr, Harrogate • 01423 565418 • www.rhs.org.uk
Ripley Castle & Gardens, Harrogate • 01423 770152 • www.ripleycastle.co.uk
Yorkshire Air Museum, Elvington • 01904 608595 • www.yorkshireairmuseum.co.uk
Ingleton Waterfalls Walk, Ingleton • 01756 795621 • www.ingletonwaterfallswalk.co.uk
Kinderland Fun, Play & Activity Park, Scarborough • 01723 354555 • wwww.kinderland.co.uk

YORK. Mrs J. Woodland, Cavalier Hotel, 39 Monkgate, York YO31 7PB (Tel & Fax: 01904 636615).

The Cavalier is an early Georgian Listed building, recently refurbished to provide very comfortable accommodation. It is ideally located close to the city centre and yards from the ancient city walls and most of the historic sites. Also convenient for touring North York Moors, Dales and East Coast resorts. Most rooms are en suite, and all have washbasins, colour TV, shaver points, radio alarms, and tea/coffee making facilities. Hairdryer and ironing facilities are available on request. Bed and full English breakfast with vegetarian options. Amenities include sauna, pay phone, garage parking, full central heating. Full Fire Certificate. Winter/Spring mini-breaks available, details on request.

- Open all year.

ETC ◆◆◆

ST GEORGE'S

6 St George's Place,
York YO24 1DR
Tel: 01904 625056
Fax: 01904 625009
e-mail: sixstgeorg@aol.com
http://members.aol.com/sixstgeorg/

St George's is a small and friendly family-run Victorian residence in a quiet cul-de-sac by York's beautiful racecourse.

- All rooms, one of which is on the ground floor, are en suite with tea/coffee tray and TV.
- Vegetarians are catered for.
- Private enclosed parking.
- Non-smoking.
- The hotel is only a 10-minute walk from the City Walls and many places of historic interest.

ETC/AA ★★★

ASCOT HOUSE

80 East Parade, York YO31 7YH
Tel: 01904 426826 • Fax: 01904 431077
ETC/AA ★★★★ • ETC SILVER AWARD

An attractive Victorian villa with easy access to the historic city centre by walking or by public transport. Most rooms have four-poster or canopy beds, and family and double rooms are en suite. All rooms have central heating, colour TV and tea/coffee facilities. Sauna available to hire by the hour. Private enclosed car park.

Singles from £30 to £60, doubles £60 to £75 including Traditional English Breakfast and VAT.

e-mail: admin@ascothouseyork.com • www.ascothouseyork.com

Pet-Friendly
Pubs, Inns & Hotels

on pages 298-311

Please note that these establishments may not feature in the main section of this book

A very warm welcome awaits you at our attractive family home set in open countryside, yet only three miles from York. Ideally situated for City, Coast, Dales and Moors.

Our comfortable bedrooms have • central heating • en suite facilities • remote-control colour TV • razor point • tea & coffee tray • radio alarm • hairdryer.

Full breakfast is served in a light airy dining room. Discounts available. Open all year. No pets. Smoking in garden only. Free, safe off-road parking. On very regular bus route to York.

Bed and full English Breakfast from £23.

Oaklands GUEST HOUSE

351 Strensall Road, Earswick, York YO32 9SW

★★★★ GUEST ACCOMMODATION

Telephone: 01904 768443

e-mail: mavmo@oaklands5.fsnet.co.uk

Church View B&B

Stockton-on-the-Forest, York YO32 9UP

This 200 year-old former farmhouse is located in the pretty village of Stockton on the Forest approximately 4 miles from York. All bedrooms are en suite and have been newly refurbished and decorated, each individually designed, from a romantic four-poster room to our popular large, ground floor family room. Cosy lounge with TV, video, music and real log fire on chilly evenings (you are welcome to bring your own wine). Breakfast of your choice, made with local produce, and home made jams will set you up for the day. The Fox Inn is just a stroll away, serving a good selection of local ales. Forest Park Golf Course lies to the rear of the house. We are ideally located for visiting the North Yorkshire Moors, East Coast (30 minutes by bus) and many more attractions. Many guests return - we hope to see you soon. Prices from £25pp.

AA ♦♦♦♦ Guest Accommodation

Lynn & Alan Manners, tel: 01904 400403; mobile: 07752 273371

e-mail: manners@87churchview.fsnet.co.uk • www.bandbyork.co.uk

YORK. Cumbria House, 2 Vyner Street, Haxby Road, York YO31 8HS (01904 636817).

A warm and friendly welcome awaits you at Cumbria House - an elegant, tastefully decorated Victorian guest house, where comfort and quality are assured. We are convenient for the city, being only 15 minutes' walk from York's historic Minster and yet within minutes of the northern by-pass (A1237). A launderette, post office and children's park are close by. All rooms have colour TV, radio alarms and tea/coffee facilities. Most are en suite and all are non-smoking. Central heating. Fire Certificate. Guests' car park. Full English breakfast or vegetarian alternative.

Rates: £25 to £30 per person.

• Non-smoking.

ETC/AA ♦♦♦

e-mail: candj@cumbriahouse.freeserve.co.uk **www.cumbriahouse.com**

YORK. Mrs J.W. Harrison, Fairthorne, 356 Strensall Road, Earswick, York YO32 9SW (Tel & Fax: 01904 768609). John and Joan Harrison invite you for a restful holiday in a peaceful country setting - a dormer bungalow with central heating, TV, shaver points, tea making facilities and en suite in bedrooms; TV lounge and dining room. Pleasant family atmosphere. Situated three miles north of York, within easy reach of East Coast and Yorkshire Moors and near golf course. Bus stop 50 yards if required. Private car park and large garden.

Rates: Bed and Breakfast from £24 per night.

• Reductions for children • Open all year.

ETC ♦♦♦

Please mention **FHG Guides** when making enquiries about accommodation featured in these pages

West Yorkshire

HALIFAX. Mrs L. White, Staups House, Staups Lane, Shibden, Halifax HX3 7AB (01422 362866).
Staups House is a beautiful Grade II* Listed manor house built in 1684 by John Crowther. The house has a facinating history and boasts many original features such as the magnificent oak staircase and inglenook fireplaces. The whole house is furnished to a very high standard. Set in peaceful surroundings, but handy for Leeds, Bradford and Haworth (Brontë country). M62 only five minutes away. A generous breakfast to suit your times and needs. One double en suite, one family suite, comprising double with four-poster, one single and private bathroom.
Rates: Bed and Breakfast from £25 to £35 per person
e-mail: rikki.white@lineone.net
www.staupshouse.co.uk

Free or reduced rate entry to
Holiday Visits and Attractions – see our
READERS' OFFER VOUCHERS on pages 9-42

Ratings & Awards

For the first time ever the AA, VisitBritain, VisitScotland, and the Wales Tourist Board will use a single method of assessing and rating serviced accommodation. Irrespective of which organisation inspects an establishment the rating awarded will be the same, using a common set of standards, giving a clear guide of what to expect. The RAC is no longer operating an Hotel inspection and accreditation business.

Accommodation Standards: Star Grading Scheme

Using a scale of 1-5 stars the objective quality ratings give a clear indication of accommodation standard, cleanliness, ambience, hospitality, service and food, This shows the full range of standards suitable for every budget and preference, and allows visitors to distinguish between the quality of accommodation and facilities on offer in different establishments. All types of board and self-catering accommodation are covered, including hotels, B&Bs, holiday parks, campus accommodation, hostels, caravans and camping, and boats.

The more stars, the higher level of quality

★★★★★
exceptional quality, with a degree of luxury

★★★★
excellent standard throughout

★★★
very good level of quality and comfort

★★
good quality, well presented and well run

★
acceptable quality; simple, practical, no frills

VisitBritain and the regional tourist boards, **enjoyEngland.com, VisitScotland** and **VisitWales,** and **the AA** have full details of the grading system on their websites

National Accessible Scheme

If you have particular mobility, visual or hearing needs, look out for the National Accessible Scheme. You can be confident of finding accommodation or attractions that meet your needs by looking for the following symbols.

Typically suitable for a person with sufficient mobility to climb a flight of steps but would benefit from fixtures and fittings to aid balance

Typically suitable for a person with restricted walking ability and for those that may need to use a wheelchair some of the time and can negotiate a maximum of three steps

Typically suitable for a person who depends on the use of a wheelchair and transfers unaided to and from the wheelchair in a seated position. This person may be an independent traveller

Typically suitable for a person who depends on the use of a wheelchair in a seated position. This person also requires personal or mechanical assistance (eg carer, hoist).

Scotland

-Leven Guest House, Ballachulish, Argyll

Inveresk House, Musselburgh, Lothian

Hunters Lodge Hotel, Gretna, Dumfries & Galloway

The Scottish smoke-free legislation forbids smoking in enclosed places used by the public or where people work.

This means that it is now illegal to smoke inside any building, vehicle or structure like a marquee or caravan apart from your own home or car.

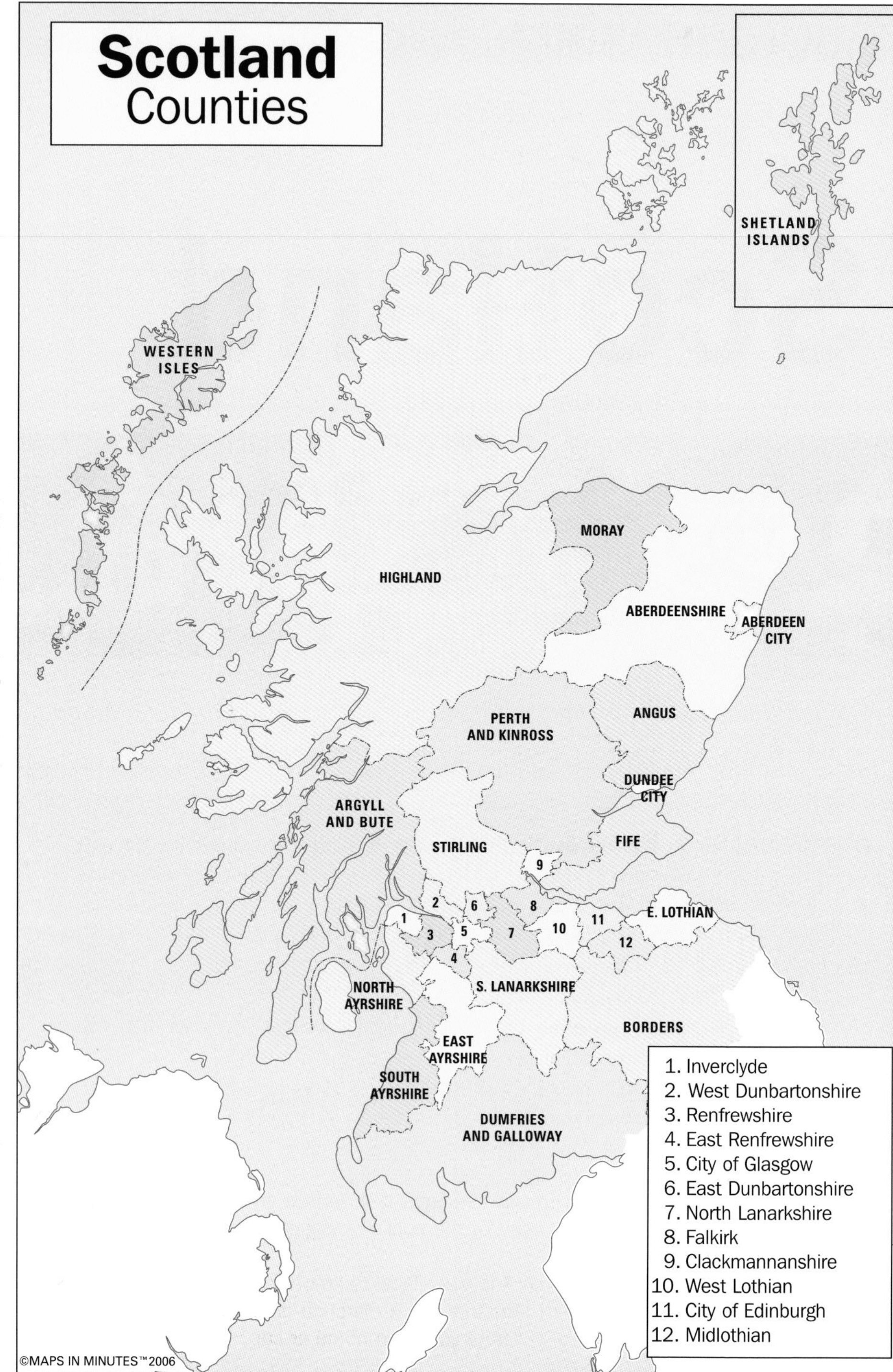
Scotland
Counties
SHETLAND ISLANDS
WESTERN ISLES
HIGHLAND
MORAY
ABERDEENSHIRE
ABERDEEN CITY
ANGUS
PERTH AND KINROSS
DUNDEE CITY
ARGYLL AND BUTE
STIRLING
FIFE
9
2
6
8
1
3
5
7
10
11
E. LOTHIAN
12
4
NORTH AYRSHIRE
S. LANARKSHIRE
BORDERS
EAST AYRSHIRE
SOUTH AYRSHIRE
DUMFRIES AND GALLOWAY
1. Inverclyde
2. West Dunbartonshire
3. Renfrewshire
4. East Renfrewshire
5. City of Glasgow
6. East Dunbartonshire
7. North Lanarkshire
8. Falkirk
9. Clackmannanshire
10. West Lothian
11. City of Edinburgh
12. Midlothian
©MAPS IN MINUTES™2006

Aberdeenshire, Banff & Moray

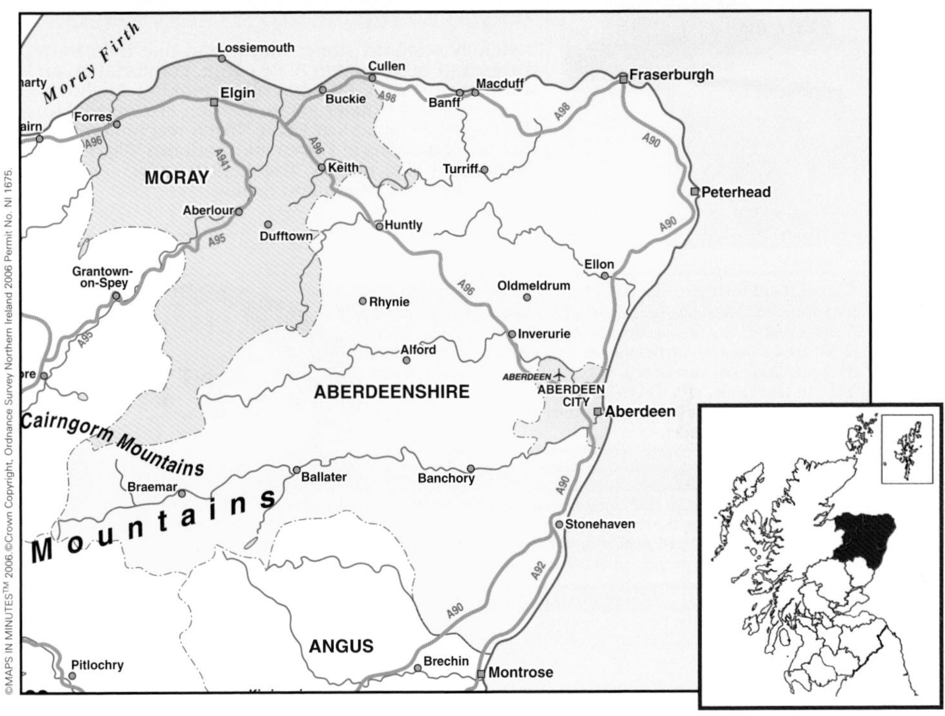

Aberdeenshire, Banff & Moray - one of the easiest ways to explore the area is by following one of the signposted tourist routes and theme trails. Perhaps the most famous of these is the Malt Whisky Trail around magnificent Speyside which links the award winning Speyside Cooperage and eight famous distilleries. Aberdeenshire is very much Scotland's "Castle Country" and 13 of the region's finest castles and great houses are located along Scotland's only Castle Trail. A lesser known feature of Scotland's North East is the fact that 10% of Scotland's Standing Stones are to be found here. Archaeolink, Scotland's prehistory park, interprets the early history of Grampian and promotes a journey through time for all ages. Royal Deeside has many attractions associated with Queen Victoria and a succession of British monarchs. There are many well known sites in this part of the region along the Victorian Heritage Trail including Balmoral Castle, home to royalty for 150 years, Crathie Church, Royal Lochnagar Distillery and Loch Muick. Around the Coastal Trail you will find some of Europe's best coastline, visually stunning, clean air and clear seawater. There are delightful villages such as the "Local Hero" village of Pennan, picturesque harbours, spectacular cliff formations, 150 miles of unspoilt beaches and fabulous golf courses such as Cruden Bay, Royal Tarlair, Duff House Royal and many more along the Moray Firth, as well as the company of the area's wildlife from dolphins to seals and seabirds.

Photo courtesy VisitScotland Aberdeen & Grampian

Argyll & Bute

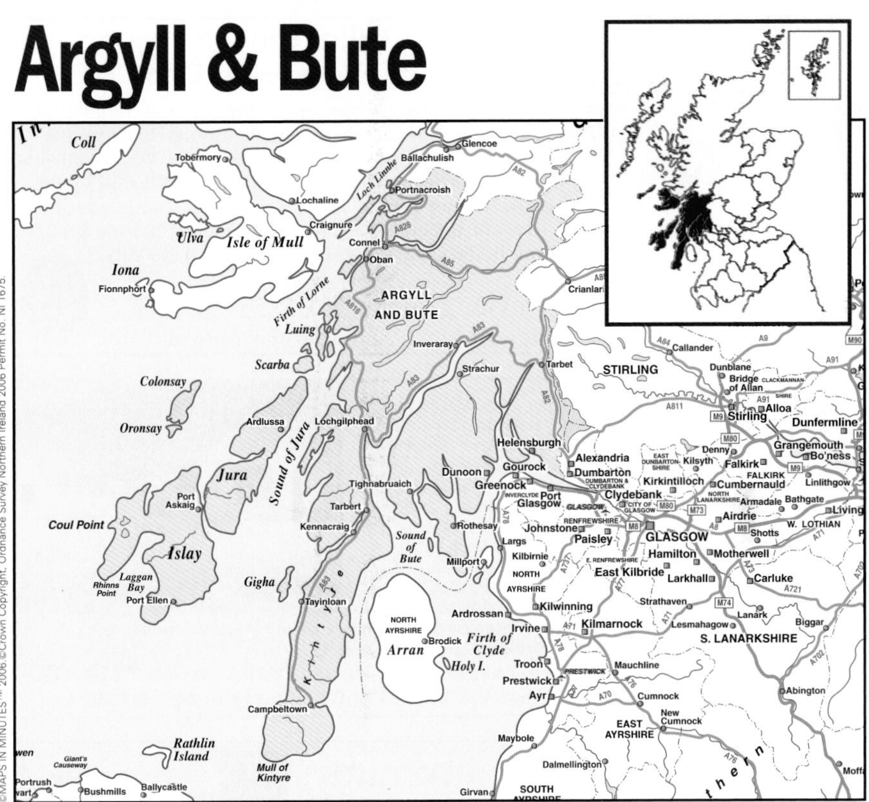

Argyll & Bute is a wonderfully unspoilt area, historically the heartland of Scotland and home to a wealth of fascinating wildlife. Here you may be lucky enough to catch a glimpse of an eagle, a wildcat or an osprey, or even a fine antlered stag. At every step the sea fringed landscape is steeped in history, from prehistoric sculpture at Kilmartin, to the elegant ducal home of the once feared Clan Campbell. There are also reminders of pre-historic times with Bronze Age cup-and-ring engravings, and standing stone circles. On the upper reaches of Loch Caolisport can be found St Columba's Cave, and more recent times are illustrated at the Auchindrain Highland Township south of Inveraray, a friendly little town with plenty to see, including the Jail, Wildlife Park and Maritime Museum.

Bute is the most accessible of the west coast islands, and Rothesay is its main town. Explore the dungeons and grand hall of Rothesay Castle, or visit the fascinating Bute Museum. The town offers a full range of leisure facilities, including a fine swimming pool and superb golf course, and there are vast areas of parkland where youngsters can safely play.

Free or reduced rate entry to
Holiday Visits and Attractions – see our
READERS' OFFER VOUCHERS on pages 9-42

Fern Villa Guest House

Loanfern, Ballachulish PH49 4JE

A warm welcome awaits you at our cosy and comfortable Victorian villa. Gentle strolls and Munro climbs on the doorstep. Ideally positioned for touring the West Highlands with Glencoe just over a mile away, Fort William 13 miles and Oban just over 30 miles. Relax in the lounge after your day out and enjoy the fabulous sunsets. Make our home your home while you enjoy your stay at Fern Villa.

Non-smoking.

Scottish Tourist Board ★★★ Guest House

Catherine and David Susans • 01855 811393

e-mail: ghfernvilla@aol.com • www.fernvilla.org.uk

AA/RAC ◆◆◆◆

Lyn-Leven, a superior, award-winning licensed guest house overlooking Loch Leven, with every comfort, in the beautiful Highlands of Scotland, is situated one mile from historic Glencoe village. Four double, two twin and two family bedrooms, all rooms en suite; sittingroom and diningroom. Central heating. Excellent and varied home cooking served daily. Children welcome at reduced rates. An ideal location for touring. Fishing, walking and climbing in the vicinity. The house is open all year except Christmas. Car not essential but private car park provided.

Bed and Breakfast from £25 • Dinner, Bed and Breakfast from £220 to £245 per person per week
Credit and debit cards accepted

Mr & Mrs J.A. MacLeod, Lyn-Leven Guest House, Ballachulish PA39 4JW
Tel: 01855 811392 • Fax: 01855 811600 • www.lynleven.co.uk

Minard Castle, Inveraray

Stay in style in our 19th Century Scottish castle which stands in its own grounds in beautiful countryside beside Loch Fyne, three-quarters-of-a-mile from the A83 Inveraray to Lochgilphead road. A peaceful location for a quiet break, you can stroll in the grounds, walk by the loch, explore the woods, or use Minard Castle as your base for touring this beautiful area with its lochs, hills, gardens, castles and historic sites. Breakfast in the Morning Room and relax in the Drawing Room. The comfortable bedrooms have colour television, tea/coffee making facilities and en suite bathrooms.

No smoking in the house • Evening Meals available within five miles.

Bed and Breakfast £55 per person, children half price • Open April to October • We offer a warm welcome in a family home • Self-catering property also available, £150 to £370 per week.

Reinold & Anne Gayre, Minard Castle, Minard PA32 8YB • Tel & Fax: 01546 886272
e-mail: reinoldgayre@minardcastle.com • www.minardcastle.com

Killean Farmhouse is located just a few miles outside Inveraray. Ideally situated for walking, climbing, pony trekking or just touring. There is fishing for trout, pike or salmon, and opportunities to enjoy boating, water skiing or windsurfing. The whole area is steeped in history and the town of Inveraray itself is a classic example of 18th century Scottish town planning. With all this in mind, the cottages provide high quality accommodation for family holidays.

Mrs Semple, Killean Farmhouse, Inveraray PA32 8XT
Tel: 01499 302474

One of Scotland's Best Kept Secrets

Accommodation, Bar, Restaurant, Function Suite, Four-Poster Bridal Suite with Jacuzzi

Ideal base for touring and visiting Mid-Argyll

www.staghotel.com
staghotel@btconnect.com

Tel: 01546 602496 • Fax: 01546 603549

THE STAG HOTEL & RESTAURANT, ARGYLL STREET, LOCHGILPHEAD, ARGYLL PA31 8NE

The hotel enjoys magnificent views standing in its own grounds overlooking Oban Bay and is the first hotel that visitors meet when entering on the A85. Most bedrooms are en suite with colour TV and hospitality tray. The elegant Kings Rest lounge bar has a Highland theme and is ideal for a cosy dram before dinner in the Knoll restaurant, which specialises in fresh local produce. Oban is ideally located for visiting the Western Isles and exploring the spectacular local scenery.

Scottish Tourist Board ★★★ HOTEL

Dunollie Road, Oban PA34 5JH
Tel: 01631 562536 • Fax: 01631 566101
e-mail: info@kingsknollhotel.co.uk
www.kingsknollhotel.co.uk

Palace Hotel

GEORGE STREET, OBAN, ARGYLL PA34 5SB
Tel: 01631 562294 • Fax: 01631 562863
www.thepalacehotel.activehotels.com

A small family hotel offering personal supervision situated on Oban's sea front with wonderful views over the Bay, to the Mull Hills beyond. All rooms en suite, with colour TV, tea/coffee making facilities, all non-smoking. The Palace is an ideal base for a real Highland holiday. By boat you can visit the islands of Kerrera, Coll, Tiree, Lismore, Mull and Iona, and by road Glencoe, Ben Nevis and Inveraray. Fishing, golf, horse riding, sailing, tennis and bowls all nearby. Children and pets welcome. Reductions for children. Please write or telephone for brochure. Competitive rates.

• • • some fun days out in ARGYLL & BUTE

Scottish Sea Life Sanctuary, Oban • 01631 720386 • www.sealsanctuary.co.uk
Oban Rare Breeds Park, Oban • 01631 770608 • www.obanrarebreeds.com
Inveraray Castle, Inveraray • 01499 302203 • www.inveraray-castle.com

A warm welcome awaits you in this delightful bungalow set in 20 acres of farmland where we breed our own Highland cattle which graze at the front. It is a peaceful location as we are set back from the road, and an ideal spot for touring, with the main ferry terminal at Oban just 10 minutes away. Our luxurious rooms have their own special sitting room attached where you can enjoy your coffee or a glass of wine in peace, and we also have our own restaurant where you can dine.

Mrs J. Currie, Hawthorn, 5 Keil Crofts, Benderloch, Oban PA37 1QS • 01631 720452
e-mail: june@hawthorncottages.com • www.hawthorncottages.com

The Barriemore

Corran Esplanade, Oban PA34 5AQ
Tel: 01631 566356 • Fax: 01631 571084

The Barriemore enjoys a splendid location on the Oban seafront. Built in 1895, the house exudes an opulence in keeping with its late Victorian origins. All bedrooms are beautifully and individually styled and have en suite facilities. The elegant lounge is an ideal spot for quiet relaxation, while the attractive dining room, overlooking Oban Bay, is the perfect place to enjoy full Scottish breakfasts including locally produced smoked haddock and kippers.

e-mail: reception@barriemore-hotel.co.uk
www.barriemore-hotel.co.uk

Rhu House • Tarbert

Rhu House is found in a quiet rural location, set in mature gardens, on the shore of West Loch Tarbert. Situated four miles south of Tarbert on the Campbeltown Road, close to Kennacraig Ferry Terminal. Ideal base for exploring the Kintyre Peninsula or making day trips to the Southerly Hebrides. This is a non-smoking establishment. En suite facilities available, all rooms have scenic views, tea/coffee making facilities and TV. There is a spacious residents' lounge with television. Ample parking, but sorry no dogs in the house. *Prices from £26 per person.*

Mrs Linda Whyatt, Rhu House, Tarbert PA29 6YF
Tel & Fax: 01880 820231
e-mail: rhuhouse@ukonline.co.uk
www.rhu-house.co.uk

Visit the FHG website
www.holidayguides.com
for details of the wide choice of accommodation featured in the full range of FHG titles

Ayrshire & Arran

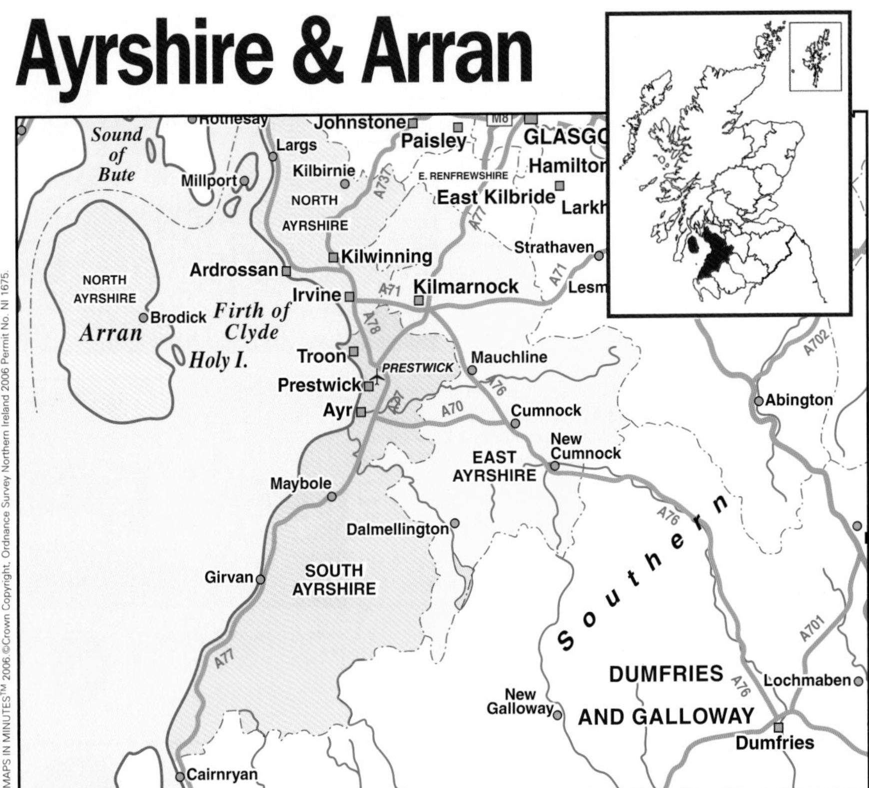

Ayrshire and Arran has always held a special affinity with families and this is reflected in the many fun attractions and activities geared towards children. These include farm parks, theme parks with daring funfair rides, and many sports and leisure centres. There's plenty to see and do with features like the Vikingar Viking Centre at Largs and The Scottish Industrial Railway Centre at Dalmellington adding to established attractions like Culzean Castle and the thriving business built on the life, loves and works of Scotland's best-loved poet, Robert Burns. A visit to the Secret Forest at Kelburn Country Centre is a must – its canopy of trees hides a multitude of surprises, the green man, the spirit of the forest, a Chinese garden with pagoda, and a crocodile swamp. Older visitors may enjoy a visit to Ayr Racecourse, enjoy a shopping spree, or treat themselves to a round on one the area's 44 golf courses. Whether the pace is leisurely or frantic, it's got to be Ayrshire and the Isle of Arran.

Traditional stone-built farmhouse on working mixed farm with extensive sea views to Arran. Convenient for golf, walking and Burns Country. Also convenient for Culzean Castle and Prestwick Airport.

From Ayr take A719 coast road past Haven Craig Tara; farm is five miles south of Ayr.

Accommodation comprises one double and one twin en suite, ground floor bedrooms with TV and tea/coffee making facilities. Central heating throughout. Children welcome. Pets by arrangement.

Please write, telephone or fax for further information. WELCOME HOST.

Prices from £20 to £25. Also self catering.

Mrs L. Wilcox, Fisherton Farm, Dunure, Ayr KA7 4LF
Tel & Fax: 01292 500223
www.fishertonfarm.homestead.com

Comfortable friendly accommodation is offered on this 200 acre dairy farm well situated for the A736 Glasgow to Irvine road and for the A737; well placed to visit golf courses, country parks, or leisure centre, also ideal for the ferry to Arran or Millport and for many good shopping centres all around.

A high standard of cleanliness is assured by Mrs Gillan who is a first class cook holding many awards, food being served in the diningroom with its beautiful picture windows.

Three comfortable bedrooms (double en suite, family and twin), all with tea-making facilities, central heating and electric blankets. Two bathrooms with shower; sittingroom with colour TV. Children welcome.

Bed and Breakfast from £18 double room; en suite from £23. Dinner can be arranged.

Mrs Jane Gillan, Shotts Farm, Beith KA15 1LB
Tel & Fax: 01505 502273 • e-mail: shotts.farm@btinternet.com

Open all year
Terms from £18.50pppn

A friendly welcome to Sunnyside, a comfortably furnished bungalow, with one double en suite and one twin-bedded B&B accommodation. Enjoy a wholesome cooked breakfast, or lighter alternatives, and drink in the beautiful unrestricted views over the suntrap garden and across the bonny Clyde.

Scottish TOURIST BOARD ★★★ B&B

The peaceful hamlet of King's Cross - off the beaten track, yet easily accessible - is just 15 minutes away from the ferry terminal at Brodick. Natural beauty and history combine to make it an ideal base for exploring Arran: some 56 miles round by road, and aptly described as 'Scotland in miniature'. Sunnyside has full central heating, washbasin, tea/coffee making facilities and colour TV in both rooms, and each having bath and shower. It is fully non-smoking, with private parking.

Mrs Evelyn Coles, "Sunnyside", King's Cross KA27 8RG
Tel: 01770 700422

FHG Guides

publish a large range of well-known accommodation guides.

We will be happy to send you details or you can use the order form at the back of this book.

Useful Guidance for Guests and Hosts

Every year literally thousands of holidays, short breaks and overnight stops are arranged through our guides, the vast majority without any problems at all. In a handful of cases, however, difficulties do arise about bookings, which often could have been prevented from the outset.

It is important to remember that when accommodation has been booked, both parties – guests and hosts – have entered into a form of contract. We hope that the following points will provide helpful guidance.

Guests

- **When enquiring about accommodation, be as precise as possible. Give exact dates, numbers in your party and the ages of any children.**
- **State the number and type of rooms wanted and also what catering you require – bed and breakfast, full board etc. Make sure that the position about evening meals is clear – and about pets, reductions for children or any other special points.**
- **Read our reviews carefully to ensure that the proprietors you are going to contact can supply what you want. Ask for a letter confirming all arrangements, if possible.**
- **If you have to cancel, do so as soon as possible. Proprietors do have the right to retain deposits and under certain circumstances to charge for cancelled holidays if adequate notice is not given and they cannot re-let the accommodation.**

Hosts

- **Give details about your facilities and about any special conditions. Explain your deposit system clearly and arrangements for cancellations, charges etc. and whether or not your terms include VAT.**
- **If for any reason you are unable to fulfil an agreed booking without adequate notice, you may be under an obligation to arrange suitable alternative accommodation or to make some form of compensation.**

Borders

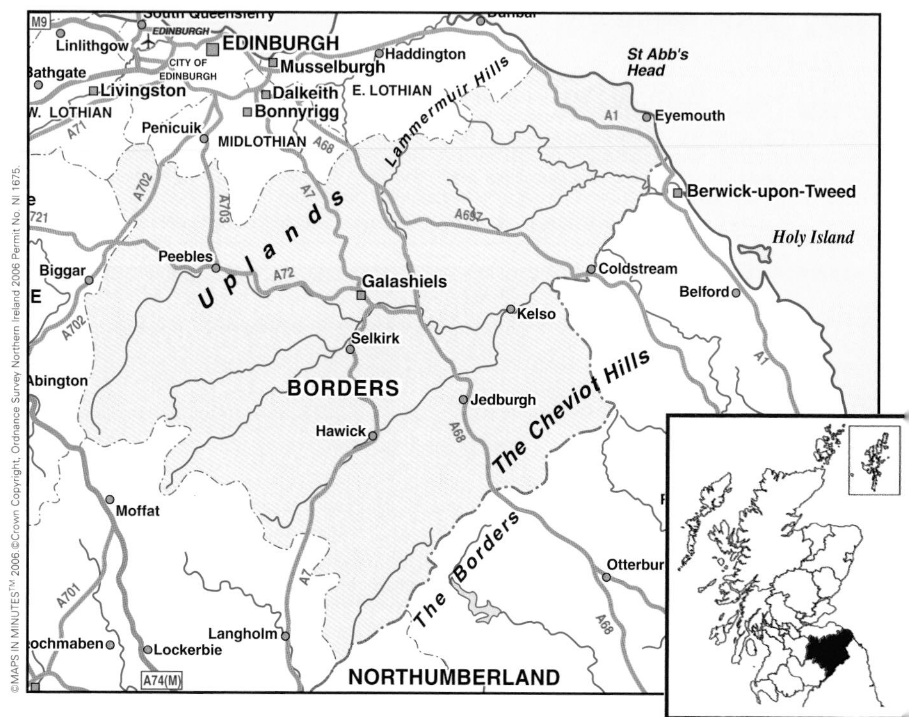

Covering about eighteen hundred miles, **The Scottish Borders** stretch from the rolling hills and moorland in the west, through gentler valleys to the rich agricultural plains of the east, and the rocky Berwickshire coastline with its secluded coves and picturesque fishing villages. Through the centre, tracing a silvery course from the hills to the sea, runs the River Tweed which provides some of the best fishing in Scotland. As well as fishing there is golf – 18 courses in all, riding or cycling and some of the best modern sports centres and swimming pools in the country. Friendly towns and charming villages are there to be discovered, while castles, abbeys, stately homes and museums illustrate the exciting and often bloody history of the area. It's this history which is commemorated in the Common Ridings and other local festivals, creating a colourful pageant much enjoyed by visitors and native Borderers alike.

One of the delights of travelling is finding gifts and keepsakes with a genuine local flavour, and dedicated souvenir hunters will find a plentiful supply of traditional delicacies, from drinks to baking and handmade sweets. Handcrafted jewellery, pottery, glass and woodwork, as well as beautiful tweeds and high quality knitwear can be found in the many interesting little shops throughout the area.

Scottish Borders eating establishments take pride in providing particularly good food and service and the choice of hotels, inns restaurants and cafes make eating out a real pleasure.

Glenbank is set in its own grounds with ample private car parking. Guests can relax in one of the en suite bedrooms, all comfortably furnished with central heating, television and tea/coffee making facilities. We have a cosy, well-stocked lounge bar with a wide selection of malt whiskies, wines, liqueurs, spirits, beers and soft drinks. Bar lunches and evening meals are served in our 30-seater à la carte restaurant, where the extensive menus use local produce according to season. Jedburgh offers an attractive setting for a well-deserved break. With town trails, riverside walks, renovated buildings, Mill shops, Visitor Centres as well as numerous castles and abbeys nearby – there is plenty to keep you occupied!

Castlegate, Jedburgh TD8 6RD • 01835 862258 • Fax: 01835 863697
e-mail: enquiries@glenbankhotel.co.uk • www.glenbankhotel.co.uk

Ferniehirst Mill Lodge

Built in 1980, Ferniehirst Mill Lodge has all the amenities required for your comfort whilst blending with the existing mill buildings and stables. Just south of Jedburgh, situated in a secluded valley, the Lodge is a haven for bird life. Ideal for walking, fishing and horse riding. 8 bedrooms, all with en suite bathroom or shower, tea and coffee making facilities and telephone. Central heating throughout and the spacious lounge has a log fire for chillier evenings. Full cooked breakfast and dinner are served in the attractive pine dining room. The emphasis is on home cooking using local produce. There is a small bar for residents. Personal service and warm hospitality from owners Alan and Christine.

Jedburgh TD8 6PQ
Tel: 01835 863279
ferniehirstmill@aol.com • www.ferniehirstmill.co.uk

• • • some fun days out in THE BORDERS

Hirsel Country Park, Coldstream • 01890 882834 • www.hirselcountrypark.co.uk
Halliwell's House Museum, Selkirk • 01750 20096 • www.scotborders.gov.uk
Manderston, Duns • 01361 882636 • www.manderston.co.uk
Floors Castle, Kelso • 01573 223333 • www.floorscastle.com

e-mail: mary@marysweeney.wanadoo.co.uk

Tastefully converted steading with spacious rooms peacefully situated on an elevated position with panoramic views over Peebles. Surrounded by countryside, yet only a short distance from the town centre.

The Steading
Venlaw Castle Road, Peebles EH45 8QG
Tel: 01721 720293

Scottish Tourist Board ★★★★ B&B

Two double and one twin room, all en suite, with hairdryer, TV and tea/coffee making facilities. Large garden and cobbled courtyard. Ideal base for touring. Ample parking. Pets welcome. Non-smoking. Details from Mrs Mary Sweeney.

Lyne Farmhouse

LYNE FARM, PEEBLES EH45 8NR

Victorian farmhouse with character and spectacular views overlooking Stobo Valley. Tastefully decorated throughout, bedrooms all upstairs, double or twin beds with tea/coffee facilities and TV. Walled garden to sit in, hillwalking, picnic areas, Lyne Roman Fort and site of early Christian graves all on farm. Many sports amenities (The Hub), Glentress Cycling Centre, Icelandic pony trekking, golfing, fishing and swimming. Picturesque Peebles 4 miles with its many restaurants, pubs, museum and Eastgate Theatre, shows and plays every week. B&B from £24 pppn.

Tel & Fax: 01721 740255 • e-mail: lynefarmhouse@btinternet.com • website: www.lynefarm.co.uk

Other specialised holiday guides from FHG

Recommended **INNS & PUBS** OF BRITAIN

Recommended **COUNTRY HOTELS** OF BRITAIN

Recommended **SHORT BREAK HOLIDAYS** IN BRITAIN

The bestselling and original **PETS WELCOME!**

The GOLF GUIDE, *Where to Play, Where to Stay* IN BRITAIN & IRELAND

COAST & COUNTRY HOLIDAYS

SELF-CATERING HOLIDAYS IN BRITAIN

CARAVAN & CAMPING HOLIDAYS

CHILDREN WELCOME! Family Holiday & Days Out Guide

BRITAIN'S BEST **LEISURE & RELAXATION GUIDE**

Published annually: available in all good bookshops or direct from the publisher:

FHG Guides, Abbey Mill Business Centre, Seedhill, Paisley PA1 1TJ

Tel: 0141 887 0428 • Fax: 0141 889 7204

e-mail: admin@fhguides.co.uk • www.holidayguides.com

Dumfries & Galloway

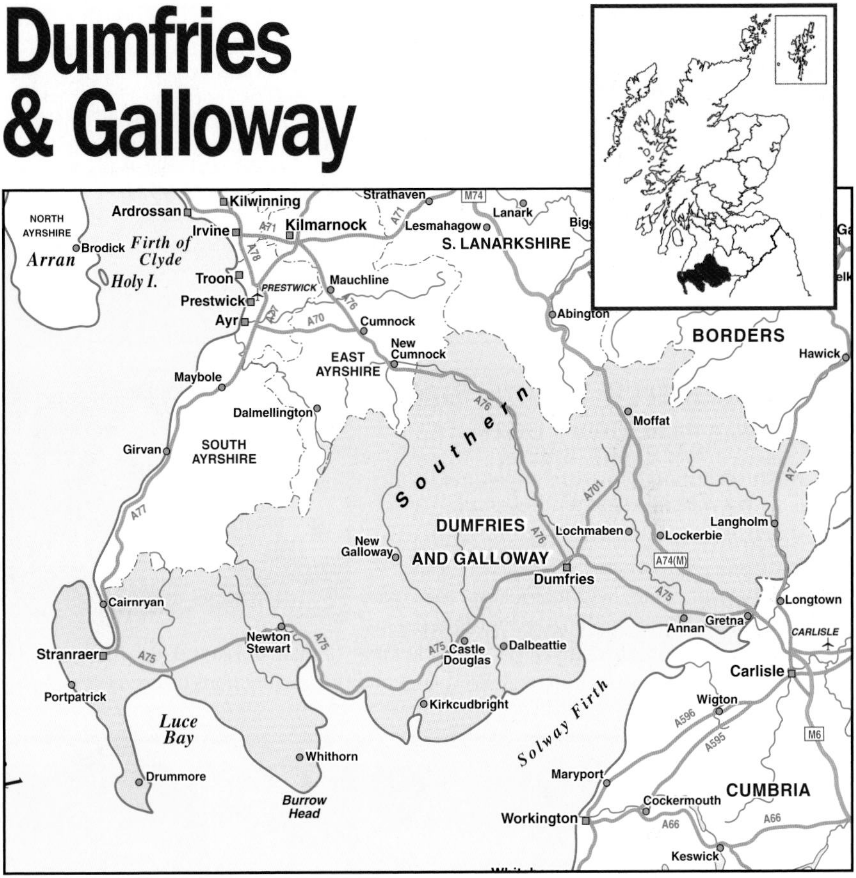

Dumfries & Galloway is a mixture of high moorland and sheltered glens, and presents abundant opportunities for hill walking, rambling, fishing for salmon and sea trout, cycling, bird watching and field sports. There are at least 32 golf courses, ranging from the challenging Stranraer course at Creachmore to the scenic, clifftop course at Port Patrick. The Stranraer course has the distinction of being the last course designed by James Braid. The warming influence of the Gulf Stream ensures a mild climate which makes touring a pleasure, and many visitors come here to visit the dozens of interesting castles, gardens, museums and historic sites. In addition, pony trekking and riding plus a never-ending succession of ceilidhs, village fairs, country dances, classical music concerts and children's entertainment guarantee plenty of scope for enjoyment. Discover the many hidden secrets of this lovely and unspoilt landscape such as the pretty little villages along the coast or visit some of the interesting towns in the area including Stranraer, the principal town and ferry port with its busy shopping streets, park and leisure centre. Those who love 'the written word' must surely visit the book town of Wigtown, and the gourmet amongst us will love the new concept of Castle Douglas, the recently designated 'Food Town'.

A charming country house, tastefully furnished, with a warm, friendly, welcoming atmosphere. The spacious en suite bedrooms (two double/family and one twin) have lovely views over garden and countryside. Beautifully appointed, each room has colour satellite TV plus video, tea/coffee making facilities, shower and toilet, and full central heating. Small health suite, steam room and sauna available for guests' use.

Situated in peaceful countryside only three miles from Dumfries town centre with excellent shopping, swimming pool, ice bowl for curling, green bowling, fishing and golf. Hill and forest walks, birdwatching, cycling and mountain bike trails all nearby.

Bed and Breakfast from £28 per person.

Mr & Mrs G. Hood, Wallamhill House, Kirkton, Dumfries DG1 1SL
Tel: 01387 248249 • e-mail: wallamhill@aol.com • www.wallamhill.co.uk

The Hunters Lodge Hotel

Annan Road, Gretna DG16 5DL
Tel: 01461 338214
e-mail: reception@hunterslodgehotel.co.uk
www.hunterslodgehotel.co.uk

Situated in the heart of Gretna, and the nearest hotel to the world famous Gretna Registration Office

◆ All rooms en suite, with colour TV, tea/coffee making and modern furnishings ◆ Private residents' lounge ◆ Comfortable lounge bar with a wide range of malt whiskies ◆ Bar meals or à la carte dinners served each evening ◆ Weddings and private functions catered for.

BARRASGATE HOUSE

Millhill, Gretna Green DG16 5HU

Tel: 01461 337577
e-mail: info@barrasgate.co.uk
www.barrasgate.co.uk

AA ♦♦♦ Guest Accommodation

Surrounded by broad-leaved woodland and with country views, the accommodation at Barrasgate House is on ground and first floors, with disabled access. Our en suite bathrooms and shower rooms are equipped with soft fluffy towels. To help you relax after a long drive, our Gold Room has a spa shower. Five minutes from the M74 or A7, our central location is ideal for exploring Hadrian's Wall, the Borders, the Lakes and the beautiful Solway Coast. Local produce is used in our menus, and farmhouse baking will appeal to most tastes. Short breaks Spring/Autumn: three nights from £99.

Kirkcroft Guest House

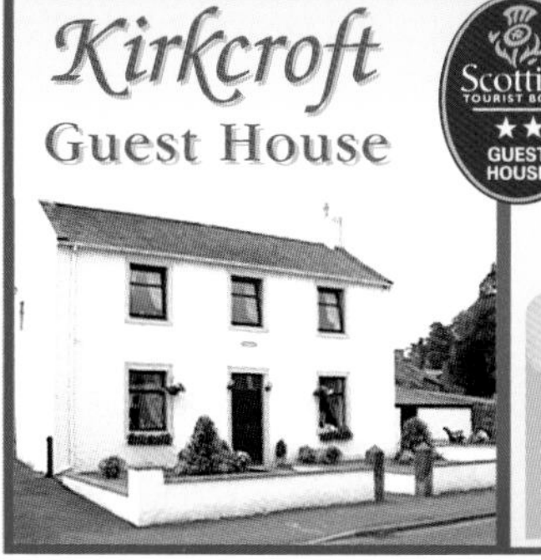

Scottish Tourist Board ★★ Guest House

Situated in the heart of Gretna Green, Kirkcroft Guest House, a detached house built in 1836, was once used as the local Post Office, and is now a comfortable and friendly Bed and Breakfast. Gretna Green is well placed for touring. To the south lies the Lake District with all its attractions, and to the west, the lovely Galloway coast towards Stranraer on the Gulf Stream. There is also easy access to the Scottish Border towns, and Kielder Water and Forest in Northumberland.

Double/twin en suite from £49.00 per room
• DISCOUNTS FOR LONGER STAYS •

Glasgow Road, Gretna Green DG16 5DU
Tel: 01461 337403
e-mail: info@kirkcroft.co.uk • www.kirkcroft.co.uk

BARNHILL SPRINGS
Country Guest House, Moffat DG10 9QS

Barnhill Springs is an early Victorian country house standing in its own grounds and overlooking some of the finest views of Upper Annandale. Situated on the Southern Upland Way, half-a-mile from the A74/M, the house and its surroundings retain an air of remote peacefulness. Comfortable accommodation, residents' lounge with open fire, all decorated and furnished to an exceptionally high standard of comfort. Ideal centre for touring South-West Scotland and the Borders, or for an overnight stop. Pets free of charge. Bed & Breakfast from £25; Evening Meal (optional) from £18.

Mr & Mrs W. Gray • 01683 220580

Limetree House
Eastgate, Moffat
DG10 9AE
Tel: 01683 220001

Limetree House is a Georgian Grade B Listed building situated in stunning countryside.

- **One family, two double, two twin, and master bedroom with king-size sleigh bed • All bedrooms are en suite**
- **Colour TV/DVD, tea/coffee making facilities in all rooms**
- **Private parking**
- **Open all year except Christmas and New Year**
- **No smoking**
- **Pets by arrangement**

e-mail: info@limetreehouse.co.uk
www.limetreehouse.co.uk/

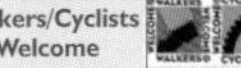

Situated just five minutes' walk from Moffat town centre and one mile off the M74, Annandale House is a haven of peace, surrounded by mature gardens with private parking and storage for cycles. The three well appointed spacious bedrooms all have central heating, tea/coffee making facilities hairdryers and colour TVs. There is one en suite double with king-size bed, one twin and one family room. An ideal base for exploring south-west Scotland and the Scottish Borders.

Well behaved pets welcome • Open all year • No smoking in house
Self-catering cottage also available

Bed and Breakfast from £19.50pppn (reduced rates for children).
Short Breaks available.

Mrs Deakins, Annandale House, Moffat DG10 9SA • Tel: 01683 221460
e-mail: june@annandalehouse.com • www.annandalehouse.com

• • • some fun days out in DUMFRIES & GALLOWAY

Mabie Farm Park, Near Dumfries • 01387 259666 • www.mabiefarm.co.uk
Threave Gardens & Estate, Castle Douglas • 01556 502575 • www.nts.org.uk
Gem Rock Museum, Creetown • 01671 820357 • www.gemrock.net

Edinburgh & Lothians

Edinburgh & Lothians - Scotland's Capital is home to a wide range of attractions offering something for visitors of all ages. The Royal Mile holds many of the most historic sights, but within a short distance there are fine gardens to visit or the chance to sample the latest in interactive technology. A network of signposted paths allow walkers of all abilities to enjoy the contrasts of the area, whether for a leisurely stroll or at a more energetic pace. The annual Festival in August is part of the city's tradition and visitors flock to enjoy the performing arts, theatre, ballet, cinema and music, and of course "The Tattoo" itself. At the Festival Fringe there are free shows and impromptu acts, a jazz festival and book festivals. Other events take place throughout the year, including children's festivals, science festivals, the famous Royal Highland Show and the Hogmanay street party. East Lothian has beautiful countryside and dramatic coastline, all only a short distance from Edinburgh. Once thriving fishing villages, North Berwick and Dunbar now cater for visitors who delight in their traditional seaside charm. In Midlothian you can step back in time with a visit to Rosslyn Chapel or Borthwick and Crichton Castles, or seize the chance to brush up on your swing at one of the excellent courses in the area. The Almond Valley Heritage Centre in Livingston has a museum, friendly farmyard animals and children's activities, while the Butterfly and Insect World at Lasswade offers a fabulous tropical display.

A relaxed and friendly base is provided at Cruachan from which to explore central Scotland. The centre of Edinburgh can be reached by train in only 30 minutes from nearby Bathgate, and Glasgow is only 35 minutes by car. All rooms en suite/private facilities, full hospitality tray, fresh towels daily, colour TV and central heating. Hosts Kenneth and Jacqueline ensure you receive the utmost in quality of service, meticulously presented accommodation and of course a full Scottish breakfast. They look forward to having the pleasure of your company.

Bed and Breakfast from £27.50 per person per night.

Scottish Tourist Board ★★★ B&B

AA ★★★ Guest Accommodation

78 East Main Street, Blackburn EH47 7QS
Tel: 01506 655221 • Fax: 01506 652395
e-mail: cruachan.bb@virgin.net • www.cruachan.co.uk

EDINBURGH. The Ivy Guest House, 7 Mayfield Gardens, Edinburgh EH9 2AX (0131-667 3411; Fax: 0131-620 1422). Bed and Breakfast in a comfortable Victorian villa. Private car park. Close to city centre and all its cultural attractions with excellent public transport and taxi services available on the door step. Many local sports facilities (booking assistance available). All rooms have central heating, washbasins, colour TV, tea/coffee, and hairdryers. Choice of en suite or standard rooms, all power showers. Public phone. Large selection of eating establishments nearby. A substantial Scottish breakfast and warm welcome is assured, courtesy of Dolly Green.

Rates: terms from £25 per person per night.

- Open all year round.

STB ★★★ *GUEST HOUSE*

e-mail: dolly@ivyguesthouse.com
www.ivyguesthouse.com

EDINBURGH. Mr Ian McCrae, 44 East Claremont Street, Edinburgh EH7 4JR (Tel & Fax: 0131-556 2610). Situated in the Victorian part of Edinburgh's New Town, McCrae's is only 15 minutes' walk from the city centre giving easy access to all attractions. The comfortable accommodation comprises three twin/double rooms, all at ground level. All rooms have en suite facilities, central heating, colour TV, radio/alarm, fridge, hairdryer and tea/coffee trays. Iron available on request. A full traditional breakfast is served using fresh local produce. Unrestricted on-street parking immediately outside. Visa/Mastercard accepted.

Rates: from £24.50pppn sharing or from £28.50 for single occupation. Reductions available for long stays.

- Open all year.

STB ★★★ *B&B*

e-mail: mccraes.bandb@lineone.net
http://website.lineone.net/~mccraes.bandb

Spylaw Bank House
Elegant Georgian Country House built around 1790, situated within the city of Edinburgh. It has a secluded position in walled gardens close to Colinton village and three miles from the city centre. Luxuriously appointed en suite bedrooms with many personal touches. Relax in the original drawing room with its open fire and antique furnishings and take breakfast in the period dining room.
Ideally situated for sightseeing in Edinburgh and touring the Borders, Fife and Perthshire. Five miles from airport, one from city by-pass. Ample parking. Frequent buses to city centre - a 15 minute journey.
www.spylawbankhouse.com
Bed and Breakfast from £30 per person.
Scottish Tourist Board ★★★★ B&B
David Martin, Spylaw Bank House, 2 Spylaw Avenue, Colinton, Edinburgh EH13 0LR
0131-441 5022 • mobile: 07981 923017 • e-mail: davidsmartin@blueyonder.co.uk

CASTLE PARK GUEST HOUSE 75 Gilmore Place, Edinburgh EH3 9NU

Tel: 0131 229 1215 • e-mail: castlepark@btconnect.com

A warm and friendly welcome awaits you at Castle Park Guest House, a charming Victorian Guest House ideally situated close to King's Theatre and city centre. Travel along the Royal Mile with Edinburgh Castle at one end and the Palace of Holyrood House, the Official Scottish Residence of the Queen, at the other end.

Centrally heated throughout, colour TV in all rooms, en suite facilities available, tea/coffee hospitality tray, full Scottish/Continental breakfast. Children welcome – special prices. Off-street parking. STB classification.

www.castleparkguesthouse.co.uk

Blossom House is a traditional stone-built town house attractively situated within the Newington district of Edinburgh, less than one mile from the City Centre and on a main bus route. All bedrooms are tastefully furnished, with colour TV and tea/coffee hospitality tray; most have en suite facilities. Some rooms enjoy attractive views towards the extinct volcano of Arthur's Seat. Full Scottish breakfasts are served in the spacious dining room. Many fine restaurants are situated nearby, providing a wide range of cuisine to suit everyone's taste and pocket. Central heating. Private car park. B&B from £20 per person per night.

Mrs Kay, Blossom House, 8 Minto Street, Edinburgh EH9 1RG
Tel: 0131-667 5353 • Fax: 0131-667 2813
e-mail: blossom_house@hotmail.com • www.blossomguesthouse.co.uk

INTERNATIONAL GUEST HOUSE • EDINBURGH

Conveniently situated 1½ miles south of Princes Street on the main A701, on the main bus route. Private parking. All bedrooms en suite, with direct-dial telephone, colour television and tea/coffee making facilities. Some rooms enjoy magnificent views across to the extinct volcano of Arthur's Seat. The full Scottish breakfasts served on the finest bone china are a delight. Contact Mrs Niven for details. ***AA*** ★★★★

B&B from £30 to £65 single; £50 to £120 double

37 Mayfield Gardens, Edinburgh EH9 2BX • Tel: 0131 667 2511 • Fax: 0131 667 1112
e-mail: intergh1@yahoo.co.uk • www.accommodation-edinburgh.com

Family-Friendly

Pubs, Inns & Hotels

See the Supplement on pages 293-297 for establishments which *really* welcome children.

Please note that these establishments may not feature in the main section of this book

Comfortable and relaxed family-run Victorian house. Central situation in a peaceful location near the Union Canal in historic Linlithgow - only five minutes' walk from the town centre, Linlithgow Palace and railway station. Open March to November inclusive. Excellent base for visiting Edinburgh, Stirling, Glasgow and the Falkirk Wheel.

Early booking advisable. Credit cards accepted.
Terms from £30 per person.

WINNER AA 'BEST BREAKFAST' SCOTLAND AWARD, RECOMMENDED BY "WHICH?" B&B GUIDE

Mr and Mrs R. Inglis, Thornton, Edinburgh Road, Linlithgow EH49 6AA • 01506 844693
e-mail: inglisthornton@hotmail.com • www.thornton-scotland.co.uk

AA ♦♦♦♦ Guest Accommodation

Inveresk House

Inveresk Village, Musselburgh EH21 7UA

Historic mansion house and award-winning Bed & Breakfast. Family-run "home from home". Situated in three acres of garden and woodland. Built on the site of a Roman settlement from 150 AD, the remains of a bathhouse can be found hidden in the garden. Three comfortable en suite rooms. Original art and antiques adorn the house. Edinburgh's Princes Street seven miles from Inveresk House. Good bus routes. Families welcome. Off-street parking. Telephone first. B&B from £90 double, £65 single. Family room £100 to £120.

e-mail: chute.inveresk@btinternet.com
website: http://travel.to/edinburgh

Tel: 0131-665 5855
Fax: 0131-665 0578

We are situated on the A68, three miles south of Pathhead at the picturesque village of Fala. The house is an 18th century coaching inn (Listed building). All bedrooms have washbasins and tea/coffee making facilities; one is en suite. All the rooms are comfortably furnished. We are within easy reach of Edinburgh and the Scottish Borders. A warm welcome is extended to all our guests – our aim is to make your stay a pleasant one.

Cost is from £20 per person;
children under 12 years £13.

Mrs Anne Gordon, "Fairshiels",
Blackshiels, Pathhead EH37 5SX
Tel: 01875 833665
e-mail: anne@fairshiels.fsnet.co.uk

Please note

All the information in this book is given in good faith in the belief that it is correct. However, the publishers cannot guarantee the facts given in these pages, neither are they responsible for changes in policy, ownership or terms that may take place after the date of going to press. Readers should always satisfy themselves that the facilities they require are available and that the terms, if quoted, still apply.

Fife

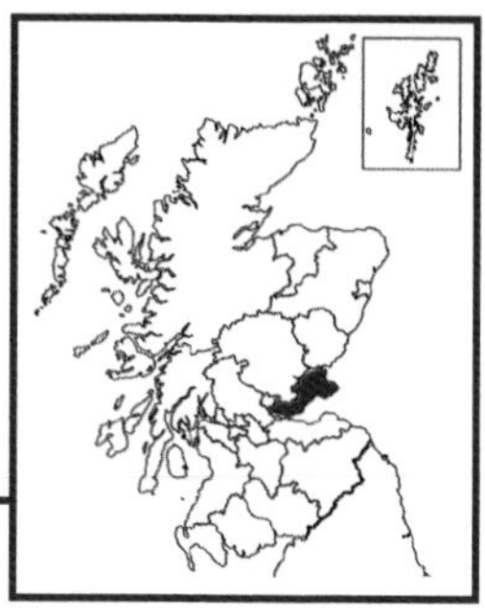

Fife - whether as 'County', 'Region' or more traditionally 'Kingdom', Fife has always been a prosperous and self-contained part of Scotland. The coast, with small ports such as Crail, Anstruther, Pittenweem, St Monance, Elie and the more commercial Methil, Burntisland and Kirkcaldy, has always been interesting and important. St Andrews with its university, castle, cathedral and golf, is the best known and most visited town. Dunfermline has a historic past with many royal associations and was the birthplace of the philanthropist, Andrew Carnegie. Medieval buildings have been restored by the National Trust in nearby Culross. Cupar, Falkland, Kinross (for Loch Leven), Auchtermuchty and Leuchars are amongst the many other historic sites in Fife, and at North Queensferry is one of Fife's newest and most popular attractions, Deep Sea World. The picturesque seaside village of Aberdour with its own castle is nearby.

Culross, Kirkcaldy

This quiet Victorian former rectory provides the ideal location for touring. Ideal base for golf enthusiasts, within easy reach of 46 golf courses and only 14 miles from St Andrews. 40 minutes from Edinburgh Airport, Perth and 30-35 minutes from Dundee.

Mrs Pam MacDonald, Dunclutha Guest House, 16 Victoria Road, Leven KY8 4EX
Tel: 01333 425515 • Fax: 01333 422311
e-mail: pam.leven@blueyonder.co.uk
website: www.dunclutha.myby.co.uk

Facilities include three en suite rooms – one double, one twin, one family (sleeps three to four), one family (sleeps three) with private bathroom. Colour TV and tea/coffee facilities in all rooms, cot available. Visitors' lounge with TV. Most credit cards accepted. Open all year. Terms from £28pppn. Non-smoking.

AA ♦♦♦♦

Only two miles from St Andrews on the picturesque A917 road to Crail, Spinkstown is a uniquely designed farmhouse with views of the sea and surrounding countryside. Bright and spacious, it is furnished to a high standard. Accommodation consists of double and twin rooms, all en suite, with tea/coffee making facilities and colour TV; diningroom and lounge. Substantial farmhouse breakfast to set you up for the day. The famous Old Course, historic St Andrews and several National Trust properties are all within easy reach, as well as swimming, tennis, putting, bowls, horse riding, country parks, nature reserves, beaches and coastal walks. Plenty of parking available. Bed and Breakfast from £27.

Scottish Tourist Board ★★★★ B&B

AA ♦♦♦♦ Guest Accommodation

e-mail: anne@spinkstown.com
website: www.spinkstown.com
Mrs Anne Duncan, Spinkstown Farmhouse, St Andrews KY16 8PN
Tel & Fax: 01334 473475

• • • some fun days out in FIFE

Deep Sea World, North Queensferry • 01383 411880 • www.deepseaworld.com
Scottish Fisheries Museum, Anstruther • 01333 310628 • www.scotfishmuseum.org
British Golf Museum, St Andrews • 01334 460046 • www.britishgolfmuseum.co.uk
Scottish Deer Centre, Cupar • 01337 810391 • www.thedeercentre.co.uk

Glasgow & District

Glasgow & District -in one of Europe's most dynamic cultural centres, there's so much to see and do – from the City of Glasgow itself, alive with heritage, entertainment and nightlife, to the charm of the bustling towns, scenic villages and countryside of the surrounding districts. Entertainment and sport feature in an exciting year-round calendar that encompasses opera and theatre, Scottish ceilidhs and top sporting events. Glasgow is home to a multitude of shops, from boutiques and specialist stores to High Street favourites and shopping malls, such as Buchanan Galleries and Princes Square. The city is brimming over with restaurants, cafes, bars and bistros. Culinary treats include many Scottish dishes, plus a wide range of international cuisine, with prices to suit every pocket. The famous River Clyde links city life to country life as it flows from its source in the Lowther Hills to the maritime towns and villages of Inverclyde and Renfrewshire.

Glasgow, Kilsyth

GLASGOW. Mrs P. Wells, "Avenue End" B&B, 21 West Avenue, Stepps, Glasgow G33 6ES (0141-779 1990; Fax: 0141-779 1951).

Stepps village is situated north-east of Glasgow just off the A80. This self-built family home nestles down a quiet leafy lane offering the ideal location for an overnight stay or touring base with the main routes to Edinburgh, Stirling and the North on our doorstep. Easy commuting to Loch Lomond, the Trossachs or Clyde Valley. M8 exit 12 from the south, or A80 Cumbernauld Road from the north. Glasgow only ten minutes away, Glasgow Airport 12 miles. Ample parking. All rooms offer colour TV, compliments tray and en suite or private facilities. Generous Continental-style breakfast included. Home from Home – warm welcome assured!

Rates: from £25 to £35 per person per night.

• Self-catering also available.

STB ★★★ *B&B*

e-mail: avenueEnd@aol.com

www.avenueend.co.uk

A working family farm situated close to the town of Kilsyth at the foot of the Kilsyth Hills, a great base to explore central Scotland. Glasgow, Stirling 20 minutes. Croy Station is just five minutes' drive away, where a short train journey will take you into the centre of Edinburgh. Golf, fishing, hill walking and a swimming pool are all within half a mile plus Cumbernauld and Kirkintilloch five minutes away.

Scottish Tourist Board ★★★ B&B

One twin/family room, one single room, both with TV and tea/coffee facilities. B&B from £22-£25. Open all year.

Libby MacGregor, Allanfauld Farm, Kilsyth, Glasgow G65 9DF
Tel & Fax: 01236 822155 • e-mail: allanfauld@hotmail.com

Highlands

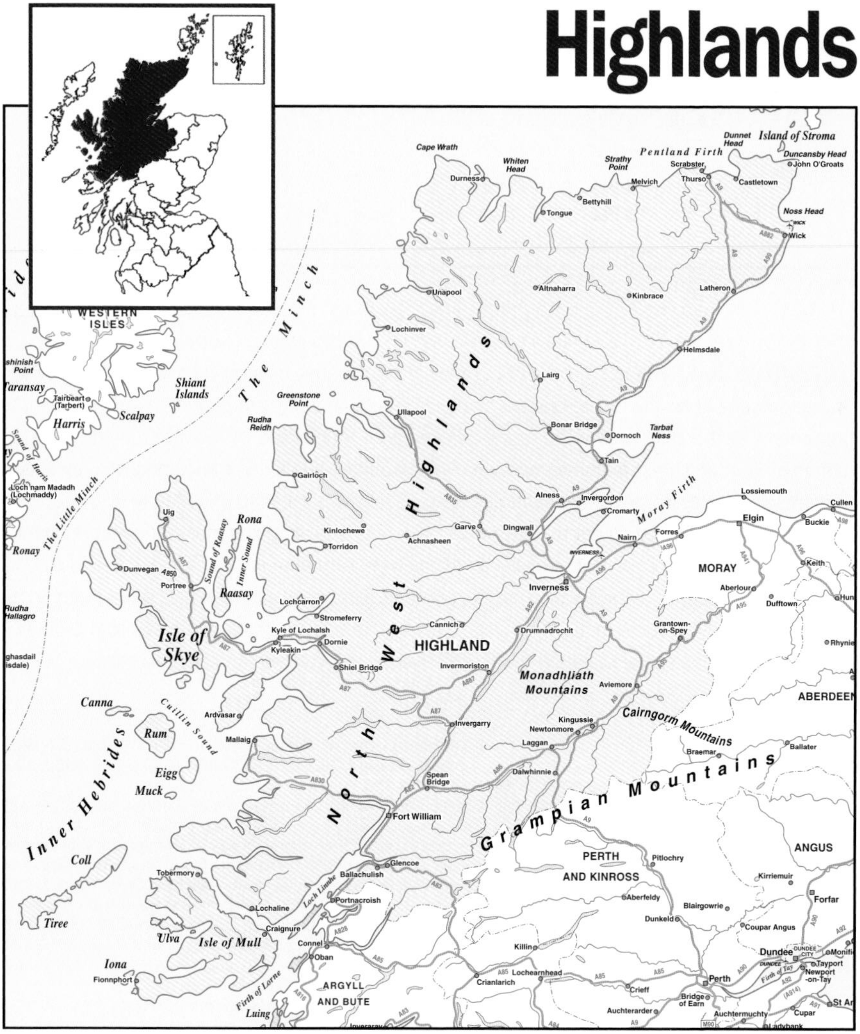

©MAPS IN MINUTES™ 2006.©Crown Copyright, Ordnance Survey Northern Ireland 2006 Permit No. NI 1675.

Apart from the stunning scenery, the major attraction of **The Scottish Highlands** is that there is so much to see and do, whatever the season. Stretching from Fort William in the south, to Wick in the far north, there is a wealth of visitor attractions and facilities. Loch Ness, home of the famous monster, is perhaps the most well-known of these attractions and the Loch Ness Visitor Centre also provides a variety of souvenirs, including kilts and whisky. The Clansman Centre, The Rare Breeds Park and The Caledonian Canal Heritage Centre are also worth a visit. Fort William in the Western Highlands is a busy town with a wide range of shops and services, pubs, restaurants and Scottish entertainment. The West Highland Museum in the town illustrates the tale of Bonnie Prince Charlie and the Jacobites. The North West Highlands is home to the Nations first Geopark, underlining the importance of the area's geological past. The famous Inverewe Gardens with its wonderful array of foreign plants, more formal borders and lovely views everywhere is worth a visit at any season. John O'Groats is, of course, the ultimate destination of most travellers as it was for the Norsemen centuries ago, whose heritage is preserved in the Northlands Viking Centre at Auckengill. The main towns in this sparsely populated area are Dornoch, Golspie, Brora and Helmsdale.

Opportunities exist throughout the Highlands for all kinds of water sports, and the Caledonian Canal is ideal for cruising holidays, or yachting. Other activities include walking, cycling, pony trekking and golf, and anglers will find good sea fishing, as well as some great value day permits for fresh water fishing.

Highlands (North)

Dornoch

This peaceful village is the perfect base from which to tour the northern Highlands. Our home overlooks Loch Shin and is ten minutes' walk from the shops, pub etc. It's perfect for walkers, wildlife enthusiasts, cyclists, bikers and those who just need a break! All three rooms have private bathrooms and TVs. Superb vegan breakfasts that everyone loves! No smoking indoors.

Please call for prices (from £18pppn depending upon time of year, length of stay, two sharing room etc.)

Caroline Snow, Carnbren Vegan Guest House, Station Road, Lairg IV27 4AY • 01549 402259
e-mail: highlandvegan@aol • www.carnbren-vegan.highland-guesthouse.co.uk

LOCHINVER. Arthur and Meryl Quigley, Ardglas Guest House, Inver, Lochinver IV27 4LJ (01571 844257 or 01571 844632).

The guest house gives panoramic views of Lochinver village, the loch, the harbour and the mountains around, including Suilven, in an area distinguished for its walking and angling. We can advise on local walks and attractions. Accommodation comprises one single, five double/twin rooms and two family rooms, with shared facilities. Guest lounge. Ample parking.

Rates: from £21 per person, children under four years free, age four to 11 half price.

- Open all year.

STB ★★★ *GUEST HOUSE.*

e-mail: art@ardglas.co.uk **www.ardglas.co.uk**

Polcraig Guest House nestles on the hillside, centrally in Lochinver village. Family-run, with six very comfortable en suite bedrooms (three twin and three double). Each room is equipped with tea/coffee tray, colour TV, hairdryer and shaving point.

Enjoy hearty breakfasts in our dining room, with local produce used whenever possible. Generous helpings of fresh salmon, smoked haddock, sausage, bacon, eggs and black pudding will set you up nicely for the day ahead. The area is a paradise for anglers (permits available), climbers, walkers, birdwatchers and photographers. Drying area. Car park.

Mr C. MacLeod, Polcraig Guest House, Lochinver IV27 4LD
Tel & Fax: 01571 844429 • e-mail: cathelmac@aol.com
www.smoothhound.co.uk/hotels/polcraig.html

Sordale House, Sordale, Halkirk, Caithness KW12 6XB

Our location is 4½ miles/7 km south of Thurso on the A9, overlooking the river Thurso and the mountains to the south. Accommodation consists of one twin room en suite and one double room with private facilities. We are ideally placed for river and loch fishing, golf and bird watching. The Castle of Mey and the ferries to Orkney are all within a 10 to 30 minute drive. Enjoy motoring once again - no jams or queues, beautiful scenery which Caithness is famed for, peace, quiet and big skies. We welcome dogs by prior arrangement. Private parking. Terms from £25 pppn. For reduced rates please enquire.

Mrs V. Rodgers • 01847 831270 • e-mail: pete.sordale@talktalk.net

Highlands (Mid)

A warm welcome awaits at Heatherdale, situated on the outskirts of Gairloch, overlooking the harbour and bay beyond. Within easy walking distance of the golf course and sandy beaches. Ideal base for hill walking. All rooms have en suite facilities, some with sea view. Excellent eating out facilities nearby. Ample parking. Residents' lounge with open fire.

Scottish Tourist Board ★★★★ B&B

Bed and Breakfast prices from £22 per person per night.

Mrs A. MacIver, Heatherdale, Charleston, Gairloch IV21 2AH
Tel: 01445 712388 • e-mail: BrochoD1@aol.com

PLOCKTON. Margaret & Gerry Arscott, Soluis Mu Thuath Guest House, Braeintra, by Achmore, Lochalsh IV53 8UP (01599 577219).
A warm welcome awaits guests at this family-run guesthouse. All rooms are spacious with lovely views over mountain and forest, en suite facilities, central heating, televisions and hospitality trays. Situated about ten miles north of Kyle of Lochalsh, we offer traditional Scottish hospitality. Whether you are touring, biking, walking or just soaking up the atmosphere, Soluis Mu Thuath is in the ideal location for exploring some of the most dramatic scenery in the Western Highlands. Visit Skye, Plockton, Torridon, Applecross and Glenelg or enjoy some of the many challenging (and less challenging) walks.
Rates: from £25.

- Two of the ground floor rooms are suitable for disabled visitors • Non-smoking

STB ★★ *GUEST HOUSE.*

e-mail: soluismuthuath@btopenworld.com **www.highlandsaccommodation.co.uk**

Pet-Friendly
Pubs, Inns & Hotels

on pages 298-311

Please note that these establishments may not feature in the main section of this book

FHG Guides

publish a large range of well-known accommodation guides. We will be happy to send you details or you can use the order form at the back of this book.

Highlands (South)

A family-run Bed and Breakfast, situated in a quiet cul-de-sac in the centre of Aviemore

Ideal base for a holiday, whether it is fishing, skiing, sailing, bird watching, climbing or any other outdoor pursuit – we cater for all.
Purpose-built drying room and secure storage to protect vital outdoor equipment.
Pick-up/drop-off service to and from the Ski Centre or local glens.
Packed lunches and dinners by prior arrangement.
Luxurious guest lounge with blazing log fire. Private off-road parking.
All rooms are en suite or have their own private bathroom, with king and queen-size beds, TV, radio, hairdryers, controllable electric heating, and a host of other extras.

Complete No Smoking policy • Pets accepted by prior arrangement.

We hope that you arrive as a guest and leave as a friend

Craig-na-gower Avenue, Aviemore PH22 1RW • Tel: 01479 810717
e-mail: enquiry@eriskay-aviemore.co.uk • www.eriskay-aviemore.co.uk

Boat of Garten

Tel: 01479 831234

Heathbank House, Drumuillie Road, Boat of Garten, Inverness-shire PH24 3BD

With a friendly welcome, Heathbank House is the perfect base for your short break or longer stay in an unhurried and relaxed atmosphere. The house, which is non-smoking throughout, has six en suite rooms, two with four-poster beds. Dinner menus change daily and are served in a Charles Rennie Mackintosh style licensed dining room. Alternatively, recline on an Italian leather sofa and sip a whisky in front of our Carrera marble fireplace. Heathbank House is well situated for an array of activities in the region. We are Silver Award Winners in the Green Tourism Business Scheme.

e-mail: enquiries@heathbankhotel.co.uk
www.heathbankhotel.co.uk

Escape to the Scottish Highlands for peace and tranquillity and stay in our comfortable, friendly hotel with fantastic views of Loch Meiklie and Glen Urquhart. The hotel nestles in six acres of wooded grounds close to Loch Ness and Glen Affric nature reserve and is ideally suited for touring the Highlands. Most rooms are en suite and all have tea/coffee making facilities, hairdryer, colour TV, plus video in family rooms. There is a residents' lounge warmed by a log fire, restaurant serving freshly cooked meals and a cosy bar with ample supply of malt whiskies. Bikes can be hired and there is fishing available.

Carol and Ewan Macleod, Glenurquhart House Hotel, Balnain, Drumnadrochit IV63 6TJ
Tel: 01456 476234
e-mail: info@glenurquhart-house-hotel.co.uk
www.glenurquhart-house-hotel.co.uk

Free or reduced rate entry to Holiday Visits and Attractions – see our **READERS' OFFER VOUCHERS on pages 9-42**

FORT WILLIAM. John and Jeanette Mooney, Ben Nevis View Bed and Breakfast, Station Road, Corpach, Fort William PH33 7JH (01397 772131).

Bed and Breakfast establishment located adjacent to the Caledonian Canal basin on the outskirts of Fort William, affording superb views across the water to Ben Nevis. Providing all the modern comforts for today's traveller, Ben Nevis View caters for two to six people in one double and one family room (one double and two single beds), both en suite with colour TV, hairdryer and tea/coffee making facilities. Enjoy a hearty cooked breakfast in our bright, cheery dining room in true Scottish style.

Rates: from £20 to £25 per person per night, subject to season. Family room prices available on request. •

Open from February to October • Non-smoking • Sorry, no dogs

STB ★★★ *B&B.*

e-mail: bennevisview@amserve.net **www.bennevisview.co.uk**

FORT WILLIAM. Stuart & Mandy McLean, Distillery Guest House & Cottages, North Road, Nevis Bridge, Fort William PH33 6LR (01397 700103; Fax: 01397 702980).

Set in the extensive grounds of the former Glenlochy Distillery with its fine distinctive distillery buildings forming a backdrop to one of the most attractive areas in Fort William. The house is situated on the banks of the River Nevis, at the entrance to Glen Nevis and the West Highland Way, but only five minutes' walk from the town centre, railway and bus stations. Seven very well equipped guest rooms, all with en suite facilities, TV, central heating, tea/coffee facilities and hairdryer. Lovely home cooked traditional breakfast. Full fire certificate. Car parking. We look forward to welcoming you.

Rates: from £22.50 to £38.00 per person per night.

• Non-smoking policy in bedrooms. • Open all year. • Self-catering accommodation also available.

STB ★★★★ *GUEST HOUSE,* **AA ◆◆◆◆, RAC ◆◆◆◆** *SPARKLING DIAMOND AWARD. WALKERS AND CYCLISTS WELCOME*

e-mail: DistHouse@aol.com **www.stayinfortwilliam.co.uk**

Melantee

Achintore Road, Fort William PH33 6RW

Melantee is a bungalow situated 1½ miles south of the town on the A82 with views of Loch Linnhe. Ideal centre for touring the Highlands, Inverness, Aviemore, Oban, Mallaig, Kyle of Lochalsh, Skye or walk to the top of Britain's highest mountain, Ben Nevis, via the tourist path.

One double, one twin, one triple and one single room, two shared bathrooms with showers. Tea and coffee facilities in all bedrooms. Access to house at all times. Ample parking. Open all year round. Fire Certificate held. Non-smoking.

Terms from £19 per adult for B&B. Reductions for children in family rooms. Welcome Host.

Mrs F. Cook

Scottish Tourist Board ★★ B&B

Tel: 01397 705329 • Fax: 01397 700453 • e-mail: melanteeftwm@aol.com • www.melantee.co.uk

An Cala is a lovely Victorian granite house set in half an acre and offers comfort in a friendly and cosy atmosphere, only a ten minute walk from the town centre.

Four delightful en suite guest bedrooms with tea/coffee tray and colour TV, hairdryers. Doubles have king-size beds.

Ideally situated for Spey walks, Munros, RSPB Reserves at Boat of Garten and Loch Insh, the Whisky Trail and as a base for visiting castles and most places in the Highlands. Excellent local golf and tennis clubs. Non-smoking. On-site parking. Terms from £30 to £33 per person.

Mrs Val Dickinson, An Cala Guest House, Woodlands Terrace, Grantown-on-Spey PH26 3JU • 01479 873293
e-mail: ancala@globalnet.co.uk

Rossmor Guest House

Built in 1887, the Rossmor is an elegant Victorian villa, with six en suite rooms, one with a Tudor Four-Poster bed. Each room is equipped with a hairdryer, colour TV and complimentary tray. From the elegant lounge and dining room there is a beautiful view of the Cromdale Hills and the Curling Pond. Within easy walking distance of the town, the Rossmor is also ideally situated to visit the Cairngorm Mountains, distilleries and the many attractions the Highlands has to offer. Off-road parking. Non-smoking. Open all year. Credit/Debit cards accepted. Tariff from £26pppn.

The MacDonalds, Rossmor Guest House, Woodlands Terrace, Grantown-on-Spey PH26 3JU
Tel: 01479 872201 • e-mail: RossmorGrantown@yahoo.com • www.rossmor.co.uk

LIVELY • FRIENDLY • STYLISH

Heathmount Hotel

Kingsmills Road, Inverness IV2 3JU
Tel: 01463 235877 • Fax: 01463 715749
e-mail: info@heathmounthotel.com • www.heathmounthotel.com

- Close to the centre of Inverness
- Individually designed bedrooms with LCD TV, DVD and Sky
- Popular restaurant
- Lively bar • Heated patio • Free WiFi throughout

Rates from £75pp single • £47.59pp twin/double
£55pp four-poster • £110 family

Bay View is set in a rural area on famous Culloden Moor, offering comfortable homely accommodation in one twin-bedded room with en suite shower, one double room with en suite bathroom, and one double room with private bathroom.

An excellent touring base for the Highlands of Scotland and many famous historic sites.
All home made food, local produce used.
Choice of Breakfast.
Bed and Breakfast from £22.

Mrs Margaret Campbell, Bay View, Westhill, By Inverness IV2 5BP
01463 790386 • www.bayviewguest.com

e-mail: sunnyholm@aol.com

INVERNESS. Mrs A. Gordon, Sunnyholm Guest House, 12 Mayfield Road, Inverness IV2 4AE (01463 231336). Sunnyholm is situated in a large mature, secluded garden in a pleasant residential area within six or seven minutes walking distance of the town centre, tourist information office and all essential holiday amenities. The front of the house overlooks the garden, with the rear allowing easy access to guests private parking. All rooms are ground floor level and bedrooms are all en suite with colour TV, tea/coffee making facilities, hairdryers, central heating and double glazing. The lounge is a spacious tastefully furnished room with bay window overlooking the garden, as is the diningroom which overlooks the conservatory and garden beyond. ***Rates: Double/Twin from £24pppn, single from £32pppn.***
STB ★★★ *GUEST HOUSE.*
www.invernessguesthouse.com

The Whins

114 Kenneth Street, Inverness IV3 5QG
Tel: 01463 236215

Comfortable, small, homely, non-smoking accommodation awaits you here. Ten minutes bus and railway stations, with easy access to many golf courses, walking and cycling areas, and a great base for touring North, East and West by car, rail or bus. Two double/twin rooms with TV, tea making, washbasins and heating off season. Bathroom, shared toilet and shower; £17 per person. Write or phone for full details.

B&B in 1827 Telford Manse and two timber self-catering cottages in superb rural location in the Cairngorms National Park.
Aviemore 10 minutes • Inverness 45 minutes.
Ideal for many outdoor activities and good touring base. Family, double, twin and single rooms available. Family and pet friendly.

Insh House

Insh House, Kincraig,
By Kingussie PH21 1NU
01540 651377
e-mail: inshhouse@btinternet.com
www.kincraig.com/inshhouse

A former hunting lodge situated within two acres of private grounds, Ardselma has magnificent views of the Cairngorm Mountains. Accommodation comprises two family and one double en suite rooms, one twin room with private facilities, and one single and one twin room with shared facilities. TV lounge available with tea/coffee making facilities; central heating. A three minute walk to the high street or to the golf course.

- Groups catered for, discounts available
- Children and pets welcome • Safe cycle storage • Bed and Breakfast from £20pppn.

Valerie J. Johnston, Ardselma, The Crescent, Kingussie PH21 1JZ
Mobile: 07786 696384 • e-mail: valerieardselma@aol.com

MACDONALD HOTEL

FORT WILLIAM ROAD, KINLOCHLEVEN PH50 4QL

TEL: 01855 831539
FAX: 01855 831416

Ideally located between Glencoe and Ben Nevis at the foot of the Mamores, this family-run hotel has all en suite bedrooms with 8-channel digital TV and Wi-Fi available.

Scottish Tourist Board ★★★ Hotel

The Bothy Bar has great mountain and loch views and serves over 40 malt whiskies, local real ale and fine wines. A pool table, big screen tv and internet access are also available.

Food is served in the bar or the restaurant and fresh local produce is used when available. Dogs are welcome! Also, there is a small campsite and nine climbers' cabins - see our website for more details.

Walkers Welcome

e-mail: enquiries@macdonaldhotel.co.uk
www.macdonaldhotel.co.uk

Situated in the hamlet of Inchree in the village of Onich, eight miles south of Fort William (nearest town). This is a Swedish design bungalow with full central heating. Two twin-bedded rooms and a family room which sleeps four available, with tea making facilities, TV and central heating. One public bathroom plus extra toilet. Bed and breakfast from £18 per person. Children in family rooms half price.

Mrs J. MacLean,

Forester's Bungalow,

Inchree, Onich PH33 6SE

01855 821285

TOMATIN. Robert Coupar & Lesley Smithers, Glenan Lodge (Licensed), Tomatin IV13 7YT Tel & Fax: 0845 6445793. The Glenan Lodge is a typical Scottish Lodge situated in the midst of the Monadhliath Mountains in the valley of the Findhorn River, yet only one mile from the A9. It offers typical Scottish hospitality, home cooking, warmth and comfort. The seven bedrooms, including two family rooms, are all en suite, with central heating, tea-making facilities and colour TV. There is a large comfortable lounge and a homely dining room. The licensed bar is well stocked with local malts for the guests. Glenan Lodge caters for the angler, birdwatcher, hillwalker, stalker and tourist alike whether passing through or using as a base. Bed and Breakfast; Dinner optional. Credit cards accepted.

• Non-smoking. • Open all year round.

AA ★★★

e-mail: glenanlodgecouk@hotmail.com **www.glenanlodge.co.uk**

WHITEBRIDGE HOTEL

Whitebridge, Loch Ness South
IV2 6UN • 01456 486226

Proprietors David & Sarah welcome you to Whitebridge Hotel, where an atmosphere of comfort and quiet goes hand in hand with traditional character. The hotel has stunning views of the Monadhliath Mountains. 12 en suite bedrooms, all with colour TV and tea/coffee making. • Excellent home-prepared food served in the cosy dining room. Comfortable residents' lounge. • Two bars.

AA ★★ HOTEL

Excellent brown trout fishing in the area, also pony trekking, riding, boating, windsurfing, golf, off-road driving.

e-mail: info@whitebridgehotel.co.uk • www.whitebridgehotel.co.uk

Family-Friendly

Pubs, Inns & Hotels

See the Supplement on pages 293-297 for establishments which *really* welcome children.

Please note that these establishments may not feature in the main section of this book

Perth & Kinross

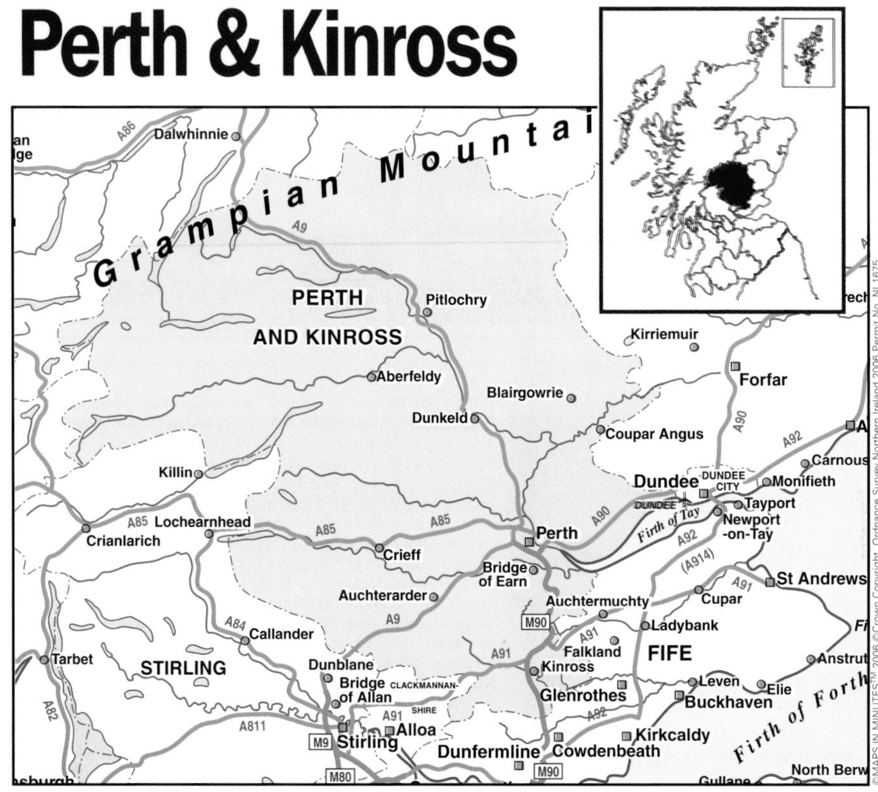

Perth & Kinross embraces both Highland and Lowland. Close to where the two Scotlands meet, a cluster of little resort towns have grown up: Crieff, Comrie, Dunkeld, Aberfeldy, and Pitlochry, set, some say, right in the very centre of Scotland. Perthshire touring is a special delight, as north-south hill roads drop into long loch-filled glens - Loch Rannoch, Loch Tay or Loch Earn, for example. No matter where you base yourself, from Kinross by Loch Leven to the south to Blairgowrie by the berry-fields on the edge of Strathmore, you can be sure to find a string of interesting places to visit. If your tastes run to nature wild, rather than tamed in gardens, then Perthshire offers not only the delights of Caledonian pinewoods by Rannoch and the alpine flowers of the Lawers range, but also wildlife spectacle such as nesting ospreys at Loch of the Lowes by Dunkeld. There are viewing facilities by way of hides and telescopes by the lochside. Water is an important element in the Perthshire landscape, and it also plays a part in the activities choice. Angling and sailing are two of the 'mainstream' activities on offer, though if you are looking for a new experience, then canyoning is a Perthshire speciality on offer from a number of activity operators. Enjoy a round of golf on any of Perthshire's 40 courses, including those at Gleneagles by Auchterarder.

The main town of Perth has plenty of shops with High Street names as well as specialist outlets selling everything from Scottish crafts to local pearls. With attractions including an excellent repertory theatre and a great choice of eating places, this is an ideal base to explore the true heartland of Scotland.

Kirkmichael, Blairgowrie, Perthshire PH10 7NA

Unique, family-run hotel, set in the picturesque hills of Perthshire, less than half-an-hour from Glenshee, Pitlochry and Blairgowrie. The bar is fully licensed, with a good range of malt whiskies; guests can enjoy panoramic views of Strathardle from the dining room. All bedrooms are en suite.

A good central base for touring Perthshire and beyond; many golf courses are within easy reach; skiing at Glenshee in the winter; ideal for walking holidays.

Pets and children welcome.

Please call for brochure for further information.

Bed and Breakfast from £25 pppn.

Scottish Tourist Board ★★ HOTEL

Ideally situated at the gateway to the Highlands, yet only one hour from Edinburgh and Glasgow. Dating from 1700, this charming family-run Inn offers excellent accommodation, an atmospheric dining experience at Willoughby's Restaurant or supper in the Bothy Bar with it s fine range of real ales. We are listed in the Good Beer Guide, Good Pub Guide and Rough Guide to Britain and many more publications.

Tel - 01764 681451
email - bookings@muthillvillagehotel.com
web - www.muthillvillagehotel.com

Ashbank House is a traditional stone and slate built Victorian villa providing comfortable guest accommodation within easy reach of local services and amenities, but with a private rural feel. Two double bedrooms and one twin room, all with en suite/private bathroom facilities. A large mature garden offers you privacy, with beautiful views over woodland and mountains. Relax on the patio or take a stroll along the burn. Private off-road parking, secure storage and drying facilities. This area offers a wide range of recreational pursuits including walking, golf, climbing, cycling, motor biking, water sports, fishing, whisky tasting and many more. There is also a Salmon leap - a well established local attraction.

B&B from £23 to £30 per person.

Ashbank House, 14 Tomcroy Terrace, Pitlochry PH16 5JA • 01796 472711
e-mail: ashbankhouse@btinternet.com • www.ashbankhouse.co.uk

A family-run farm on the A9, 6 miles north of Perth. Accommodation comprises double and twin en suite rooms and a family room (sleeps 4), with private bathroom. The centrally heated farmhouse has a real coal fire in the lounge. There is a large garden and free secure parking. Situated in the area known as "The Gateway to the Highlands", the farm is ideally placed for those seeking some of the best unspoilt scenery in Western Europe. The numerous castles and historic ruins are testimony to Scotland's turbulent past. There are many famous golf courses and trout rivers in the Perth area, and it is only one hour's drive to both Edinburgh and Glasgow.

Newmill Farm, Stanley PH1 4PS
Mrs Ann Guthrie • 01738 828281

e-mail: guthrienewmill@sol.co.uk
www.newmillfarm.co.uk

Renfrewshire

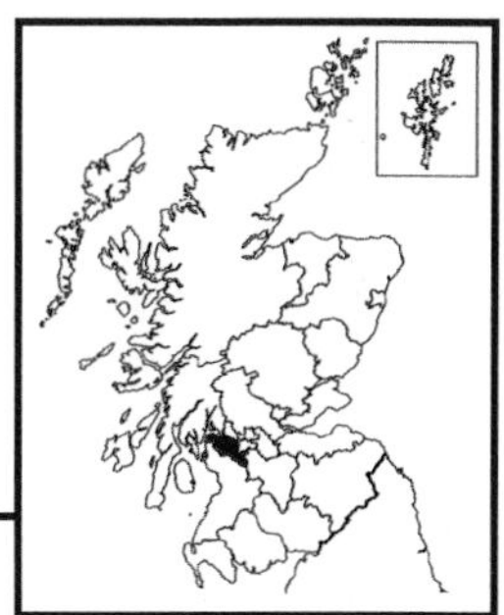

Renfrewshire & Inverclyde - these areas have witnessed the full force of the rise and fall of the Industrial Revolution in Scotland and now host a thriving computer industry and Glasgow's airport. Greenock and Gourock stand at the 'Tail of the Bank' of the Clyde, with ferries to Dunoon and Argyll. The Erskine Bridge across the river commands the road route to Loch Lomond, Oban and the West. Paisley is a busy shopping centre, and the 12th century abbey is well worth a visit. A day out at the RSPB Centre in Lochwinnoch is easy by train or by car. There are nature trails, birdwatching hides and an observation tower. Trains leave Glasgow Central at regular intervals and there is also a frequent bus service.

The district of Inverclyde lies just twenty miles to the west of Glasgow and is ideal for coastal walks starting at Greenock Esplanade. Just off the A78, a winding road leads up to Loch Thom and the Cornalees Nature Trails. Before leaving Inverclyde, stop at Finlaystone Estate in Langbank, a country park with woodland walks.

Paisley

Free or reduced rate entry to
Holiday Visits and Attractions – see our
READERS' OFFER VOUCHERS on pages 9-42

Useful Guidance for Guests and Hosts

Every year literally thousands of holidays, short breaks and overnight stops are arranged through our guides, the vast majority without any problems at all. In a handful of cases, however, difficulties do arise about bookings, which often could have been prevented from the outset.

It is important to remember that when accommodation has been booked, both parties – guests and hosts – have entered into a form of contract. We hope that the following points will provide helpful guidance.

Guests

- When enquiring about accommodation, be as precise as possible. Give exact dates, numbers in your party and the ages of any children.
- State the number and type of rooms wanted and also what catering you require – bed and breakfast, full board etc. Make sure that the position about evening meals is clear – and about pets, reductions for children or any other special points.
- Read our reviews carefully to ensure that the proprietors you are going to contact can supply what you want. Ask for a letter confirming all arrangements, if possible.
- If you have to cancel, do so as soon as possible. Proprietors do have the right to retain deposits and under certain circumstances to charge for cancelled holidays if adequate notice is not given and they cannot re-let the accommodation.

Hosts

- Give details about your facilities and about any special conditions. Explain your deposit system clearly and arrangements for cancellations, charges etc. and whether or not your terms include VAT.
- If for any reason you are unable to fulfil an agreed booking without adequate notice, you may be under an obligation to arrange suitable alternative accommodation or to make some form of compensation.

Stirling & The Trossachs

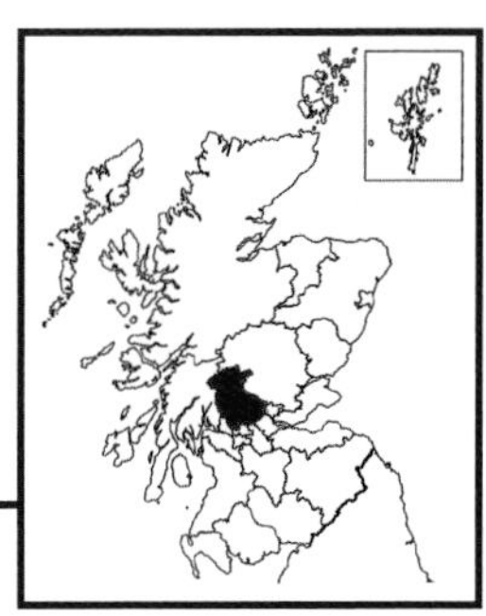

At the heart of Scotland, **Stirling & The Trossachs** has played a central role in most aspects of the nation's life. History and geography have converged here in road and rail routes, in decisive sieges and battles, in important industrial developments and heritage. The county enjoys the natural riches of the Forth valley and the economic wealth of Grangemouth and Falkirk. The town of Stirling itself is a natural tourist centre, both for its own attractions, such as the historic castle and the excellent shopping facilities, and as a base for other visitor attractions close at hand. Villages and small towns such as Drymen, Killearn, Fintry and Kippen offer hospitality and interesting outings. Loch Lomond and The Trossachs National Park is less than an hour from Glasgow, yet feels worlds apart from the bustle of city life. Explore wild glens and sparkling lochs, and for the more energetic, low-level walking, cycling, hill walking, and the new sport of canyoning can be enjoyed.

Blairlogie, Callander

BLAIRLOGIE. Mrs Margaret Logan, Blairmains Farm, Manor Loan, Blairlogie, Stirling FK9 5QA (01259 761338). Charming, traditional stone farmhouse set in attractive gardens on a working farm. Adjacent to a picturesque conservation village and close to the Wallace Monument and Stirling University. Three-and-a-half miles from Stirling. Edinburgh airport is 30 minutes' drive and Glasgow airport 45 minutes. Ideal base for touring and walking. Accommodation is in one double and two twin rooms with shared bathroom. Very comfortable TV lounge. Ample private parking. A warm Scottish welcome awaits you.
Rates: Bed and Breakfast - double or twin £22.50pp; single £25. Room only £20.

- Working farm.
- Children welcome.
- Sorry, no pets.
- Non-smoking.

Riverview House

Leny Road, Callander FK17 8AL
Tel: 01877 330635 • Fax: 01877 339386

Excellent accommodation in the Trossachs area which forms the most beautiful part of Scotland's first National Park. Ideal centre for walking and cycling holidays, with cycle storage available. In the guest house all rooms are en suite, with TV and tea-making. Private parking. Also available self-catering stone cottages, sleep 3 or 4. Sorry, no smoking and no pets. Call Drew or Kathleen Little for details.

e-mail: drew@visitcallander.co.uk
website: www.visitcallander.co.uk

B&B from £25.
Low season and long stay discounts available.
Self-catering cottages from £150 per week (STB 3 & 4 Stars).

Scottish Islands

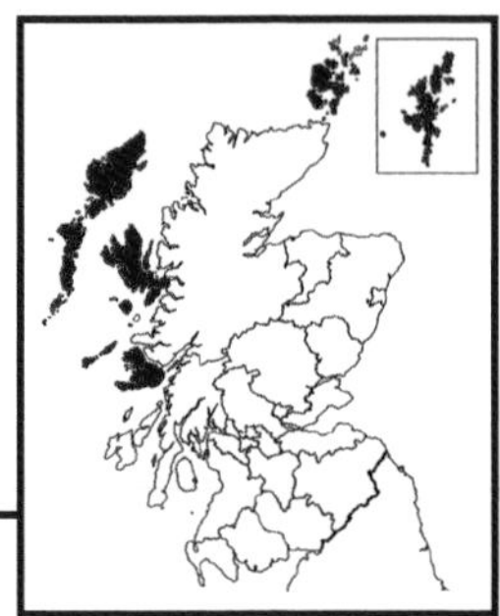

Isle of Skye

The Isle of Skye is the most scenic of the Western Isles, both on the coast and inland, where the Cuillin Mountains are steep and impressive. Access is easy over the famous bridge, and you can still travel 'over the sea to Skye' by taking the "Road to the Isles' from Fort William, then sailing to Armadale. During the summer months, a ferry runs between Glenelg and Kylerhea. While the main appeal of the island is undoubtedly the scenery and the wealth of outdoor activities available, visitor attractions such as the Heritage Centre at Portree, the Talisker Distillery at Carbost, and the Clan Donald Centre at Armadale Castle are worth visiting, as well as the seat of Clan MacLeod at Dunvegan Castle, home of the famous Fairy Flag.

Portree

Set overlooking the picturesque harbour of Portree, The Royal Hotel offers you a quiet, relaxing retreat during your stay on Skye. Accommodation consists of 21 well appointed rooms, most overlooking the harbour and featuring private bathroom facilities and colour TV. Room service is available as well as a fitness centre and sauna for guests to use. The Royal Hotel offers a wide and varied menu serving sea food, lamb, venison and tender Highland beef. Vegetarians are also catered for. There is something for everyone, from walking, climbing and watersports to good food, great local arts & crafts, colourful museums and places of interest.

THE ROYAL HOTEL • Portree, Isle of Skye IV51 9BU
Tel: 01478 612525 • Fax: 01478 613198
e-mail: info@royal-hotel-skye.com • www.royal-hotel-skye.com

The FHG Directory of Website Addresses

on pages 313-346 is a useful quick reference guide for holiday accommodation with e-mail and/or website details

Orkney Islands

Orkney - Less than 10 miles from the Scottish mainland across the Pentland Firth, the 70-odd islands of Orkney are rich in pre-history, but thinly populated in present times. Kirkwall, the capital, is on Mainland, the largest island, where the most accessible and best-known ancient sites are found, inlcuding Maes Howe and Skara Brae. The ruins of Notland Castle on the northern island of Westray, and the famous sheltered harbour of Scapa Flow are other Orkney landmarks.

Kirkwall

KIRKWALL. John D. Webster, Lav'rockha Guest House, Inganess Road, Kirkwall KW15 1SP (Tel & Fax: 01856 876103).

Situated a short walk from the Highland Park Distillery and Visitor Centre, and within reach of all local amenities. Lav'rockha is the perfect base for exploring and discovering Orkney. We offer high quality accommodation at affordable rates. All our rooms have en suite WC and power shower, tea/coffee tray, hairdryer, radio alarm clock and remote-control colour TV. Those with young children will appreciate our family room with reduced children's rates, children's meals and child minding service. We also have facilities for the disabled, with full unassisted wheelchair access from our private car park. All our meals are prepared to a high standard using fresh, local produce as much as possible.

Rates: Bed and Breakfast from £28 per person. Special winter break prices available.

• Children welcome. • Wheelchair access.

STB ★★★★ *GUEST HOUSE, WINNER OF BEST B&B ORKNEY; FOOD AWARDS, TASTE OF SCOTLAND ACCREDITED.*

e-mail: lavrockha@orkney.com **www.lavrockha.co.uk**

Pet-Friendly
Pubs, Inns & Hotels
on pages 298-311
Please note that these establishments may not feature in the main section of this book

Shetland

Shetland -Over 60 miles north of Orkney are the Shetland Isles, where the principal island has the airport at its southern tip at Sumburgh Head. More than 100 islands, just 15 of them inhabited, boast abundant wildlife, a spectacular coastline, and many major archaeological sites. Regular ferries and air services link Shetland with mainland Scotland, as well as the Scandinavian countries, which have close links with the islands. A network of roads, inter-island ferries and bridges make it easy to explore by car from the capital, Lerwick. The vibrant cultural life includes internationally famous events such as the annual Folk Festival, and the Up Helly Aa fire festival.

Brae, Lerwick

BRAE. Mrs E. Wood, Westayre Bed and Breakfast, Muckle Roe, Brae ZE2 9QW (01806 522368).
A warm welcome awaits you at our working croft on the picturesque island of Muckle Roe, where we have breeding sheep, pet lambs, ducks and cats. The island is joined to the mainland by a small bridge and is an ideal place for children. The accommodation is of a high standard and has en suite facilities. Guests can enjoy good home cooking and baking. In the evening sit by the open peat fire and enjoy the views looking out over Swarbacks Minn. Spectacular cliff scenery and clean safe sandy beaches, bird watching and hill walking and also central for touring North Mainland and North Isles.

Rates: Bed and Breakfast from £22 (standard room), £26 (en suite), £25 single.

- Working farm. • Children welcome

STB ★★★★ *B&B*

e-mail: westayre@ukonline.co.uk

www.westayre.shetland.co.uk

Glen Orchy House
Glen Orchy House
20 Knab Road, Lerwick
Shetland ZQE1 0AX
e-mail: glenorchy.house@virgin.net
www.guesthouselerwick.com

Built in 1904 by the Episcopalian church as a convent, and later a Rectory, it was sold into private ownership in 1969. Since then the house has been sympathetically renovated and extended in keeping with the original style, whilst providing every modern comfort for the discerning guest. 5 double rooms, 6 single, 7 twin (one on the ground floor with facilities for disabled) and 4 family rooms. All are en suite. The lounge on the ground floor contains an 'honesty bar' where guest can enjoy drinks before or after meals. There are also board games and a selection of books. Situated on the south side of Lerwick overlooking the Knab and 9-hole golf course (free to the public), it is ideal for birdwatchers, photographers, artists and walkers alike and yet still close to the town centre for business or browsing. Pets and well behaved children welcome.

Please mention **FHG Guides** when making enquiries about accommodation featured in these pages

Wales

lifawr Hotel & Cottages, Newport

Brynderwen Farm B&B, Brecon, Powys

Hafod-y-Garreg, Builth Wells, Powys

Ratings & Awards

For the first time ever the AA, VisitBritain, VisitScotland, and the Wales Tourist Board will use a single method of assessing and rating serviced accommodation. Irrespective of which organisation inspects an establishment the rating awarded will be the same, using a common set of standards, giving a clear guide of what to expect. The RAC is no longer operating an Hotel inspection and accreditation business.

Accommodation Standards: Star Grading Scheme

Using a scale of 1-5 stars the objective quality ratings give a clear indication of accommodation standard, cleanliness, ambience, hospitality, service and food, This shows the full range of standards suitable for every budget and preference, and allows visitors to distinguish between the quality of accommodation and facilities on offer in different establishments. All types of board and self-catering accommodation are covered, including hotels, B&Bs, holiday parks, campus accommodation, hostels, caravans and camping, and boats.

The more stars, the higher level of quality

★★★★★
exceptional quality, with a degree of luxury

★★★★
excellent standard throughout

★★★
very good level of quality and comfort

★★
good quality, well presented and well run

★
acceptable quality; simple, practical, no frills

VisitBritain and the regional tourist boards, **enjoyEngland.com, VisitScotland** and **VisitWales,** and **the AA** have full details of the grading system on their websites

enjoy**England**.com

visit**Wales**.com

National Accessible Scheme

If you have particular mobility, visual or hearing needs, look out for the National Accessible Scheme. You can be confident of finding accommodation or attractions that meet your needs by looking for the following symbols.

 Typically suitable for a person with sufficient mobility to climb a flight of steps but would benefit from fixtures and fittings to aid balance

 Typically suitable for a person with restricted walking ability and for those that may need to use a wheelchair some of the time and can negotiate a maximum of three steps

 Typically suitable for a person who depends on the use of a wheelchair and transfers unaided to and from the wheelchair in a seated position. This person may be an independent traveller

 Typically suitable for a person who depends on the use of a wheelchair in a seated position. This person also requires personal or mechanical assistance (eg carer, hoist).

Anglesey & Gwynedd

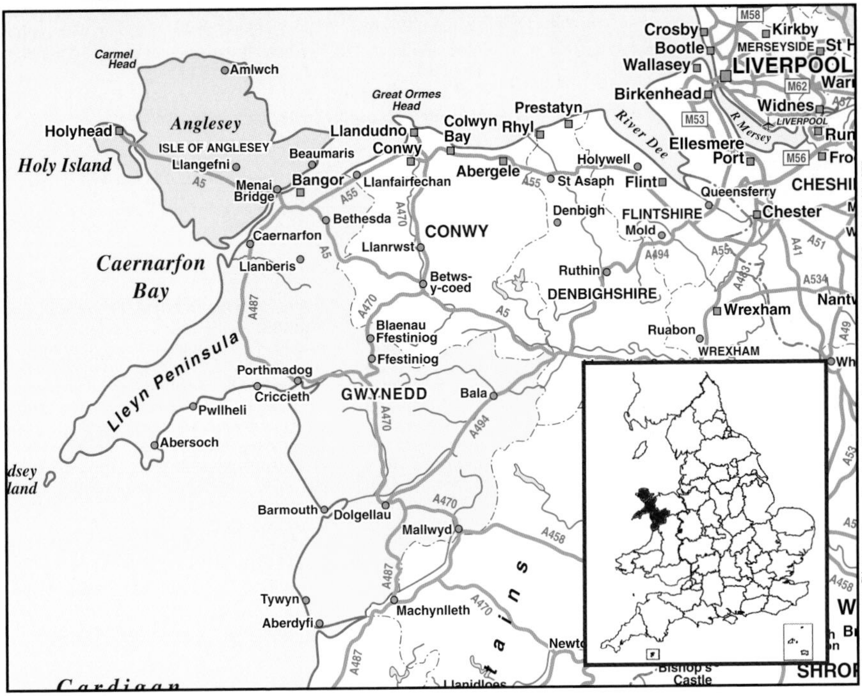

ANGLESEY & GWYNEDD, the northernmost area of Wales, bordered by the Irish sea, has something for everyone. Its beautiful coastline has glorious sandy beaches which offer safe bathing, and there are quaint coastal resorts with attractive harbours and maritime activities, The stunning Snowdonia National Park, right at its centre, covers 823 miles of beautiful, unspoilt countryside and a wide range of leisure activities can be enjoyed. Natural attractions abound throughout the area - mountains, forests, lakes, rivers and waterfalls all wait to be explored, and man-made attractions include castles, railways and industrial archaeology.

Visit the FHG website
www.holidayguides.com
for details of the wide choice of accommodation featured in the full range of FHG titles

Ingledene

A large Edwardian seaside home with magnificent views across Trearddur Bay provides a warm and friendly welcome for your stay. Spacious twin/double rooms (three en suite), most with sea views. Relax and watch the glorious sunsets and wake up to the sound of the waves. All rooms are centrally heated with colour TV and tea/coffee making facilities. Parking at rear, with ample space for boats, etc. Holyhead ferry terminal is only 10 minutes away, with day trips to Ireland from £12.

Bed and Breakfast from £25 per person. Open all year. Self-catering cottage (sleeps 2+2) also available.

Richard and Shirley Murphy, Ingledene, Ravenspoint Road, Trearddur Bay LL65 2YU
Tel: 01407 861026
e-mail: info@ingledene.co.uk • www.ingledene.co.uk

BALA. Mrs C. A. Morris, Tai'r Felin Farm, Frongoch, Bala LL23 7NS (01678 520763).
Tai'r Felin Farm is a working farm, situated three miles north of Bala (A4212 and B4501). Double and twin bedrooms available with beverage tray and clock radio. Beamed lounge with colour TV, diningroom. Central heating. Excellent base for touring Snowdonia National Park, watersports, walking, fishing, and sailing Bala Lake. National White Water Centre one mile. Hearty breakfast. Recommended for excellent cooking and friendly atmosphere. Relax and enjoy a homely welcome. Walkers and cyclists welcome. Car essential.
Rates: Bed and Breakfast from £24.
• Working farm.
WTB ★★ *FARM*

Seaspray is a large, non-smoking Victorian terrace house, situated on the sea front, on the west side of Criccieth Castle on the Lleyn Peninsula. Some rooms are en suite, others have private facilities. Sea views across Cardigan Bay. Pets are welcome. Criccieth is only a short distance away from the Snowdonia National Park, which boasts some of the most beautiful and spectacular scenery in the country. Ample facilities are available for golfers, sailors, fishermen and ramblers. B&B from £23.50 pppn.

Mrs Parker, Seaspray, 4 Marine Terrace, Criccieth LL52 0EF • Tel: 01766 522373
www.seasprayguesthouse.co.uk

Ivy House

FINSBURY SQUARE, DOLGELLAU LL40 1RF
Tel: 01341 422535 • Fax: 01341 422689
e-mail: marg.bamford@btconnect.co.uk
www.ivyhouse-dolgellau.co.uk

A country town guesthouse offering a welcoming atmosphere and good homemade food. Guest accommodation consists of six double rooms, four with en suite toilet facilities, all with colour TV, tea/coffee making facilities and hair dryer. The diningroom has a choice of menu, including vegetarian dishes. The lounge has tourist information literature and there are maps available to borrow. Dolgellau is an ideal touring, walking and mountain biking region in the southern area of the Snowdonia National Park.

Bed and Breakfast from £25, en suite from £30.

WTB ★★ *Guest House* • **AA ★★★**

Boathouse Hotel

Tranquil setting overlooking the harbour • Ferry terminal 4 minutes On the edge of country park and marina • Luxury en suite bedrooms at affordable prices • Seafood a speciality • Bar snacks and chef's specials • Lunches and afternoon teas • Ample free parking

BOATHOUSE HOTEL • NEWRY BEACH • HOLYHEAD • ANGLESEY LL65 1YF
Tel: 01407 762094 • e-mail: boathousehotel@supanet.com
www.holyhead.org/boathouse.html

Gwesty Minffordd Hotel

Talyllyn, Anglesey LL36 9AJ

Tel: 01654 761665 • Fax: 01654 761517

This 17th century Country House Hotel is situated at the foot of Cader Idris mountain in the Snowdonia National Park. There are seven en suite bedrooms, two of which are downstairs(well behaved dogs allowed); two lounges for residents' use, one with real fire. The restaurant is open most evenings and serves freshly prepared meals using local Welsh produce; the small public bar also serves a good selection of home made bar meals. There is a pleasant sitting area outside, and a two acre paddock with stream. Children welcome. Open during Christmas and New Year. Special winter rates available.

e-mail: hotel@minffordd.com • www.minffordd.com

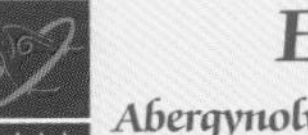

Eisteddfa

Abergynolwyn, Tywyn LL36 9UP

Eisteddfa offers you the comfort of a newly-built bungalow on the Tan-y-coed Ucha Farm, situated adjacent to the farmhouse but with all the benefits of Bed and Breakfast accommodation. The bungalow, which has been designed to accommodate disabled guests, is conveniently situated between Abergynolwyn and Dolgoch Falls with Talyllyn Narrow Gauge Railway running through the farmland. Three bedrooms, two en suite and the third with a shower and washbasin suitable for a disabled person. The toilet is located in the adjacent bathroom. Tea/coffee tray and TV are provided in the bedrooms as are many other extras. We also cater for Coeliac Diets.

Mrs Gweniona Pugh • 01654 782385 • Fax: 01654 782228

North Wales

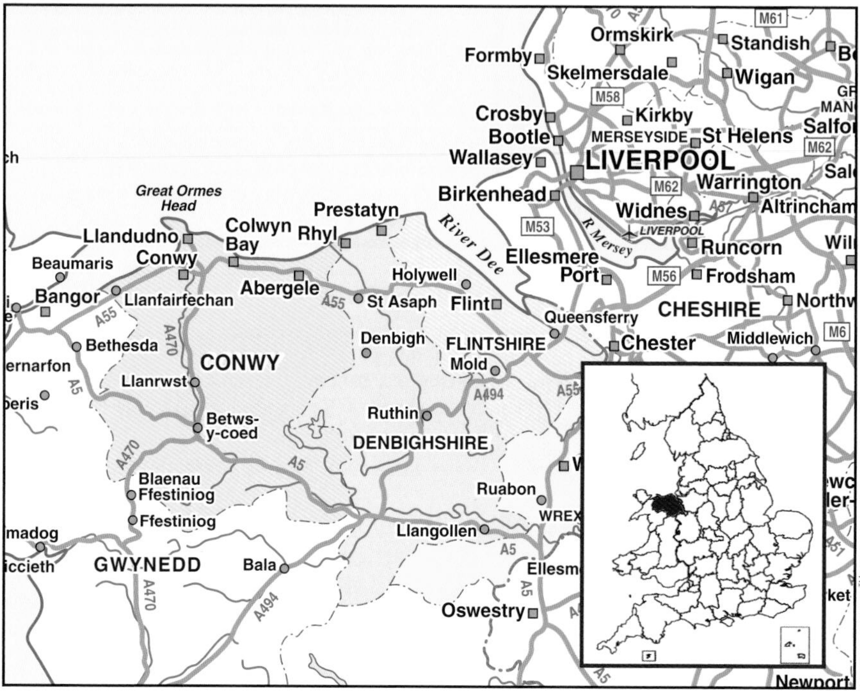

Great Ormes Head
Llandudno
Colwyn Bay
Prestatyn
Rhyl
Beaumaris
Conwy
Abergele
Holywell
Bangor
Llanfairfechan
St Asaph
Flint
Bethesda
Denbigh
FLINTSHIRE
CONWY
Mold
Llanrwst
Ruthin
Betws-y-coed
DENBIGHSHIRE
Blaenau Ffestiniog
Ffestiniog
Ruabon
Llangollen
GWYNEDD
Bala
Oswestry
Formby
Ormskirk
Standish
Skelmersdale
Wigan
Crosby
Kirkby
Bootle
MERSEYSIDE
St Helens
Salford
Wallasey
LIVERPOOL
Birkenhead
Warrington
Altrincham
Widnes
River Dee
R Mersey
LIVERPOOL
Ellesmere Port
Runcorn
Frodsham
Queensferry
CHESHIRE
Chester
Middlewich
A55 A470 A5 A494 M61 M58 M62 M53 M56 M6

Peaceful and quiet, but with a friendly atmosphere, this sheep farm of 181 acres, with scenic views, is situated five miles from Betws-y-Coed. Ideal for touring, within easy reach of Snowdon, Bodnant Gardens, Caernarvon Castle, Llandudno, Black Rock Sands, Ffestiniog Railway, Llechwedd Slate Mines and the Swallow and Conwy Falls. Accommodation comprises one double and one twin bedroom, both with washbasins and tea/coffee making facilities; bath and shower, two toilets. Use of colour TV lounge. Sorry no pets. Car essential, parking for three/four cars. Bed and Breakfast from £20. Open May to October.

MRS E.A. JONES, PANT GLAS, PADOC, PENTREFOELAS ROAD, BETWS-Y-COED LL24 0PG 01690 770248

Mount Garmon View GUESTHOUSE

Located in the centre of Betws-y-Coed, this is an ideal base for relaxing in the picturesque Snowdonia National Park. Whether walking, horse riding, birdwatching, touring, mountain biking, canoeing, fishing, or playing golf, there is something for everyone, including shops, cafes and restaurants. Mount Garmon View provides totally non-smoking accommodation. Four double and one single en suite bedrooms, one twin with private bathroom. All rooms with colour TV, beverage tray, radio alarm, hairdryer and many other thoughtful extras. Excellent choice of breakfast menu; special diets can be catered for by prior arrangement. Drying room facilities available. Large private car park.

WTB ★★★★ B&B

Holyhead Road, Betws-y-Coed, Conwy LL24 0AN
Tel: 01690 710335
www.mount-garmon.co.uk

Bron Celyn Guest House, Lôn Muriau, Llanrwst Road, Betws-y-Coed LL24 0HD • Tel: 01690 710333 • Fax: 01690 710111

A warm welcome awaits you at this delightful guest house overlooking the Gwydyr Forest and Llugwy/Conwy Valleys and village of Betws-y-Coed in Snowdonia National Park. Ideal centre for touring, walking, climbing, fishing and golf. Also excellent overnight stop en route for Holyhead ferries. Easy walk into village and close to Conwy/Swallow Falls and Fairy Glen.

Most rooms en suite, all with colour TV and beverage makers. Lounge. Full central heating. Garden. Car park. Open all year. Full hearty breakfast, packed meals, evening meals - special diets catered for. Walkers and Cyclists Welcome.

B&B from £24 to £30, reduced rates for children under 12 years. Special out of season breaks.

Jim and Lilian Boughton

e-mail: welcome@broncelyn.co.uk • www.broncelyn.co.uk

★★★★

BRYN BELLA GUEST HOUSE

Lôn Muriau, Llanrwst Road, Betws-y-Coed LL24 0HD
Tel & Fax: 01690 710627
e-mail: welcome@bryn-bella.co.uk

www.bryn-bella.co.uk

Bryn Bella is a small but select Victorian guest house in an elevated position overlooking the beautiful village of Betws-y-Coed and the Snowdonia National Park. All rooms have en suite shower facilities, colour TV, microwave, electronic safe, fridge and tea/coffee making facilities. The house enjoys glorious views of the village and surrounding mountains, and has parking for every room. Secure garaging for motorcycles and mountain bikes also available. Free internet connection available in guest lounge.

AA

Non-smoking throughout • Open all year • On-line booking • *Contact Mark and Joan Edwards for details.*

♦♦♦♦ ***B&B from £25pppn. Midweek breaks available October-March, summer breaks April-September.***

Fairy Glen Hotel offers you a warm and friendly welcome, comfortable accommodation and excellent home-cooked food, in a relaxed and convivial atmosphere. All our rooms are well equipped with central heating, colour TV, alarm clock-radio, hairdryer and tea/ coffee making facilities. We have a TV lounge, and cosy licensed bar for our residents to relax in. Our private car park is for guests only. Evening meals available from £15.00 per person. Bed and Breakfast from £26.00 per person per night.

Brian and Enid Youe, Fairy Glen Hotel, Beaver Bridge, Betws-y-Coed LL24 0SH • 01690 710269
e-mail: fairyglen@youe.fsworld.co.uk
www.fairyglenhotel.co.uk

CONWY. Park Hill Hotel/Gwesty Bryn Parc, Llanrwst Road, Betws-y-Coed, Conwy LL24 0HD (Tel & Fax: 01690 710540). OUR HOTEL IS YOUR CASTLE. Family-run country house hotel. Ideally situated in Snowdonia National Park. Breathtaking views of Conwy/Llugwy Valleys. Renowned for excellent service, cuisine and its teddy bear collection. Indoor heated swimming pool with sauna free and exclusively for our guests. Secluded free car park. Golf course and village within six minutes' walking distance. Walkers welcome; guided walks on request. Free shuttle service to nearest railway stations. All our rooms with en suite bathroom facilities, coffee/tea tray, CTV etc. Full cooked English Breakfast. Multilingual staff.
Rates: Bed and Breakfast from £28 per person per night.
WTB ★★★ *HOTEL*, **AA/RAC ★★**. *SPECIAL HOSPITALITY AWARD. ASHLEY COURTENAY AND WHICH? RECOMMENDED.*

e-mail: welcome@park-hill.co.uk
www.park-hill.co.uk

LLANDUDNO. Mrs Ruth Hodkinson, Cranleigh, Great Orme's Road, West Shore, Llandudno LL30 2AR (01492 877688).
A comfortable, late Victorian private residence and family home situated on the quieter West Shore of Llandudno. Only yards from beach and magnificent Great Orme Mountain. Parking: no problem. Town centre is a short pleasant walk away. Many places of interest in surrounding area, and opportunities for sports and recreational activities. Excellent home cooked food. Two en suite rooms with bath and wc, both with views of sea and mountains. Conforms to high standards of S.I. 1991/474. Most highly recommended.
Rates: Bed and Breakfast £25 per person.

LLANDUDNO. Chilterns for Non-Smokers, 19 Deganwy Avenue, Llandudno LL30 2YB (01492 875457).
Catering specifically, and only, for non-smokers, Chilterns is well placed close to the Great Orme, promenade, beach and shops. Our forecourt provides invaluable parking in this beautiful seaside town. We provide Bed and Breakfast accommodation in centrally heated, en suite rooms with king-size beds, hairdryers, alarm clocks, colour TV and beverage trays.
Rates: tariff from £20 per person per night.
• Non-smokers only.
WTB ★★★ *GUEST HOUSE*.
e-mail: info@chilternsguesthouse.co.uk
www.chilternsguesthouse.co.uk

RHOS-ON-SEA. Sunnydowns Hotel, Rhos-on-Sea, Colwyn Bay, Conwy LL28 4NU (01492 544256; Fax: 01492 543223).
A three star hotel, situated close to the beach and shops, with car park, bar, games room, sauna, restaurant and TV lounge. All rooms en suite with remote-control TV, video and satellite channels, radio, tea/coffee facilities, hairdryer, mini-bar/ refrigerator, safe and telephone. The towns of Llandudno, Colwyn Bay and Conwy are only five minutes' drive away and it is just ten minutes to the mountains and castles of Snowdonia.

- Dogs welcome.

e-mail: sunnydowns-hotel@tinyworld.co.uk
www.hotelnorthwales.co.uk

TREFRIW. Mrs B. Cole, Glandwr, Trefriw, Near Llanrwst LL27 0JP (01492 640431).
Large country house on the outskirts of Trefriw Village overlooking the Conwy River and its Valley, with beautiful views towards the Clwydian Hills. Good touring area; Llanrwst, Betws-y-Coed and Swallow Falls five miles away. Fishing, walking, golfing and pony trekking all close by. Comfortable rooms, lounge with TV, dining room. Good home cooking using local produce whenever possible. Parking.
Rates: Bed and Breakfast from £25.

Family-Friendly
Pubs, Inns & Hotels
See the Supplement on pages 293-297 for establishments which *really* welcome children.

Please note that these establishments may not feature in the main section of this book

Carmarthenshire

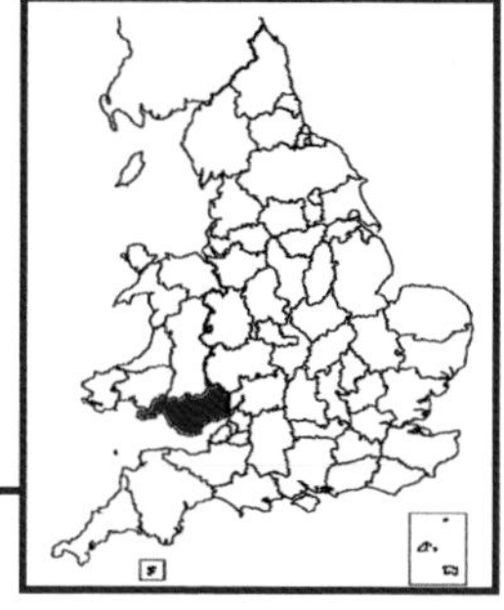

Situated six miles west of Carmarthen town along the A40 towards St Clears. Quiet location, ideal touring base. Working farm run by the Thomas family for the past 100 years. Very spacious, comfortable farmhouse.

All rooms have tea/coffee making facilities, colour TV and full central heating. TV lounge. Evening meals available at local country inn nearby. Good golf course minutes away. Plas Farm is en route to Fishguard and Pembroke Ferries. Ample safe parking.

B&B from £25 per person. Children under 16 years sharing family room half price. A warm welcome awaits. "Welcome Host"

Mrs Margaret Thomas, Plas Farm, Llangynog, Carmarthen SA33 5DB • Tel & Fax: 01267 211492
www.plasfarm.co.uk

The Diplomat Hotel

Felinfoel Road, Aelybryn, Llanelli SA15 3PJ
Tel: 01554 756156 • Fax: 01554 751649
AA/WTB ★★★

The Diplomat Hotel offers a rare combination of charm and character, with excellent well appointed facilities to ensure your comfort. Explore the Gower Peninsula and the breathtaking West Wales coastline. Salmon & trout fishing, horse riding, golf, and motor racing at Pembrey are all within reach.

e-mail: reservations@diplomat-hotel-wales.com
www.diplomat-hotel-wales.com

FHG Guides

publish a large range of well-known accommodation guides. We will be happy to send you details or you can use the order form at the back of this book.

Ceredigion

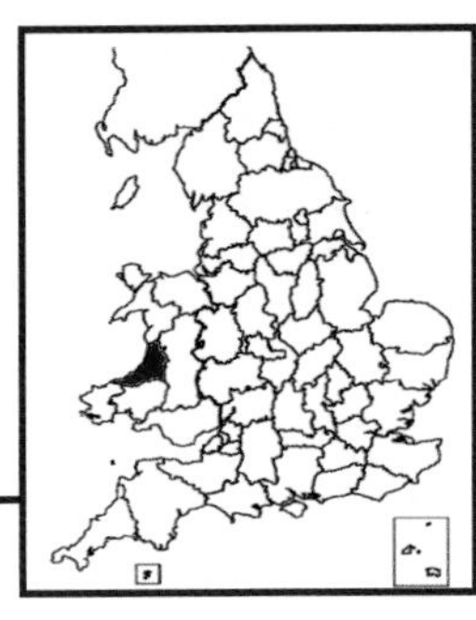

ABERYSTWYTH. Marine Hotel, The Promenade, Marine Terrace, Aberystwyth SY23 2BX (Freephone: 0800 0190020; Tel: 01970 612444; Fax: 01970 617435).
Large seafront hotel with a lift to all floors. Bars, restaurant, bistro and lounges all on ground level. This family-run hotel is highly recommended for its warm, friendly atmosphere, good home cooking, and attention to guests' comfort. The 42 en suite refurbished bedrooms have TV and tea/coffee making facilities, and most have magnificent views of Cardigan Bay. Complimentary use of leisure suite with sauna, steam room, jacuzzi and gym. The hotel has facilities for disabled guests. Bargain breaks and mini-holidays offer excellent value. Golf parties welcome.

- Disabled facilities.

WTB ★★ *HOTEL*

e-mail: marinehotel1@btconnect.com **www.marinehotelaberystwyth.co.uk**

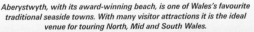

• • • some fun days out in CEREDIGION

Animalarium, Borth • 01970 871224 • www.animalarium.co.uk
New Quay Honey Farm, Llandysul • 01545 560822 • www.thehoneyfarm.co.uk
Llwernog Silver-lead Mine, Ponterwyd • 01545 570823 • www.silverminetours.co.uk

Pembrokeshire

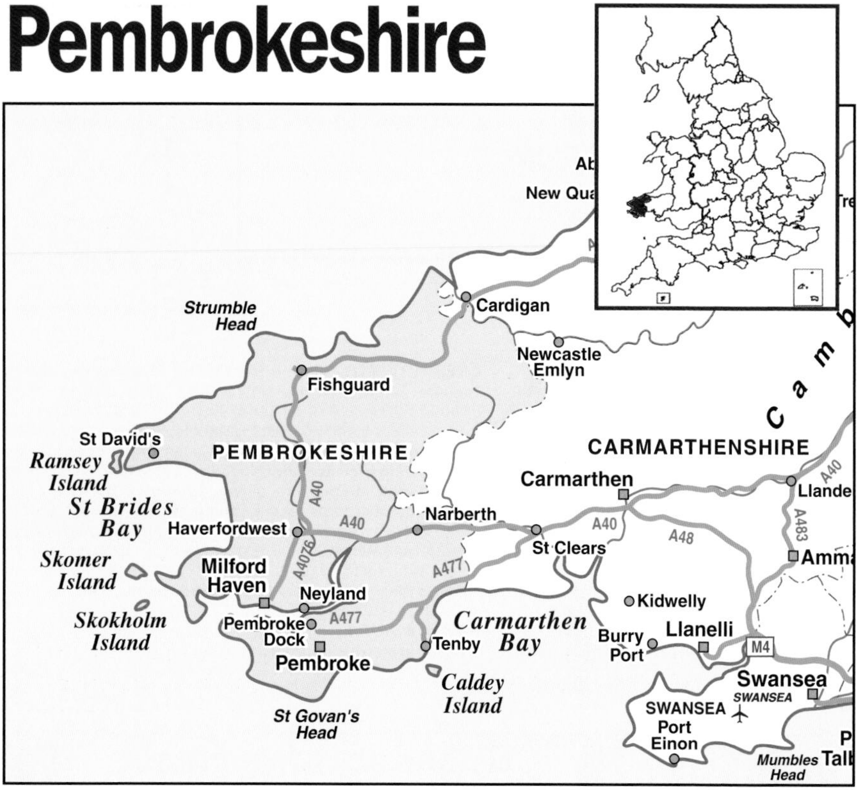

PEMBROKESHIRE'S entire coastline is a designated National Park, with its sheltered coves and wooded estuaries, fine sandy beaches and some of the most dramatic cliffs in Britain. The islands of Skomer, Stokholm and Grasholm are home to thousands of seabirds, and Ramsey Island, as well as being an RSPB Reserve boasts the second largest grey seal colony in Britain. Pembrokeshire's mild climate and the many delightful towns and villages, family attractions and outdoor facilities such as surfing, water skiing, diving, pony trekking and fishing make this a favourite holiday destination.

Welcome to Ivybridge

Situated down a leafy lane, Ivybridge is a modern guesthouse waiting to welcome you. All rooms en suite with TV/hot drinks tray. Swim in our indoor pool, relax in our lounge/bar. Good home cooking, vegetarian and special diets catered for. Ample off-road parking. Close by are quiet walks to the sea which you and your pet will enjoy. Please ring for brochure.

New for 2007 - The Ivybridge Spa

Ivybridge, Drim Mill, Dyffryn, Goodwick SA64 0JT
Tel: 01348 875366 • Fax: 01348 872338
e-mail: ivybridge@cwcom.net • www.ivybridge.cwc.net

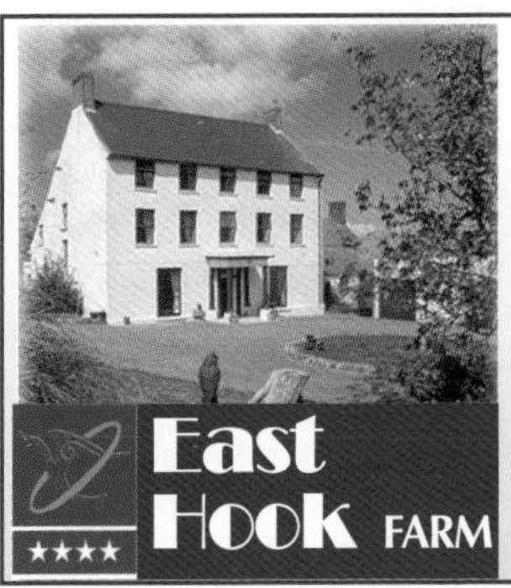

Howard and Jen welcome you to their Georgian Farmhouse surrounded by beautiful countryside, four miles from the coastline and three miles from Haverfordwest. Double, twin and family suite available, all en suite. Ground floor rooms available. Pembrokeshire produce used for dinner and breakfast. Dinner £18pp. Bed and Breakfast from £25 to £30 pp.

Cottage conversion also available from Christmas 2005 – caters for 2 to 8 people.

Mr and Mrs Patrick, East Hook Farm,
Portfield Gate, Haverfordwest, Pembroke SA62 3LN
01437 762211 • www.easthookfarmhouse.co.uk

THE DIAL INN

Ridgeway Road, Lamphey, Pembroke,
Pembrokeshire SA71 5NU
Tel: 01646 672426 • e-mail: info@dialinn.co.uk

The Dial Inn is situated in Lamphey village, two miles east of Pembroke, and only a stone's throw from the Bishop's Palace. This elegant, interesting and deceptively large village pub has excellent bar food, a daily blackboard menu, and an imaginative dining room menu. All food is freshly prepared and cooked. Also available are fine wines and cask-conditioned ales, and the inn is open for coffee, lunch, dinner and bar meals. Accommodation is available in five luxury en suite bedrooms. Open all year.

It is listed in all the best food and beer guides including 'Which?' and the AA. CAMRA.

The FHG Directory of Website Addresses

on pages 313-346 is a useful quick reference guide for holiday accommodation with e-mail and/or website details

Free or reduced rate entry to
Holiday Visits and Attractions – see our
READERS' OFFER VOUCHERS on pages 9-42

GELLIFAWR HOTEL & COTTAGES

This 19th century stone farmhouse has been lovingly restored, ensuring a warm welcome to this family-run hotel. The seven en suite bedrooms are spacious, and have tea/coffee making facilities and colour TV. The non-smoking restaurant offers varied à la carte and bistro menus, and is open to non-residents. There is also a well-stocked bar (non-smoking), where a log-burning fire and friendly staff will ensure an enjoyable visit.

★★★

Self-catering accommodation is available in double glazed, centrally heated cottages (one to three bedrooms), set around a landscaped courtyard, with modern kitchens and all the comforts of home. This scenic area is ideal for walking, birdwatching, cycling, or just relaxing.

Pontfaen, Newport SA65 9TX
Tel: 01239 820343
e-mail: reservations@gellifawr.co.uk
www.gellifawr.co.uk

Vine Cottage Guesthouse

Saundersfoot SA69 9LA
(Non-smoking)

Coastal village outskirts. Sandy beaches and coast path nearby.
Comfortable accommodation, hearty breakfast.
All rooms en suite. Award-winning garden. Pets by arrangement.

AA ★★★★ **01834 814422** **www.vinecottageguesthouse.co.uk**

★★★

LANGDON FARM GUEST HOUSE, SAUNDERSFOOT AND TENBY

Beautifully appointed, idyllic farm guesthouse on working farm overlooking two small lakes in a perfect location close to Saundersfoot and Tenby. All bedrooms en suite with central heating, colour TV and tea/coffee/hot chocolate making facilities. Separate guest sitting room with colour TV. Conservatory/breakfast room overlooking pretty gardens and rolling countryside where horses and sheep leisurely graze while you enjoy your delicious breakfast. Local fresh farm produce used when available. Vegetarians catered for. Perfect base for walking and touring the beautiful beaches, countryside and attractions of Pembrokeshire. Many excellent eating establishments within a short distance, from local Welsh Inns to specialist fish restaurants. Ample parking. Open January 15th - November 15th.

Bed and Breakfast £25 - £29 pppn (based on two sharing). *Welcome Host Gold Award.*

Kilgetty, Near Saundersfoot SA68 0NJ • 01834 814803
e-mail: mail@stayinpembrokeshire.co.uk • www.stayinpembrokeshire.co.uk

Please note

All the information in this book is given in good faith in the belief that it is correct. However, the publishers cannot guarantee the facts given in these pages, neither are they responsible for changes in policy, ownership or terms that may take place after the date of going to press. Readers should always satisfy themselves that the facilities they require are available and that the terms, if quoted, still apply.

Powys

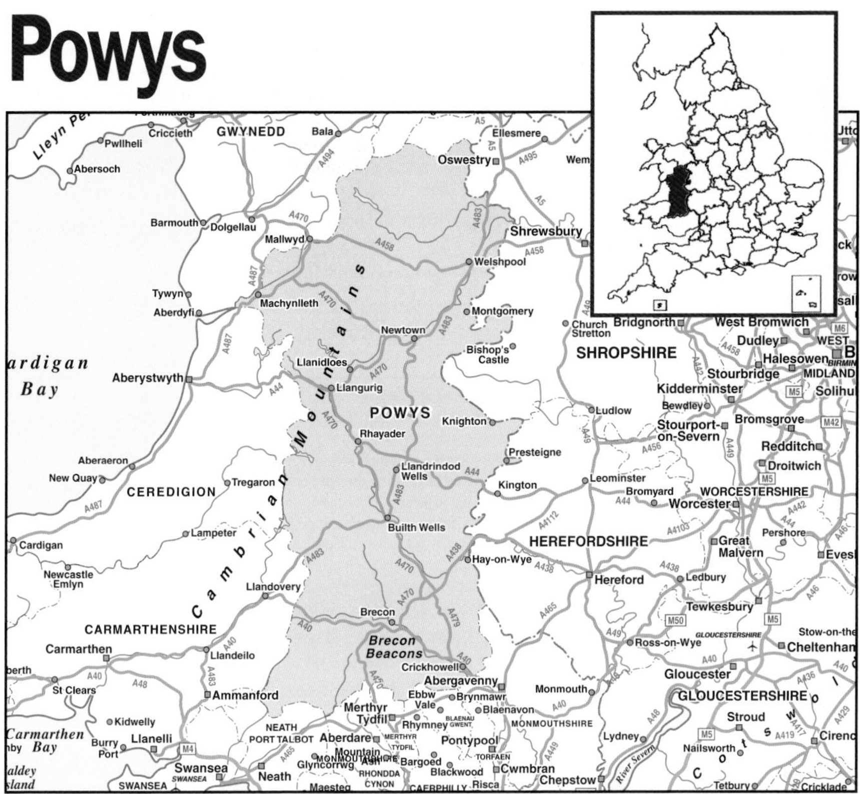

POWYS is situated right on England's doorstep and boasts some of the most spectacular scenery in Europe. Ideal for an action packed holiday with fishing, golfing, pony trekking, sailing and canal cruising readily available, and walkers have a choice of everything from riverside trails to mountain hikes. Offa's Dyke Path and Glyndwr's Way pass through the region. Offa's Dyke Path runs for 177 miles through Border country, often following the ancient earthworks, while Glyndwr's Way takes in some of the finest landscape features in Wales on its journey from Knighton to Machynlleth and back to the borders at Welshpool.

There are border towns with Georgian architecture and half-timbered black and white houses to visit, or wander round the wonderful shops in the book town of Hay, famous for its Literary Festival each May. There are Victorian spa towns too, with even the smallest of places holding festivals and events throughout the year.

Brynderwen

Peaceful smallholding four miles from Brecon, set in the Brecon Beacons National Park, two miles from Llangorse Lake, with pony trekking, walking and mountain biking available locally. A full cooked breakfast is served - healthy option also available, and the village pub serves good meals. All rooms are en suite. Free tea/coffee is provided and newspapers are available in the morning. TV lounge area and outside seating area.

Views of the surrounding countryside - say 'hello' to the sheep!

Terms - adults £30 pppn, children (under 12 years) £15 pppn. Non-smoking. No pets.

Horses may be accommodated in our paddock (£5 per night), but no stabling available.

Mr R Price, Brynderwen Farm Bed & Breakfast, Brynderwen, Talyllyn, Brecon LD3 7SY • 01874 658247

Caebetran Farm

A warm welcome, a cup of tea and home-made cakes await you when you arrive at Caebetran. Well off the beaten track, where there are breathtaking views of the Brecon Beacons and the Black Mountains, and just across a field is a 400 acre common, ideal for walking, bird-watching or just relaxing. The rooms are all en suite and have colour TV and tea making facilities. The dining room has separate tables, there is also a comfortable lounge with colour TV and video. Caebetran is an ideal base for exploring this beautiful, unspoilt part of the country with pony trekking, walking, birdwatching, wildlife, hang-gliding and so much more. For a brochure and terms please write, telephone or fax.

"Arrive as visitors and leave as our friends".

Winners of the 'FHG Diploma' for Wales 1998/99. Welcome Host.

Gwyn and Hazel Davies Caebetran Farm, Felinfach, Brecon, Powys LD3 0UL • Tel: 01874 754460

e-mail: hazelcaebetran@aol.com • www.caebetranfarmhousebedandbreakfastwales.com

BRECON. Mrs Joy Bloss, Beech Copse, 2 Pentrebach Cottage, Trallong, Brecon LD3 8HS (01874 636125). Comfort and tranquillity in a delightful cottage on the edge of the Brecon Beacons National Park. Lovely double en suite room, comfortable adult put-you-up also available. Good food; traditional and vegetarian breakfasts; special diets catered for (please notify in advance). Ideal location for varied walking in the National Park. Abundant wildlife; red kite and buzzard country. A40 approximately one mile; Brecon ten minutes' drive (theatre, restaurants, markets, leisure centre etc). Cyclists and walkers welcome; drying facilities, lifts. Packed lunches, home-cooked evening meals (£7) by prior arrangement.We look forward to welcoming you!

Rates: B&B £22.50 to £30.00, DB&B £29.50 to £37.00.

• No smoking • Children welcome

VisitWales ★★★

e-mail: alan.bloss@talktalk.net

www.beechcopsebb.co.uk

• • • some fun days out in POWYS

Centre for Alternative Technology, Machynlleth • 01654 705950 • www.cat.org.uk

King Arthur's Labyrinth, Corris • 01654 761584 • www.kingarthurslabyrinth.com

WTB/AA ◆◆◆

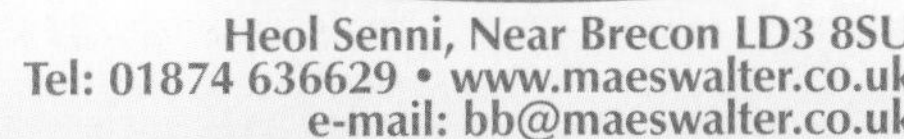

Heol Senni, Near Brecon LD3 8SU
Tel: 01874 636629 • www.maeswalter.co.uk
e-mail: bb@maeswalter.co.uk

Maeswalter is a 300-year-old farmhouse in the mountainous Brecon Beacons National Park. There are four tastefully decorated bedrooms: three en suite and one twin with private bathroom. The comfortable lounge/dining room features exposed timbers. Visitors can roam freely through the grounds where there are seats to sit and admire the scenery and wildlife. Also private apartment (en suite double bedroom and private sitting room). The apartment and all bedrooms have colour TV and beverage trays with tea/coffee/ chocolate and biscuits.

Twin room with private bathroom £30pppn • double en suite £28pppn • private suite £35pppn.

Hafod-y-Garreg

The oldest house in Wales, Henry IV's Hunting Lodge, nestling on a wooded hillside and well off the beaten track, above, reputedly, the most picturesque part of the River Wye. A short drive from Hay-on-Wye 'Town of Books', and Brecon and the Beacons National Park. Alternatively, leave your car and step through our gate into a walkers' paradise, steeped in ancient Celtic history. Drink spring water from the tap, and have an enormous breakfast with our free-range eggs. Enjoy a delicious candlelit supper with log fires in the massive inglenook. Bed and Breakfast £55 per double en suite, dinner available at £17.50 per person.

Annie and John McKay, Hafod-y-Garreg,
Erwood, Builth Wells LD2 3TQ • 01982 560400
www.hafodygarreg.co.uk
e-mail: john-annie@hafod-y.wanadoo.co.uk

Set in 3 acres of beautiful Welsh countryside and close to the famous Elan Valley. Accommodation includes touring pitches and fully equipped motel units which have either a twin or double bedroom, shower room, and kitchen with a dinette that converts to a double bed. Sleeping up to 4, they can be booked for either self-catering or B&B. On-site facilities include restaurant, bar and snug, TV lounge/reading room. Well behaved pets are very welcome.

- *self-catering chalets (max.4 persons)*
- *bed & breakfast*
- *all bedding & towels provided*
- *touring caravan pitches*
- *tent pitches*
- *restaurant (carvery on Sundays and extensive home-cooked food menu, bar snacks, takeaway)*
- *functions (up to 50 seated)*
- *group bookings*

www.parkmotel.co.uk

FOREST CABIN BARGAIN BREAKS

Tel: 02920 754887

Arguably as like the Canadian Rockies as you will find in this country. High in the majestic mountains and forests of Mid-Wales. Enjoy the sheer exhilaration of mountain air so pure it sparkles like champagne! Pets very welcome.

www.victoriawells.org.uk

3 nights from £83, 7 nights from £199

Gwernstablau is a tranquil 17th century farmhouse set in its own five acre grounds. It tastefully combines the old world charm of a wealth of beamed ceilings and open log fires with the convenience of modern central heating and en suite accommodation.

Dinner can be enjoyed in the distinctive dining room with its galleried landing, crystal chandelier and antique furniture.

Bed and Breakfast £26. Enjoy a short break or longer stay. Individual attention assured.

www.gwern-stablau.com

NEWTOWN. Mrs Vi Madeley, Greenfields, Kerry, Newtown SY16 4LH (01686 670596; mobile: 07971 075687; Fax: 01686 670354).

A warm welcome awaits you at Greenfields. All rooms are tastefully decorated and are spacious in size, each having panoramic views of the rolling Kerry hills. There is a good choice of breakfast menu and evening meals can be provided by prior arrangement; packed lunches are also available. Licensed for residents. Accommodation available in twin, double, family and single rooms, all en suite (twin rooms let as singles if required). Hostess tray and TV in all rooms. The diningroom has individual tables. A good place for stopping for one night, a short break or longer holiday. Excellent off-road parking. Brochure available.

Rates: Bed and Breakfast from £45 double or twin room, from £26 single and £70 family room.

WTB ★★★ *GUEST HOUSE.*

e-mail: info@greenfields-bb.co.uk **www.greenfields-bb.co.uk**

Once a workhouse and now a beautiful and very comfortable hotel, Brynafon has great character and charm. It is set against the dramatic backdrop of Gwastedyn Hill and the Druid's Circle, and is a stone's throw from the River Wye. Sitting in the very heart of the beautiful and still yet undiscovered Elan Valley, Brynafon is a must to visit any time of year. We cook fresh food each day, and change our set two and three-course menus five times per week, as well as offering a daily specials board. Our aim is to have a balanced menu which always has several vegetarian, meat and fish options. Brynafon has a total of 20 en suite bedrooms; three are family suites containing an extra bedroom, which brings the total number of bedrooms to 23. All are different, and most have beautiful views of the surrounding countryside.

B&B prices range from £61-£88 for two sharing, with family suites from £88. Brochure and tariff on request.

South Wales

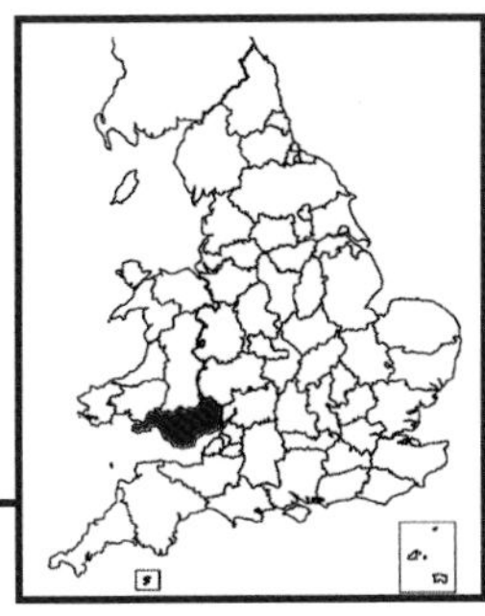

Culver House Hotel, Port Eynon, Gower SA3 1NN

01792 390755 • www.culverhousehotel.co.uk

Nestling against the sand dunes, Culver House enjoys an idyllic location overlooking the beautiful "Blue Flag" beach at Port Eynon. The bay is extensively used for swimming and watersports and access to the beach and dunes is easy.

An ideal base to explore Gower, our quiet, family-run hotel offers a licensed bar and comfortable lounge equipped with a library of interesting books to delight walkers, nature lovers and bird watchers alike. We welcome singles and do not charge a supplement.

All bedrooms have en suite or private facilities, most have sea views. Ground floor rooms available. Non-smoking.

Tallizmand Guest House

Llanmadoc, Gower, Swansea SA3 1DE

Tel: 01792 386373

Tastefully furnished en suite rooms. Packed lunches. Near to beautiful secluded beaches, lined by pine forests and salt marshes. Coastal and inland walks, flowers, birds. Open all year. No smoking.

B&B from £27.50pppn

WTB ★★★★

e-mail: tallizmandbb@aol.com • www.tallizmand.co.uk

A spacious and homely 16th century (Grade II Listed) former farmhouse with oak beams and inglenook fireplaces, set in large attractive garden with stream. An excellent base for visiting the Wye Valley, Forest of Dean and Black Mountains. All nine bedrooms are en suite or have private facilities. Own car park • Terrace, barbecue • Colour TV • Non-smoking.

Bed and Breakfast from £24 to £28 per person, Evening Meals by arrangement.

Rosemary and Derek Ringer, Church Farm Guest House, Mitchel Troy, Monmouth NP25 4HZ • 01600 712176

www.churchfarmmitcheltroy.co.uk

info@churchfarmguesthouse.eclipse.co.uk

SPECIAL WELCOME SUPPLEMENT

Are you looking for a guest house where smoking is banned, a farmhouse that is equipped for the disabled, or a hotel that will cater for your special diet? If so, you should find this supplement useful. Its three sections, NON-SMOKERS, DISABLED, and SPECIAL DIETS, list accommodation where these particular needs are served. Brief details of the accommodation are provided in this section; for a fuller description you should turn to the appropriate place in the main section of the book.

Non-smoking • England

LONDON, HAMMERSMITH. Anne and Sohel Armanios, 67 Rannoch Road, Hammersmith, London W6 9SS (020 7385 4904; Fax: 020 7610 3235). Comfortable, centrally located Edwardian family home. Great base for sightseeing. Excellent transport access. Bed and Continental Breakfast £25 pppn Double; £36 single. Smoking only in garden.

CAMBRIDGESHIRE, BURWELL. Mrs H. Marsh, The Meadow House, 2a High Street, Burwell CB5 0HB (01638 741926; Fax: 01638 741861). Bed and Breakfast in spacious rooms. Variety of en suite accommodation, all have TV, central heating and tea/coffee making facilities. Car parking. No smoking. **ETC ◆◆◆◆**

CAMBRIDGESHIRE, ELY. Mrs C. Bennett, Stockyard Farm B&B, Wisbech Road, Welney, Wisbech PE14 9RQ (01354 610433). Between Ely and Wisbech, ideal for touring, birdwatching. Two bedrooms; guest lounge. Vegetarians and vegans welcome. Free-range produce. Pets by arrangement. Non-smoking throughout.

CHESHIRE, CHESTER. Brian and Hilary Devenport, White Walls, Village Road, Christleton, Chester CH3 7AS (Tel & Fax: 01244 336033). Two miles Chester, off the A41, close to A55, M53 and North Wales. En suite double bedroom, twin-bedded room with washbasin, all including English Breakfast. Non-smoking. Sorry, no children or pets.

CORNWALL, POLZEATH. Mrs P. White, Seaways, Polzeath PL27 6SU (01208 862382). small family guest house, 250 yards from safe, sandy beach. All bedrooms with en suite or private bathrooms, comprising one family, two double, two twin and a single room. Chldren welcome. Non-smoking establishment. Open all year round. **AA ◆◆◆**

CORNWALL, ST IVES. Angela and Barrie Walker, Rivendell, 7 Porthminster Terrace, St Ives TR26 2DQ (Tel & Fax: 01736 794923). Highly recommended non-smoking guest house with a reputation for excellent meals prepared by Barrie, our chef. Superb location with sea views from many rooms. Parking available. Open all year. **RAC ◆◆◆◆**, *SPARKLING DIAMOND AWARD, DINING AWARD.*

CUMBRIA, AMBLESIDE. Broadview Guest House, Lake Road, Ambleside LA22 0DN (015394 32431). Quality, friendly guest house with 6 comfortable bedrooms (most en suite). Broadview is perfect for a holiday or short break. Special diets catered for. Non smoking. **AA ★★★★**

CUMBRIA, AMBLESIDE. Ferndale Lodge, Lake Road, Ambleside LA22 0DB (015394 32207). Small, family-run guest house with 10 attractive en suite bedrooms, several with views of fells. Good home-cooked English or vegetarian breakfast. Open all year. Non-smoking. **ETC ◆◆◆**

CUMBRIA, AMBLESIDE. Rothay House, Rothay Road, Ambleside LA22 0EE (Tel & Fax: 015394 32434). Attractive modern guest house; all bedrooms en suite. Within easy walking distance of village centre. Open all year. Children over 4 years welcome; sorry, no pets. Strictly non-smoking.

CUMBRIA, APPLEBY. Barbara and Derick Cotton, Glebe House, Bolton, Appleby-in-Westmorland CA16 6AW (017683 61125). Centrally heated former farmhouse; two double (one en suite) and one twin room all with tea-making facilities. Hearty breakfasts served, special diets catered for. Children welcome. Non-smoking. **ETC ◆◆◆◆**

CUMBRIA, BOWNESS-ON-WINDERMERE. Annisgarth B&B, 48 Craig Walk, Bowness-on-Windermere LA23 2JT (015394 43866). Three double bedrooms, one twin, one family room and a deluxe room with a jacuzzi bath and lake view. All diets are catered for including vegetarian and vegan. All produce is local with free range eggs. Exclusively non-smoking.

CUMBRIA, COCKERMOUTH. Amanda Vickers, Mosser Heights, Mosser, Cockermouth CA13 0SS (01900 822644). Comfortable, spacious en suite bedroom, cosy lounge and dining room with log fires. On family-run farm, close to fells and lakes of Loweswater and Cockermouth. Hearty breakfast.

CUMBRIA, PENRITH. Greenah Crag, Troutbeck, Penrith CA11 0SQ (017684 83233). Two double bedrooms with bathroom en suite, and one twin-bedded room with washbasin, all with tea/coffee making facilities. A full breakfast is served in the oak-beamed diningroom. Regret no pets or smoking in the house.

CUMBRIA, WINDERMERE. St John's Lodge, Lake Road, Windermere LA23 2EQ (015394 43078; Fax: 015394 88054). Pretty Lakeland B&B, exclusively for non-smokers, situated close to all amenities. Extremely wide choice of breakfasts. Free access to nearby luxury leisure club. Free internet access. **AA** *3 RED DIAMONDS*.

CUMBRIA, WINDERMERE. The Firgarth, Ambleside Road, Windermere LA23 1EU (015394 46974; Fax: 015394 42384). Elegant Victorian house; all bedrooms en suite with tea/coffee making and colour TV. Guest lounge. Ample private parking. Good selection of restaurants nearby. Non-smoking establishment.

CUMBRIA, WINDERMERE. Beckmead House, 5 Park Avenue, Windermere LA23 2AR (Tel & Fax: 015394 42757). Small, family-run guest house with quality accommodation, delicious breakfasts, and a relaxed, friendly atmosphere. All rooms en suite or with private bathrooms. Comfortable residents' lounge. **ETC ◆◆◆◆**

DERBYSHIRE, WINSTER. Mrs Jane Ball, Brae Cottage, East Bank, Winster DE4 2DT (01629 650375). 300-year-old cottage offering independent en suite accommodation across paved courtyard. Furnished and equipped to a high standard. Ample private parking. Non-smoking throughout. **ETC ◆◆◆◆** *SILVER AWARD*.

DEVON, ASHBURTON (Dartmoor). Mrs Joy Hasler, Riversmead, Newbridge, Near Ashburton TQ13 7NT (01364 631224). Quality en suite accommodation with stunning views. Full central heating, tea/coffee making facilities. Ample parking. Non-smoking. Children over 12. Dogs by arrangement. Open all year.

DEVON, BIDEFORD. The Mount, Northdown Road, Bideford EX39 3LP (01237 473748). Small, interesting Georgian building, full of character and charm with quiet, restful bedrooms, (single, double, twin and family); all en suite. Tea and coffee making facilities are available. All rooms have TV. Non-smoking. **ETC/AA ◆◆◆◆**

DEVON. BIDEFORD. Graham and Liz White, Bulworthy Cottage, Stoney Cross, Alverdiscott, Near Bideford EX39 4PY (01271 858441). Three 17th century miner's cottages sympathetically renovated to modern standards whilst retaining many original features. Good choice of breakfasts and evening meals. **ETC** ★★★★ *SILVER AWARD*.

DEVON, CHUDLEIGH. Jill Shears, Glen Cottage, Rock Road, Chudleigh TQ13 0JJ (01626 852209). 17th century thatched cottage idyllically set in secluded garden, with stream surrounded by woods. Outdoor swimming pool. Tea/coffee all rooms.

DEVON, CROYDE. Audrey Isaac, Crowborough Farmhouse, Georgeham, Braunton EX33 1JZ (01271 891005). Quiet and secluded old farmhouse two miles from Croyde. Enjoy exploring beaches, coastal walks and countryside. Three bedrooms, two bathrooms; breakfast/sitting room. No children or pets.

DEVON, ILFRACOMBE. Wentworth House, 2 Belmont Road, Ilfracombe EX34 8DR (Tel & Fax: 01271 863048). Friendly family-run private hotel only minutes from the town and harbour. En suite rooms with colour TV, tea/coffee making facilities. Home cooked food, packed lunches on request. Private parking. No smoking. Open all year.

DEVON, LYNMOUTH. Tricia and Alan Francis, Glenville House, 2 Tors Road, Lynmouth EX35 6ET (01598 752202). Delightful Victorian house built in local stone, full of character and lovingly refurbished. Award-winning garden. Picturesque village, enchanting harbour. Enjoy a four-course breakfast in our attractive dining room. Non-smoking. Licensed. **AA ◆◆◆◆**

DEVON, LYNTON. Pine Lodge, Lynway, Lynton EX35 6AX (01598 753230). Set in landscaped gardens a short stroll from Lynton. Spacious en suite rooms and comfortable lounge; ground floor bedrooms available. Children over 12 welcome. Licensed. Non-smoking. **AA ★★★★**

DEVON, MORETONHAMPSTEAD. Great Sloncombe Farm, Moretonhampstead Devon TQ13 8QF (01647 440595). Comfortable double and twin rooms with en suite facilities, TV, central heating and coffee/tea making facilities. Delicious Devonshire breakfasts with new baked bread. No smoking. Open all year. **ETC/AA ◆◆◆◆, ETC** *SILVER AWARD*

DEVON, TORQUAY. Aveland Hotel, Aveland Road, Babbacombe, Torquay TQ1 3PT (Tel/Minicom: 01803 326622; Fax: 01803 328940). Family-run, licensed hotel in quiet, level location. Panoramic views. All rooms en suite. Evening meal optional. Non-smoking Silver Award. **AA ★★★★**

DEVON, YELVERTON. Linda Landick, Eggworthy Farm, Sampford Spiney, Yelverton PL20 6LJ (01822 852142). One double en suite room, one family suite, both with colour TV, tea/coffee facilities and fridge. Full English breakfast. Non-smoking. Pets welcome. Open all year except Christmas. Brochure available. **ETC ◆◆◆**

DORSET, BEAMINSTER. Caroline and Vincent Pielesz, The Walnuts, 2 Prout Bridge, Beaminster DT8 3AY (01308 862211). Very well situated in this medieval town, the house has been very tastefully refurbished with en suite rooms, tea and coffee making facilities, all the comforts of home. Totally non smoking. **ETC ◆◆◆◆** *SILVER AWARD.*

DORSET, BOURNEMOUTH. Hazel & Keith Ingram, Woodside Hotel, 29 Southern Road, Southbourne, Bournemouth BH6 3SR (01202 427213). Situated on a quiet tree-lined road within two minutes of 'Blue Flag' beach. All rooms en suite, with tea/coffee making facilities, colour TV and shaver point. **ETC ◆◆◆◆**

DORSET, BRIDPORT. Britmead House Hotel, West Bay Road, Bridport DT6 4EG (01308 422941; Fax: 01308 422516). Elegant Edwardian house ideally situated between Bridport and West Bay Harbour. En suite rooms (two ground floor). Lounge and dining room. Non-smoking.

DORSET, DORCHESTER. Churchview Guest House, Winterbourne Abbas, Dorchester DT2 9LS (Tel & Fax: 01305 889296). Beautiful 17th Century Licensed Guest House set in the heart of West Dorset, character bedrooms, delightful period dining room, two lounges and bar. Ideal base for touring. Non-smoking. Short breaks available. **ETC ◆◆◆◆**

DORSET, LULWORTH COVE. John and Jenny Aldridge, Applegrove, West Road, West Lulworth, Wareham BH20 5RY (01929 400592). Comfortable accommodation in central yet quiet position. Two double rooms and one twin/super king (with balcony), all en suite. Generous traditional English, Vegetarian or Vegan breakfast using home grown produce and eggs. Open all year except Christmas and New year. **ETC ◆◆◆**

HAMPSHIRE, LYMINGTON. Mrs R Sque, Harts Lodge, 242 Everton Road, Lymington SO41 0HE (01590 645902). Bungalow set in three acres. Accommodation comprising double, twin and family en suite rooms, each with tea/coffee making facilities and colour TV. Horse riding, golf and fishing are nearby. Pets welcome. **AA ★★★★**

LANCASHIRE, BLACKPOOL. Elsie and Ron Platt, Sunnyside and Holmsdale Hotel, 25-27 High Street, North Shore, Blackpool FY1 2BN (01253 623781). Two minutes from North Station, five minutes from Promenade, all shows and amenities. Colour TV lounge. Central heating. No smoking.

NORTHUMBERLAND, SEAHOUSES. Paul and Donna, Wyndgrove House, 156 Main Street, Seahouses NE68 7UA (01665 722855). Quietly situated within short walking distance of sea front. Newly refurbished, comfortable rooms all with en suite facilities. Ground floor rooms available. No smoking. Vegetarian breakfast on request.

SOMERSET, BATH. Michael and Carole Bryson, Walton Villa, 3 Newbridge Hill, Bath BA1 3PW (01225 482792; Fax: 01225 313093). All bedrooms tastefully decorated and furnished with en suite facilities, hospitality tray, colour TV, hairdryer and central heating. No smoking policy throughout. **ETC ◆◆◆◆**

STAFFORDSHIRE, OAKAMOOR. Mrs D. Bickle, Crowtrees Farm, Oakamoor, Stoke-on-Trent ST10 3DY (Tel & Fax: 01538 702260). Working family farm offering comfortable accommodation in four en suite bedrooms and family rooms in a converted barn. Within easy reach of Alton Towers. Special short breaks available. Non-smoking. **AA ★★★★**

SURREY, GATWICK. Carole and Adrian Grinsted, The Lawn Guest House, 30 Massetts Road, Horley RH6 7DF (01293 775751; Fax: 01293 821803). Imposing Victorian house, five minutes from Gatwick Airport. All rooms en suite with TV, hairdryer, tea/coffee/chocolate tray, direct dial phone and computer modem sockets. Central heating. Children welcome. Totally non-smoking.

SUSSEX (EAST), HASTINGS. Peter Mann, Grand Hotel, Grand Parade, St Leonards, Hastings TN38 0DD (Tel & Fax: 01424 428510 or 0870 2257025). Seafront family-run hotel; some rooms with colour TV, radio; some en suite. Wi-fi broadband access throughout. Unrestricted/disabled parking. Non-smoking restaurant. Licensed bar. **ETC ◆◆◆**

NORTH YORKSHIRE, RIPON. Mrs L. Hitchen, St George's Court, Old Home Farm, High Grantley, Ripon HG4 3PJ (01765 620618). Five ground floor en suite rooms round a pretty courtyard, all full of character - oak beams etc., with modern facilities and views over countryside. Private fishing lake. **AA ◆◆◆◆**

NORTH YORKSHIRE, SCARBOROUGH. Sue and Tony Hewitt, Harmony Country Lodge, Limestone Road, Burniston, Scarborough YO13 0DG (0800 2985840; Tel & Fax: 01723 870276). Relaxing octagonal retreat, superb 360° views of the National Park and sea. Licensed, private parking, completely non-smoking. Warm and friendly. **ETC ★★★★**

Non-smoking • Scotland

AYRSHIRE, LARGS. Mrs M. Watson, South Whittlieburn Farm, Brisbane Glen, Largs KA30 8SN (01475 675881). Superb farmhouse accommodation, enormous delicious breakfasts, warm, friendly hospitality. Nominated for "AA LANDLADY OF THE YEAR 2005", and chosen by "WHICH BEST BED & BREAKFAST". All rooms en suite. Open all year except Christmas. **STB ★★★★** *B&B,* **AA ◆◆◆◆**

Non-smoking • Wales

NORTH WALES, LLANDUDNO. Chilterns for Non-Smokers, 19 Deganwy Avenue, Llandudno LL30 2YB (01492 875457). Centrally placed Bed & Breakfast accommodation in en suite rooms with king-size beds, hairdryers, alarm clocks, colour TVs and beverage trays. **WTB ★★★** *GUEST HOUSE.*

Disabled • England

SUSSEX (EAST), HASTINGS. Peter Mann, Grand Hotel, Grand Parade, St Leonards, Hastings TN38 0DD (Tel & Fax: 01424 428510 or 0870 2257025). Seafront family-run hotel; some rooms with colour TV, radio; some en suite. Wi-fi broadband access throughout.Unrestricted/disabled parking. Non-smoking restaurant. Licensed bar. **ETC ◆◆◆**

Special Diets • England

LONDON, HAMMERSMITH. Anne and Sohel Armanios, 67 Rannoch Road, Hammersmith, London W6 9SS (020 7385 4904; Fax: 020 7610 3235). Comfortable, centrally located Edwardian family home. Great base for sightseeing. Excellent transport access. Bed and Continental Breakfast £25 pppn Double; £36 single. Smoking only in garden.

CAMBRIDGESHIRE, ELY. Mrs C. Bennett, Stockyard Farm B&B, Wisbech Road, Welney, Wisbech PE14 9RQ (01354 610433). Between Ely and Wisbech, ideal for touring, birdwatching. Two bedrooms; guest lounge. Vegetarians and vegans welcome. Free-range produce. Pets by arrangement. Non-smoking throughout.

CUMBRIA, AMBLESIDE. Broadview Guest House, Lake Road, Ambleside LA22 0DN (015394 32431). Quality, friendly guest house with 6 comfortable bedrooms (most en suite). Broadview is perfect for a holiday or short break. Vegetarian, vegan and most special diets catered for by prior arrangement. Non smoking. **AA ★★★★**

CUMBRIA, AMBLESIDE. Ferndale Lodge, Lake Road, Ambleside LA22 0DB (015394 32207). Small, family-run guest house with 10 attractive en suite bedrooms, several with views of fells. Good home-cooked English or vegetarian breakfast. Open all year. Non-smoking. **ETC ◆◆◆**

CUMBRIA, BOWNESS-ON-WINDERMERE. Annisgarth B&B, 48 Craig Walk, Bowness-on-Windermere LA23 2JT (015394 43866). Three double bedrooms, one twin, one family room and a deluxe room with a jacuzzi bath and lake view. All diets are catered for including vegetarian and vegan. All produce is local with free range eggs. Exclusively non-smoking.

DEVON, ASHBURTON (Dartmoor). Mrs Joy Hasler, Riversmead, Newbridge, Near Ashburton TQ13 7NT (01364 631224). Quality en suite accommodation with stunning views. Full central heating, tea/coffee making facilities. Ample parking. Non-smoking. Children over 12. Dogs by arrangement. Open all year.

DEVON, TORQUAY. Aveland Hotel, Aveland Road, Babbacombe, Torquay TQ1 3PT (Tel/Minicom: 01803 326622; Fax: 01803 328940). Family-run, licensed hotel in quiet, level location. Panoramic views. All rooms en suite. Evening meal optional. Non-smoking Silver Award. **AA ★★★★**

NORTHUMBERLAND, SEAHOUSES. Paul and Donna, Wyndgrove House, 156 Main Street, Seahouses NE68 7UA (01665 722855). Quietly situated within short walking distance of sea front. Newly refurbished, comfortable rooms all with en suite facilities. Ground floor rooms available. No smoking. Vegetarian breakfast on request.

STAFFORDSHIRE, OAKAMOOR. Mrs D. Bickle, Crowtrees Farm, Oakamoor, Stoke-on-Trent ST10 3DY (Tel & Fax: 01538 702260). Working family farm offering comfortable accommodation in four en suite bedrooms and family rooms in a converted barn. Within easy reach of Alton Towers. Special short breaks available. Non-smoking. **AA ★★★★**

SUSSEX (EAST), HASTINGS. Peter Mann, Grand Hotel, Grand Parade, St Leonards, Hastings TN38 0DD (Tel & Fax: 01424 428510 or 0870 2257025). Seafront family-run hotel; some rooms with colour TV, radio; some en suite. Wi-fi broadband access throughout.Unrestricted/disabled parking. Non-smoking restaurant. Licensed bar. **ETC ◆◆◆**

Special Diets • Scotland

AYRSHIRE, LARGS. Mrs M. Watson, South Whittlieburn Farm, Brisbane Glen, Largs KA30 8SN (01475 675881). Superb farmhouse accommodation, enormous delicious breakfasts, warm, friendly hospitality. Nominated for "AA LANDLADY OF THE YEAR 2005", and chosen by "WHICH BEST BED & BREAKFAST". All rooms en suite. Open all year except Christmas. Packed lunches and special diets. **STB ★★★★** *B&B,* **AA ◆◆◆◆**

Special Diets • Wales

POWYS, BRECON. Mrs Joy Bloss, Beech Copse, 2 Pentrebach Cottage, Trallong, Brecon LD3 8HS (01874 636125). Comfort and tranquillity in a delightful cottage on the edge of the Brecon Beacons National Park. Lovely double en suite room. Good food; traditional and vegetarian breakfasts; special diets catered for (please notify in advance). No smoking.

The FHG Directory of Website Addresses

on pages 313-346 is a useful quick reference guide for holiday accommodation with e-mail and/or website details

Country Inns

Bedfordshire

Leighton Buzzard

THE Globe INN

Globe Lane, Stoke Road, Old Linslade,
Leighton Buzzard, Bedfordshire LU7 7TA

★ Canal-side location with access over own bridge.
★ Beer garden with outdoor eating facilities
★ Bar/Lounge open all day, every day
★ Children welcome ★ Children's play area
★ Dining area with non-smoking section
★ Excellent choice of food served12 noon to 9pm daily
★ Cask Marque Accredited 2005
★ Booking Highly Recommended

Tel: 01525 373338 • Fax: 01525 850551

Cheshire

Congleton

The Plough at Eaton

Macclesfield Road, Eaton,
Near Congleton, Cheshire CW12 2NH
Tel: 01260 280207 • Fax: 01260 298377

e-mail: theploughinn@hotmail.co.uk • www.plough-eaton.co.uk

Traditional oak beams and blazing log fires in winter reflect the warm and friendly atmosphere of this half-timbered former coaching inn which dates from the 17th century. The heart of the 'Plough' is the kitchen where food skilfully prepared is calculated to satisfy the most discerning palate. Luncheons and dinners are served seven days a week with traditional roasts on Sundays. In peaceful, rolling countryside near the Cheshire/Staffordshire border, this is a tranquil place in which to stay and the hostelry has elegantly colour-co-ordinated guest rooms, all with spacious bathrooms, LCD colour television, direct-dial telephone and tea and coffee-making facilities amongst their impressive appointments. Wireless internet access available.

Cornwall

Liskeard

COLLIFORD TAVERN

Colliford Lake, Near St Neot, Liskeard,
Cornwall PL14 6PZ • Tel: 01208 821335
e-mail: info@colliford.com • www.colliford.com

Set in attractive grounds which include a children's play area, ponds and a working waterwheel, this delightfully furnished free house offers good food and bar snacks. Sprucely-appointed guest rooms are spacious and have en suite shower, colour television, radio alarm, beverage maker and numerous thoughtful extras. An unusual feature of the tavern is a 37' deep granite well. In the midst of the scenic splendour of Bodmin Moor, this is a relaxing country retreat only a few minutes' walk from Colliford Lake, so popular with fly fishermen. Both north and south coasts are within easy driving distance and terms are most reasonable.

Cumbria

Brampton, Carlisle

Talkin Village, Brampton, Cumbria CA8 1LE
Tel: 016977 3452 • Fax: 016977 3396
e-mail: blacksmithsarmstalkin@yahoo.co.uk
www.blacksmithstalkin.co.uk

The Blacksmith's Arms offers all the hospitality and comforts of a traditional country inn. Enjoy tasty meals served in the bar lounges, or linger over dinner in the well-appointed restaurant. The inn is personally managed by the proprietors, Anne and Donald Jackson, who guarantee the hospitality one would expect from a family concern. Guests are assured of a pleasant and comfortable stay. There are eight lovely bedrooms, all en suite. Peacefully situated in the beautiful village of Talkin, the inn is convenient for the Borders, Hadrian's Wall and the Lake District. There is a good golf course, walking and other country pursuits nearby.

GRAHAM ARMS HOTEL

Longtown, Near Carlisle, Cumbria CA6 5SE

A warm welcome awaits at this 180-year-old former Coaching Inn. Situated six miles from the M6 (J44) and Gretna Green, The Graham Arms makes an ideal overnight stop or perfect touring base for the Scottish Borders, English Lakes, Hadrian's Wall and much more. 16 comfortable en suite bedrooms, including four-poster and family rooms with TV, radio etc. Meals and snacks served throughout the day. Friendly 'local's bar' and new 'Sports bar' serving real ale, extra cold lagers, cocktails and a fine selection of malt whiskies. Secure courtyard parking for cars, cycles and motorcycles. Beautiful woodland and riverside walks!

Visit our website on www.grahamarms.com • Tel: 01228 791213 • Fax: 01228 794110
Email: office@grahamarms.com • Website: www.grahamarms.com
Bed and full traditional breakfast £32– £36. Special rates for weekend and midweek breaks. RAC ★★

Ennerdale Bridge

With an informal and relaxed atmosphere on one of the most attractive stretches of Wainwright's Coast to Coast footpath, this splendid small hotel presents first-rate food and accommodation. Several real ales are served and there is an extensive bar menu including daily 'specials'. Traditional comforts are very much in evidence and bedrooms have central heating, digital colour television, direct-dial telephone and tea and coffee-makers. Although one of the smaller lakes, Ennerdale can fairly claim to be the most beautiful. From here, valley paths, forest tracks and lake shores offer a variety of rewarding walks suitable for all ages and capabilities. Other activities available include fishing, canoeing, bird watching and pony trekking.

Shepherd's Arms Hotel

Ennerdale Bridge, Lake District National Park CA23 3AR
Tel: 01946 861249
e-mail: shepherdsarms@btconnect.com
website: www.shepherdsarmshotel.co.uk

Gloucestershire

Lydney

THE FOUNTAIN INN & LODGE

Parkend, Royal Forest of Dean, Gloucestershire GL15 4JD.

Traditional village inn, well known locally for its excellent meals and real ales. A Forest Fayre menu offers such delicious main courses as Lamb Steak In Woodland Berry Sauce and Gloucester Sausage in Onion Gravy, together with a large selection of curries, vegetarian dishes, and other daily specials.

Centrally situated in one of England's foremost wooded areas, the inn makes an ideal base for sightseeing, or for exploring some of the many peaceful forest walks nearby.

All bedrooms (including one specially adapted for the less able) are en suite, decorated and furnished to an excellent standard, and have television and tea/coffee making facilities. Various half-board breaks are available throughout the year.

Tel: 01594 562189 • Fax: 01594 564438 • e-mail: thefountaininn@aol.com • www.thefountaininnandlodge.com

Shropshire

Ludlow

LUDLOW The Church Inn, Buttercross SY8 1AW (01584 872174, Fax: 01584 877146).

This historic inn has undergone several changes of name over the centuries – it was originally called the "Cross Keys" – but retains the fine old-fashioned traditions of good ale and good food which have ensured its lasting popularity through the ages. Nine cosy en suite bedrooms all with telephone and modem points, provide first-rate overnight accommodation, and a full range of catering, from freshly cut sandwiches to succulent steaks, ensures that appetites large and small will be amply satisfied. Regularly changing guest beers supplement the already extensive range of wines, spirits and ales on offer. The ancient town of Ludlow is an ideal base for exploring the Border counties and the Welsh Marches, and is conveniently located for road and rail links to the Midlands.

• Children welcome.

ETC/AA/RAC ◆◆◆◆, *CAMRA.*

www.thechurchinn.com

Surrey

Haslemere

Readers are requested to mention this guidebook when making enquiries about accommodation.

Useful Guidance for Guests and Hosts

Every year literally thousands of holidays, short breaks and ovemight stops are arranged through our guides, the vast majority without any problems at all. In a handful of cases, however, difficulties do arise about bookings, which often could have been prevented from the outset.

It is important to remember that when accommodation has been booked, both parties – guests and hosts – have entered into a form of contract. We hope that the following points will provide helpful guidance.

Guests

- When enquiring about accommodation, be as precise as possible. Give exact dates, numbers in your party and the ages of any children.
- State the number and type of rooms wanted and also what catering you require – bed and breakfast, full board etc. Make sure that the position about evening meals is clear – and about pets, reductions for children or any other special points.
- Read our reviews carefully to ensure that the proprietors you are going to contact can supply what you want. Ask for a letter confirming all arrangements, if possible.
- If you have to cancel, do so as soon as possible. Proprietors do have the right to retain deposits and under certain circumstances to charge for cancelled holidays if adequate notice is not given and they cannot re-let the accommodation.

Hosts

- **Give details about your facilities and about any special conditions. Explain your deposit system clearly and arrangements for cancellations, charges etc. and whether or not your terms include VAT.**
- **If for any reason you are unable to fulfil an agreed booking without adequate notice, you may be under an obligation to arrange suitable alternative accommodation or to make some form of compensation.**

Family-Friendly Pubs and Inns

This is a selection of establishments which make an extra effort to cater for parents and children. The majority provide a separate children's menu or they may be willing to serve small portions of main course dishes on request; there are often separate outdoor or indoor play areas where the junior members of the family can let off steam while Mum and Dad unwind over a drink.
For more details, please see individual entries under county headings.

NB: Many other inns, pubs and hotels listed in the main section of the book but not included in this Supplement also welcome children – please see individual entries.

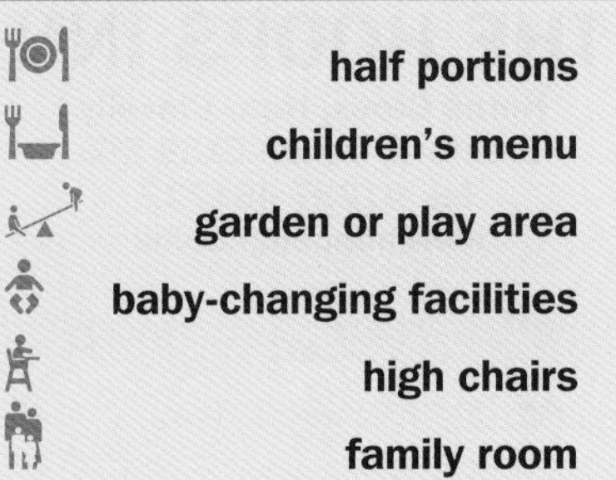

THE CROWN HOTEL
16 High Street, Amersham,
Buckinghamshire HP7 0DH
01494 721541
www.dhillonhotels.co.uk

CROWN & PUNCHBOWL
Hligh Street, Horningsea,
Cambridgeshire CB5 9JG
Tel: 01223 860643
www.cambscuisine.com

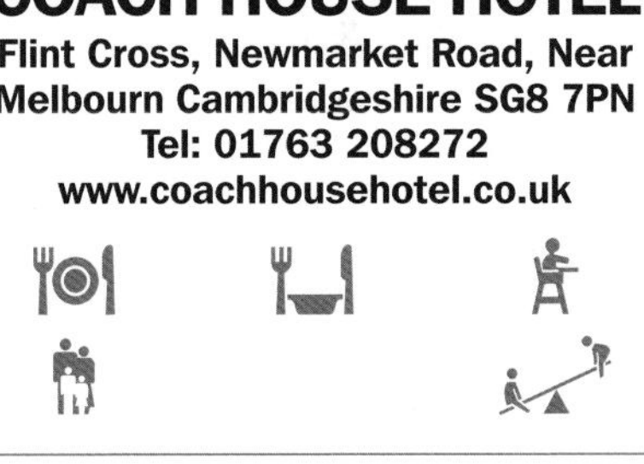

COACH HOUSE HOTEL
Flint Cross, Newmarket Road, Near
Melbourn Cambridgeshire SG8 7PN
Tel: 01763 208272
www.coachhousehotel.co.uk

THE DOG INN

Wellbank Lane, Over Peover, Near Knutsford, Cheshire WA16 8UP
Tel: 01625 861421
www.doginn-overpeover.co.uk

COLEDALE INN
Braithwaite, Near Keswick,
Cumbria CA12 5TN
Tel: 017687 78272
www.coledale-inn.co.uk

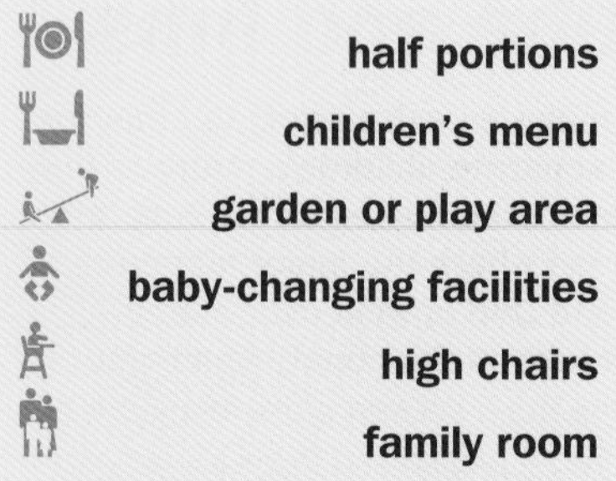

BROTHERSWATER INN

Patterdale, Penrith,
Cumbria CA11 0NZ
Tel: 017684 82239
www.sykeside.co.uk

NEW INN HOTEL

High Street, Clovelly, Near
Bideford, Devon EX39 5TQ
Tel: 01237 431303
www.clovelly.co.uk

THE HOOPS INN

Horns Cross, Near Clovelly,
Bideford, Devon EX39 5DL
Tel: 01237 451222
www.hoopsinn.co.uk

WHITE HART HOTEL

Fore Street, Okehampton,
Devon EX20 1HD
Tel: 01837 52730/54514
www.thewhitehart-hotel.com

THE BELL HOTEL

The Quay, Sandwich,
Kent CT13 9EF
Tel: 01304 613388
www.bellhotelsandwich.co.uk

ANGEL & ROYAL HOTEL

4-5 High Street, Grantham,
Lincolnshire NG31 6PN
Tel: 01476 565816
www.angelandroyal.co.uk

THE TALLY HO INN

Aswarby, Near Sleaford,
Lincolnshire NG34 8SA
Tel: 01529 455205
www.tally-ho-aswarby.co.uk

THE OLD RAM INN

Ipswich Road (A140),
Tivetshall St Mary, Norfolk NR15 2DE
Tel: 01379 676794
www.theoldram.com

THE TOM MOGG INN

Station Road, Burtle,
Near Bridgwater, Somerset TA7 8NU
Tel: 01278 722399
www.tommogg.co.uk

THE CROWN HOTEL

Exford, Exmoor National Park,
Somerset TA24 7PP
Tel: 01643 831554/5
www.crownhotelexmoor.co.uk

LORD POULETT ARMS

High Street, Hinton St George,
Somerset TA17 8SE
Tel: 01460 73149
www.lordpoulettarms.com

THE FOUNTAIN INN

1 St Thomas Street, Wells,
Somerset BA5 2UU
Tel: 01749 672317
www.fountaininn.co.uk

THE CROWN AT WELLS

Market Place, Wells,
Somerset BA5 2RP
Tel: 01749 673457
www.crownatwells.co.uk

THE SIX BELLS

The Green, Bardwell, Bury St
Edmunds, Suffolk IP13 1AW
Tel: 01359 250820
www.sixbellsbardwell.co.uk

WORSLEY ARMS HOTEL

Hovingham, North Yorkshire YO62 4LA
Tel: 01653 628234
www.worsleyarms.com

WHITE ROSE HOTEL

Leeming Bar, Northallerton,
North Yorkshire DL7 9AY
Tel: 01677 422707/424941
www.whiterosehotel.co.uk

WHITE SWAN INN

Market Place, Pickering, North
Yorkshire YO18 7AA
Tel: 01751 472288
www.white-swan.co.uk

MURRAY ARMS HOTEL

Gatehouse of Fleet, Castle Douglas,
Kirkcudbrightshire DG7 2HY
Tel: 01557 814207
www.murrayarmshotel.co.uk

LAIRD & DOG HOTEL

5 High Street, Lasswade, Near
Edinburgh, Midlothian EH18 1NA
Tel: 0131 663 9219
www.lairdanddog.btinternet.co.uk

OAK TREE INN

Balmaha, Loch Lomond, G63 0JQ
Tel: 01360 870357
www.oak-tree-inn.co.uk

WATERHOUSE INN

The Square, Balloch Road,
Balloch G83 8LE
Tel: 01389 752120
www.waterhouseinn.co.uk

THE BELLACHROY

Dervaig, Isle of Mull PA75 6QW
Tel: 01688 400314
www.thebellachroy.co.uk

HUNTER'S MOON INN

Llangattock Lingoed, Near
Abergavenny, NP7 8RR
Tel: 01873 821499
www.hunters-moon-inn.co.uk

KING ARTHUR HOTEL

Higher Green, Reynoldston,
Swansea, South Wales SA31 1AD
Tel: 01792 390775
www.kingarthurhotel.co.uk

Readers are requested to mention this guidebook when making enquiries about accommodation.

Looking for Holiday Accommodation?

FHG
K·U·P·E·R·A·R·D

for details of hundreds of properties throughout the UK visit our website

www.holidayguides.com

'et-Friendly Pubs and Inns

ease note that these establishments may not feature in the man section of this book

ENGLAND

BERKSHIRE

UNCLE TOM'S CABIN
Hills Lane, Cookham Dean, Berkshire (01628 483339).
Dogs allowed throughout.
Pet Regulars: Flossie and Ollie (Old English Sheepdog). Free dog biscuit pub.

THE GREYHOUND (known locally as 'The Dog')
The Walk, Eton Wick, Berkshire (01753 863925).
Dogs allowed throughout the pub.
Pet Regulars: Harvey (Retriever), retrieves anything, including Beer mats. Tully - German Shepherd.

THE OLD BOOT
Stanford Bingley, Berkshire (01189 744292).
Pets welcome in bar area.
Pet Regulars: Resident dog Skip - Black Labrador.

THE TWO BREWERS
Park Street, Windsor, Berkshire (01753 855426).
Dogs allowed, public and saloon bars.
Pet Regulars: Molly (Newfoundland), Bear (Black Labrador), Rufus (Springer Spaniel), Mr Darcy (Poodle), Rosie (Chocolate Labrador), Lilly (English Bulldog), Molly (Fox Terrier), McIntosh (Highland Terrier) and Lulu & Paddy (Cocker Spaniels).

Publisher's note

While every effort is made to ensure accuracy, we regret that FHG Guides cannot accept responsibility for errors, misrepresentations or omissions in our entries or any consequences thereof. Prices in particular should be checked.
We will follow up complaints but cannot act as arbiters or agents for either party.

Pet-Friendly Pubs and Inns

BUCKINGHAMSHIRE

WHITE HORSE
Village Lane, Hedgerley, Buckinghamshire SL2 3UY (01753 643225).
Dogs allowed at tables on pub frontage, beer garden (on leads), public bar.

FROG AT SKIRMETT
Skirmett, Henley-on-Thames, Buckinghamshire RG9 6TG (01491 638996)
Dogs welcome, pet friendly.

GEORGE AND DRAGON
High Street, West Wycombe, Buckinghamshire HP14 3AB (01494 464414)
Pet friendly.

CAMBRIDGESHIRE

YE OLD WHITE HART
Main Street, Ufford, Peterborough, Cambridgeshire (01780 740250).
Dogs allowed in non-food areas.

CHESHIRE

THE GROSVENOR ARMS
Chester Road, Aldford, Cheshire CH3 6HJ (01244 620228)
Pet friendly.
Pet Regulars: resident dog "Sadie" (Labrador).

CORNWALL

DRIFTWOOD SPARS HOTEL
Trevaunance Cove, St Agnes, Cornwall (01872 552428).
Dogs allowed everywhere except the restaurant.
Pet Regulars: Buster (Cornish Labrador cross with a Seal) - devours anything.

JUBILEE INN
Pelynt, Near Looe, Cornwall PL13 2JZ (01503 220312).
Dogs allowed in all areas except restaurant; accommodation for guests with dogs.

THE MILL HOUSE INN
Trebarwith Strand, Tintagel, Cornwall PL34 OHD (01840 770200).
Pet friendly.

THE MOLESWORTH ARMS HOTEL
Molesworth Street, Wadebridge, Cornwall PL27 7DP (01208 812055).
Dogs allowed in all public areas and in hotel rooms.
Pet Regulars: Thomson Cassidy (Black Lab), Ruby Cassidy and Lola (Black Lab).

CUMBRIA

THE BRITANNIA INN
Elterwater, Ambleside, Cumbria LA22 9HP (015394 37210).
Dogs allowed in all areas except dining room and residents' lounge.
Pet Friendly.

THE MORTAL MAN HOTEL
Troutbeck, Windermere, Cumbria LA23 IPL (015394 33193).
Pets allowed everywhere except restaurant.

STAG INN
Dufton, Appleby, Cumbria (017683 51608).
Dogs allowed in non-food bar, beer garden, village green plus cottage.
Pet Regulars: Sofie (Labrador) and Jeanie (Terrier).

WATERMILL INN
School Lane, Ings, Near Staveley, Kendal, Cumbria (01539 821309).
Dogs allowed in beer garden, Wrynose bottom bar.
Pet Regulars: Blot (sheepdog), Finn (mongrel) and Pub dog Shelley (German Shepherd). Owners cannot walk dogs past pub, without being dragged in! Biscuits and water provided.

DERBYSHIRE

THE GEORGE HOTEL
Commercial Road, Tideswell, Near Buxton, Derbyshire SK17 8NU (01298 871382).
Dogs allowed in snug and around the bar, water bowls provided.

DOG AND PARTRIDGE COUNTRY INN & MOTEL
Swinscoe, Ashbourne, Derbyshire (01335 343183).
Dogs allowed throughout, except restaurant.
Pet Regulars: Include Mitsy (57); Rusty (Cairn); Spider (Collie/GSD) and Rex (GSD).

DEVONSHIRE ARMS
Peak Forest, Near Buxton, Derbyshire SK17 8EJ (01298 23875)
Pet friendly.

DEVON

THE SHIP INN

Axmouth, Devon EX12 4AF (01297 21838).
A predominantly catering pub, so dogs on a lead please.
Pet Regulars: Kym (Boxer), Soxy (cat). Also 2 Japanese Quail, 2 Cockatiels and 2 Kaki Riki (New Zealand Lovebirds).

BRENDON HOUSE

Brendon, Lynton, North Devon EX35 6PS (01598 741206).
Dogs very welcome and allowed in tea gardens, guest bedrooms by arrangement.
Owner's dogs - Drummer, Piper and Angus (Labradors).

THE BULLERS ARMS

Chagford, Newton Abbot, Devon (01647 432348).
Dogs allowed throughout pub, except dining room/kitchen. "More than welcome".

CROWN AND SCEPTRE

2 Petitor Road, Torquay, Devon TQ1 4QA (01803 328290).
Dogs allowed in non-food bar, family room, lounge. All dogs welcome.
Pet Regulars: Two Jack Russells - Scrappy Doo and Minnie Mouse.

THE JOURNEY'S END INN

Ringmore, Near Kingsbridge, South Devon TQ7 4HL (01548 810205).
Dogs allowed throughout the pub.

PALK ARMS INN

Hennock, Bovey Tracey, Devon TQ13 9QS (01626 836584).
Pets welcome.

THE ROYAL OAK INN

Dunsford, Near Exeter, Devon EX6 7DA (01647 252256).
Dogs allowed in bars, beer garden, accommodation for guests with dogs.
Pet Regulars: Kizi. Resident Dogs - Connie and Posie.

THE POLSHAM ARMS

Lower Polsham Road, Paignton, Devon (01803 558360).
Dogs allowed throughout the pub.
Pet Regulars: Patch, owner brings his supply of dog biscuits, and Bracken (German Shepherd).

THE SEA TROUT INN

Staverton, Near Totnes, Devon TQ9 6PA (01803 762274).
Dogs welcome in lounge and public bar, beer garden, owners' rooms (but not on beds).
Pet Regulars: Buster (resident dog) partial to Guiness.

THE DEVONSHIRE INN
Sticklepath, Okehampton, Devon EX20 2NW (01837 840626).
Dogs allowed in non-food bar, car park, beer garden, family room and guest rooms.
Pet Regulars: Clarrie and Rosie (Terriers).

THE TROUT & TIPPLE
(A386 - Tavistock to Okehampton Road), Parkwood Road, Tavistock,
Devon PL10 0JS (01822 618886)
Dogs welcome at all times in bar, games room and patio.
Pet regulars include: Connor and Fenrhys (Black Labradors) - sometimes misbehave. Casey (Bronze Springer) - always after food. Border, Chaos and Mischief (Border Collies), Snoopy (Rhodesian Ridgeback) likes his beef dinners. Also, our own dog - Dave (Lurcher).

DORSET

THE ANVIL HOTEL
Sailsbury Road, Pimperne, Blandford, Dorset DT11 8UQ (01258 453431).
Pets allowed in bar, lounge and bedrooms.

THE SQUARE AND COMPASS
Swanage, Dorset BH19 3LF (01929 439229).
Well-behaved dogs allowed - but beware of the chickens!

DRUSILLA'S INN
Wigbeth, Horton, Dorset (01258 840297).
Well-behaved dogs welcome.

DURHAM

MOORCOCK INN
Hill Top, Eggleston, Teesdale, County Durham DL12 9AU (01833 650395).
Pet Regulars: Thor, the in-house hound dog, and Raymond, the resident hack, welcome all equine travellers; Gem (Jack Russell); Arnie (Ginger Tom); Poppy (Jack Russell); Haflinger - the horse.

TAP AND SPILE
27 Front Street, Framwellgate Moor, Durham DH1 5EE (0191 386 5451).
Dogs allowed throughout the pub.

THE ROSE TREE
Low Road West, Shincliff, Durham DH1 2LY (0191-386 8512).
Pets allowed in bar area and garden.
Pet Regulars: "Benson" (Boxer), "Ben" (Miniature White Poodle) and "Oliver" (King Charles).

THE SEVEN STARS
High Street North, Shincliff, Durham (0191-384 8454).
Dogs welcome in bar area only.

ESSEX

WHITE HARTE

The Quay, Burnham-on-Crouch, Essex CM0 8AS (01621 782106).
Pets welcome.
Pet Regulars: Resident dog "Tilly" (Collie).

THE OLD SHIP

Heybridge Basin, Heybridge, Maldon, Essex (01621 854150).
Dogs allowed downstairs only, on lead.

GLOUCESTERSHIRE

THE OLD STOCKS HOTEL

The Square, Stow on the Wold, Gloucestershire GL54 1AF (01451 830666).
Dogs allowed in the beer garden, accommodation for dogs and their owners also available.
Pet Regulars: Ben (Labrador) enjoys bitter from the drip trays and Casey (Doberman) often gets carried out as he refuses to leave.

GREATER LONDON

THE PHOENIX

28 Thames Street, Sunbury on Thames, Middlesex (01932 785358).
Dogs allowed on lead in beer garden, family room. Capability 2 Grading.
Pet Regulars: Sammy (Black Labrador).

THE TIDE END COTTAGE

Ferry Road, Teddington, Middlesex (0208 977 7762).
Dogs allowed throughout the pub, except dining area.
Pet Regulars: Mimi (Labrador), Toffee (Terrier), Gracie (Guide Dog) and Fiona.

HAMPSHIRE

THE SUN

Sun Hill, Bentworth, Alton, Hampshire GU34 5JT (01420 562338)

Pets welcome throughout the pub.

Pet Regulars: Willow (Collie), Hazel and Purdey (Jack Russells) and "Dilweed" the cat.

HIGH CORNER INN

Linwood, Near Ringwood, Hampshire BH24 3QY (01425 473973).

Dogs, and even horses, are catered for here.

THE CHEQUERS

Ridgeway Lane, Lower Pennington, Lymington, Hants (01590 673415).

Dogs allowed in non-food bar, outdoor barbecue area (away from food).

Pet Regulars: Rusty Boyd - parties held for him. Resident pet - D'for (Labrador).

THE VICTORY

High Street, Hamble-le-Rice, Southampton, Hampshire (023 80 453105).

Dogs allowed.

Pet Regulars: Chester (Boxer).

HERTFORDSHIRE

THE BLACK HORSE

Chorley Wood Common, Dog Kennel Lane, Rickmansworth, Herts (01923 282252).

Dogs very welcome and allowed throughout the pub, on a lead.

THE RED LION

Chenies Village, Rickmansworth, Hertfordshire WD3 6ED (01923 282722).

Pets welcome in bar area only.

Pet Regulars: Resident dog Bobby (Collie mixture), Paddy and Mollie (Boxers).

THE ROBIN HOOD AND LITTLE JOHN

Rabley Heath, near Codicote, Hertfordshire (01438 812361).

Dogs allowed in non-food bar, car park tables, beer garden.

Pet Regulars: Pongo (Dalmation) and Eailey (Labrador). The locals of the pub have close to 50 dogs between them, most of which visit from time to time. The team includes a two Labrador search squad dispatched by one regular's wife to indicate time's up. When they arrive he has five minutes' drinking up time before all three leave together.

FREE or REDUCED RATE entry to Holiday Visits and Attractions – see our READERS' OFFER VOUCHERS on pages 5-32

Pet-Friendly Pubs and Inns

KENT

KENTISH HORSE
Cow Lane, Mark Beech, Edenbridge, Kent (01342 850493).
Dogs allowed in reserved area on lead, outside included.

THE SWANN INN
Little Chart, Kent TN27 0QB (01233 840702).
Dogs allowed - everywhere except restaurant.

LANCASHIRE

Assheton Arms
Downham, Clitheroe
BB7 4BJ
01200 441227
e-mail: asshetonarms@aol.com
www.assheton-arms.co.uk

Popular but unspoilt pub in traditional village with stone cottages. Good walks. Food served Mon-Sat 12pm-2pm, Sun 12pm-2.30pm and 7pm-10pm.
Children and dogs welcome. Disabled access.

MALT'N HOPS
50 Friday Street, Chorley, Lancashire PR6 0AH (01257 260967).
Dogs allowed throughout pub if kept under control.

LINCOLNSHIRE

THE BLUE DOG INN
Main Street, Sewstern, Grantham, Lincs NG33 5QR (01476 860097).
Dogs allowed.
Pet Regulars: Cassie (Scottie) shares biscuits with Beth (pub cat); Nelson (Terrier), Diesel (Springer Spaniel) and Ted (Spaniel).

Note

All the information in this guide is given in good faith in the belief that it is correct. However, the publishers cannot guarantee the facts given in these pages, neither are they responsible for changes in ownership or facilities that may take place after the date of going to press.
Readers should always satisfy themselves that the facilities they require are available and that the terms, if quoted, still apply.

MERSEYSIDE

THE SCOTCH PIPER

Southport Road, Lydiate, Merseyside (0151 526 0503).

Dogs allowed throughout the pub.

NORFOLK

THE OLD RAILWAY TAVERN

Eccles Road, Quidenham, Norwich, Norfolk NR16 2JG (01953 888223).

Dogs allowed, must be on lead.

Pet Regulars: Pub dogs Flo (German Shepherd) and Benji (Jack Russell).

THE HOSTE ARMS

The Green, Burnham Market, King's Lynn, Norfolk PE31 8HD (01328 738777).

Dogs allowed throughout the pub, except restaurant.

Pet Regulars: "Augustus" and "Sweep" (Black Labradors).

THE ROSE AND CROWN

Nethergate Street, Harpley, King's Lynn, Norfolk (01485 520577).

Well behaved dogs welcome.

OXFORDSHIRE

THE BELL

Shenington, Banbury, Oxfordshire OX15 6NQ (01295 670274).

Pets allowed throughout.

Pet Regulars: Resident pub dogs "Oliver" (Great Dane) and "Daisy" (Labrador).

THE PLOUGH INN

High Street, Finstock, Chipping Norton, Oxfordshire (01993 868333).

Dogs more than welcome.

Pet Regulars: Zac (Sheepdog), Strumpet and Trollop (Labradors).

THE BELL INN

High Street, Adderbury, Oxon (01295 810338).

Dogs allowed throughout the pub.

Owner's dogs: Murphy and Dizzy (Lancashire Heelers) and Rika (Rottweiler).

SHROPSHIRE

THE TRAVELLERS REST INN

Church Stretton, Shropshire (01694 781275).

Well-mannered pets welcome - but beware of the cats!

LONGMYND HOTEL

Cunnery Road, Church Stretton, Shropshire SY6 6AG (01694 722244).

Dogs allowed in owners' hotel bedrooms but not in public areas.

Pet Regulars: Bruno and Frenzie; and owner's dogs, Sam and Sailor.

SOMERSET

CASTLE OF COMFORT HOTEL
Dodington, Nether Stowey, Bridgwater, Somerset TA5 1LE (01278 741264).
Pet friendly.

THE SPARKFORD INN
High Street, Sparkford, Somerset BA22 7JN (01963 440218).
Dogs allowed in bar areas but not in restaurant; safe garden and car park.

THE BUTCHERS ARMS
Carhampton, Somerset (01643 821333).
Dogs allowed in bar. B&B accommodation available.

HOOD ARMS
Kilve, Somerset TA5 1EA (01278 741210)
Pets welcome.

THE SHIP INN
High Street, Porlock, Somerset (01643 862507).
Dogs allowed throughout and in guests' rooms.
Pet Regulars: Include Silver (Jack Russell); Sam (Black Lab) and Max (Staffordshire). Resident Pets include Brit (Spaniel) and Holly (Belgian Shepherd).

STAFFORDSHIRE

The Hollybush Inn

Denford Road, Denford, Leek, Staffordshire ST13 7JT

Dating back to the 17th century, this former corn mill is a favourite with people cruising the Caldon Canal. Features include quarry-tiled floors, open fires, copper and brass ornaments, and old oak beams. Open all day, the Inn has a good selection of beers, wines, ales and other refreshments. Food is also available seven days a week, all dishes prepared in the inn's own kitchens, using fresh, locally sourced produce whenever possible.

The Inn works hard to make sure that all its customers feel welcome, including its four-legged friends.

Tel: 01538 371819

SUFFOLK

THE KINGS HEAD
High Street, Southwold, Suffolk IP18 6AD (01502 724517).
Well-behaved dogs welcome.

SIX BELLS AT BARDWELL
The Green, Bardwell, Bury St Edmunds, Suffolk IP31 1AW (01359 250820).
Dogs allowed in guest bedrooms by arrnagement but not allowed in bar and restaurant.

SURREY

THE PLOUGH
South Road, Woking, Surrey GU21 4JL (01483 714105).
Pets welcome in restricted areas.

THE SPORTSMAN
Mogador Road, Mogador, Surrey (01737 246655).
Adopted dogs congregate at this pub.
Pet Regulars: Meesha (Border Collie) and Max (German Shepherd).

THE CRICKETERS
12 Oxenden Road, Tongham, Farnham, Surrey (01252 333262).
Dogs allowed in beer garden on lead.

SUSSEX

THE FORESTERS ARMS
High Street, Fairwarp, Near Uckfield, East Sussex TN22 3BP (01825 712808).
Dogs allowed in the beer garden and at car park tables, also inside.
Dog biscuits always available.

THE PLOUGH
Crowhurst, Near Battle, East Sussex TN33 9AY (01424 830310).
Dogs allowed in non-food bar, car park tables, beer garden.

QUEENS HEAD
Village Green, Sedlescombe, East Sussex (01424 870228).
Dogs allowed throughout the pub.

THE SLOOP INN

Freshfield Lock, Haywards Heath, West Sussex RH17 7NP (01444 831219).

Dogs allowed in public bar and garden.

THE SPORTSMAN'S ARMS

Rackham Road, Amberley, Near Arundel, West Sussex BN18 9NR (01798 831787).
Dogs allowed in the bar area.

WILTSHIRE

THE HORSE AND GROOM

The Street, Charlton, Near Malmesbury, Wiltshire (01666 823904).
Dogs welcome in bar.
Pet Regulars: Troy and Gio (Labradors).

THE PETERBOROUGH ARMS

Dauntsey Lock, Near Chippenham, Wiltshire SN15 4HD (01249 890409).
All pets welcome in bar.
Resident pets - Poppy, Holly, Lilly and Dotty (4 generations of Jack Russell).

THE THREE HORSESHOES

High Street, Chapmanslade, Near Westbury, Wiltshire (01373 832280).
Dogs allowed in non-food bar and beer garden.
Three horses overlooking the beer garden.

YORKSHIRE

BARNES WALLIS INN

North Howden, Howden, East Yorkshire (01430 430639).
Guide dogs only

KINGS HEAD INN

Barmby on the Marsh, East Yorkshire DN14 7HL (01757 630705).
Dogs allowed in non-food bar.
Pet Regulars: Many and varied!

THE FORESTERS ARMS

Kilburn, North Yorkshire YO6 4AH (01347 868386).
Dogs allowed throughout, except restaurant.
Pet Regulars: Ainsley (Black Labrador).

NEW INN HOTEL

Clapham, Near Settle, North Yorkshire LA2 8HH (015242 51203).
Dogs allowed in bar, beer garden, bedrooms.

SIMONSTONE HALL

Hawes, North Yorkshire DL8 3LY (01969 667255).
Dogs allowed except dining area.
Dogs of all shapes, sizes and breeds welcome.
-*

THE SPINNEY

Forest Rise, Balby, Doncaster, South Yorkshire DN4 9HQ (01302 852033).
Dogs allowed throughout the pub.
Pet Regulars: Wyn (Labrador) a guide dog and Buster (Staff). Resident dog Paddy (Irish Setter).

THE ROCKINGHAM ARMS
8 Main Street, Wentworth, Rotherham, South Yorkshire S62 7LO (01226 742075).
Pets welcome.
Pet Regulars: Sheeba (Springer Spaniel), Charlie and Gypsy (Black Labradors), Sally (Alsatian) and Rosie (Jack Russell).

THE GOLDEN FLEECE
Lindley Road, Blackley, near Huddersfield, West Yorkshire (01422 372704).
Guide Dogs only.

WALES

ANGLESEY & GWYNEDD

THE GRAPES HOTEL
Maentwrog, Blaenau Ffestiniog, Gwynedd LL41 4HN (01766 590365).
Pets allowed in bar area only.

THE BUCKLEY HOTEL
Castle Street, Beaumaris, Isle of Anglesey LL58 8AW (01248 810415).
Dogs allowed throughout the pub, except in the dining room and bistro.
Pet Regulars: Cassie (Springer Spaniel) and Rex (mongrel), dedicated 'companion' dogs, also Charlie (Spaniel).

NORTH WALES

THE WEST ARMS HOTEL
Llanarmon Dyffryn Ceiriog, Llangollen, North Wales LL20 7LD (01691 600665).
Welcome pets.

PEMBROKESHIRE

THE FARMERS
14-16 Goat Street, St David's, Pembrokeshire (01437 721666).
Pets welcome in the pub area.

POWYS

SEVERN ARMS HOTEL
Penybont, Llandrindod Wells, Powys LD1 5UA (01597 851224).
Dogs allowed in the bar, but not the restaurant, and in the rooms - but not on the beds.

Please note

All the information in this book is given in good faith in the belief that it is correct. However, the publishers cannot guarantee the facts given in these pages, neither are they responsible for changes in policy, ownership or terms that may take place after the date of going to press. Readers should always satisfy themselves that the facilities they require are available and that the terms, if quoted, still apply.

SCOTLAND

ABERDEEN, BANFF & MORAY

THE CLIFTON BAR

Clifton Road, Lossiemouth, Moray (01343 812100).
Dogs allowed in beer garden only.

ROYAL OAK

Station Road, Urquhart, Elgin, Moray (01343 842607).
Dogs allowed throughout pub.
Pet Regulars: Jack (Collie).

ARGYLL & BUTE

CAIRNDOW STAGECOACH INN

Cairndow, Argyll PA26 8BN (01499 600286).
Pets welcome.

THE BALLACHULISH HOTEL

Ballachulish, Argyll PA39 4JY (01855 811606).
Dogs allowed in the lounge and guests' bedrooms, excluding food areas.

EDINBURGH & LOTHIANS

JOHNSBURN HOUSE

Johnsburn Road, Balerno, Lothians EH14 7BB (0131-449 3847).
Pets welcome in bar area only.
Pet Regulars: Resident dog "Topaz" (Great Dane).

LAIRD & DOG

Lasswade, Midlothian (0131-663 9219).
Dogs allowed in bar.
Pet Regulars: Fleetwood (cat). Many pet regulars. Drinking bowls .

PERTH & KINROSS

FOUR SEASONS HOTEL

St Fillans, Perthshire (01764 685333).
Dogs allowed in all non-food areas.

THE MUNRO INN

Main Street, Strathyre, Perthshire FK18 8NA (01877 384333).
Dogs allowed throughout pub, lounge, games room, beer garden and bedrooms (except restaurant).
Pet Regulars: Residents Jess (black mongrel with brown eyes) and Jules (white lurcher with blue eyes). Bring your dog to visit! Water and dog biscuits always available.

Readers are requested to mention this FHG guidebook when seeking accommodation

DIRECTORY OF WEBSITE AND E-MAIL ADDRESSES

A quick-reference guide to holiday accommodation with an e-mail address and/or website, conveniently arranged by country and county, with full contact details.

Holiday Parks/Touring & Camping
Cinque Ports Leisure
• **website: www.cplholidays.com**

•LONDON

B & B
Sohel & Anne Armanios, 67 Rannoch Road, Hammersmith, LONDON W6 9SS
Tel: 020 7385 4904
• **website: www.thewaytostay.co.uk**

Hotel
Athena Hotel, 110-114 Sussex Gardens, Hyde Park, LONDON W2 1UA
Tel: 020 7706 3866
• **e-mail: athena@stavrouhotels.co.uk**
• **website: www.stavrouhotels.co.uk**

Hotel
Barry House Hotel, 12 Sussex Place, Hyde Park, LONDON W2 2TP Tel: 0207 723 7340
• **e-mail: hotel@barryhouse.co.uk**
• **website: www.barryhouse.co.uk**

Hotel
Elizabeth Hotel, 37 Eccleston Square, LONDON SW1V 1PB Tel: 020 7828 6812
• **e-mail: info@elizabethhotel.com**
• **website: www.elizabethhotel.com**

Hotel
The Elysee Hotel, 25-26 Craven Terrace, LONDON W2 3EL Tel: 020 7402 7633
• **e-mail: information@hotelelysee.co.uk**
• **website: www.hotelelysee.co.uk**

Hotel
Gower Hotel, 129 Sussex Gardens, Hyde Park, LONDON W2 2RX
Tel: 020 7262 2262
• **e-mail: gower@stavrouhotels.co.uk**
• **website: www.stavrouhotels.co.uk**

Hotel
Lincoln House Hotel, 33 Gloucester Place, Marble Arch, LONDON W1V 8HY
Tel: 0207 486 7630
• **e-mail: reservations@lincoln-house-hotel.co.uk**
• **website: www.lincoln-house-hotel.co.uk**

B & B
Manor Court Hotel, 7 Clanricarde Gardens, LONDON W2 4JJ Tel: 020 7792 3361 or 020 7727 5407
• **e-mail: enquiries@manorcourthotel.com**
• **website: www.abc-london.com**
www.123europe-londonhotels.com

Hotel
Queens Hotel, 33 Anson Road, Tufnell Park, LONDON N7 Tel: 020 7607 4725
• **e-mail: queens@stavrouhotels.co.uk**
• **website: www.stavrouhotels.co.uk**

•BEDFORDSHIRE

Self-Catering
Bluegate Farm Holiday Cottages
Bluegate Farm, Stanbridge,
LEIGHTON BUZZARD, Beds LU7 9JD
Tel: 01525 210621
• **e-mail: enquiries@bluegatecottages.co.uk**
• **website: www.bluegatecottages.co.uk**

Farmhouse / B & B / Self-Catering Cottages
Mrs M. Codd, Highfield Farm,
Tempsford Road, SANDY, Beds SG19 2AQ
Tel: 01767 682332
• **e-mail: margaret@highfield-farm.co.uk**
• **website: www.highfield-farm.co.uk**

•BERKSHIRE

Inn
Julie Plastow, The Greyhound,
16 Common Road,
ETON WICK, Berkshire SL4 6JE
Tel: 01753 863 925
• **e-mail: thegreyhoundpub@hotmail.com**
• **website: thegreyhoundetonwick.co.uk**

Hotel

Clarence Hotel, 9 Clarence Road, WINDSOR, Berkshire SL4 5AE
Tel: 01753 864436

- **e-mail: enquiries@clarence-hotel.co.uk**
- **website: www.clarence-hotel.co.uk**

•BUCKINGHAMSHIRE

B & B / Self-Catering Cottages

Poletrees Farm, Ludgershall Road, Brill, AYLESBURY, Buckinghamshire HP18 9TZ
Tel: 01844 238276

- **e-mail: poletrees.farm@virgin.net**
- **web: www.countryaccom.co.uk/poletrees-farm**

•CAMBRIDGESHIRE

B & B

Hilary & Brian Marsh, The Meadow House 2A High Street, BURWELL, Cambridgeshir CB5 0HB Tel: 01638 741 926

- **e-mail: hilary@themeadowhouse.co.uk**
- **website: www.themeadowhouse.co.uk**

Guest House

Dykelands Guest House, 157 Mowbray Road,CAMBRIDGE, Cambridgeshire CB1 7SP
Tel: 01223 244300

- **website: www.dykelands.com**

Self-Catering

Mrs J. Farndale, Cathedral House, 17 St Mary's Street, ELY, Cambridgeshire CB7 4ER
Tel: 01352 662124

- **e-mail: farndale@cathedralhouse.co.uk**
- **website: www.cathedralhouse.co.uk**

B & B

Chequer Cottage, 43 Streetly End, HORSEHEATH, Cambridgeshire CB1 6RP
Tel: 01223 891 522

- **e-mail: stay@chequercottage.com**
- **website: www.chequercottage.com**

•CHESHIRE

Guest House / Self-Catering

Mrs Joanne Hollins, Balterley Green Farm, Deans Lane, BALTERLEY, near Crewe Cheshire CW2 5QJ Tel: 01270 820 214

- **e-mail: greenfarm@balterley.fsnet.co.uk**
- **website: www.greenfarm.freeserve.co.uk**

Guest House

Mitchell's of Chester, 28 Hough Green, CHESTER, Cheshire CH4 8JQ
Tel: 01244 679 004

- **e-mail: mitoches@dialstart.net**
- **website: www.mitchellsofchester.com**

Guest House / Self-Catering

Mrs Angela Smith, Mill House and Granary, Higher Wych, MALPAS, Cheshire SY14 7JR
Tel: 01948 780362

- **e-mail: angela@videoactive.co.uk**
- **website: www.millhouseandgranary.co.uk**

Farm House / B & B

Jean Callwood, Lea Farm, Wrinehill Road, Wybunbury, NANTWICH, Cheshire CW5 7NS. Tel: 01270 841429

- **e-mail: contactus@leafarm.freeserve.co.uk**
- **website: www.leafarm.co.uk**

•CORNWALL

Self-catering

Graham Wright, Guardian House, Barras Street, Liskeard, Cornwall PL14 6AD
Tel: 01579 344080

Self-Catering

Cornish Traditional Cottages, Blisland, BODMIN, Cornwall PL30 4HS
Tel: 01208 821666

- **e-mail: info@corncott.com**
- **website: www.corncott.com**

Self-Catering

Mrs Angela Clark, Darrynane Cottages, Darrynane, St Breward, BODMIN, Cornwall PL30 4LZ. Tel: 01208 850885

- **e-mail: enquiries@darrynane.co.uk**
- **website: www.darrynane.com**

Self-Catering

Penrose Burden Holiday Cottages, St Breward, BODMIN, Cornwall PL30 4LZ
Tel: 01208 850277 or 01208 850617

- **website: www.penroseburden.co.uk**

Self-Catering

Trevella, Treveighan, St Teath, BODMIN, Cornwall PL30 3JN
Tel: 01208 850 529

- **e-mail: david.trevella@btconnect.com**
- **website: www.trevellacornwall.co.uk**

Readers are requested to mention this FHG guidebook when seeking accommodation

Touring Caravan & Camping Park
Budemeadows Touring Park, BUDE, Cornwall EX23 0NA Tel: 01288 361646
- **e-mail: holiday@budemeadows.com**
- **website: www.budemeadows.com**

Self-Catering
Langfield Manor, Broadclose, BUDE, Cornwall EX23 8DP Tel: 01288 352 415
- **e-mail: info@langfieldmanor.co.uk**
- **website: www.langfieldmanor.co.uk**

Guest House
Stratton Gardens, Cot Hill, Stratton, BUDE, Cornwall EX23 9DN Tel: 01288 352500
- **e-mail: moira@stratton-gardens.co.uk**
- **website: www.stratton-gardens.co.uk**

Farm
Mrs Margaret Short, Langaton Farm, Whitstone, Holsworthy, BUDE, Cornwall EX22 6TS Tel: 01288 341 215
- **e-mail: langatonfarm@hotmail.com**
- **website: www.langaton-farm-holidays.co.uk**

Self-Catering Cottage
Lower Kitleigh Cottage, Week St Mary, near BUDE, Cornwall
Contact: Mr & Mrs T. Bruce-Dick, 114 Albert Street, London NW1 7NE
Tel: 0207 485 8976
- **e-mail: timbrucedick@yahoo.co.uk**
- **website: www.tbdarchitects.co.uk**

Hotel
Wringford Down Hotel, Hat Lane, CAWSAND, Cornwall PL10 1LE
Tel: 01752 822287
- **e-mail: a.molloy@virgin.net**
- **website: www.cornwallholidays.co.uk**

Self-Catering
Mineshop Holiday Cottages, CRACKINGTON HAVEN, Bude, Cornwall EX23 0NR Tel: 01840 230338
- **e-mail: info@mineshop.co.uk**
- **website: www.mineshop.co.uk**

Self-Catering
Delamere Holiday Bungalows, DELABOLE, Cornwall
Contact: Mrs J. Snowden Tel: 01895 234144
- **website: www.delamerebungalows.com**

Self-Catering
Cornish Holiday Cottages, Killibrae, West Bay, Maenporth, FALMOUTH, Cornwall TR11 5HP Tel: 01326 250 339
- **e-mail: info@cornishholidaycottages.net**
- **website: www.cornishholidaycottages.net**

Self-Catering
Mr M. Watson, Creekside Holiday Cottages, Strangwith House, Restronguet, FALMOUTH, Cornwall TR11 5ST
Tel: 01326 375972
- **e-mail: martin@creeksidecottages.co.uk**
- **website: www.creeksidecottages.co.uk**

Self-Catering
Colin Kemp, Pantiles, 6 Stracey Road, FALMOUTH, Cornwall TR11 4DW Tel: 01326 211838
- **e-mail: colinkemp@lineone.net**
- **website: www.falmouthapartments.co.uk**

Hotel
Rosemullion Hotel, Gyllyngvase Hill, FALMOUTH, Cornwall TR11 4DF
Tel: 01326 314 690
- **e-mail: gail@rosemullionhotel.demon.co.uk**
- **www.SmoothHound.co.uk/hotels/rosemullion.**

Self-Catering
Mrs K Terry, "Shasta", Carwinion Road, Mawnan Smith, FALMOUTH, Cornwall TR11 5JD Tel: 01326 250775
- **e-mail: katerry@btopenworld.com**
- **website: www.cornwallonline.com**

Guest House
Jenny Lake, Wickham Guest House, 21 Gyllyngvase Terrace, FALMOUTH, Cornwall TR11 4DL Tel: 01326 311140
- **e-mail: enquiries@wickhamhotel.freeserve.co.uk**
- **website: www.wickham-hotel.co.uk**

Self-Catering
Mrs Furniss, Lancrow Farm, near FOWEY, Cornwall PL24 2SA Tel: 01726 814 263
- **e-mail: sarahfurniss@aol.com**
- **website: www.foweyvacations.com**

Self-Catering
Mrs S. Trewhella, Mudgeon Vean Farm, St Martin, HELSTON Cornwall TR12 6DB
Tel: 01326 231341
- **e-mail: mudgeonvean@aol.com**
- **website: www.cornwall-online.co.uk/mudgeon-vean/ctb.html**

Self-Catering
Mrs W.J. Morris, Bossava Cottage, LAMORNA, Penzance, Cornwall TR19 6XG
Tel: 01736 732 420
- **e-mail: junekernow@aol.com**
- **website: www.lamornaholidays.com**

Hotel / Lodges
Trethorne Golf Club, Kennards House, LAUNCESTON, Cornwall PL15 8QE
Tel: 01566 86903
- **e-mail: jon@trethornegolfclub.com**
- **website: www.trethornegolfclub.com**

Self-Catering Cottages

Swallows & Meadow Cottage, Lower Dutson Farm, LAUNCESTON, Cornwall PL15 9SP Tel: 01566 776456

- **e-mail: francis.broad@farm-cottage.co.uk**
- **website: www.farm-cottage.co.uk**

Self-Catering

Celia Hutchinson, Caradon Country Cottages, East Taphouse, LISKEARD, Cornwall PL14 4NH Tel: 01579 320355

- **e-mail: celia@caradoncottages.co.uk**
- **website: www.caradoncottages.co.uk**

Self-Catering

Mr Lowman, Cutkive Wood Holiday Lodges, St Ive, LISKEARD, Cornwall PL14 3ND Tel: 01579 362216

- **e-mail: holidays@cutkivewood.co.uk**
- **website: www.cutkivewood.co.uk**

Holiday Home Caravans / Tents & Touring

Mullion Holiday Park, Near Helston, LIZARD, Cornwall TR12 7LT Tel: 0870 444 0080

- **e-mail: bookings@weststarholidays.co.uk**
- **website: www.weststarholidays.co.uk**

Caravan Park

Looe Bay Holiday Park, LOOE, Cornwall PL13 1NX Tel: 0870 444 0080

- **e-mail: bookings@weststarholidays.co.uk**
- **website: www.weststarholidays.co.uk**

Self-Catering

Mr P. Brumpton, Talehay Holiday Cottages, Pelynt, Near LOOE, Cornwall PL13 2LT Tel: 01503 220252

- **e-mail: paul@talehay.co.uk**
- **website: www.talehay.co.uk**

Self-Catering

Tremaine Green Country Cottages, Tremaine Green, Pelynt, Near LOOE, Cornwall PL13 2LT. Tel: 01503 220333

- **e-mail: stay@tremainegreen.co.uk**
- **website: www.tremainegreen.co.uk**

Self-Catering

Mr & Mrs Holder, Valleybrook Holidays, Peakswater, Lansallos, LOOE, Cornwall PL13 2QE Tel: 01503 220493

- **e-mail: admin@valleybrookholidays.co.uk**
- **website: www.valleybrookholidays.co.uk**

Self-Catering Cottages

Wringworthy Cottages, LOOE, Cornwall PL13 1PR Tel: 01503 240 685

- **e-mail: pets@wringworthy.co.uk**
- **website: www.wringworthy.co.uk**

Self-Catering

St Anthony Holidays, St Anthony, MANACCAN, Helston, Cornwall TR12 6JW Tel: 01326 231357

- **e-mail: info@stanthony.co.uk**
- **website: www.stanthony.co.uk**

Hotel

Blue Bay Hotel, Trenance, MAWGAN PORTH, Cornwall TR8 4DA Tel: 01637 860324

- **e-mail: hotel@bluebaycornwall.co.uk**
- **website: www.bluebaycornwall.co.uk**

B & B

Mrs Dawn Rundle, Lancallan Farm, MEVAGISSEY, St Austell,Cornwall PL26 6EW Tel: 01726 842 284

- **e-mail: dawn@lancallan.fsnet.co.uk**
- **website: www.lancallanfarm.co.uk**

B & B

Mr & Mrs M. Limer, Alicia, 136 Henver Road, NEWQUAY, Cornwall TR7 3EQ Tel: 01637 874328

- **e-mail: aliciaguesthouse@mlimer.fsnet.co.uk**
- **website: www.alicia-guesthouse.co.uk**

Guest House

Pensalda Guest House, 98 Henver Road, NEWQUAY, Cornwall TR7 3BL Tel: 01637 874 601

- **e-mail: karen_pensalda@yahoo.co.uk±**
- **website: www.pensalda-guesthouse.co.uk**

Hotel

St George's Hotel, 71 Mount Wise, NEWQUAY, Cornwall TR7 2BP Tel: 01637 873010

- **e-mail: enquiries@stgeorgeshotel.free-online.co.uk**
- **website: www.st-georges-newquay.co.uk**

Caravan & Camping / Self-Catering

Quarryfield Caravan & Camping Park, Crantock, NEWQUAY, Cornwall Contact: Mrs A. Winn, Tretherras, Newquay, Cornwall TR7 2RE

Tel: 01637 872 792

- **website: www.quarryfield.co.uk**

Hotel

Tregea Hotel, 16-18 High Street, PADSTOW, Cornwall PL28 8BB Tel: 01841 532 455

- **e-mail: info@tregea.co.uk**
- **website: www.tregea.co.uk**

B & B

Mrs Owen, Penalva Private Hotel, Alexandra Road, PENZANCE, Cornwall TR18 4LZ Tel: 01736 369 060

- **website: www.penalva.co.uk**

Holiday Park
Perran Sands Holiday Park, PERRANPORTH, Cornwall TR6 0AQ Tel: 01872 573742
• **website: www.touringholidays.co.uk**

Hotel / Inn
Cornish Arms, Pendoggett, PORT ISAAC, Cornwall PL30 3HH Tel: 01208 880263
• **e-mail: info@cornisharms.com**
• **website: www.cornisharms.com**

Guest House
Mrs E. Neal, Tamarind, 12 Shrubberies Hill, PORTHLEVEN, Cornwall TR13 9EA
Tel: 01326 574303
• **e-mail: lizzybenzimra@hotmail.com**
• **www.web-direct.co.uk/porthleven/tamarind.html**

Hotel
Rosevine Hotel, Porthcurnick Beach, PORTSCATHO, Near St Mawes, Cornwall TR2 5EW Tel: 01872 580206
• **e-mail: info@rosevine.co.uk**
• **website: www.rosevine.co.uk**

Caravan & Camping
Globe Vale Holiday Park, Radnor, REDRUTH, Cornwall TR16 4BH Tel: 01209 891183
• **e-mail: info@globevale.co.uk**
• **website: www.globevale.co.uk**

Hotel
Penventon Park Hotel, West End, REDRUTH, Cornwall TR15 1TE Tel: 01209 20 3000
• **e-mail: enquiries@penventon.com**
• **website: www.penventon.com**

Caravan & Camping
Wheal Rose Caravan & Camping Park, Scorrier, REDRUTH, Cornwall TR16 5DD
Tel: 01209 891496
• **e-mail: whealrose@aol.com**
• **website: www.whealrosecaravanpark.co.uk**

Guest House
Mrs Merchant, Woodpeckers, RILLA MILL, Callington, Cornwall PL17 7NT
Tel: 01579 363717
• **e-mail: alison.merchant@virgin.net**
• **website: www.woodpeckersguesthouse.co.uk**

Hotel
The Beacon Country House Hotel, Goonvrea Road, ST AGNES, Cornwall TR5 0NW Tel:01872 552 318
• **e-mail: info@beaconhotel.co.uk**
• **website: www.beaconhotel.co.uk**

Caravan & Camping / Holiday Park
Chiverton Park, Blackwater, ST AGNES, Cornwall TR4 8HS Tel: 01872 560667
• **e-mail: info@chivertonpark.co.uk**
• **website: www.chivertonpark.co.uk**

Hotel / Inn
Driftwood Spars Hotel, Trevaunance Cove, ST AGNES, Cornwall TR5 0RT
Tel: 01872 552428/553323
• **website: www.driftwoodspars.com**

Hotel / B & B
Penkerris, Penwinnick Road, ST AGNES, Cornwall TR5 0PA Tel: 01872 552262
• **e-mail: info@penkerris.co.uk**
• **website: www.penkerris.co.uk**

Guest House
Mr Gardener, The Elms, 14 Penwinnick Road, ST AUSTELL, Cornwall PL25 5DW
Tel: 01726 74981
• **website: www.edenbb.co.uk**

Farmhouse
Mrs Diana Clemes, Tregilgas Farm, Gorran, ST AUSTELL, Cornwall PL26 6ND
Tel: 01726 842342
• **e-mail: dclemes88@aol.com**

Self-Catering
Big-Picture Holiday Apartments, ST IVES, Cornwall Tel: 07803 129918
• **e-mail: sarah@bigpictureholidays.co.uk**
• **website: www.bigpictureholidays.co.uk**

Self-Catering
R.G. Pontefract, The Links Holiday Flats, Church Lane, Lelant, ST IVES, Cornwall TR26 3HY Tel: 01736 753326
• **e-mail: jackpontefract@aol.com**

Guest House
Angela & Barrie Walker, Rivendell, 7 Porthminster Terrace, ST IVES, Cornwall TR26 2DQ Tel: 01736 794923
• **e-mail: rivendellstives@aol.com**
• **website: www.rivendell-stives.co.uk**

Self-Catering
Sandbank Holidays, ST IVES BAY, Hayle, St Ives, Cornwall TR27 5BL
Tel: 01736 752594
• **website: www.sandbank-holidays.co.uk**

Self-Catering
Mr & Mrs C.W. Pestell, Hockadays, Tregenna, Near Blisland, ST TUDY, Cornwall PL30 4QJ Tel: 01208 850146
• **e-mail: holidays@hockadaysholidaycottages.co.uk**
• **website: www.hockadaysholidaycottages.co.uk**

Self-Catering
Mrs R. Reeves, Polstraul, Trewalder, Delabole, ST TUDY, Cornwall PL33 9ET
Tel: 01840 213 120
• **e-mail: aandr.reeves@virgin.net**
• **website: www.maymear.co.uk**

Self-Catering

Mrs Susan Tanzer, Trewithian Farm, ST WENN, Bodmin, Cornwall PL30 5PH
Tel: 01208 895 181

- **e-mail: trewithian@hotmail.co.uk**
- **www.cornwall-online.co.uk/trewithianfarm**

Self-Catering

Mrs Sandy Wilson, Salutations, Atlantic Road, TINTAGEL, Cornwall PL34 0DE
Tel: 01840 770287

- **e-mail: sandyanddave@tinyworld.co.uk**
- **website: www.salutationstintagel.co.uk**

Touring Caravan Park

Summer Valley Touring Park, Shortlanesend, TRURO, Cornwall TR4 9DW
Tel: 01872 277878

- **e-mail: res@summervalley.co.uk**
- **website: www.summervalley.co.uk**

Farm / B & B / Self-Catering Cottages

Mrs P. Carbis. Trenona Farm Holidays, Ruan High Lanes, TRURO, Cornwall TR2 5JS
Tel: 01872 501339

- **e-mail: info@trenonafarmholidays.co.uk**
- **website: www.trenonafarmholidays.co.uk**

Farm

Pengelly Farmhouse, Pengelly Farm, Burlawn, WADEBRIDGE, Cornwall PL27 7LA
Tel: 01208 814 217

- **e-mail: hodgepete@hotmail.com**
- **website: www.pengellyfarm.co.uk**

•CUMBRIA

Inn

The Britannia Inn, Elterwater, AMBLESIDE, Cumbria LA22 9HP Tel: 015394 37210

- **e-mail: info@britinn.co.uk**
- **website: www.britinn.co.uk**

Hotel

Crow How Country House, Rydal Road, AMBLESIDE, Cumbria LA22 9PN
Tel: 015394 32193

- **e-mail: stay@crowhowcountryhouse.co.uk**
- **website: www.crowhowcountryhouse.co.uk**

Caravan Park

Greenhowe Caravan Park, Great Langdale, AMBLESIDE, Cumbria LA22 9JU
Tel: 015394 37231

- **e-mail: enquiries@greenhowe.com**
- **website: www.greenhowe.com**

Hotel / Guest House

Ian & Helen Burt, The Old Vicarage, Vicarage Road, AMBLESIDE, Cumbria LA22 9DH. Tel: 015394 33364

- **e-mail: info@oldvicarageambleside.co.uk**
- **website: www.oldvicarageambleside.co.uk**

B & B

Broom House, Long Martin, APPLEBY-IN-WESTMORLAND, Cumbria CA16 6JP
Tel: 01768 361 318

- **website: www.broomhouseappleby.co.uk**

Guest House

Barbara & Derick Cotton, Glebe House, Bolton, APPLEBY-IN-WESTMORLAND, Cumbria CA16 6AW Tel: 01768 361125

- **e-mail: derick.cotton@btinternet.com**
- **website: www.glebeholidays.co.uk**

B & B

Sharon Moore, Annisgarth B & B, 48 Craig Walk, BOWNESS-ON-WINDERMERE, Cumbria LA23 2JT Tel: 015394 43866

- **website: www.annisgarth.co.uk**

Self-Catering

Lakelovers, Belmont House, Lake Road, BOWNESS-ON-WINDERMERE, Cumbria LA23 3BJ Tel: 015294 88855

- **e-mail: bookings@lakelovers.co.uk**
- **website: www.lakelovers.co.uk**

Self-Catering / Farm

Mrs J. M. Almond, Irton House Farm, Isel, COCKERMOUTH, Cumbria CA13 9ST
Tel: 017687 76380

- **e-mail: almond@farmersweekly.net**
- **website: www.irtonhousefarm.com**

B & B

Mosser Heights, Mosser, COCKERMOUTH, Cumbria CA13 0SS Tel: 01900 822644

- **e-mail: AmandaVickers@aol.com**

Guest House

Rose Cottage Guest House, Lorton Road, COCKERMOUTH, Cumbria CA13 9DX
Tel: 01900 822189

- **website: www.rosecottageguest.co.uk**

B & B

Birkhow Cottage, ESKDALE, Cumbria
Contact: Sally Tel: 017687 76836

- **e-mail: sally@hollinhead.co.uk**

Guest House

Mr & Mrs J. D. Bromage, Forest How Guest House, ESKDALE GREEN, Cumbria CA19 1TR
Tel: 019467 23201

- **website: www.foresthow.co.uk**

Holiday Park
Lakeland Leisure Park, Moor Lane, Flookburgh, Near GRANGE-OVER-SANDS, Cumbria LA11 7LT Tel: 01539 558556
- **website: www.touringholidays.co.uk**

Farm / Self-Catering
Mr P. Brown, High Dale Park Farm, High Dale Park, Salterthwaite, Ulverston, GRIZEDALE FOREST, Cumbria LA12 8LJ
Tel: 01229 860226
- **e-mail: peter@lakesweddingmusic.com**
- **www.lakesweddingmusic.com/accomm**

Self-Catering Cottages
Hideaways, The Square, HAWKSHEAD, Cumbria LA22 0NZ Tel: 015394 42435
- **e-mail: bookings@lakeland-hideaways.co.uk**
- **website: www.lakeland-hideaways.co.uk**

Hotel
Ivy House Hotel, Main Street, HAWKSHEAD, Cumbria LA22 0NS Tel: 015394 36204
- **e-mail: ivyhousehotel@btinternet.com**
- **website: www.ivyhousehotel.com**

Self-Catering
Keswick Cottages, 8 Beechcroft, Braithwaite, KESWICK, Cumbria CA12 5RS
Tel: 017687 78555
- **e-mail: info@keswickcottages.co.uk**
- **website: www.keswickcottages.co.uk**

Guest House
Rickerby Grange Guest House, Portinscale, KESWICK, Cumbria CA12 5RH
Tel: 017687 72344
- **e-mail: stay@rickerbygrange.co.uk**
- **website: www.rickerbygrange.co.uk**

Self-Catering
Mrs S.J. Bottom, Crossfield Cottages, KIRKOSWALD, Penrith, Cumbria CA10 1EU
Tel: 01768 898711
- **e-mail: info@crossfieldcottages.co.uk**
- **website: www.crossfieldcottages.co.uk**

Self-Catering
Routen House & Little Paddock, LAKE DISTRICT, Cumbria
Contact: Mrs J. Green Tel: 01604 626383
- **e-mail: joanne@routenhouse.co.uk**
- **website: www.routenhouse.co.uk**

Farm
Esthwaite How Farmhouse, NEAR SAWREY, Ambleside, Cumbria LA22 0LB
Tel: 01539 436 450
- **e-mail: elizabeth@esthwaitehow.co.uk**
- **website: www.esthwaitehow.co.uk**

B & B
Mr Bell, Albany House, 5 Portland Place, PENRITH, Cumbria CA11 7QN
Tel: 01768 863072
- **e-mail: info@albany-house.org.uk**
- **website: www.albany-house.org.uk**

Guest House
Blue Swallow Guest House, 11 Victoria Road, PENRITH, Cumbria CA11 8HR Tel: 01768 866335
- **e-mail: blueswallow@tiscali.co.uk**
- **website: www.blueswallow.co.uk**

Self-Catering
Mr & Mrs Iredale, Carrock Cottages, Carrock House, Hutton Roof, PENRITH, Cumbria CA11 0XY Tel: 01768 484111
- **e-mail: info@carrockcottages.co.uk**
- **website: www.carrockcottages.co.uk**

Self-Catering
Mark Cowell, Church Court Cottages, Gamblesby, PENRITH, Cumbria CA10 1HR
Tel: 01768 881682
- **e-mail: markcowell@tiscali.co.uk**
- **website: www.gogamblesby.co.uk**

B & B
Greenah Crag, Troutbeck, PENRITH, Cumbria CA11 0SQ Tel: 017684 83233
- **e-mail: greenahcrag@lineone.net**
- **website: www.greenahcrag.co.uk**

Golf Club
Seascale Golf Club, The Banks, SEASCALE, Cumbria CA20 1QL Tel: 01946 728202
- **e-mail: seascalegolfclub@btconnect.com**
- **website: www.seascalegolfclub.co.uk**

Self-Catering / Caravan & Camping
Tanglewood Caravan Park, Causeway Head, SILLOTH-ON-SOLWAY, Cumbria CA7 4PE
Tel: 016973 31253
- **e-mail: tanglewoodcaravanpark@hotmail.com**
- **website: www.tanglewoodcaravanpark.co.uk**

Hotel
Golf Hotel, SILLOTH-ON-SOLWAY, Cumbria CA7 4AB Tel: 016973 31438
- **e-mail: golf.hotel@virgin.net**
- **website: www.golfhotelsilloth.co.uk**

Self-Catering / Caravan
Fell View Holidays, Glenridding, Penrith, ULLSWATER, Cumbria CA11 0PJ
Tel: 01768 482342; Evening: 01768 867420
- **e-mail: enquiries@fellviewholidays.com**
- **website: www.fellviewholidays.com**

B & B / Self-Catering

Barbara Murphy, Land Ends Country Lodge, Watermillock, Near Penrith, ULLSWATER, Cumbria CA11 0NB Tel: 01768 486438
- **e-mail: infolandends@btinternet.com**
- **website: www.landends.co.uk**

Guest House

Fir Trees Guest House, Lake Road, WINDERMERE, Cumbria LA23 2EQ Tel: 015394 42272
- **e-mail: enquiries@fir-trees.com**
- **website: www.fir-trees.com**

Guest House

Green Gables, 37 Broad Street, WINDERMERE LA23 2AB Tel: 015394 43886
- **e-mail: greengables@fsbdial.co.uk info@greengablesguesthouse.co.uk**

Guest House

Josette & Mark Bayley, Holly-Wood Guest House, Holly Road, WINDERMERE, Cumbria LA23 2AF Tel: 015394 42219
- **e-mail: info@hollywoodguesthouse.co.uk**
- **website: www.hollywoodguesthouse.co.uk**

Guest House

Meadfoot Guest House, New Road, WINDERMERE, Cumbria LA23 2LA Tel: 015394 42610
- **website: www.meadfoot-guesthouse.co.uk**

• DERBYSHIRE

B & B

Compton House, 27- 31 Compton, ASHBOURNE, Derbyshire DE6 1BX Tel: 01335 343100
- **e-mail: enquiries@comptonhouse.co.uk**
- **website: www.comptonhouse.co.uk**

B & B

Mrs M Harris, The Courtyard, Dairy House Farm, Alkmonton, Longford, ASHBOURNE, Derbyshire DE6 3DG Tel: 01335 330187
- **e-mail: michael@dairyhousefarm.org.uk**
- **website: www.dairyhousefarm.org.uk**

Inn

The Dog & Partridge Country Inn, Swinscoe, ASHBOURNE, Derbyshire DE6 2HS Tel: 01335 343183
- **e-mail: info@dogandpartridge.co.uk**
- **website: www.dogandpartridge.co.uk**

B & B

Mrs A.M. Whittle, Stone Cottage, Green Lane, Clifton, ASHBOURNE, Derbyshire DE6 2BL Tel: 01335 343377
- **e-mail: info@stone-cottage.fsnet.co.uk**
- **website: www.stone-cottage.fsnet.co.uk**

B&B

Mrs J. Salisbury, Turlow Bank, Hognaston, ASHBOURNE, Derbyshire DE6 1PW Tel: 01335 370299
- **e-mail: turlowbank@w3z.co.uk**
- **website: www.turlowbank.co.uk**

Self-Catering

P. Skemp, Cotterill Farm, BIGGIN-BY-HARTINGTON, Buxton, Derbyshire SK17 0DJ Tel: 01298 84447
- **e-mail: enquiries@cotterillfarm.co.uk**
- **website: www.cotterillfarm.co.uk**

Hotel

Biggin Hall Hotel, Biggin-by-Hartington, BUXTON, Derbyshire SK17 0DH Tel: 01298 84451
- **e-mail: enquiries@bigginhall.co.uk**
- **website: www.bigginhall.co.uk**

Guest House

Mr & Mrs Hyde, Braemar Guest House, 10 Compton Road, BUXTON, Derbyshire SK17 9DN Tel: 01298 78050
- **e-mail: buxtonbraemar@supanet.com**
- **website: www.cressbrook.co.uk/buxton/braemar**

Self-Catering

Mrs Gillian Taylor, Priory Lea Holiday Flats, 50 White Knowle Road, BUXTON, Derbyshire SK17 9NH Tel: 01298 23737
- **e-mail: priorylea@tiscali.co.uk**
- **website: www.cressbrook.co.uk/buxton/priorylea**

Self-Catering
Mr R. D. Hollands, Wheeldon Trees Farm, Earl Sterndale, BUXTON, Derbyshire SK17 0AA Tel: 01298 83219
- **e-mail: hollands@easterndale.fsnet.co.uk**
- **website: www.wheeldontreesfarm.co.uk**

Hotel
Charles Cotton Hotel, Hartington, Near BUXTON, Derbyshire SK17 0AL Tel: 01298 84229
- **e-mail: info@charlescotton.co.uk**
- **website: www.charlescotton.co.uk**

Caravan & Camping Park
Newhaven Caravan & Camping Park, Newhaven, NEAR BUXTON, Derbyshire SK17 0DT Tel: 01298 84300
- **website: www.newhavencaravanpark.com**

Farm / B & B
Mrs Catherine Dicken, Bonehill Farm, Etwall Road, Mickleover, DERBY, Derbyshire DE3 0DN Tel: 01332 513553
- **website: www.bonehillfarm.co.uk**

Farm / Self-Catering
J. Gibbs, Wolfscote Grange, HARTINGTON, Near Buxton, Derbyshire SK17 0AX Tel: 01298 84342
- **e-mail: wolfscote@btinternet.com**
- **website: www.wolfscotegrangecottages.co.uk**

Guest House
Ivy House Farm, Stanton-by-Bridge, NEAR MELBOURNE, Derby, Derbyshire DE73 7HT Tel: 01332 863152
- **e-mail: mary@guesthouse.fsbusiness.co.uk**
- **website: www.ivy-house-farm.com**

Self-Catering
Angela Kellie, Shatton Hall Farm, Bamford, Hope Valley, PEAK DISTRICT, Derbyshire S33 0BG Tel: 01433 620635
- **e-mail: ahk@peakfarmholidays.co.uk**
- **website: www.peakfarmholidays.co.uk**

•DEVON

Self-Catering
Farm & Cottage Holidays, DEVON Tel: 01237 479698
- **e-mail: enquiries@farmcott.co.uk**
- **website: www.holidaycottages.co.uk**

Self-Catering
Helpful Holidays, Mill Street, Chagford, DEVON TQ13 8AW Tel: 01647 433593
- **e-mail: help@helpfulholidays.com**
- **website: www.helpfulholidays.com**

Self-Catering
Toad Hall Cottages, DEVON Tel: 01548 853089 (24 Hours)
- **e-mail: thc@toadhallcottages.com**
- **website: www.toadhallcottages.com**

Self-Catering
Robin & Wren Cottages, ASHBURTON, Devon Contact: Mrs M. Phipps, Newcott Farm, Poundsgate, Newton Abbot TQ13 7PD Tel: 01364 631421
- **e-mail: enquiries@newcott-farm.co.uk**
- **website: www.newcott-farm.co.uk**

B & B
The Durant Arms, ASHPRINGTON, Totnes, Devon TQ9 7UP Tel: 01803 732240
- **e-mail: info@thedurantarms.com**
- **website: www.thedurantarms.com**

Self-Catering
Braddon Cottages, ASHWATER, Beaworthy, Holsworthy, Devon Tel: 01409 211350
- **e-mail: holidays@braddoncottages.co.uk**
- **website: www.braddoncottages.co.uk**

B & B / Self-Catering
Mrs S.J. Avis, Lea Hill, Membury, AXMINSTER, Devon EX13 7AQ Tel: 01404 881881
- **e-mail: reception@leahill.co.uk**
- **website: www.leahill.co.uk**

Self-Catering
North Devon Holiday Homes, 19 Cross Street, BARNSTAPLE, Devon EX31 1BD Tel: 01271 376322
- **e-mail: info@northdevonholidays.co.uk**
- **website: www.northdevonholidays.co.uk**

Farm / B & B
Jenny Cope, North Down Farm B & B, Pyncombe Lane, Wiveliscombe, BARNSTAPLE, Devon TA4 2BL Tel: 01984 623730
- **e-mail: jennycope@tiscali.co.uk**
- **website: www.north-down-farm.co.uk**

Hotel
Sandy Cove Hotel, Combe Martin Bay, BERRYNARBOR, Devon EX34 9SR Tel: 01271 882243/882888
- **website: www.sandycove-hotel.co.uk**

B & B / Self-Catering
Mr & Mrs Lewin, Lake House Cottages and B&B, Lake Villa, BRADWORTHY, Devon EX22 7SQ Tel: 01409 241962
- **e-mail: info@lakevilla.co.uk**
- **website: www.lakevilla.co.uk**

Caravan & Camping

Berry Barton Caravan Park, BRANSCOMBE, Seaton, Devon EX12 3BD Tel: 01297 680208

- **email: berrybarton@amserve.com**
- **website: www.berrybarton.co.uk**

Self-Catering / Organic Farm

Little Comfort Farm Cottages, Little Comfort Farm, BRAUNTON, North Devon EX33 2NJ Tel: 01271 812414

- **e-mail: info@littlecomfortfarm.co.uk**
- **website: www.littlecomfortfarm.co.uk**

Self-Catering

Marsdens Cottage Holidays, 2 The Square, BRAUNTON, Devon EX33 2JB Tel: 01271 813777

- **e-mail: holidays@marsdens.co.uk**
- **website: www.marsdens.co.uk**

Self-Catering

Devoncourt Holiday Flats, Berryhead Road, BRIXHAM, Devon TQ5 9AB Tel: 01803 853748

- **website: www.devoncourt.info**

Guest House

Woodlands Guest House, Parkham Road, BRIXHAM, South Devon TQ5 9BU Tel: 01803 852040

- **e-mail: woodlandsbrixham@btinternet.com**
- **website: www.dogfriendlyguesthouse.co.uk www.woodlandsdevon.co.uk**

Self-Catering / B & B / Caravans

Mrs Gould, Bonehayne Farm, COLYTON, Devon EX24 6SG Tel: 01404 871416/871396

- **e-mail: gould@bonehayne.co.uk**
- **website: www.bonehayne.co.uk**

Self-Catering

Watermouth Cove Cottages, Watermouth, Near COMBE MARTIN, Devon EX34 9SJ Tel: 0870 2413168

- **e-mail: stay@coastalvalleyhideaways.co.uk**
- **website: www.coastalvalleyhideaways.co.uk**

Holiday Park

Manleigh Holiday Park, Rectory Road, COMBE MARTIN, Devon EX34 0NS Tel: 01271 883353

- **e-mail: info@manleighpark.co.uk**
- **website: www.manleighpark.co.uk**

www.holidayguides.com

B & B

Miss Audrey Isaac, Crowborough, Georgeham, Braunton, CROYDE, Devon EX33 1JZ Tel: 01271 891005

- **website: www.crowboroughfarm.co.uk**

Self-Catering

Mrs S.R. Ridalls, The Old Bakehouse, 7 Broadstone, DARTMOUTH, Devon TQ6 9NR Tel: 01803 834585

- **e-mail: ridallsleisure@aol.com**
- **website: www.oldbakehousedartmouth.co.uk**

Self-Catering

Watermill Cottages, Higher North Mill, Hansel, DARTMOUTH, Devon TQ6 0LN Tel: 01803 770219

- **e-mail: graham@hanselpg.freeserve.co.uk**
- **website: www.watermillcottages.co.uk**

Farm B & B

Mrs Karen Williams, Stile Farm, Starcross, EXETER, Devon EX6 8PD Tel: 01626 890268

- **e-mail: info@stile-farm.co.uk**
- **website: www.stile-farm.co.uk**

Self-Catering

The Independent Traveller, The Bury, Thorverton, EXETER, Devon EX5 5NT Tel: 01392 860 807

- **e-mail: help@gowithit.co.uk**
- **website: www.gowithit.co.uk**

Holiday Park

Devon Cliffs Holiday Park, Sandy Bay, EXMOUTH, Devon EX8 5BT Tel: 01395 226226

- **website: www.touringholidays.co.uk**

Hotel

Devoncourt Hotel, Douglas Avenue, EXMOUTH, Devon EX8 2EX Tel: 01395 272277

- **website: www.devoncourt.com**

Caravan & Camping

Mrs Megan Daglish, Tamarstone Farm, Bude Road, Pancrasweek, HOLSWORTHY, Devon EX22 7JT Tel: 01288 381734

- **e-mail: pets@tamarstone.co.uk**
- **website: www.tamarstone.co.uk**

Hotel / Guest House

St Brannocks House, St Brannocks Road, ILFRACOMBE, Devon EX34 8EQ Tel: 01271 863873

- **e-mail: barbara@stbrannockshotel.co.uk**
- **website: www.stbrannockshotel.co.uk**

Farm / B & B

Venn Farm, Ugborough, IVYBRIDGE, Devon PL21 0PE Tel: 01364 73240

- **e-mail: info@vennfarm.co.uk**
- **website: www.vennfarm.co.uk**

Self-Catering

Beachdown Holiday Bungalows, Beachdown House, Challaborough Bay, KINGSBRIDGE, South Devon
Tel: 01548 810089

- **e-mail: enquiries@beachdown.co.uk or petswelcome@beachdown.co.uk**
- **website: www.beachdown.co.uk**

Hotel

Alford House Hotel, Alford Terrace, LYNTON, Devon EX35 6AT
Tel: 01598 752359

- **e-mail: enquiries@alfordhouse.co.uk**
- **website: www.alfordhouse.co.uk**

Caravan Park

Pennymoor Caravan Park, MODBURY, Near Ivybridge, Devon PL21 0SB
Tel: 01548 830542 or 01548 830020

- **e-mail: enquiries@pennymoor-camping.co.uk**
- **website: www.pennymoor-camping.co.uk**

Guest House

The Smugglers Rest Inn, North Morte Road, MORTEHOE, North Devon EX34 7DR
Tel: 01271 870891

- **e-mail: info@smugglersmortehoe.co.uk**
- **website: www.smugglersmortehoe.co.uk**

Farm B & B

Mrs T.M. Merchant, Great Sloncombe Farm, MORETONHAMPSTEAD, Newton Abbot, Devon TQ13 8QF Tel: 01647 440595

- **e-mail: hmerchant@sloncombe.freeserve.co.uk**
- **website: www.greatsloncombefarm.co.uk**

Hotel

Riversford Hotel, Limers Lane, NORTHAM, Bideford, Devon EX39 2RG
Tel: 01237 474239

- **e-mail: riversford@aol.com**
- **website: www.riversford.co.uk**

Self-Catering

Crab Cottage, NOSS MAYO, South Devon
Tel: 01425 471 372

- **website: www.crab-cottage.co.uk**

Farm Guest House

Mrs Ann Forth, Fluxton Farm, OTTERY ST MARY, Devon EX11 1RJ
Tel: 01404 812818

- **website: www.fluxtonfarm.co.uk**

Self-Catering

Mr & Mrs Dillon, Boswell Farm Cottages, Sidford, Near SIDMOUTH, Devon EX10 0PP
Tel: 01395 514162

- **e-mail: dillon@boswell-farm.co.uk**
- **website: www.boswell-farm.co.uk**

Caravan & Camping

Harford Bridge Holiday Park, Peter Tavy, TAVISTOCK, Devon PL19 9LS
Tel: 01822 810349

- **e-mail: enquiry@harfordbridge.co.uk**
- **website: www.harfordbridge.co.uk**

Farm / B & B

Mary & Roger Steer, Rubbytown Farm, Gulworthy, TAVISTOCK, Devon PL19 8PA
Tel: 01822 832493

- **e-mail: jimmy.steer@virgin.net**
- **website: www.rubbytown-farm.co.uk**

Guest House

Mrs Arnold, The Mill, Lower Washfield, TIVERTON, Devon EX16 9PD
Tel: 01884 255297

- **e-mail: arnold5@washfield.freeserve.co.uk**
- **website: www.washfield.freeserve.co.uk**

Hotel

Heathcliff House Hotel, 16 Newton Road, TORQUAY, Devon TQ2 5BZ
Tel: 01803 211580

- **e-mail: heathcliffhouse@btconnect.com**
- **website: www.heathcliffhousehotel.co.uk**

Hotel

The Aveland Hotel, Babbacombe,TORQUAY, Devon TQ1 3PT Tel: 01803 326622

- **e-mail: avelandhotel@aol.com**
- **website: www.avelandhotel.co.uk**

Hotel

Grosvenor House Hotel, Falkland Road, TORQUAY, Devon TQ2 5JP
Tel: 01803 294110

- **e-mail: fhg@grosvenorhousehotel.co.uk**
- **website: www.grosvenorhousehotel.co.uk**

Self-Catering

Mrs H. Carr, Sunningdale Apartments, 11 Babbacombe Downs Road, TORQUAY, Devon TQ1 3LF Tel: 01803 325786

- **e-mail: allancarr@yahoo.com**
- **website: www.sunningdaleapartments.co.uk**

Self-Catering
West Pusehill Farm Cottages, West Pusehill Farm, Pusehill, WESTWARD HO!, Devon EX39 5AH Tel: 01237 475638 or 01237 474622
- **e-mail: info@wpfcottages.co.uk**
- **website: www.wpfcottages.co.uk**

Golf Club
Royal North Devon Golf Club, Golf Links Road, WESTWARD HO!, Devon EX39 1HD Tel: 01237 473817
- **e-mail: info@royalnorthdevongolfclub.co.uk**
- **website: www.royalnorthdevongolfclub.co.uk**

Caravan & Camping
North Morte Farm Caravan & Camping Park, Mortehoe, WOOLACOMBE, Devon EX34 7EG. Tel: 01271 870381
- **e-mail: info@northmortefarm.co.uk**
- **website: www.northmortefarm.co.uk**

Self-Catering
David Mallet, Dartmoor Country Holidays, Bedford Bridge, Horrabridge, YELVERTON, Devon PL20 7RY Tel: 01822 852651
- **website: www.dartmoorcountryholidays.co.uk**

•DORSET

Self-catering
Dorset Coastal Cottages, The Manor House, Winfrith Newburgh, Dorchester, Dorset DT2 8JR Tel: 0800 980 4070
- **e-mail: hols@dorsetcoastalcottages.com**
- **website: www.dorsetcoastalcottages.com**

Self-Catering
Dorset Cottage Holidays Tel: 01929 553443
- **e-mail: enq@dhcottages.co.uk**
- **website: www.dhcottages.co.uk**

Inn
The Anvil Inn, Salisbury Road, Pimperne, BLANDFORD, Dorset DT11 8UQ Tel: 01258 453431
- **e-mail: theanvil.inn@btconnect.com**
- **website: www.anvilinn.co.uk**

Self-Catering
Iona Holiday Flat, 71 Sea Road, BOURNEMOUTH, Dorset BH5 1BG Contact: Andrew Hooper Tel: 01202 460517 or 07967 027025
- **e-mail: hoops2@ntlworld.com**
- **website: www.ionaholidayflat.co.uk**

Guest House
Cransley Hotel, 11 Knyveton Road, East Cliff, BOURNEMOUTH, Dorset BH1 3QG Tel: 01202 290067
- **e-mail: info@cransley.com**
- **website: www.cransley.com**

Hotel
Southbourne Grove Hotel, 96 Southbourne Road, BOURNEMOUTH, Dorset BH6 3QQ Tel: 01202 420 503
- **e-mail: neil@pack1462.freeserve.co.uk**

Hotel
White Topps, 45 Church Road, Southbourne, BOURNEMOUTH, Dorset B46 4BB Tel: 01202 428868
- **e-mail: thedoghotel@aol.com**
- **website: www.whitetopps.co.uk**

Guest House
Hazel & Keith Ingram, Woodside Hotel, 29 Southern Road, Southbourne, BOURNEMOUTH, Dorset BH6 3SR Tel: 01202 427213
- **e-mail: enquiries@woodsidehotel.co.uk**
- **website: www.woodsidehotel.co.uk**

Inn
The Fox & Hounds Inn, Duck Street, CATTISTOCK, Dorchester, Dorset DT2 0JH Tel: 01300 320 444
- **e-mail: info@foxandhoundsinn.com**
- **website: www.foxandhoundsinn.com**

Hotel
The Queens Armes Hotel, The Street, CHARMOUTH, Dorset DT6 6QF Tel: 01297 560339
- **e-mail: darkduck@btconnect.com**
- **website: www.queensarmeshotel.co.uk**

Golf Club
Parley Court Golf Course Ltd, Parley Green Lane, Hurn, CHRISTCHURCH, Dorset
Tel: 01202 591600
- **e-mail: info@parleygolf.co.uk**
- **website: www.parleygolf.co.uk**

Guest House
Church View Guest House, Winterbourne Abbas, DORCHESTER, Dorset DT2 9LS
Tel: 01305 889 296
- **e-mail: stay@churchview.co.uk**
- **website:www.churchview.co.uk**

Caravan Park
Giants Head Caravan & Camping Park, Old Sherborne Road, Cerne Abbas, DORCHESTER, Dorset DT2 7TR
Tel: 01300 341242
- **e-mail: holidays@giantshead.co.uk**
- **website: www.giantshead.co.uk**

Farm / Self-Catering
Tamarisk Farm, West Bexington, DORCHESTER, Dorset DT2 9DF
Tel: 01308 897784
- **e-mail: holidays@tamariskfarm.com**
- **website: www.tamariskfarm.com**

Hotel
Cromwell House Hotel, LULWORTH COVE, Dorset BH20 5RJ
Tel: 01929 400253
- **e-mail: catriona@lulworthcove.co.uk**
- **website: www.lulworthcove.co.uk**

Self-Catering
Westover Farm Cottages, Wootton Fitzpaine, Near LYME REGIS, Dorset DT6 6NE
Tel: 01297 560451/561395
- **e-mail: wfcottages@aol.com**
- **website: www.westoverfarmcottages.co.uk**

Holiday Park
Rockley Park Holiday Park, Hamworthy, POOLE, Dorset BH15 4LZ
Tel: 01202 679393
- **website: www.touringholidays.co.uk**

Holiday Park
Sandford Holiday Park, Holton Heath, POOLE, Dorset BH16 6JZ
Tel: 0870 444 0080
- **e-mail: bookings@weststarholidays.co.uk**
- **website: www.weststarholidays.co.uk**

Farm / Self-Catering
White Horse Farm, Middlemarsh, SHERBORNE, Dorset DT9 5QN
Tel: 01963 210222
- **e-mail: enquiries@whitehorsefarm.co.uk**
- **website: www.whitehorsefarm.co.uk**

Hotel
The Knoll House, STUDLAND BAY, Dorset BH19 3AW Tel: 01929 450450
- **e-mail: info@knollhouse.co.uk**
- **website: www.knollhouse.co.uk**

Hotel
The Limes Hotel, 48 Park Road, SWANAGE, Dorset BH19 2AE Tel: 01929 422664
- **e-mail: info@limeshotel.net**
- **website: www.limeshotel.net**

B & B
Fairway Bed and Breakfast, 7A Demoulham Road, SWANAGE, Dorset BH19 1NR
Tel: 01929 423 367
- **e-mail: rita@ritawaller.plus.com**
- **website: www.swanagefairway.co.uk**

Farm/ Guest House/ Caravan & Camping
Luckford Wood House, East Stoke, WAREHAM, Dorset BH20 6AW
Tel: 01929 463098/07888 719002
- **e-mail: info@luckfordleisure.co.uk**
- **website: www.luckfordleisure.co.uk**

Guest House/ Self-Catering
Glenthorne Castle Cove, 15 Old Castle Road, WEYMOUTH, Dorset DT4 8QB
Tel: 01305 777281
- **e-mail: info@glenthorne-holidays.co.uk**
- **website: www.glenthorne-holidays.co.uk**

Holiday Park
Littlesea Holiday Park, Lynch Lane, WEYMOUTH, Dorset DT4 9DT
Tel: 01305 774414
- **website: www.touringholidays.co.uk**

B & B
Mrs Karina Hill, Pebble Villa, Enkworth Road, Preston, WEYMOUTH, Dorset DT3 6JT Tel: 01305 837 469
- **e-mail: stay@pebblevilla.co.uk**
- **website: www.weymouthbedandbreakfast.net**

Holiday Park
Seaview & Weymouth Bay Holiday Parks, Preston, WEYMOUTH, Dorset DT3 6D2
Tel: 01305 833037
- **website: www.touringholidays.co.uk**

•DURHAM

Self-Catering Cottages

Low Lands Farm, Lowlands, Cockfield, BISHOP AUCKLAND, Durham DL13 5AW
Tel: 01388 718251

- **e-mail: info@farmholidaysuk.com**
- **website: www.farmholidays.com**

Hotel

The Teesdale Hotel, MIDDLETON-IN-TEESDALE, Durham DL12 0QG
Tel: 01833 640264

- **e-mail: john@teesdalehotel.co.uk**
- **website: www.teesdalehotel.co.uk**

Farm / Self-Catering Cottage

Frog Hall Cottage, Herdship Farm, Harwood Inn, TEESDALE, Durham DL12 0YB
Tel: 01833 622215

- **e-mail: kath.herdship@btinternet.com**
- **website: www.herdship.co.uk**

Hotel

Ivesley Equestrian Centre, Ivesley, WATERHOUSES, Durham DH7 9HB
Tel: 0191 373 4324

- **e-mail: ivesley@msn.com**
- **website: www.ridingholidays-ivesley.co.uk**

•ESSEX

B & B / Self-Catering

Mrs B. Lord, Pond House, Earls Hall Farm, CLACTON-ON-SEA, Essex CO16 8BP
Tel: 01255 820458

- **e-mail: brenda_lord@farming.co.uk**
- **website: www.earlshallfarm.info**

Farm

Rye Farm, Rye Lane, COLCHESTER, Essex, CO2 0JL Tel: 01206 734 350

- **e-mail: peter@buntingp.fsbusiness.co.uk**
- **website: www.buntingp.fsbusiness.co.uk**

•GLOUCESTERSHIRE

Hotel

Chester House Hotel, Victoria Street, BOURTON-ON-THE-WATER, Gloucs GL54 2BU Tel: 01451 820286

- **e-mail: info@chesterhousehotel.com**
- **website: www.chesterhousehotel.com**

Farmhouse B & B

Box Hedge Farm B & B, Box Hedge Farm Lane, Coalpit Heath, BRISTOL, Gloucs BS36 2UW Tel: 01454 250786

- **e-mail: marilyn@bed-breakfast-bristol.com**
- **website: www.bed-breakfast-bristol.com**

Lodge

Thornbury Golf Centre, Bristol Road, Thornbury, BRISTOL, Gloucs BS35 3XL
Tel: 01454 281144

- **e-mail: info@thornburygc.co.uk**
- **website: www.thornburygc.co.uk**

B & B

Mrs C. Hutsby, Holly House, Ebrington, CHIPPING CAMPDEN, Gloucs GL55 6NL
Tel: 01386 593213

- **e-mail: hutsbybandb@aol.com**
- **website: www.hollyhousebandb.co.uk**

B & B

Mrs Z.I. Williamson, Kempsford Manor, Kempsford, Near FAIRFORD, Gloucs GL7 4EQ Tel: 01285 810131

- **e-mail: ipek@kempsfordmanor.co.uk**
- **website: www.kempsfordmanor.co.uk**

B & B

Anthea & Bill Rhoton, Hyde Crest, Cirencester Road, MINCHINHAMPTON, Gloucs GL6 8PE.
Tel: 01453 731631

- **e-mail: anthea@hydecrest.demon.co.uk**
- **website: www.hydecrest.co.uk**

Self-Catering

Richard Drinkwater, Rose's Cottage, The Green, Broadwell, MORETON-IN-MARSH, Gloucs GL56 0UF
Tel: 01451 830007

- **e-mail: richard.drinkwater@ukonline.co.uk**

Self-Catering

Orion Holidays, Cotswold Water Park, Gateway Centre, Lake 6, Spine Road, SOUTH CERNEY, Gloucs GL7 5TL
Tel: 01285 861839

- **e-mail: bookings@orionholidays.com**
- **website: www.orionholidays.com**

B & B

Mrs Wendy Swait, Inschdene, Atcombe Road, SOUTH WOODCHESTER, Stroud, Gloucs GL5 5EW
Tel: 01453 873254

- **e-mail: swait@inschdene.co.uk**
- **website: www.inschdene.co.uk**

Farmhouse B & B

Robert Smith, Corsham Field Farmhouse, Bledington Road, STOW-ON-THE-WOLD, Gloucs GL54 1JH. Tel: 01541 831750

- **e-mail: farmhouse@corshamfield.co.uk**
- **website: www.corshamfield.co.uk**

www.holidayguides.com

B & B

The Limes, Evesham Road, STOW-ON-THE-WOLD, Gloucs GL54 1EN
Tel: 01451 830034 or 01451 831056
- **e-mail: thelimes@zoom.co.uk**

Farm / Self-Catering

Mrs Anne Meadows, Home Farm, Bredons Norton, TEWKESBURY, Gloucs GL20 7HA
Tel: 01684 772 332
- **e-mail: info@meadowshomefarm.co.uk**
- **website: www.meadowshomefarm.co.uk**

Hotel / Golf Club

Tewkesbury Park Hotel, Golf & Country Club, Lincoln Green lane, TEWKESBURY, Gloucs GL20 7DN Tel: 0870 609 6101
- **e-mail: tewkesburypark@corushotels.com**
- **website: www.tewkesburypark.co.uk**

•HAMPSHIRE

B & B

Mrs Arnold-Brown, Hilden B&B, Southampton Road, Boldre, BROCKENHURST, Hampshire SO41 8PT Tel: 01590 623682
- **website: www.newforestbandb-hilden.co.uk**

Campsite

Lower Tye Campsite, Copse Lane, HAYLING ISLAND, Hampshire
Tel: 02392 462479
- **e-mail: lowertye@aol.com**
- **website: www.haylingcampsites.co.uk**

Holiday Park

Hayling Island Holiday Park, Manor Road, HAYLING ISLAND, Hampshire PO11 0QS
Tel: 0870 444 0800
- **e-mail: bookings@weststarholidays.co.uk**
- **website: www.weststarholidays.co.uk**

B & B

Mrs P. Ellis, Efford Cottage, Everton, LYMINGTON, Hampshire SO41 0JD
Tel: 01590 642315
- **e-mail: effordcottage@aol.com**
- **website: www.effordcottage.co.uk**

B & B

Mr & Mrs Farrell, Honeysuckle House, 24 Clinton Road, LYMINGTON, Hampshire SO41 9EA Tel: 01590 676635
- **e-mail: skyblue@beeb.net**

Hotel

Bramble Hill Hotel, Bramshaw, Near LYNDHURST, New Forest, Hampshire SO43 7JG Tel: 02380 813165
- **website: www.bramblehill.co.uk**

Hotel

Crown Hotel, High Street, LYNDHURST, Hampshire SO43 7NF Tel: 023 8028 2922
- **e-mail: reception@crownhotel-lyndhurst.co.uk**
- **website: www.crownhotel-lyndhurst.co.uk**

Caravans for Hire

Downton Holiday Park, Shorefield Road, MILFORD-ON-SEA, Hampshire SO41 0LH
Tel: 01425 476131/01590 642515
- **e-mail: info@downtonholidaypark.co.uk**
- **website: www.downtonholidaypark.co.uk**

Self Catering

Gorse Cottage, Balmer Lawn Road, Brockenhurst, NEW FOREST, Hampshire
Contact: Mr J. Gilbert Tel: 0870 3210020
- **e-mail: info@ gorsecottage.co.uk**
- **website: www.gorsecottage.co.uk**

Hotel

Woodlands Lodge Hotel, Bartley Road, Woodlands, NEW FOREST, Southampton Hampshire SO40 7GN Tel: 023 8029 2257
- **e-mail: reception@woodlands-lodge.co.uk**
- **website: www.woodlands-lodge.co.uk**

B & B / Guest House

Michael & Maureen Burt, Fraser House, Salisbury Road, Blashford, RINGWOOD (NEW FOREST), Hampshire BH24 3PB
Tel: 01425 473958
- **e-mail: mail@fraserhouse.net**
- **website: www.fraserhouse.net**

Guest House

Mrs Thelma Rowe, Tiverton B & B, 9 Cruse Close, SWAY, Hampshire SO41 6AY
Tel: 01590 683092
- **e-mail: ronrowe@talk21.com**
- **website: www.tivertonnewforest.co.uk**

•HEREFORDSHIRE

Hotel

Hedley Lodge, Belmont Abbey, HEREFORD, Herefordshire HR2 9RZ Tel: 01432 374747
- **e-mail: hedley@belmontabbey.org.uk**
- **website: www.hedleylodge.com**

Self-catering

Mrs Williams, Radnor's End, Huntington, KINGTON, Herefordshire HR5 3NZ
Tel: 01544 370289
- **e-mail: enquiries@the-rock-cottage.co.uk**
- **website: www.the-rock-cottage.co.uk**

• ISLE OF WIGHT

Self-Catering

Island Cottage Holidays, ISLE OF WIGHT
Tel: 01929 480080

- **e-mail: enq@islandcottageholidays.com**
- **website: www.islandcottageholidays.com**

Caravan Park

Hillgrove Park, Field Lane, St Helens, RYDE, Isle of Wight PO33 1UT Tel: 01983 872802

- **e-mail: holidays@hillgrove.co.uk**
- **website: www.hillgrove.co.uk**

Guest House

Mrs V. Hudson, Strang Hall, Uplands Road, TOTLAND, Isle of Wight PO39 0DZ
Tel: 01983 753189

- **e-mail: strang_hall@hotmail.com**
- **website: www.strang-hall.co.uk**

• KENT

Self-Catering Cottages

Garden Of England

Contact: The Mews Office, 189a High Street, Tonbridge, KENT TN9 1BX
Tel: 01732 369168

- **e-mail: holidays@gardenofenglandcottages.co.uk**
- **website: www.gardenofenglandcottages.co.uk**

Self-Catering Cottages

Fairhaven Holiday Cottages, KENT
Tel: 01208 821255

- **website: www.fairhaven-holidays.co.uk**

Guest House

S. Twort, Heron Cottage, Biddenden, ASHFORD, Kent TN27 8HH. Tel: 01580 291358

- **e-mail: susantwort@hotmail.com**
- **website: www.heroncottage.info**

Farm B & B

Alison & Jim Taylor, Boldens Wood, Fiddling Lane, Stowting, FOLKESTONE, Ashford, Kent TN25 6AP Tel: 01303 812011

- **e-mail: StayoverNight@aol.com**
- **website: www.countrypicnics.com**

Hotel

Collina House Hotel, 5 East Hill, TENTERDEN, Kent TN30 6RL Tel: 01580 764852/764004

- **e-mail: enquiries@collinahousehotel.co.uk**
- **website: www.collinahousehotel.co.uk**

www.holidayguides.com

• LANCASHIRE

Hotel

The Chadwick Hotel, South Promenade, LYTHAM ST ANNES, Lancashire FY8 1NS
Tel: 01253 720061

- **e-mail: sales@thechadwickhotel.com**
- **website: www.thechadwickhotel.com**

Self-Catering

Don-Ange Holiday Apartments, 29 Holmfield Road, BLACKPOOL, Lancashire FY2 9TB Tel: 01253 355051

- **e-mail: donange@msn.com**
- **website: www.donange.cjb.net**

Holiday Park

Marton Mere Holiday Village, Mythop Road, BLACKPOOL, Lancashire FY4 4XN
Tel: 01253 767544

- **website: www.touringholidays.co.uk**

• LEICESTERSHIRE & RUTLAND

Golf Club

Birstall Golf Club, Station Road, BIRSTALL, Leicestershire LE4 3BB Tel: 0116 267 4322

- **e-mail: sue@birstallgolfclub.co.uk**
- **website: www.birstallgolfclub.co.uk**

Guest House

Richard & Vanessa Peach, The Old Rectory, 4 New Road, Belton In Rutland,OAKHAM, Rutland LE15 9LE Tel: 01572 717279

- **e-mail: bb@iepuk.com**
- **website: www.theoldrectorybelton.co.uk**

• LINCOLNSHIRE

Self-Catering

S. Jenkins, Grange Farm Riding School Holiday Cottages, Waltham Road, BARNOLDBY-LE-BECK, Grimsby, Lincolnshire DN37 0AR Tel: 01472 822216

- **e-mail: sueuk4000@netscape.net**
- **website: www.grangefarmcottages.com**

Caravan & Camping

The White Cat Caravan & Camping Park, Shaw Lane, Old Leake, BOSTON, Lincolnshire PE22 9LQ Tel: 01205 870121

- **e-mail: kevin@klannen.freeserve.co.uk**
- **website: www.whitecatpark.com**

Hotel

Branston Hall Hotel, BRANSTON, Lincolnshire LN4 1PD Tel: 01522 793305

- **e-mail: info@branstonhall.com**
- **website: www.branstonhall.com**

Holiday Park
Thorpe Park Holiday Centre, CLEETHORPES, North East Lincolnshire DN35 0PW Tel: 01472 813395
- **website: www.touringholidays.co.uk**

Self-Catering / Caravans
Woodland Waters, Willoughby Road, Ancaster, GRANTHAM, Lincolnshire NG31 3RT Tel: 01400 230888
- **e-mail: info@woodlandwaters.co.uk**
- **website: www.woodlandwaters.co.uk**

Farm B & B
Mrs C.E. Harrison, Baumber Park, Baumber, HORNCASTLE, Lincolnshire LN9 5NE Tel: 01507 578235
- **e-mail: baumberpark@amserve.com**
- **website: www.baumberpark.com**

Holiday Park
Golden Sands Holiday Park, Quebec Road, MABLETHORPE, Lincolnshire LN12 1QJ Tel: 01507 477871
- **website: www.touringholidays.co.uk**

Farmhouse B & B
S Evans, Willow Farm, Thorpe Fendykes, SKEGNESS, Lincolnshire PE24 4QH Tel: 01754 830316
- **e-mail: willowfarmhols@aol.com**
- **website: www.willowfarmholidays.co.uk**

• MERSEYSIDE

Guest House
Holme Leigh Guest House, 93 Woodcroft Road, Wavertree, LIVERPOOL, Merseyside L15 2HG Tel: 0151 734 2216
- **e-mail: info@homeleigh.com**
- **website: www.holmeleigh.com**

• NORFOLK

Self-Catering
Sand Dune Cottages, Tan Lane, CAISTER-ON-SEA, Great Yarmouth, Norfolk NR30 5DT Tel: 01493 720352
- **e-mail: sand.dune.cottages@amserve.net**
- **website: www.eastcoastlive.co.uk/sites/sanddunecottages.php**

Farmhouse B & B
Mrs M. Ling, The Rookery, Wortham, DISS, Norfolk IP22 1RB. Tel: 01379 783236
- **e-mail: russell.ling@ukgateway.net**
- **www.avocethosting.co.uk/rookery/home.htm**

Self-Catering
Idyllic Cottages at Vere Lodge, South Raynham, FAKENHAM, Norfolk NR21 7HE Tel: 01328 838261
- **e-mail: major@verelodge.co.uk**
- **website: www.idylliccottages.co.uk**

Holiday Park
Wild Duck Holiday Park, Howards Common, Belton, GREAT YARMOUTH, Norfolk NR31 9NE Tel: 01493 780268
- **website: www.touringholidays.co.uk**

Self-Catering
Blue Riband Holidays, HEMSBY, Great Yarmouth, Norfolk NR29 4HA Tel: 01493 730445
- **website: www.BlueRibandHolidays.co.uk**

Farm
Little Abbey Farm, Low Road, Pentney, KING'S LYNN, Norfolk PE32 1JF Tel: 01760 337348
- **e-mail: enquiries@littleabbeyfarm.co.uk**
- **website: www.littleabbeyfarm.co.uk**

B & B
Dolphin Lodge, 3 Knapton Road, Trunch, NORTH WALSHAM, Norfolk NR28 0QE Tel: 01263 720961
- **e-mail: dolphin.lodge@btopenworld.com**
- **website: www.dolphinlodges.net**

Hotel
Elderton Lodge Hotel, THORPE MARKET, Cromer, Norfolk NR11 8TZ Tel: 01263 833547
- **e-mail: enquiries@eldertonlodge.co.uk**
- **website: www.eldertonlodge.co.uk**

Self-Catering
Mr & Mrs Castleton, Poppyland Holiday Cottages, The Green, THORPE MARKET, Norfolk NR11 8AJ Tel: 01263 833219
- **e-mail: poppylandjc@netscape.net**
- **website: www.poppyland.com**

Self-Catering
Winterton Valley Holidays, WINTERTON-ON-SEA/CALIFORNIA, Norfolk Contact: 15 Kingston Avenue,Caister-on-Sea NR30 5ET Tel: 01493 377175
- **e-mail: info@wintertonvalleyholidays.co.uk**
- **website: www.wintertonvalleyholidays.co.uk**

Readers are requested to mention this FHG guide when seeking accommodation

•NORTHAMPTONSHIRE

Farmhouse B&B

Mrs B. Hawkins, Pear Tree Farm, Aldwincle, KETTERING, Northants NN14 3EL
Tel: 01832 720614

- **e-mail: beverley@peartreefarm.net**
- **website: www.peartreefarm.net**

•NORTHUMBERLAND

Self-Catering

Mrs M. Thompson, Heritage Coast Holidays, 6G Greensfield Court, ALNWICK, Northumberland NE66 2DE
Tel: 01665 604935

- **e-mail: info@heritagecoastholidays.com**
- **website: www.heritagecoastholidays.com**

Self-Catering Cottages

Buston Farm Holiday Cottages, Low Buston Hall, Warkworth, ALNWICK, Morpeth, Northumberland NE65 0XY
Tel: 01665 714805

- **e-mail: jopark@farming.co.uk**
- **website: www.buston.co.uk**

Hotel

The Blue Bell Hotel, Market Place, BELFORD, Northumberland NE70 7NE
Tel: 01668 213543

- **e-mail: bluebel@globalnet.co.uk**
- **website: www.bluebellhotel.com**

Self-Catering

Swinhoe Farmhouse, BELFORD, Northumberland NE70 7LJ
Tel: 016682 13370

- **e-mail: valerie@swinhoecottages.co.uk**
- **website: www.swinhoecottages.co.uk**

Hotel / Self-Catering

Riverdale Hall Hotel, BELLINGHAM, Northumberland NE48 2JT
Tel: 01434 220254

- **e-mail: reservations@riverdalehallhotel.co.uk**
- **website: www.riverdalehallhotel.co.uk**

Self-Catering

2, The Courtyard, BERWICK-UPON-TWEED
Contact: J. Morton, 1, The Courtyard, Church Street, Berwick-upon-Tweed TD15 1EE
Tel: 01289 308737

- **e-mail: jvm@patmosphere.uklinux.net**
- **website: www.berwickselfcatering.co.uk**

Hotel

The Cobbled Yard Hotel, 40 Walkergate, BERWICK-UPON-TWEED, Northumberland TD15 1DJ Tel: 01289 308407

- **e-mail: cobbledyardhotel@berwick35.fsnet.co.uk**
- **website: www.cobbledyardhotel.com**

B & B

Friendly Hound Cottage, Ford Common, BERWICK-UPON-TWEED, Northumberland TD15 2QD Tel: 01289 388554

- **e-mail: friendlyhound@aol.com**
- **website: www.friendlyhoundcottage.co.uk**

Holiday Park

Haggerston Castle Holiday Park, Beal, Near BERWICK-UPON-TWEED, Northumberland TD15 2PA Tel: 01289 381333

- **website: www.touringholidays.co.uk**

B & B / Farm / Camping

Mrs S. Maughan, Greencarts Farm, Near Humshaugh, HEXHAM, Northumberland NE46 4BW Tel: 01434 681320

- **e-mail: sandra@greencarts.co.uk**
- **website: www.greencarts.co.uk**

Self-Catering

Burradon Farm Cottages & Houses, Burradon Farm, Cramlington, NEWCASTLE-UPON-TYNE, Northumberland NE23 7ND
Tel: 0191 2683203

- **e-mail: judy@burradonfarm.co.uk**
- **website: www.burradonfarm.co.uk**

Self-Catering Cottages

Lorbottle Holiday Cottages, THROPTON, Northumberland
Contact: Leslie & Helen Far, Lorbottle, West Steads, Thropton, Near Morpeth, Northumberland NE65 7JT
Tel: 01665 574672

- **e-mail: stay@lorbottle.com**
- **website: www.lorbottle.com**

Guest House / B & B

Mrs M. Halliday, Beck'n'Call, Birling West Cottage, WARKWORTH, Northumberland NE65 0XS Tel: 01665 711653

- **e-mail: beck-n-call@lineone.net**
- **website: www.beck-n-call.co.uk**

Please mention this publication when making enquiries about accommodation featured in these pages

• NOTTINGHAMSHIRE

Farm / B & B

Mrs D. Hickling, Woodside Farm, Long Lane, BARKESTONE-LE-VALE, Nottinghamshire NG13 0HQ Tel: 01476 870336

- **e-mail: hickling-woodside@supanet.com**
- **website: www.woodsidebandb.co.uk**

Visitor Attraction

White Post Farm Centre, FARNSFIELD, Nottinghamshire NG22 8HL

Tel: 01623 882977

- **website: www.whitepostfarmcentre.co.uk**

•OXFORDSHIRE

Self-Catering

Cottage in the Country Cottage Holidays Tukes Cottage, 66 West Street, Chipping Norton, Oxfordshire OX7 5ER
Tel: 0870 027 5930

- **e-mail: enquiries@cottageinthecountry.co.uk**
- **website: www.cottageinthecountry.co.uk**

Self-Catering Cottages

Grange Farm Country Cottages, Grange Farm Estates, Godington, BICESTER, Oxfordshire OX27 9AF Tel: 01869 278 778

- **e-mail: info@grangefarmcottages.co.uk**
- **website: www.grangefarmcottages.co.uk**

Leisure Park

Cotswold Wildlife Park, BURFORD, Oxfordshire OX18 4JN Tel: 01993 823006

- **website: www.cotswoldwildlifepark.co.uk**

B & B

The Old Bakery, Skirmett, Near HENLEY-ON-THAMES, Oxfordshire RG9 6TD
Tel: 01491 410716

- **e-mail: lizzroach@aol.com**

Guest House

The Bungalow, Cherwell Farm, Mill Lane, Old Marston, OXFORD,
Oxfordshire OX3 0QF Tel: 01865 557171

- **e-mail: ros.bungalowbb@btinternet.com**
- **www.cherwellfarm-oxford-accomm.co.uk**

Guest House

Nanford Guest House, 137 Iffley Road, OXFORD, Oxfordshire, OX4 1EJ
Tel: 01865 244743

- **e-mail: b.cronin@btinternet.com**
- **website: www.nanfordguesthouse.com**

B & B

Fords Farm, Ewelme, WALLINGFORD, Oxfordshire OX10 6HU Tel: 01491 839272

- **e-mail: fordsfarm@callnetuk.com**
- **www.country-accom.co.uk/fords-farm/**

Guest House

Mrs Elizabeth Simpson, Field View, Wood Green, WITNEY, Oxfordshire OX28 1DE
Tel: 01993 705485

- **e-mail: bandb@fieldview-witney.co.uk**
- **website: www.fieldview-witney.co.uk**

B & B

Mr & Mrs N. Hamilton, Gorselands Hall, Boddington Lane, North Leigh,
between WOODSTOCK and WITNEY,
Oxfordshire OX29 6PU Tel: 01993 882292

- **e-mail: hamilton@gorselandshall.com**
- **website: www.gorselandshall.com**

•SHROPSHIRE

Golf Club / Self-Catering Cottages

Cleobury Mortimer Golf Club, Wyre Common, CLEOBURY MORTIMER, Kidderminster, Worcestershire DY14 8HQ
Tel: 01299 271112

- **e-mail: enquiries@cleoburygolfclub.com**
- **website: www.cleoburygolfclub.com**

•SHROPSHIRE

Guest House

Ron & Jenny Repath, Meadowlands, Lodge Lane, Frodesley, DORRINGTON, Shropshire SY5 7HD Tel: 01694 731350

- **e-mail: meadowlands@talk21.com**
- **website: www.meadowlands.co.uk**

Self-Catering

Clive & Cynthia Prior, Mocktree Barns Holiday Cottages, Leintwardine, LUDLOW, Shropshire SY7 0LY Tel: 01547 540441

- **e-mail: mocktreebarns@care4free.net**
- **website: www.mocktreeholidays.co.uk**

B & B / Self-Catering

Mrs E. Purnell, Ravenscourt Manor, Woofferton, LUDLOW, Shropshire SY8 4AL
Tel: 01584 711905

- **e-mail: elizabeth@ravenscourtmanor.plus.com**
- **website: www.internet-tsp.co.uk/ravenscourt**
  www.cottagesdirect.com

Inn / Hotel

The Four Alls Inn, Woodseaves, MARKET DRAYTON, Shropshire TF9 2AG
Tel: 01630 652995

- **e-mail: inn@thefouralls.com**
- **website: www.thefouralls.com**

Farmhouse / B & B

Sambrook Manor, Sambrook, NEWPORT, Shropshire TF10 8AL Tel: 01952 550256

- **website: www.sambrookmanor.com**

B & B

The Mill House, High Ercall, TELFORD, Shropshire TF6 6BE Tel: 01952 770394

- **e-mail: mill-house@talk21.com**
- **website: www.ercallmill.co.uk**

•SOMERSET

Self-Catering

The Pack Horse, ALLERFORD, Near Porlock, Somerset TA24 8HW Tel: 01643 862475

- **e-mail: holidays@thepackhorse.net**
- **website: www.thepackhorse.net**

B&B

Mrs C. Bryson, Walton Villa, 3 Newbridge Hill, BATH, Somerset BA1 3PW Tel: 01225 482792

- **e-mail: walton.villa@virgin.net**
- **website: www.walton.izest.com**

B & B / Self-Catering

Mrs P. Foster, Pennsylvania Farm, Newton-St-Loe, NEAR BATH, Somerset BA2 9JD Tel: 01225 314912

- **website: www.pennsylvaniafarm.co.uk**

Inn

The Talbot 15th Century Coaching Inn, Selwood Street, Mells, Near BATH, Somerset BA11 3PN Tel: 01373 812254

- **e-mail: roger@talbotinn.com**
- **website: www.talbotinn.com**

Farm Guest House / Self-Catering

Jackie & David Bishop, Toghill House Farm, Freezing Hill, Wick, Near BATH, Somerset BS30 5RT. Tel: 01225 891261

- **e-mail: accommodation@toghillhousefarm.co.uk**
- **website: www.toghillhousefarm.co.uk**

Self-Catering / Caravans

Beachside Holiday Park, Coast Road, BREAN, Somerset TA8 2QZ Tel: 01278 751346

- **e-mail: enquiries@beachsideholidaypark.co.uk**
- **website: www.beachsideholidaypark.co.uk**

Self-Catering

Westward Rise Holiday Park, South Road, BREAN, Burnham-on-Sea, Somerset TA8 2RD Tel: 01278 751310

- **e-mail: westwardrise@breansands.freeserve.co.uk**
- **website: www.breansands.freeserve.co.uk**

Farmhouse / Self-Catering

Josephine Smart, Leigh Farm, Old Road, Pensford, NEAR BRISTOL, Somerset BS39 4BA Tel: 01761 490281

- **website: www.leighfarm.co.uk**

Holiday Park

Burnham-On-Sea Holiday Village, Marine Drive, BURNHAM-ON-SEA, Somerset TA8 1LA Tel: 01278 783391

- **website: www.touringholidays.co.uk**

Farm / Self-Catering Cottages

Mrs Wendy Baker, Withy Grove Farm, East Huntspill, NEAR BURNHAM-ON-SEA, Somerset TA9 3NP Tel: 01278 784471

- **website: www.withygrovefarm.co.uk**

Farm / B & B

Mrs C. Bacon, Honeydown Farm, Seaborough Hill, CREWKERNE, Somerset TA18 8PL Tel: 01460 72665

- **e-mail: c.bacon@honeydown.co.uk**
- **website: www.honeydown.co.uk**

Guest House

Mrs M. Rawle, Winsbere House, 64 Battleton, DULVERTON, Somerset TA22 9HU Tel: 01398 323278

- **e-mail: info@winsbere.co.uk**
- **website: www.winsbere.co.uk**

Inn

Exmoor White Horse Inn, Exford, EXMOOR, Somerset TA24 7PY Tel: 01643 831229

- **e-mail: user@exmoor-whitehouse.co.uk**
- **website: www.exmoor-whitehorse.co.uk**

Farm Self-Catering & Camping

Westermill Farm, Exford, EXMOOR, Somerset TA24 7NJ Tel: 01643 831216 or 01643 831238

- **e-mail: fhg@westermill.com**
- **website: www.westermill.com**

Farm Self-Catering

Jane Styles, Wintershead Farm, Simonsbath, EXMOOR, Somerset TA24 7LF Tel: 01643 831222

- **e-mail: wintershed@yahoo.co.uk**
- **website: www.wintershead.co.uk**

B & B / Half-Board / Self-Catering / Towing Pitches

St Audries Bay Holiday Club, West Quantoxhead, MINEHEAD, Somerset TA4 4DY Tel: 01984 632515

- **e-mail: mrandle@staudriesbay.co.uk**
- **website: www.staudriesbay.co.uk**

Self-Catering

Wood Dairy, Wood Lane, NORTH PERROTT, Somerset TA18 7TA Tel: 01935 891532

- **e-mail: liz@acountryretreat.co.uk**
- **website: www.acountryretreat.co.uk**

Self-Catering Cottages

Knowle Farm, West Compton, SHEPTON MALLET, Somerset BA4 4PD Tel: 01749 890482

- **website: www.knowle-farm-cottages.co.uk**

Guest House / B & B
Blorenge House, 57 Staplegrove Road, TAUNTON, Somerset TA1 1DG
Tel: 01823 283005
- **e-mail: enquiries@blorengehouse.co.uk**
- **website: www.blorengehouse.co.uk**

Guest House
The Old Mill, Netherclay, Bishop's Hull, TAUNTON, Somerset TA1 5AB
Tel: 01823 289732
- **website: www.theoldmillbandb.co.uk**

Self-Catering
Mrs J Greenway, Woodlands Farm, Bathealton, TAUNTON, Somerset TA4 2AH
Tel: 01984 623271
- **website: www.woodlandsfarm-holidays.co.uk**

B & B
G. Clark, Yew Tree Farm, THEALE, Near Wedmore, Somerset BS28 4SN
Tel: 01934 712475
- **e-mail: yewtreefarm@yewtreefarmbandb.co.uk**
- **website: www.yewtreefarmbandb.co.uk**

Self-Catering
Croft Holiday Cottages, 2 The Croft, Anchor Street, WATCHET, Somerset TA23 0BY
Tel: 01984 631121
- **e-mail: croftcottages@talk21.com**
- **website: www.cottagessomerset.com**

B&B
Cricklake Farm, Bartlett Bridge, Cocklake, WEDMORE, Somerset BS28 4HH
Tel: 01934 712736
- **e-mail: info@cricklakefarm.co.uk**
- **website: www.cricklakefarm.co.uk**

Guest House
Infield House, 36 Portway, WELLS, Somerset BA5 2BN Tel: 01749 670989
- **e-mail: infield@talk21.com**
- **website: www.infieldhouse.co.uk**

B & B
Susan Crane, Birdwood House, Bath Road, WELLS, Somerset BA5 3EW
Tel: 01749 679250
- **website: www.birdwood-bandb.co.uk**

Farm / B & B
Mrs Sheila Stott, "Lana", Hollow Farm, Westbury-Sub-Mendip, NEAR WELLS, Somerset BA5 1HH Tel: 01749 870635
- **e-mail: sheila@stott2366.freeserve.co.uk**

Mrs H.J. Millard, Double-Gate B&B Ltd, Godney, WELLS, Somerset BA5 1RX
Tel: 01458 832217
- **e-mail: doublegatefarm@aol.com**
- **website: www.doublegatefarm.com**

Hotel / Self-Catering
Francesca Day, Timbertop Aparthotel, 8 Victoria Park, WESTON-SUPER-MARE, Somerset BS23 2HZ
Tel: 01934 631178 or 01934 424348
- **e-mail: stay@aparthoteltimbertop.com**
- **website: www.aparthoteltimbertop.com**

•STAFFORDSHIRE

Caravan & Camping / Holiday Park
The Star Caravan & Camping Park, Star Road, Cotton, Near ALTON TOWERS Staffordshire ST10 3DW
Tel: 01538 702219
- **website: www.starcaravanpark.co.uk**

Farm B & B / Self-Catering
Mrs M. Hiscoe-James, Offley Grove Farm, Adbaston, ECCLESHALL, Staffordshire ST20 0QB. Tel: 01785 280205
- **e-mail: accom@offleygrovefarm.freeserve.co.uk**
- **website: www.offleygrovefarm.co.uk**

Self-catering
The Raddle Log Cabins, Quarry Bank, Hollington, Near Tean, STOKE-ON-TRENT, Staffordshire ST10 4HQ Tel: 01889 507278
- **e-mail: peter@logcabin.co.uk**
- **website: www.logcabin.co.uk**

Guest House
Mrs Griffiths, Prospect House Guest House, 334 Cheadle Road, Cheddleton, LEEK, Staffordshire ST13 7BW Tel: 01782 550639
- **e-mail: prospect@talk21.com**
- **website: www.prospecthouseleek.co.uk**

•SUFFOLK

Guest House
Kay Dewsbury, Manorhouse, The Green, Beyton, BURY ST EDMUNDS, Suffolk IP30 9AF
Tel: 01359 270960
- **e-mail: manorhouse@beyton.com**
- **website: www.beyton.com**

Self-catering
Rede Hall Farm Park, Rede, BURY ST EDMUNDS, Suffolk IP29 4UG
Tel: 01284 850695
- **e-mail: oakley@soils.fsnet.co.uk**
- **website: www.redehallfarmpark.co.uk**

Self-Catering
Mr & Mrs D. Cole, The Close, Middlegate Barn, DUNWICH, Suffolk IP17 3DP
Tel: 01728 648741
- **e-mail: middlegate@aol.com**

Self-Catering
Mr P. Havers, Athelington Hall, Norham, EYE, Suffolk IP21 5EJ Tel: 01728 628233
- **e-mail: peter@logcabinholidays.co.uk**
- **website: www.logcabinholidays.co.uk**

Guest House
The Grafton Guest House, 13 Sea Road, FELIXSTOWE, Suffolk IP11 2BB
Tel: 01394 284881
- **e-mail: info@grafton-house.com**
- **website: www.grafton-house.com**

B & B / Self-Catering
Mrs Sarah Kindred, High House Farm, Cransford, Woodbridge, FRAMLINGHAM, Suffolk IP13 9PD Tel: 01728 663461
- **e-mail: b&b@highhousefarm.co.uk**
- **website: www.highhousefarm.co.uk**

Self-Catering
Kessingland Cottages, Rider Haggard Lane, KESSINGLAND, Suffolk.
Contact: S. Mahmood,
156 Bromley Road, Beckenham, Kent BR3 6PG Tel: 020 8650 0539
- **e-mail: jeeptrek@kjti.freeserve.co.uk**
- **website: www.k-cottage.co.uk**

Farm / Guest House
Sweffling Hall Farm, Sweffling, SAXMUNDHAM, Suffolk IP17 2BT
Tel: 01728 663644
- **e-mail: stephenmann@suffolkonline.net**
- **website: www.swefflinghallfarm.co.uk**

Self-Catering
Southwold Self-Catering Properties.
H.A. Adnams, 98 High Street, SOUTHWOLD, Suffolk IP18 6DP
Tel: 01502 723292
- **e-mail: haadnams_lets@ic24.net**
- **website: www.haadnams.com**

Self-Catering Cottage
Anvil Cottage, WOODBRIDGE, Suffolk
Contact: Mr & Mrs R. Blake, IA Moorfield Road, Woodbridge, Suffolk IP12 4JN
Tel: 01394 382 565
- **e-mail: robert@blake4110.fsbusiness.co.uk**

Self-Catering
Windmill Lodges Ltd, Redhouse Farm, Saxtead, WOODBRIDGE, Suffolk IP13 9RD
Tel: 01728 685338
- **e-mail: holidays@windmilllodges.co.uk**
- **website: www.windmilllodges.co.uk**

• SURREY

Guest House
The Lawn Guest House, 30 Massetts Road, Horley, GATWICK, Surrey RH6 7DF
Tel: 01293 775751
- **e-mail: info@lawnguesthouse.co.uk**
- **website: www.lawnguesthouse.co.uk**

Hotel
Chase Lodge Hotel, 10 Park Road, Hampton Wick, KINGSTON-UPON-THAMES, Surrey KT1 4AS. Tel: 020 8943 1862
- **e-mail: info@chaselodgehotel.com**
- **website: www.chaselodgehotel.com**
  www.surreyhotels.com

• EAST SUSSEX

Self-Catering
"Pekes", CHIDDINGLY, East Sussex
Contact: Eva Morris, 124 Elm Park Mansions, Park Walk, London SW10 0AR
Tel: 020 7352 8088
- **e-mail: pekes.afa@virgin.net**
- **website: www.pekesmanor.com**

Guest House
Ebor Lodge, 71 Royal Parade, EASTBOURNE, East Sussex BN22 7AQ
Tel: 01323 640792
- **e-mail: info@eborlodge.co.uk**
- **website: www.eborlodge.co.uk**

Self-Catering Cottages
Caburn Cottages, Ranscombe Farm, GLYNDE, Lewes, East Sussex BN8 6AA
Tel: 01273 858062
- **e-mail: enquiries@caburncottages.co.uk**
- **website: www.caburncottages.co.uk**

Guest House / Self-Catering
Longleys Farm Cottage, Harebeating Lane, HAILSHAM, East Sussex BN27 1ER
Tel: 01323 841227
- **e-mail: longleysfarmcottagebb@dsl.pipex.com**
- **website: www.longleysfarmcottage.co.uk**

Hotel
Grand Hotel, Grand Parade, St. Leonards, HASTINGS, East Sussex TN38 0DD
Tel: 01424 428510
- **e-mail: petermann@grandhotelhastings.co.uk**
- **website: www.grandhotelhastings.co.uk**

Bed & Breakfast
Barbara Martin, Little Saltcote, 22 Military Road, RYE, East Sussex TN31 7NY
Tel: 01797 223210
- **e-mail: info@littlesaltcote.co.uk**
- **website: www.littlesaltcote.co.uk**

Hotel
Rye Lodge Hotel, Hilders Cliff, RYE, East Sussex TN31 7LD Tel: 01797 223838
- **e-mail: chris@ryelodge.co.uk**
- **website: www.ryelodge.co.uk**

B & B
Jeake's House, Mermaid Street, RYE, East Sussex TN31 7ET Tel: 01797 222828
- **e-mail: stay@jeakeshouse.com**
- **website: www.jeakeshouse.com**

Hotel
Flackley Ash Hotel & Restaurant, Peasmarsh, Near RYE, East Sussex TN31 6YH. Tel: 01797 230651
- **e-mail: enquiries@flackleyashhotel.co.uk**
- **website: www.flackleyashhotel.co.uk**

• WEST SUSSEX

B & B
Mrs Vicki Richards, Woodacre, Arundel Road, Fontwell, ARUNDEL, West Sussex BN18 0QP Tel: 01243 814301
- **e-mail: wacrebb@aol.com**
- **website: www.woodacre.co.uk**

B & B
Broxmead Paddock, Broxmead Lane, Bolney, HAYWARDS HEATH, West Sussex RH17 5RG Tel: 01444 881458
- **e-mail: broxmeadpaddock@hotmail.com**
- **website: www.broxmeadpaddock.eclipse.co.uk**

Self-Catering
Mrs M. W. Carreck, New Hall Holiday Flat and Cottage, New Hall Lane, Small Dole, HENFIELD, West Sussex BN5 9YJ Tel: 01273 492546
- **website: www.newhallcottage.co.uk**

Touring Park
Warner Touring Park, Warner Lane, SELSEY, West Sussex PO20 9EL Tel: 01243 604499
- **website: www.bunnleisure.co.uk**

Guest House
Manor Guest House, 100 Broadwater Road, WORTHING, West Sussex BN14 8AN Tel: 01903 236028
- **e-mail: stay@manorworthing.com**
- **website: www.manorworthing.com**

•WARWICKSHIRE

Guest House / B & B
Julia & John Downie, Holly Tree Cottage, Pathlow, STRATFORD-UPON-AVON, Warwickshire CV37 0ES Tel: 01789 204461
- **e-mail: john@hollytree-cottage.co.uk**
- **website: www.hollytree-cottage.co.uk**

Guest House
The Croft, Haseley Knob, WARWICK, Warwickshire CV35 7NL Tel: 01926 484447
- **e-mail: david@croftguesthouse.co.uk**
- **website: www.croftguesthouse.co.uk**

•WEST MIDLANDS

Hotel
Featherstone Farm Hotel, New Road, Featherstone, WOLVERHAMPTON, West Midlands WV10 7NW Tel: 01902 725371
- **e-mail: info@featherstonefarm.co.uk**
- **website: www.featherstonefarm.co.uk**

•WILTSHIRE

Guest House
Alan & Dawn Curnow, Hayburn Wyke Guest House, 72 Castle Road, SALISBURY, Wiltshire SP1 3RL Tel:01722 412627
- **e-mail: hayburn.wyke@tinyonline.co.uk**
- **website: www.hayburnwykeguesthouse.co.uk**

•WORCESTERSHIRE

Farmhouse / B & B
The Barn House, BROADWAS ON TEME, Worcestershire WR6 5NS Tel: 01886 888733
- **e-mail: info@barnhouseonline.co.uk**
- **website: www.barnhouseonline.co.uk**

Guest House
Ann & Brian Porter, Croft Guest House, Bransford, GREAT MALVERN, Worcester, Worcestershire WR6 5JD Tel: 01886 832227
- **e-mail: hols@crofthousewr6.fsnet.co.uk**
- **website: www.croftguesthouse.com**

Self-Catering Cottages
Rochford Park, TENBURY WELLS, Worcestershire WR15 8SP Tel: 01584 781 372
- **e-mail: cottages@rochfordpark.co.uk**
- **website: www.rochfordpark.co.uk**

Readers are requested to mention this FHG guide when seeking accommodation

•NORTH YORKSHIRE

Self-Catering

Recommended Cottage Holidays, Eastgate House, Pickering, NORTH YORKSHIRE
Tel: 01751 475547

• **website: www.recommended-cottages.co.uk**

Farmhouse B & B

Mrs Julie Clarke, Middle Farm, Woodale, COVERDALE, Leyburn,
North Yorkshire DL8 4TY Tel: 01969 640271

• **e-mail: j-a-clarke@amserve.com**
• **www.yorkshirenet.co.uk/stayat/middlefarm**

Holiday Park

Blue Dolphin Holiday Park, Gristhorpe Bay, FILEY, North Yorkshire YO14 9PU
Tel: 01723 515155

• **website: www.touringholidays.co.uk**

Holiday Park

Primrose Valley Holiday Park, Primrose Valley, NEAR FILEY, North Yorkshire YO14 9RF Tel: 01723 513771

• **website: www.touringholidays.co.uk**

Holiday Park

Reighton Sands Holiday Park, Reighton Gap, NEAR FILEY, North Yorkshire YO14 9SH • Tel: 01723 890476

• **website: www.touringholidays.co.uk**

Farmhouse B&B

Mr & Mrs Richardson, Egton Banks Farmhouse, GLAISDALE, Whitby, North Yorkshire YO21 2QP Tel: 01947 897289

e-mail: egtonbanksfarm@agriplus.net
•**website: www.egtonbanksfarm.agriplus.net**

Country Inn

The Foresters Arms, Main Street, GRASSINGTON, Near Skipton, North Yorkshire BD23 5AA
Tel: 01756 752349

• **e-mail: theforesters@totalise.co.uk**
• **website: www.forestersarmsgrassington.co.uk**

Caravan & Camping

Bainbridge Ings Caravan & Camping Site, HAWES, North Yorkshire DL8 3NU
Tel: 01969 667354

• **e-mail: janet@bainbridge-ings.co.uk**
• **website: www.bainbridge-ings.co.uk**

Hotel

Stone House Hotel, Sedbusk, HAWES, Wensleydale, North Yorkshire DL8 3PT
Tel: 01969 667571

• **e-mail: daleshotel@aol.com**
• **website: www.stonehousehotel.com**

Guest House

The New Inn Motel, Main Street, HUBY, York, North Yorkshire YO61 1HQ
Tel: 01347 810219

• **enquiries@newinnmotel.freeserve.co.uk**
• **website: www.newinnmotel.co.uk**

Guest House

Mr B.L.F. Martin, The Old Star, West Witton, LEYBURN, North Yorkshire DL8 4LU
Tel: 01969 622949

• **e-mail: enquiries@theoldstar.com**
• **website: www.theoldstar.com**

Self-Catering

Abbey Holiday Cottages, MIDDLESMOOR. 12 Panorama Close, Pateley Bridge, Harrogate, North Yorkshire HG3 5NY
Tel: 01423 712062

• **e-mail: abbeyholiday.cottages@virgin.net**
• **website: www.abbeyholidaycottages.co.uk**

B & B

Banavie, Roxby Road, Thornton-Le-Dale, PICKERING, North Yorkshire YO18 7SX
Tel: 01751 474616

• **e-mail: info@banavie.co.uk**
• **website: www.banavie.uk.com**

Guest House / Self-Catering

Sue & Tony Hewitt, Harmony Country Lodge, 80 Limestone Road, Burniston, SCARBOROUGH, North Yorkshire YO13 0DG Tel: 0800 2985840

• **e-mail: mail@harmonylodge.net**
• **website: www.harmonylodge.net**

B & B

Beck Hall, Malham, SKIPTON, North Yorkshire BD23 4DJ Tel: 01729 830332

• **e-mail: simon@beckhallmalham.com**
• **website: www.beckhallmalham.com**

Inn

Gamekeepers Inn, Long Ashes Park, Threshfield, NEAR SKIPTON, North Yorkshire BD23 5PN Tel: 01756 752434

• **e-mail: info@gamekeeperinn.co.uk**
• **website: www.gamekeeperinn.co.uk**

Self-Catering

Mrs Jones, New Close Farm, Kirkby Malham, SKIPTON, North Yorkshire BD23 4DP
Tel: 01729 830240

• **brendajones@newclosefarmyorkshire.co.uk**
• **website: www.newclosefarmyorkshire.co.uk**

Self-Catering

Allaker in Coverdale, WEST SCRAFTON, Near Leyburn, North Yorkshire
Contact Mr A. Cave Tel: 020 8567 4862

• **e-mail: ac@adriancave.com**
• **website: www.adriancave.com/allaker**

Guest House
Ashford Guest House, 8 Royal Crescent, WHITBY, North Yorkshire YO21 3EJ
Tel: 01947 602138
• **e-mail: info@ashfordguesthouse.co.uk**
• **website: www.ashfordguesthouse.co.uk**

Self-Catering
Mrs Jill McNeil, Swallow Holiday Cottages, Long Leas Farm, Hawsker, WHITBY, North Yorkshire YO22 4LA Tel: 01947 603790
• **e-mail: jillian@swallowcottages.co.uk**
• **website: www.swallowcottages.co.uk**

Self-Catering
Mr J.N. Eddleston,
Greenhouses Farm Cottages,
Greenhouses Farm, Lealholm,
Near WHITBY, North Yorkshire YO21 2AD
Tel: 01947 897486
• **e-mail: n_eddleston@yahoo.com**
• **www.greenhouses-farm-cottages.co.uk**

Self-Catering
The Old Granary & Copper Cottage, Ravenhill Farm, Dunsley, NEAR WHITBY, North Yorkshire YO21 3TJ
Tel: 01947 893331
• **e-mail: jackie.richardson6@btopenworld.com**

Self-Catering
White Rose Holiday Cottages,
NEAR WHITBY, North Yorkshire
Contact: Mrs J. Roberts, 5 Brook Park, Sleights, Near Whitby, North Yorkshire YO21 1RT Tel: 01947 810763
• **e-mail: enquiries@whiterosecottages.co.uk**
• **website: www.whiterosecottages.co.uk**

Guest House
Mrs J.M. Wood, Ascot House,
80 East Parade, YORK, North Yorkshire YO31 7YH Tel: 01904 426826
• **e-mail: admin@ascothouseyork.com**
• **website: www.ascothouseyork.com**

Self-Catering Cottages
The Grange Farm Holiday Cottages, Bishop Wilton, York, North Yorkshire YO42 1SA Tel: 01759 369500
• **e-mail: richarddavy@supanet.com**
• **website: www.thegrangefarm.com**

Guest House / Self-Catering
Mr Gary Hudson, Orillia House, 89 The Village, Stockton on Forest, YORK, North Yorkshire YO3 9UP Tel: 01904 400600
• **e-mail: info@orilliahouse.co.uk**
• **website: www.orilliahouse.co.uk**

Guest House / Camping
Mrs Jeanne Wilson, Robeanne House, Driffield Lane, Shiptonthorpe, YORK, North Yorkshire YO43 3PW Tel: 01430 873312
• **e-mail: robert@robeanne.freeserve.com**
• **website: www.robeannehouse.co.uk**

Guest House
St George's, 6 St George's Place, YORK, North Yorkshire YO24 1DR
Tel: 01904 625056
• **e-mail: sixstgeorg@aol.com**
• **website: http://members.aol.com/sixstgeorg/**

Self-Catering
Mr N. Manasir, York Lakeside Lodges, Moor Lane, YORK, North Yorkshire YO24 2QU
Tel: 01904 702346
• **e-mail: neil@yorklakesidelodges.co.uk**
• **website: www.yorklakesidelodges.co.uk**

•SOUTH YORKSHIRE

Golf Club
Sandhill Golf Club, Middlecliffe Lane, Little Houghton, BARNSLEY, South Yorkshire S72 0HW Tel: 01226 753444
• **e-mail: vwistow@sandhillgolfclub.co.uk**
• **website: www.sandhillgolfclub.co.uk**

B & B
Padley Farm Bed & Breakfast, Dungworth Green, Bradfield, SHEFFIELD,
South Yorkshire S6 6HE Tel: 01142 851427
• **e-mail: info@padleyfarm.co.uk**
• **website: www.padleyfarm.co.uk**

•WEST YORKSHIRE

Farm / B & B / Self-Catering Cottages
Currer Laithe Farm, Moss Carr Road, Long Lee, KEIGHLEY, West Yorkshire BD21 4SL
Tel: 01535 604387
• **website: www.currerlaithe.co.uk**

•SCOTLAND

Self-Catering Cottages

Islands & Highlands Cottages, Bridge Road, Portree, Isle of Skye, SCOTLAND IV51 9ER

Tel: 01478 612123

- **website: www.islands-and-highlands.co.uk**

•ABERDEEN, BANFF & MORAY

Hotel

Banchory Lodge Hotel, BANCHORY, Kincardineshire AB31 5HS

Tel: 01330 822625

- **e-mail: enquiries@banchorylodge.co.uk**
- **website: www.banchorylodge.co.uk**

B & B

Davaar B & B, Church Street, DUFFTOWN, Moray, AB55 4AR Tel: 01340 820464

- **e-mail: davaar@cluniecameron.co.uk**
- **website: www.davaardufftown.co.uk**

Self-catering

Newseat & Kirklea, FRASERBURGH, Aberdeenshire.
Contact: Mrs E.M. Pittendrigh, Kirktown, Tyrie, Fraserburgh AB43 7DQ. Tel: 01346 541231

- **e-mail: pittendrigh@supanet.com**

Golf Club

Moray Golf Club, Stotfield Road, LOSSIEMOUTH, Moray IV31 6QS

Tel: 01343 812018

- **e-mail: secretary@moraygolf.co.uk**
- **website: www.moraygolf.co.uk**

Self-Catering

Val & Rob Keeble, Lighthouse Cottages, RATTRAY HEAD, Peterhead, Aberdeenshire AB42 3HB Tel: 01346 532236

- **e-mail: enquiries@rattrayhead.net**
- **website: www.rattrayhead.net**

Self-Catering

Simon Pearse, Forglen Cottages, Forglen Estate, TURRIFF, Aberdeenshire AB53 4JP Tel: 01888 562918

- **e-mail: reservations@forglen.co.uk**
- **website: www.forglen.co.uk**

•ARGYLL & BUTE

Self-Catering

Ardtur Cottages, APPIN, Argyll PA38 4DD
Tel: 01631 730223

- **e-mail: pery@btinternet.com**
- **website: www.selfcatering-appin-scotland.com**

Inn

Mr D. Fraser, Cairndow Stagecoach Inn, CAIRNDOW, Argyll PA26 8BN
Tel: 01499 600286

- **e-mail: cairndowinn@aol.com**
- **website: www.cairndow.com**

Self-Catering

Catriona O'Keeffe, Blarghour Farm Cottages, Blarghour Farm, By DALMALLY, Argyll PA33 1BW Tel: 01866 833246

- **e-mail: blarghour@btconnect.com**
- **website: www.self-catering-argyll.co.uk**

Guest House / Self-Catering

Rockhill Guesthouse & Self-Catering Cottages, DALMALLY, Argyll PA33 1BH
Tel: 01866 833218

- **website: www.rockhill@lochawe.co.uk**

Hotel

West End Hotel, West Bay, DUNOON, Argyll PA23 7HU Tel: 01369 702907

- **e-mail: mike@westendhotel.com**
- **website: www.westendhotel.com**

Self-Catering

B & M Phillips, Kilbride Croft, Balvicar, ISLE OF SEIL, Argyll PA34 4RD
Tel: 01852 300475

- **e-mail: kilbridecroft@aol.com**
- **website: www.kilbridecroft.co.uk**

Self-Catering

Robin Malcolm, Duntrune Castle, KILMARTIN, Argyll PA31 8QQ
Tel: 01546 510283

- **website: www.duntrune.com**

Caravans

Caolasnacon Caravan Park, KINLOCHLEVEN, Argyll PH50 4RJ Tel: 01855 831279

- **e-mail: caolasnacon@hotmail.co.uk**
- **website: www.kinlochlevencaravans.com**

Readers are requested to mention this FHG guidebook when seeking accommodation

Self-Catering
Castle Sween Bay (Holidays) Ltd, Ellary, LOCHGILPHEAD, Argyll PA31 8PA
Tel: 01880 770232
- **e-mail: info@ellary.com**
- **website: www.ellary.com**

Self-Catering
Linda Battison,
Cologin Country Chalets & Lodges, Lerags Glen, OBAN, Argyll PA34 4SE
Tel: 01631 564501
- **e-mail: info@cologin.co.uk**
- **website: www.cologin.co.uk**

Self-Catering
Colin Mossman, Lagnakeil Lodges, Lerags, OBAN, Argyll PA34 4SE
Tel: 01631 562746
- **e-mail: info@lagnakeil.co.uk**
- **website: www.lagnakeil.co.uk**

Self-Catering
Mrs Barker, Barfad Farm, TARBERT, Loch Fyne, Argyll PA29 6YH
Tel: 01880 820549
- **e-mail: vbarker@hotmail.com**
- **website: www.tarbertlochfyne.com**

Golf Club
Taynuilt Golf Club, TAYNUILT, Argyll PA35 1JE Tel: 01866 822429
- **website: www.taynuiltgolfclub.co.uk**

• AYRSHIRE & ARRAN

Caravan Park
Laggan House Leisure Park, BALLANTRAE, Near Girvan, Ayrshire KA26 0LL
Tel: 01465 831229
- **e-mail: lhlp@lagganhouse.co.uk**
- **website: www.lagganhouse.co.uk**

Farmhouse / B & B
Mrs Nancy Cuthbertson, West Tannacrieff, Fenwick, KILMARNOCK, Ayrshire KA3 6AZ
Tel: 01560 600258
- **e-mail: westtannacrieff@btopenworld.com**
- **website: www.smoothhound.co.uk/hotels/westtannacrieff.html**

Self-Catering
Bradan Road, TROON, Ayrshire
Contact: Mr Ward Brown
Tel: 07770 220830
- **e-mail: stay@bradan.info**
- **website: www.bradan.info**

• BORDERS

Self-Catering
The Old Barn, High Letham, BERWICK-UPON-TWEED.
Contact: Richard & Susan Persse, High Letham Farmhouse, High Letham, Berwick-upon-Tweed, Borders TD15 1UX
Tel: 01289 306585
- **e-mail: r.persse-highl@amserve.com**
- **website: www.oldbarnhighletham.co.uk**

Self-Catering
Wauchope Cottages, BONCHESTER BRIDGE, Hawick, Borders TD9 9TG
Tel: 01450 860630
- **e-mail: wauchope@btinternet.com**
- **website: www.wauchopecottages.co.uk**

Self-Catering / Caravan & Camping
Neuk Farm Cottages & Chesterfield Caravan Park, Neuk Farmhouse, COCKBURNSPATH, Berwickshire TD13 5YH Tel: 01368 830459
- **e-mail: info@chesterfieldcaravanpark.co.uk**
- **website: www.chesterfieldcaravanpark.co.uk**

Guest House
Ferniehirst Mill Lodge, JEDBURGH, Borders TD8 6PQ Tel: 01835 863279
- **e-mail: ferniehirstmill@aol.com**
- **website: www.ferniehirstmill.co.uk**

Self-Catering
Mill House Cottage, JEDBURGH.
Contact: Mrs A. Fraser, Overwells, Jedburgh, Borders TD8 6LT
Tel: 01835 863020
- **e-mail: abfraser@btinternet.com**
- **website: www.overwells.co.uk**

Hotel
George & Abbotsford Hotel, High Street, MELROSE, Borders TD6 9PD
Tel: 01896 822308
- **e-mail: enquiries@georgeandabbotsford.co.uk**
- **website: www.georgeandabbotsford.co.uk**

Farm B & B/ Self Catering / Inn
Mrs J. P. Copeland, Bailey Mill, Bailey, NEWCASTLETON, Roxburghshire TD9 0TR
Tel: 01697 748617
- **e-mail: pam@baileymill.fsnet.co.uk**
- **www.baileycottages/riding/racing.com**

Self-Catering
Mrs C. M. Kilpatrick, Slipperfield House, WEST LINTON, Peeblesshire EH46 7AA
Tel: 01968 660401
- **e-mail: cottages@slipperfield.com**
- **website: www.slipperfield.com**

•DUMFRIES & GALLOWAY

Hotel

Hetland Hall Hotel, CARRUTHERSTOWN, Dumfries & Galloway DG1 4JX
Tel: 01387 840201

- **e-mail: info@hetlandhallhotel.co.uk**
- **website: www.hetlandhallhotel.co.uk**

Farm

Celia Pickup, Craigadam, CASTLE DOUGLAS, Kirkcudbrightshire DG7 3HU Tel: 01556 650233

- **website: www.craigadam.com**

Self-Catering

Rusko Holidays, Gatehouse of Fleet, CASTLE DOUGLAS, Kirkcudbrightshire DG7 2BS Tel: 01557 814215

- **e-mail: info@ruskoholidays.co.uk**
- **website: www.ruskoholidays.co.uk**

B & B

Langlands Bed & Breakfast, 8 Edinburgh Road, DUMFRIES DG1 1JQ
Tel: 01387 266549

- **e-mail: langlands@tiscali.co.uk**
- **website: www.langlands.info**

Farm / Camping & Caravans / Self-Catering

Barnsoul Farm Holidays, Barnsoul Farm, Shawhead, DUMFRIES, Dumfriesshire
Tel: 01387 730249

- **e-mail: barnsouldg@aol.com**
- **website: www.barnsoulfarm.co.uk**

Guest House

Kirkcroft Guest House, Glasgow Road, GRETNA GREEN, Dumfriesshire DG16 5DU
Tel: 01461 337403

- **e-mail: info@kirkcroft.co.uk**
- **website: www.kirkcroft.co.uk**

B & B

June Deakins, Annandale House, MOFFAT, Dumfriesshire DG10 9SA
Tel: 01683 221460

- **e-mail: june@annandalehouse.com**
- **website: www.annandalehouse.com**

Camping & Touring Site

Drumroamin Farm Camping and Touring Site, 1 South Balfern, Kirkinner, NEWTON STEWART, Wigtownshire DG8 9DB
Tel: 01988 840613 or 077524 71456

- **e-mail: lesley.shell@btinternet.com**
- **website: www.drumroamin.co.uk**

Caravan Park

Whitecairn Caravan Park, Glenluce, NEWTON STEWART, Wigtownshire DG8 0NZ Tel: 01581 300267

- **e-mail: enquiries@whitecairncaravans.co.uk**
- **website: www.whitecairncaravans.co.uk**

• DUNBARTONSHIRE

Self-Catering

Inchmurrin Island Self-Catering Holidays, Inchmurrin Island, LOCH LOMOND, Dunbartonshire G63 0JY Tel: 01389 850245

- **e-mail: scotts@inchmurrin-lochlomond.com**
- **website: www.inchmurrin-lochlomond.com**

•EDINBURGH & LOTHIANS

B & B

Cruachan B&B, 78 East Main Street, BLACKBURN, By Bathgate, West Lothian EH47 7QS Tel: 01506 655221

- **e-mail: cruachan.bb@virgin.net**
- **website: www.cruachan.co.uk**

B & B

Mrs Kay, Blossom House, 8 Minto Street, EDINBURGH EH9 1RG Tel: 0131 667 5353

- **e-mail: blossom_house@hotmail.com**
- **website: www.blossomguesthouse.co.uk**

Guest House

Kenvie Guest House, 16 Kilmaurs Road, EDINBURGH EH16 5DA Tel: 0131 6681964

- **e-mail: dorothy@kenvie.co.uk**
- **website: www.kenvie.co.uk**

Guest House

International Guest House, 37 Mayfield Gardens, EDINBURGH EH9 2BX
Tel: 0131 667 2511

- **e-mail: intergh1@yahoo.co.uk**
- **website: www.accommodation-edinburgh.com**

B & B

McCrae's B&B, 44 East Claremont Street, EDINBURGH EH7 4JR Tel: 0131 556 2610

- **e-mail: mccraes.bandb@lineone.net**
- **http://website.lineone.net/~mccraes.bandb**

Holiday Park

Seton Sands Holiday Village, LONGNIDDRY, East Lothian EH32 0QF Tel: 01875 813333

- **website: www.touringholidays.co.uk**

Self-Catering / Caravan & Camping

Drummohr Caravan Park, Levenhall, MUSSELBURGH, East Lothian EH21 8JS
Tel: 0131 6656867

- **e-mail: bookings@drummohr.org**
- **website: www.drummohr.org**

•FIFE

Hotel

The Lundin Links Hotel, Leven Road, LUNDIN LINKS, Fife KY8 6AP
Tel: 01333 320207
- **e-mail: info@lundin-links-hotel.co.uk**
- **website: www.lundin-links-hotel.co.uk**

Self-Caterting

Balmore, 3 West Road, NEWPORT-ON-TAY, Fife DD6 8HH Tel: 01382 542274
- **e-mail: allan.ramsay@ukgateway.net**
- **website: www.thorndene.co.uk**

Self-Catering

Kingask Cottages, Kingask House, ST ANDREWS, Fife KY16 8PN
Tel: 01334 472011
- **e-mail: info@kingask-cottages.co.uk**
- **website: www.kingask-cottages.co.uk**

B & B

Mrs Duncan, Spinkstown Farmhouse, ST ANDREWS, Fife KY16 8PN
Tel: 01334 473475
- **e-mail: anne@spinkstown.com**
- **website: www.spinkstown.com**

•GLASGOW & DISTRICT

B & B

Mrs P. Wells, Avenue End B & B, 21 West Avenue, Stepps, GLASGOW G33 6ES
Tel: 0141 7791990
- **website: www.avenueend.co.uk**

•HIGHLANDS

Accommodation in the HIGHLANDS.
- **website: www.Aviemore.com**

Self-Catering

Linda Murray, 29 Grampian View, AVIEMORE, Inverness-shire PH22 1TF
Tel: 01479 810653
- **e-mail: linda.murray@virgin.net**
- **website: www.cairngorm-bungalows.co.uk**

Self-Catering

Pink Bank Chalets, Dalfaber Road, AVIEMORE, Inverness-shire PH22 1PX
Tel: 01479 810000
- **e-mail: pinebankchallets@btopenworld.com**
- **website: www.pinebankchalets.co.uk**

Self Catering / Caravans

Speyside Leisure Park, Dalfaber Road, AVIEMORE, Inverness-shire PH22 1PX
Tel: 01479 810236
- **e-mail: fhg@speysideleisure.com**
- **website: www.speysideleisure.com**

Self-Catering

The Treehouse, BOAT-OF-GARTEN, Highlands
Contact: Mrs Mather Tel: 0131 337 7167
- **e-mail: fhg@treehouselodge.plus.com**
- **website: www.treehouselodge.co.uk**

Guest House

Mrs Lynn Benge, The Pines Country House, Duthil, CARRBRIDGE, Inverness-shire PH23 3ND Tel: 01479 841220
- **e-mail: lynn@thepines-duthil.co.uk**
- **website: www.thepines-duthil.fsnet.co.uk**

Hotel

The Clan MacDuff Hotel, Achintore Road, FORT WILLIAM PH33 6RW
Tel: 01397 702341
- **e-mail: reception@clanmacduff.co.uk**
- **website: www.clanmacduff.co.uk**

Hotel

Invergarry Hotel, INVERGARRY, Inverness-shire PH35 4HJ Tel: 01809 501206
- **e-mail: info@invergarryhotel.co.uk**
- **website: www.invergarryhotel.co.uk**

Self-Catering

Invermoriston Holiday Chalets, INVERMORISTON, Glenmoriston, Inverness, Inverness-shire IV63 7YF
Tel: 01320 351254
- **website: www.invermoriston-holidays.com**

Caravan & Camping

Auchnahillin Caravan & Camping Park, Daviot East, INVERNESS, Inverness-shire IV2 5XQ Tel: 01463 772286
- **e-mail: info@auchnahillin.co.uk**
- **website: www.auchnahillin.co.uk**

Self-Catering

Mrs A MacIver, The Sheiling, Achgarve, LAIDE, Ross-shire IV22 2NS
Tel: 01445 731487
- **e-mail: stay@thesheilingholidays.com**
- **website: www.thesheilingholidays.com**

Self-Catering

Wildside Highland Lodges, Whitebridge, By LOCH NESS, Inverness-shire IV2 6UN
Tel: 01456 486373
- **e-mail: info@wildsidelodges.com**
- **website: www.wildsidelodges.com**

B & B / Self-Catering Chalets

D.J. Mordaunt, Mondhuie, NETHY BRIDGE, Inverness-shire PH25 3DF Tel: 01479 821062

- **e-mail: david@mondhuie.com**
- **website: www.mondhuie.com**

Self-Catering

Crubenbeg Holiday Cottages, NEWTONMORE, Inverness-shire PH20 1BE Tel: 01540 673566

- **e-mail: enquiry@crubenbeg.com**
- **website: www.crubenbeg.com**

Self-Catering

Mr A. Urquhart, Crofters Cottages, 15 Croft, POOLEWE, Ross-shire IV22 2JY Tel: 01445 781268

- **e-mail: croftcottages@btopenworld.com**
- **website: www.croftcottages.btinternet.co.uk**

Hotel

Whitebridge Hotel, WHITEBRIDGE, Inverness IV2 6UN Tel: 01456 486226

- **e-mail: info@whitebridgehotel.co.uk**
- **website: www.whitebridgehotel.co.uk**

•LANARKSHIRE

Self-Catering

Carmichael Country Cottages, Carmichael Estate Office, Westmains, Carmichael, BIGGAR, Lanarkshire ML12 6PG Tel: 01899 308336

- **e-mail: chiefcarm@aol.com**
- **website: www.carmichael.co.uk/cottages**

Guest House

Blairmains Guest House, Blairmains, HARTHILL, Lanarkshire ML7 5TJ Tel: 01501 751278

- **e-mail: heather@blairmains.freeserve.co.uk**
- **website: www.blairmains.co.uk**

•PERTH & KINROSS

Self-Catering

Loch Tay Lodges, Remony, Acharn, ABERFELDY, Perthshire PH15 2HR Tel: 01887 830209

- **e-mail: remony@btinternet.com**
- **website: www.lochtaylodges.co.uk**

Hotel

Lands of Loyal Hotel, ALYTH, Perthshire PH11 8JQ Tel: 01828 633151

- **e-mail: info@landsofloyal.com**
- **website: www.landsofloyal.com**

Self-Catering

Laighwood Holidays, Laighwood, Butterstone, BY DUNKELD, Perthshire PH8 0HB Tel: 01350 724241

- **e-mail: holidays@laighwood.co.uk**
- **website: www.laighwood.co.uk**

Self-catering

East Cottage, Roro Estate, GLEN LYON. Contact: E. Thompson LLP, 76 Overhaugh Street, Galashiels TD1 1DP Tel: 01896 751300

- **e-mail: Galashiels@edwin-thompson.co.uk**

B & B

Brochanach, 43 Fingal Road, KILLIN, Perthshire FK21 8XA Tel: 01567 820028

- **e-mail: alifer@msn.com**
- **website: www.s-h-systems.co.uk/hotels/brochanach.html**

Self-Catering

Gill Hunt, Wester Lix Cottage, Wester Lix, KILLIN, Perthshire FK21 8RD Tel: 01567 820990

- **e-mail: gill@westerlix.net**
- **website: www.westerlix.net**

Hotel

Balrobin Hotel, Higher Oakfield, PITLOCHRY, Perthshire PH16 5HT Tel: 01796 472901

- **e-mail: info@balrobin.co.uk**
- **website: www.balrobin.co.uk**

Guest House

Jacky & Malcolm Catterall, Tulloch, Enochdhu, By Kirkmichael, PITLOCHRY, Perthshire PH10 7PW Tel: 01250 881404

- **e-mail: maljac@tulloch83.freeserve.co.uk**
- **website: www.maljac.com**

B & B

Mrs Ann Guthrie, Newmill Farm, STANLEY, Perthshire PH1 4QD Tel: 01738 828281

- **e-mail: guthrienewmill@sol.co.uk**
- **website: www.newmillfarm.co.uk**

B & B / Self-Catering

Ardoch Lodge, STRATHYRE, Near Callander FK18 8NF Tel: 01877 384666

- **e-mail: ardoch@btinternet.com**
- **website: www.ardochlodge.co.uk**

•STIRLING & TROSSACHS

Camping & Caravan Park

Riverside Caravan Park, Dollarfield, DOLLAR, Clackmannanshire FK14 7LX Tel: 01259 742896

- **e-mail: info@riverside-caravanpark.co.uk**
- **website: www.riverside-caravanpark.co.uk**

Guest House

Croftburn Bed & Breakfast, Croftamie, DRYMEN, Loch Lomond G63 0HA
Tel: 01360 660796

- **e-mail: enquiries@croftburn.co.uk**
- **website: www.croftburn.co.uk**

•SCOTTISH ISLANDS

•SKYE

Hotel & Restaurant

Royal Hotel, Bank Street, PORTREE, Isle of Skye IV51 9BU Tel: 01478 612585

- **e-mail: info@royal-hotel-skye.com**
- **website: www.royal-hotel-skye.com**

•WALES

Self-Catering

Quality Cottages, Cerbid, Solva, HAVERFORDWEST, Pembrokeshire SA62 6YE Tel: 01348 837871

- **website: www.qualitycottages.co.uk**

•ANGLESEY & GWYNEDD

Self-Catering / Caravan Park

Mrs A. Skinner, Ty Gwyn, Rhyduchaf, BALA, Gwynedd LL23 7SD Tel: 01678 521267

- **e-mail: richard.skin@btinternet.com**

Caravan & Camping Site

Glanllyn Lakeside Caravan & Camping Park, Llanuwchllyn, BALA, Gwynedd LL23 7ST
Tel: 01678 540227

- **e-mail: info@glanllyn.com**
- **website: www.glanllyn.com**

Caravan Park

Parc Caerelwan, Talybont, BARMOUTH, Gwynedd LL43 2AX Tel: 01341 247236

- **e-mail: parc@porthmadog.co.uk**
- **website: www.porthmadog.co.uk/parc/**

Country House

Sygun Fawr Country House, BEDDGELERT, Gwynedd LL55 4NE Tel: 01766 890258

- **e-mail: sygunfawr@aol.com**
- **website: www.sygunfawr.co.uk**

Holiday Park

Greenacres Holiday Park, Black Rock Sands, Morfa Bychan, Porthmadog, CAERNARFON, Gwynedd LL49 9YF Tel: 01766 512781

- **website: www.touringholidays.co.uk**

Self-Catering / Caravans

Plas-y-Bryn Chalet Park, Bontnewydd, CAERNARFON, Gwynedd LL54 7YE
Tel: 01286 672811

- **www.plasybrynholidayscaernarfon.co.uk**

Self-Catering within a Castle

BrynBras Castle, Llanrug, Near CAERNARFON, Gwynedd LL55 4RE
Tel: 01286 870210

- **e-mail: holidays@brynbrascastle.co.uk**
- **website: www.brynbrascastle.co.uk**

Self-Catering

Mrs A. Jones, Rhos Country Cottages, Betws Bach, Ynys, CRICCIETH, Gwynedd LL52 0PB Tel: 01758 720047

- **e-mail: cottages@rhos.freeserve.co.uk**
- **website: www.rhos-cottages.co.uk**

Caravan & Chalet Park/ Self-Catering

Parc Wernol Parc, Chwilog, Pwllheli, Near CRICCIETH, Gwynedd LL53 6SW
Tel: 01766 810506

- **e-mail: catherine@wernol.com**
- **website: www.wernol.com**

Guest House

Mrs M. Bamford, Ivy House, Finsbury Square, DOLGELLAU, Gwynedd LL40 1RF. Tel: 01341 422535

- **e-mail: marg.bamford@btconnect.com**
- **website: www.ukworld.net/ivyhouse**

Guest House

Fron Deg Guest House, LLanfair, HARLECH, Gwynedd LL46 2RB Tel: 01766 780448

- **website: www.bedandbreakfast-harlech.co.uk**

Caravan & Camping

Mr John Billingham, Islawrffordd Caravan Park, Tal-y-Bont, MERIONETH, Gwynedd LL43 2BQ Tel: 01341 247269

- **e-mail: info@islawrffordd.co.uk**
- **website: www.islawrffordd.co.uk**

Golf Club

Anglesey Golf Club Ltd, Station Road, RHOSNEIGR, Anglesey LL64 5QX
Tel: 01407 811127 ext 2

- **e-mail: info@theangleseygolfclub.com**
- **website: www.angleseygolfclub.co.uk**

•NORTH WALES

Hotel

Fairy Glen Hotel, Beaver Bridge, BETWS-Y-COED, Conwy, North Wales LL24 0SH Tel: 01690 710269

- **e-mail: fairyglen@youe.fsworld.co.uk**
- **website: www.fairyglenhotel.co.uk**

Country House

Hafod Country House, Trefrin, Llanrwst, CONWY VALLEY, North Wales LL27 0RQ Tel: 01492 640029

- **e-mail: hafod@breathemail.net**
- **website: www.hafod-house.co.uk**

Guest House

The Park Hill / Gwesty Bryn Parc, Llanrwst Road, Betws-y-Coed, CONWY, North Wales LL24 0HD Tel: 01690 710540

- **e-mail: welcome@park-hill.co.uk**
- **website: www.park-hill.co.uk**

Guest House

Sychnant Pass House, Sychnant Pass Road CONWY, North Wales LL32 8BJ Tel: 01492 596868

- **e-mail: bre@sychnant-pass-house.co.uk**
- **website: www.sychnant-pass-house.co.uk**

Golf Club

Denbigh Golf Club, Henllan Road, DENBIGH, North Wales LL16 5AA Tel: 01745 816669

- **e-mail: denbighgolfclub@aol.com**
- **website: www.denbighgolfclub.co.uk**

Golf Club

North Wales Golf Club, 72 Bryniau Road, West Shore, LLANDUDNO, North Wales LL30 2DZ Tel:01492 875325 or 01492 876878

- **e-mail: golf@nwgc.freeserve.co.uk**
- **website: www.northwalesgolfclub.co.uk**

Hotel / Inn

The Golden Pheasant Country Hotel & Inn, Llwynmawr, Glyn Ceiriog, Near LLANGOLLEN, North Wales LL20 7BB Tel: 01691 718281

- **e-mail: goldenpheasant@micro-plus-web.net**
- **website: goldenpheasanthotel.co.uk**

Self-Catering Cottages

Glyn Uchaf, Conwy Old Road, PENMAENMAWR, North Wales LL34 6YS Tel: 01492 623737

- **e-mail: john@baxter6055.freeserve.co.uk**
- **website: www.glyn-uchaf.co.uk**

Holiday Park

Presthaven Sands Holiday Park, Gronaut, PRESTATYN, North Wales LL19 9TT Tel: 01745 856471

website: www.touringholidays.co.uk

•CARMARTHENSHIRE

Self-Catering

Maerdy Cottages, Taliaris, LLANDEILO, Carmarthenshire SA19 7BD Tel: 01550 777448

- **e-mail: mjones@maerdyholidaycottages.co.uk**
- **website: www.maerdyholidaycottages.co.uk**

•CEREDIGION

Holiday Village

Gilfach Holiday Village, Llwyncelyn, Near ABERAERON, Ceredigion SA46 0HN Tel: 01545 580288

- **e-mail: info@stratfordcaravans.co.uk**
- **website: www.selfcateringholidays.com www.stratfordcaravans.co.uk**

• PEMBROKESHIRE

Farm Self- Catering

Holiday House, BROAD HAVEN, Pembrokeshire.
Contact: L.E. Ashton, 10 St Leonards Road, Thames Ditton, Surrey KT7 0RJ Tel: 020 8398 6349

- **e-mail: lejash@aol.com**
- **website: www.33timberhill.com**

Hotel / Guest House

Ivybridge, Drim Mill, Dyffryn, Goodwick, FISHGUARD, Pembrokeshire SA64 0JT Tel: 01348 875366

- **e-mail: ivybridge@cwcom.net**
- **website: www.ivybridge.cwc.net**

Caravans & Camp Site

Brandy Brook Caravan & Camping Site, Rhyndaston, Hayscastle, HAVERFORDWEST, Pembrokeshire SA62 5PT
Tel: 01348 840272
• **e-mail: f.m.rowe@btopenworld.com**

Farmhouse B & B

Mrs Jen Patrick, East Hook Farm, Portfield Gate, HAVERFORDWEST, Pembrokeshire SA62 3LN
Tel: 01437 762211
• **e-mail: jen.patrick@easthookfarmhouse.co.uk**
• **website: www.easthookfarmhouse.co.uk**

Inn

The Dial Inn, Ridgeway Road, LAMPHEY, Pembroke, Pembrokeshire SA71 5NU
Tel: 01646 672426
• **e-mail: info@dialinn.co.uk**

Hotel

Trewern Arms Hotel, Nevern, NEWPORT, Pembrokeshire SA42 0NB
Tel: 01239 820395
• **e-mail: info@trewern-arms-pembrokeshire.co.uk**
• **www.trewern-arms-pembrokeshire.co.uk**

Self-catering

Ffynnon Ddofn, ST DAVIDS, Pembrokeshire. Contact: Mrs B. Rees White, Brick House Farm, Burnham Road, Woodham Mortimer, Maldon, Essex CM9 6SR
Tel: 01245 224611
• **website: www.ffynnonddofn.co.uk**

Self-Catering

T. M. Hardman, High View, Catherine Street, ST DAVIDS, Pembrokeshire SA62 6RJ
Tel: 01437 720616
• **e-mail: enquiries@stnbc.co.uk**
• **website: www.stnbc.co.uk**

Farm Guest House

Mrs Morfydd Jones, Lochmeyler Farm Guest House, Llandeloy, Pen-y-Cwm, Near SOLVA, St Davids, Pembrokeshire SA62 6LL
Tel: 01348 837724
• **e-mail: stay@lochmeyler.co.uk**
• **website: www.lochmeyler.co.uk**

Holiday Park

Kiln Park Holiday Centre, Marsh Road, TENBY, Pembrokeshire SA70 7RB
Tel: 01834 844121
• **website: www.touringholidays.co.uk**

• POWYS

Farm

Caebetran Farm, Felinfach, BRECON, Powys LD3 0UL Tel: 01874 754460
• **e-mail: hazelcaebetran@aol.com**
• **website: caebetranfarmhousebedandbreakfastwales.com**

Guest House

Maeswalter, Heol Senni, Near BRECON, Powys LD3 8SU Tel: 01874 636629
• **e-mail: joy@maeswalter.fsnet.co.uk**
bb@maeswalter.co.uk
• **website: www.maeswalter.co.uk**

Self-Catering

Mrs Jones, Penllwyn Lodges, GARTHMYL, Powys SY15 6SB
Tel: 01686 640269
• **e-mail: daphne.jones@onetel.net**
• **website: www.penllwynlodges.co.uk**

B & B

Annie McKay, Hafod-y-Garreg, Erwood, Builth Wells, Near HAY-ON-WYE, Powys LD2 3TQ
Tel: 01982 560400
• **website: www.hafodygarreg.co.uk**

Self-Catering

Oak Wood Lodges, Llwynbaedd, RHAYADER, Powys LD6 5NT
Tel: 01597 811422
• **e-mail: info@oakwoodlodges.co.uk**
• **website: www.oakwoodlodges.co.uk**

Self-Catering

Ann Reed, Madog's Wells, Llanfair Caereinion, WELSHPOOL, Powys SY21 0DE
Tel: 01938 810446
• **e-mail: madogswells@btinternet.com**
• **website: www.madogswells.co.uk**

• SOUTH WALES

Narrowboat Hire

Castle Narrowboats, Church Road Wharf, Gilwern, Monmouthshire NP7 0EP
Tel: 01873 832340
• **info@castlenarrowboats.co.uk**
• **website: www.castlenarrowboats.co.uk**

Guest House / Self-Catering Cottages

Mrs Norma James, Wyrloed Lodge, Manmoel, BLACKWOOD, Caerphilly, South Wales NP12 0RN Tel: 01495 371198
• **e-mail: norma.james@btinternet.com**
• **website: www.btinternet.com/~norma.james/**

Self-Catering

Cwrt-y-Gaer, Wolvesnewton, CHEPSTOW, Monmouthshire NP16 6PR Tel: 01291 650700

- **e-mail: johnllewellyn11@btinternet.com**
- **website: www.cwrt-y-gaer.co.uk**

Hotel

Culver House Hotel, Port Eynon, GOWER, Swansea, South Wales SA3 1NN Tel: 01792 390755

- **e-mail: stay@culverhousehotel.co.uk**
- **website: www.culverhousehotel.co.uk**

Guest House

Rosemary & Derek Ringer, Church Farm Guest House, Mitchel Troy, MONMOUTH, South Wales NP25 4HZ Tel: 01600 712176

- **e-mail: info@churchfarmguesthouse.eclipse.co.uk**
- **website: www.churchfarmmitcheltroy.co.uk**

Golf Club

St Mellons Golf Club, ST MELLONS, Cardiff, South Wales Tel: 01633 680408

- **e-mail: stmellons@golf2003.fs.co.uk**
- **website: www.stmellonsgolfclub.co.uk**

Hotel

Egerton Grey Country House Hotel, Porthkerry, Barry, VALE OF GLAMORGAN, South Wales CF62 3BZ Tel: 01446 711666

- **e-mail: info@egertongrey.co.uk**
- **website: www.egertongrey.co.uk**

• IRELAND

Self-Catering Cottages

Imagine Ireland
Tel: 0870 112 77 32

- **e-mail: info@imagineireland.com**
- **website: www.imagineireland.com**

CO. CLARE

Self-Catering

Ballyvaughan Village & Country Holiday Homes, BALLYVAUGHAN.
Contact: George Quinn, Frances Street, Kilrush, Co. Clare Tel: 00 353 65 9051977

- **e-mail: sales@ballyvaughan-cottages.com**
- **website: www.ballyvaughan-cottages.com**

• CHANNEL ISLANDS

GUERNSEY

Self-Catering Apartments

Swallow Apartments, La Cloture, L'Ancresse, GUERNSEY Tel: 01481 249633

- **e-mail: swallowapt@aol.com**
- **website: www.swallowapartments.com**

Index of Towns and Counties

Note

All the information in this guide is given in good faith in the belief that it is correct. However, the publishers cannot guarantee the facts given in these pages, neither are they responsible for changes in ownership or facilities that may take place after the date of going to press.
Readers should always satisfy themselves that the facilities they require are available and that the terms, if quoted, still apply.

OTHER FHG TITLES FOR 2007

FHG Guides Ltd have a large range of attractive holiday accommodation guides for all kinds of holiday opportunities throughout Britain. They also make useful gifts at any time of year. Our guides are available in most bookshops and larger newsagents but we will be happy to post you a copy direct if you have any difficulty. POST FREE for addresses in the UK. We will also post abroad but have to charge separately for post or freight.

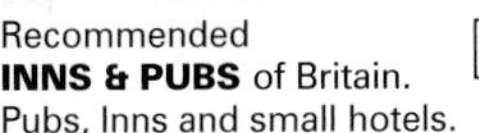

Recommended
INNS & PUBS of Britain.
Pubs, Inns and small hotels.

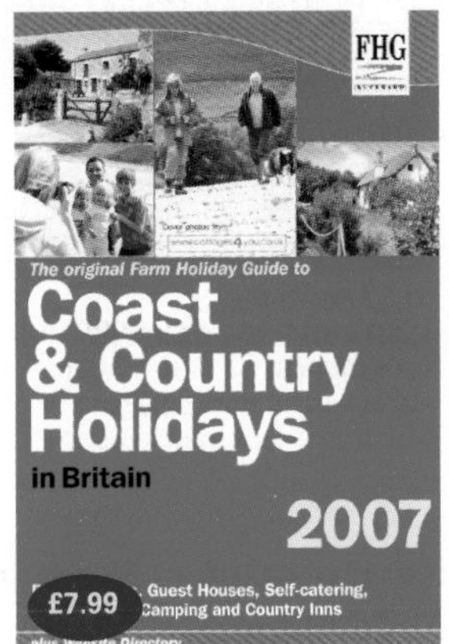

The original
Farm Holiday Guide to
COAST & COUNTRY HOLIDAYS in England, Scotland, Wales and Channel Islands. Board, Self-catering, Caravans/Camping Holidays.

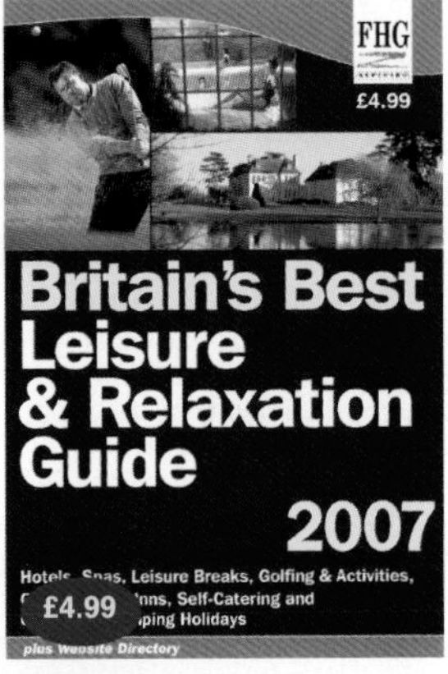

BRITAIN'S BEST LEISURE & RELAXATION GUIDE
A quick-reference general guide for all kinds of holidays.

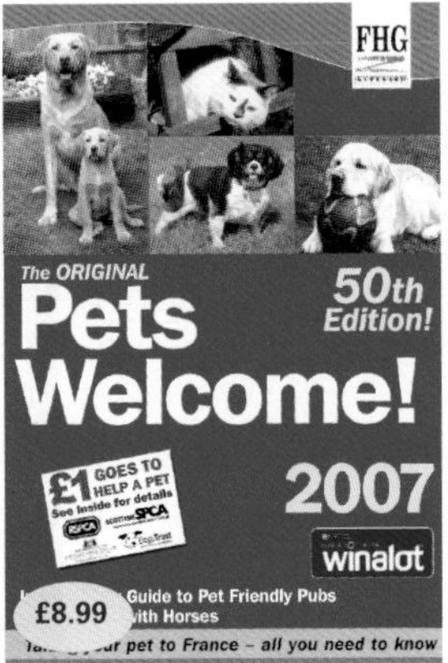

The Original
PETS WELCOME!
The bestselling guide to holidays for pet owners and their pets.

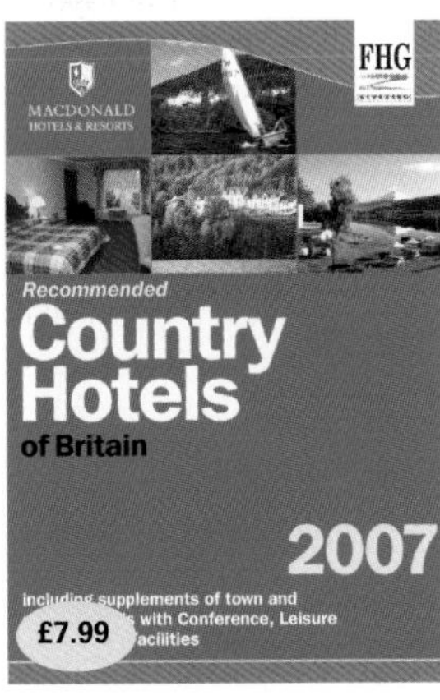

Recommended
COUNTRY HOTELS
of Britain
Including Country Houses, for the discriminating.

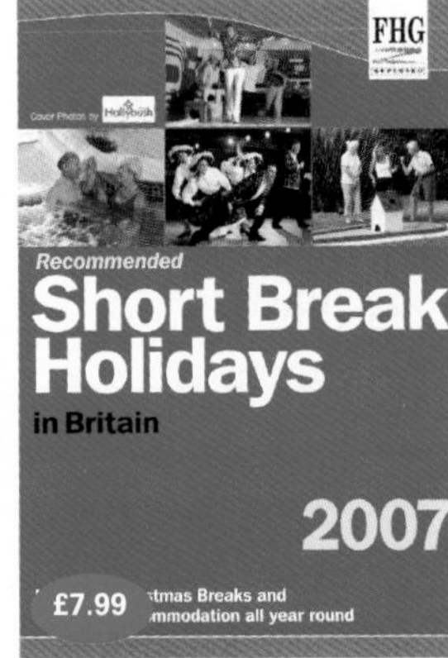

Recommended
SHORT BREAK HOLIDAYS IN BRITAIN
"Approved" accommodation for quality bargain breaks.

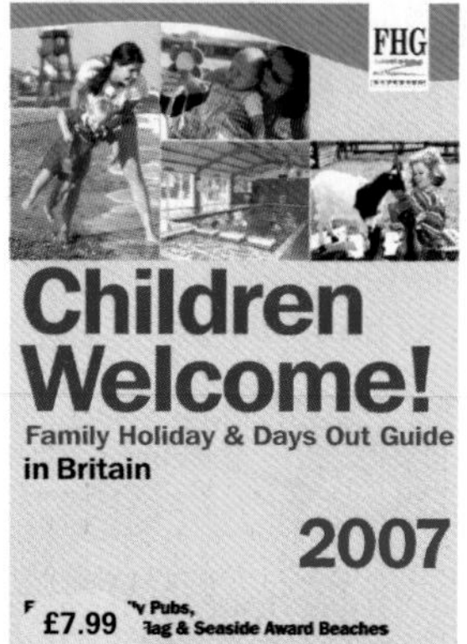

CHILDREN WELCOME! ☐
Family Holidays and Days Out guide.
Family holidays with details of amenities for children and babies.

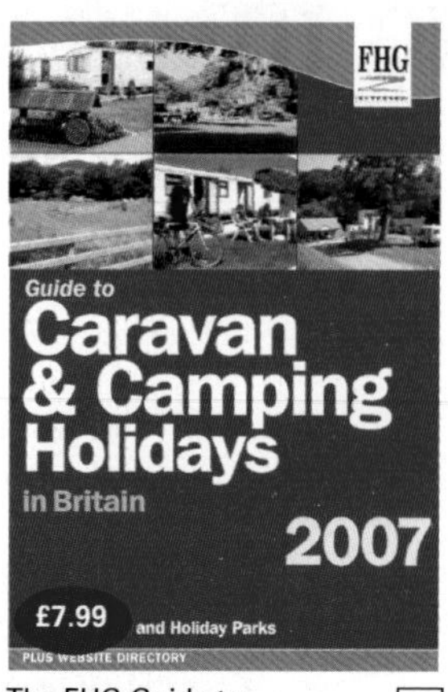

The FHG Guide to
CARAVAN & CAMPING HOLIDAYS, ☐
Caravans for hire, sites and holiday parks and centres.

SELF-CATERING HOLIDAYS ☐
in Britain
Over 1000 addresses throughout for self-catering and caravans in Britain.

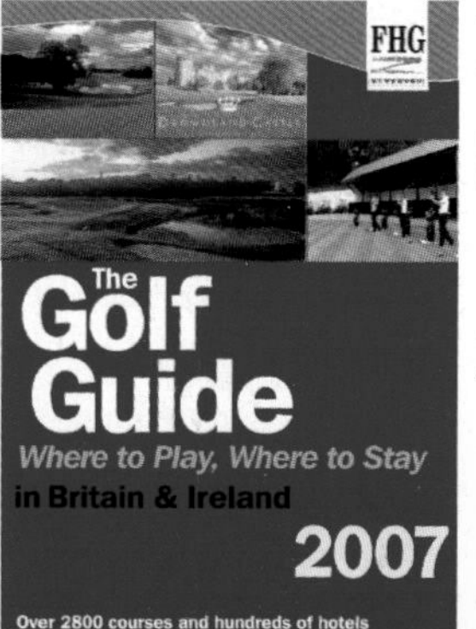

The GOLF GUIDE –
Where to play Where to stay
£9.99
In association with GOLF MONTHLY. Over 2800 golf courses in Britain with convenient accommodation. Holiday Golf in France, Portugal, Spain, USA, South Africa and Thailand. ☐

Tick your choice above and send your order and payment to

FHG Guides Ltd. Abbey Mill Business Centre
Seedhill, Paisley, Scotland PA1 1TJ
TEL: 0141- 887 0428 • FAX: 0141- 889 7204
e-mail: admin@fhguides.co.uk

Deduct 10% for 2/3 titles or copies; 20% for 4 or more.

Send to: NAME ....

FHG KUPERARD

ADDRESS ....

....

....

POST CODE ....

I enclose Cheque/Postal Order for £ ....

SIGNATURE ....DATE ....

Please complete the following to help us improve the service we provide.
How did you find out about our guides?:

☐ Press ☐ Magazines ☐ TV/Radio ☐ Family/Friend ☐ Other